The Limits
and Possibilities
of Schooling

AN INTRODUCTION TO
THE SOCIOLOGY OF EDUCATION

SECOND EDITION

Christopher J. Hurn
University of Massachusetts

Allyn and Bacon, Inc.

Boston   London   Sydney   Toronto

Library of Congress Cataloging in Publication Data
Hurn, Christopher J., date
   The limits and possibilities of schooling.
   Bibliography: p.
   Includes index.
   1. Educational sociology.   I. Title.
LC189.H87   1985   370.19   84-20331
ISBN 0-205-08400-1

Production Administrator: *Jane Schulman*
Production Coordinator: *Helyn Pultz*
Production Services: *TKM Productions*
Cover Coordinator: *Christy Rosso*
Cover Designer: *Lynne Beighley Abell*

Printed in the United States of America

10 9 8 7 6 5 4 3 2   89 88 87 86

contents

This second edition covers much of the same literature as the first edition, but it is essentially a new book. Over 80 percent of the text has been changed, and almost all these revisions are substantive rather than editorial. Chapters 1, 7, and 9 are entirely new; only two of the original chapters have escaped wholesale revision and reorganization. The result, I hope, is a clearer and more focused book (though no less argumentative than the original) that better achieves the two objectives I set myself almost ten years ago: to synthesize and interpret theory and research in the sociology of education for the student and the professional reader, and provide some tentative answers to broader questions about the accomplishments, limits, and possibilities of formal education in modern societies. I am interested not only in summarizing a body of literature, though a great deal of research is described in what follows, but also in drawing implications from that sociological work for a set of issues of general concern: questions about the limits of schools as agencies of socialization and instruments for creating a society of equal opportunity, questions about why our hopes for schools in these respects so often seem to have been disappointed, and finally, questions about the possibility that different kinds of schools in the future may make it necessary to revise recent rather pessimistic assessments of what schools can and cannot do.

This is in many ways a different book from the first edition because of developments within the sociology of education and in educational research in general. Quantitative research on schooling and its effects is more sophisticated than it was ten years ago. Considerable advances have been made in understanding the process of achievement within schools, the role of tracking in shaping that achievement, the relationship of tracking to inequality, and, more generally, the relationship between social origins, school success, and future socioeconomic status. Progress has also been made in comparative studies of social mobility, school outcomes in different societies, and the effects of schooling on cognitive skills in non-Western cultures. All of this research has important implications for the central themes of this book. By contrast, other traditions of research, including several for which high hopes were held in the mid-1970s, have not made similarly dramatic progress. The promise of phenomenological research, for example, has not been fulfilled, and despite quite general agreement that more qualitative observational studies of classroom interaction are urgently needed, surprisingly little research of this kind has appeared in the last ten years. I am uncertain that this trend toward the increasing preponderance of "hard" versus "soft" data is to be applauded; inevitably, however, this change is partly reflected in the revisions I have made.

Theoretical developments are no less significant than changes in empirical research. In the mid-1970s, neo-Marxist theories and the works of such radical critics as Ivan Illich and Paulo Freire stood almost alone as alternative interpretations to the dominant functional interpretation of schooling. Sociologists and educators who rejected that orthodox and politically liberal view—which depicted the expansion of schooling as a necessary and rational response to societal complexity and the schools as essentially emancipatory in character—tended to embrace a theory of recent educational history as manipulation of masses by elites, and existing schools as necessarily repressive of the human potential. Thanks to the work of Randall Collins and John Meyer, the alternatives are less stark today. Radical and neo-Marxist theories retain more than a foothold within the academy, though their influence is less widespread than ten years ago. But both these theories and the functional interpretation have recently been challenged by ideas that owe more to Weber, and even to Goffman, than to either Marx or Durkheim. The new conflict theories of education are profoundly skeptical of both functional and neo-Marxist accounts of the effects of schools on their students, stressing that employers and the general public respond to the prestige of educational credentials rather than to any substantial differences in skills or attitudes schools have produced. Thus these conflict theories strike at the heart of both the conventional liberal and radical wisdom about the role of schooling in modern societies including, of course, the currently popular view that improving educational quality is a key to future economic growth and national competitiveness.

Some of the most significant changes in the new edition are a response to changes in the last ten years in the broader intellectual and social climate rather than to developments within the discipline. In education these changes can be symbolized by the replacement of many of the catchwords and key phrases of the 1970s—*student needs, growth and development, relevance, individualization*—by a new set of terms with a distinctly more conservative resonance: *excellence, quality education, basic skills, standards.* The signs of these changes in the educational climate were visible by the mid-1970s; few could have anticipated, however, how dramatically the educational agenda would shift in the next ten years and how remote many of the concerns of the late 1960s and early 1970s now appear. I should make it clear that I do not share many of the priorities of the new educational reform movement, and, in particular, the relegation of problems of equality to the back burner of public attention. Nonetheless, behind the current debate over educational reform lie important questions that, until recently, have been almost entirely neglected by sociologists and educational researchers. How have schools, particularly high schools, changed in the last twenty years, and in what ways are these changes connected to the apparent decline in academic achievement during that time? How has the authority of the school to control and to inspire young people—as evidenced in increasing rates of absenteeism, vandalism, and violence—been eroded in recent decades? Are these changes temporary results of the strain of accommodating unprecedentedly large numbers of increasingly diverse students during the 1960s and early 1970s? Or do they represent a long-term shift in the traditional school's ability to mold the hearts and minds of the young, a trend accelerated by the unusual developments of the 1960s and 1970s but not easily reversed?

I have no ready answers to these questions, and much of the research that might help us answer them has not yet been done. But I am convinced that these and similar questions, along with our traditional concerns about schooling and inequality, will occupy a central place in our discipline over the next decade.

I would like to thank those many readers of the first edition of this book who shared their comments and criticisms with me, and my colleagues and students for their patience and generosity over the past four years with what must have seemed to them to be my obsessive concerns. As before, my largest debts are to Charles Page for getting me started on this ambitious enterprise and encouraging me to believe I might pull it off, and to Arnold Feldman for teaching me the difference between what is sociologically important and what is trivial. If I appear to have wandered far afield from the work Ackie taught me to do, whatever intellectual merit this book possesses owes much to him.

chapter 1

The Sociological
Approach
to Schooling

When I first began work on the original version of this book in the early 1970s, there was, as there is today, a mood of great public urgency about the problems of schooling and the large number of policy initiatives directed toward solving those problems. The popular media featured frequent articles on the crisis in schooling, and a number of best selling books and television documentaries explored the roots of this crisis and illustrated its nature with graphic examples of neglect and incompetence. And then, as now, federal and state governments attempted to solve the problems of schooling by earmarking substantial amounts of money for school reform.[1] Paradoxically, however, the crisis in schooling in 1972 or 1973 meant something very different from the crisis in schooling in 1984 or 1985. The educational catchwords or cliches of the early 1970s (and late 1960s) were *equality, relevance, individualization,* and *growth and development.*[2] The crisis to which these terms referred involved essentially two ideas that are heard much less frequently today. First, schools were failing to provide a minimally adequate education for disadvantaged students and the promise of equal opportunity had been betrayed. Second, traditional schools, instead of meeting the students' needs for growth and development, regimented and controlled students in an essentially authoritarian manner which stifled intellectual and emotional growth. The school reform movements of the time were shaped by this diagnosis. Schools were asked to *individualize* instruction, introduce new *relevant* curricula, provide more *options* and electives for students, and become far more sensitive to the special *needs* of minority and disadvantaged students.

Today, of course, the crisis in schooling is defined quite differently. Schools are attacked for encouraging educational mediocrity rather than excellence. The relevant courses of the seventies have become the frill courses of the eighties; elective courses that were designed to meet the students' individual needs are now seen as interfering with concentration on basic subjects; open admissions and liberal promotion practices that were advocated as ways of maximizing educational opportunities are now decried as symbols of the abandonment of academic standards.[3] Not so long ago, schools were attacked because they were authoritarian institutions, regimenting and controlling student behavior in unnecessary ways and interfering with the development of each student's unique personality; now they are attacked because they do not exercise *enough* authority over students. The currently popular argument asserts that educators no longer insist students learn the basic subjects, nor do they hold students responsible for even a modicum of effort and self-discipline.[4]

There are other examples in American history of sharp changes in a relatively short period of time in what people see as the major problems of schooling. In the late 1950s, for example, criticisms of the schools contained many of the same themes that are prominent today.[5] Invidious comparisons were made between American and Soviet schools (though today the fashion leans toward comparisons with Japanese schools), and books with titles like *Educational Wastelands*[6] dramatized the claim that progressive educators had captured the schools and eroded much of their serious academic content in favor of an emphasis on life adjustment. However, that crisis contrasted as strongly with the perceived problems of schooling in the 1930s and 1940s as the diagnosis of the eighties differed from that of the early seventies.[7]

To be sure, not everyone agreed at any given time with the particular diagnosis that was currently dominant; today many liberal educators reject the current preoccupation with improving academic standards just as most conservatives never accepted the criticisms that were popular in the early 1970s.[8] In other words, to say that a particular set of problems dominates public discussion of education does not imply that almost everyone accepts those definitions of what is wrong. Nevertheless, each of these differing diagnoses set the framework for public discussion of schooling in a particular era and had important effects on the direction of educational policy during that time. In the early

1970s, for example, the federal government made considerable amounts of money available for programs designed to individualize instruction and create "open" classrooms. In the 1980s those who still favor this policy, like those who favor open admissions experiments, will most likely have to search for funding in vain.

These fluctuations in the nature of the crises in schooling raise a large number of questions. Why do the major themes of educational criticism change so dramatically every fifteen or twenty years? Are these changes merely swings in the educational pendulum from progressive to conservative and hence of little more significance than changes in fashions of dress? Or do they reflect changes in what is objectively wrong with schools? Are we to regard whatever is defined as the current crisis as the real crisis, or should we take the more skeptical long-range view that while fashions in educational criticism may change, schools themselves change rather little? Most fundamentally, perhaps, why do Americans seem to be so chronically dissatisfied with schools and what is it about these institutions that produces, every decade or so, an outpouring of calls for their urgent reform and reconstruction? Are our expectations for schools simply too high, so high in fact that no realistically conceivable schools could satisfy them? Are we asking educators to do different things at different periods of our history, so that reforms that satisfy or resolve one set of problems create another set of problems for the next generation of reformers? Or is the problem, finally, that we do not know how to reform schools to achieve any of our objectives in any predictable manner?

Whatever our answers to these questions, and I shall consider each of them in this book, one thing is clear. The present crisis in schooling will not be the last, and if the past is any guide to the future, the next crisis will take a different form than the present one. Thus if we accept at face value the criticisms of schooling that are currently most popular, it is likely that many of our ideas will, in the future, be regarded with something akin to amused tolerance.[9] This does not imply we should ignore the problems of schooling as presently defined, or that these problems are insignificant or only simply a passing fashion; however, it does imply if we are trying to say something about schools that will have lasting value we would be well advised to step back from the current scene and take a somewhat broader perspective than that offered by the latest magazine article, television documentary, or reports of national commissions. That broader perspective will not lead in itself to solutions for our pressing problems, and initially it may even lead to doubt that any solutions exist. In the long run, however, our best hope for reform of schooling lies in the slow and painstaking search for knowledge about these institutions rather than in immediate action to change schools now. To gain this knowledge we must step back from the controversies and issues of the present and instead ask more general questions than are currently fashionable: questions about the nature of the educational process as well as how to improve it, and questions about the character of the institutions that we call schools as well as how to change them for the better.

The sociology of education offers our best hope for gaining this kind of knowledge about schooling. Sociological research provides partial and tentative answers to some of the most commonly asked questions about schooling: questions about the effects of schools on their students, questions about why students from different social origins often differ in how well they do in school, and questions about the likely effect of different kinds of educational policies. Even more important, the sociological perspective allows us to look at schools in a broader and more complex way than that afforded by common sense, and suggests new kinds of questions that can deepen our understanding of schooling. Let me describe this sociological perspective and show how it illuminates some of our most common preoccupations with schools.

CULTURAL TRANSMISSION AND EDUCATION

For the sociologist, education is defined as the more or less deliberate process of transmitting the culture of the adult world to the young. It is the process by which all societies select what they consider to be the most important and significant parts of their cultural heritage, whether they may be skills, facts, values, and attitudes, and attempt to teach them to the young. In this sense, all societies educate the young, whether or not the societies possess those institutions we call schools. While a good part of the cultural heritage in every society— from language to standards of taste and manners—is simply absorbed by the young without formal instruction, no society is content to leave matters there. In pre-literate societies, for example (and indeed in perhaps the majority of societies before quite recent times), religious knowledge and religious beliefs are almost always singled out for special and quite formal instruction.[10] In those societies, children might pick up hunting or food-gathering skills by observing their parents, without much explicit instruction; but they would almost certainly receive formal teaching in the religious beliefs and rituals of their society. Hence, what distinguishes education from the broader concept of socialization is that education involves the selection of certain ideals, values, and skills that are deemed of sufficiently great importance not to be left to chance and therefore must be deliberately and intentionally conveyed to the young.

Societies vary enormously, of course, in what values, ideals, and kinds of knowledge they attempt to teach the young. It is hard to deny that in modern societies the role of formal instruction in knowledge and the production of cognitive skills is of much greater importance than it was in the past. Nonetheless, it would be a great mistake to underestimate the importance of the transmission of values and ideals in the modern world. Contemporary societies, like all previous societies, can only persist if they successfully provide the young with the opportunity to share in and subscribe to the particular values and ideals that make each society distinctive. Thus children in the United States are taught about the American Revolution and to revere the names of Washington and Jefferson for much the same reasons that our pre-literate ancestors learned the names of their illustrious forebearers and the founding myths of their society; and Soviet children are told the story of the Revolution of 1917 and taught to emulate the life of Lenin in rather the same way that British children learn about the Norman Conquest of 1066 and the Glorious Revolution of 1688. In other words, all modern societies take considerable pains to ensure that the young learn what might be called the founding myths of the culture: crucial historical events and key figures that exemplify or teach its distinctive ideals and principles.

The formal teaching of history and such ceremonies as the pledge of allegiance are only a part of this process of conveying values and ideals. The organization of the classroom, the way students are evaluated, and even the demeanor and manner of the teacher convey implicit messages that teach students what kinds of conduct are appropriate. Soviet teachers often require the faster student to help the slower ones with their homework.[11] Such implicit teaching of the Soviet ideal of the individual's responsibility for the welfare of others is probably more effective than explicit pronouncements that children must put other people's interests ahead of their own. Similarly, American schools, by their stress on the competition for grades and their strict prohibitions against cheating, convey the implicit message that individuals are responsible for their own success or failure and that individual competition spurs people to greater effort.[12] In some contemporary U.S. high schools, students' desks are no longer arranged in rows but in a horseshoe or a circle, and teachers, instead of sitting behind their desks in traditional style, sometimes lead discussions from a highly informal "perching position" on top of their desks with their legs dangling in front of the students. In France or Japan, such informality would be hardly conceivable.[13] In those countries the rows of desks often bolted to the floor, the formal dress and bearing of the teacher, and the respectful silence that accompanies the lesson convey what is, by American standards, the extraordinary importance of instilling in the child respect for the authority of the teacher, and the school as representative of the society.

Through both implicit and explicit teaching, therefore, societies convey their distinctive values and ideals to the young. We consequently need to look at schools not only as places where skills and particular knowledge are taught, but as institutions that mold and shape members of a particular culture. The organization of the American classroom, the way in which students are evaluated, the rules governing student behavior or school grades, and the demeanor and deportment of teachers convey implied messages to students about what kinds of values are most precious and what kinds of goals are worth striving for, and, in the broadest sense, what it means to be an American. Thus there is more continuity between education in modern society and education in simpler pre-literate societies than we might at first suppose. The role of formal instruction in cognitive skills and knowledge is greater in the modern world than in the past, but the fundamental process of education remains similar. Modern societies, like pre-literate societies, take great pains to ensure the young will learn the fundamental values and ideals of the culture. We arrange and structure the experience of young people in order to achieve that goal.

Cultural Diversity and Educational Controversy

No modern society is culturally homogeneous. From the point of view of foreign observers, perhaps, it may make a great deal of sense to talk about American values, the British way of life, or Japanese cultural ideals, but from the perspective of someone inside these cultures the picture looks rather different. Every modern society, and the United States more than others, is a divided society, with different conceptions of the ideal man or woman, the heroes that should be emulated, and the values we should strive to realize in our lives. Furthermore, most of these differences are related to the ethnic, class, religious, or regional differences between groups. Thus we need to address the values and ideals of southern fundamentalist Protestants, or upper middle-class professionals, or lower-class white ethnics as well as the values and ideals of Americans as a whole. We also need to examine how political divisions between radicals, liberals, and conservatives, which often correspond to differences in class, education, and age, affect broader views about the kind of society we want our children to inherit.

For this reason education in any society is almost always controversial. The transmission of culture involves a struggle between competing values and competing conceptions of the ideal society, and arguments about education are almost always shaped by that larger debate. Indeed, schools themselves often become the major focus of societal disputes about the relative priority of different values and ideals. Almost any educational issue, from the admissions standards of colleges to

ed diff —
symbolic struggles
larger

the elective system, or from the teaching of evolution to methods of teaching reading, can come to symbolize a larger struggle between different groups, each trying to ensure *their* values and their ideals will be the ones the young will come to emulate.

The recent controversy over sex education serves as an example of how educational issues cannot be understood apart from wider social and political debates and how education is inevitably controversial in modern society.[14] Sex education in contemporary American schools might not seem to be particularly problematic for most liberals. Objective and reliable knowledge about human sexuality, they may reason, is greatly preferable to the often inaccurate and misleading information teenagers acquire on their own. Since many parents do not routinely teach their children about these matters, it seems entirely appropriate that this information should be included in the school curriculum. For many conservatives, however, and particularly for those conservatives who are also Christian fundamentalists, sex education in the schools is anathema. They see courses in sex education as corrupting the morals of the young, encouraging premarital sex, and undermining the authority of the home. For some conservatives the very discussion of human sexuality in the school implies that the religious and moral rules, which used to make public discussion of such matters taboo, are under attack. A textbook discussion of teenage sexuality, for example, although by no means endorsing premarital sexual behavior, nonetheless may raise the possibility that such behavior might be appropriate in some circumstances and, therefore, is not always wrong in some absolute sense.

The particular issue of sex education is not all that is at stake, however. Behind the clash over what, if anything, students should be taught in school about sexuality is a larger debate over what kind of values should be taught to the young.[15] For liberals and progressive educators, it is self-evident that students need up-to-date and objective information to enable them to cope with the complex choices they will face in a rapidly changing society. To deny this information and prohibit discussion of its implications is, from this point of view, to neglect our responsibilities to the next generation. For many and perhaps most conservatives, on the other hand, schools have the task of perpetuating, or at the very least, should not undermine, a set of clear moral precepts about right and wrong or moral and immoral conduct. In a world where these eternal verities are everywhere on the defensive, the task of schools should be to conserve and pass on traditions rather than to debunk them, and to reinforce parental authority rather than to encourage students to question it.

Conflicts over the curriculum, however, are only the most obvious issues dividing people who hold opposing views of what kind of values and ideals should be taught to the young. Virtually any part of what

sociologists call the social organization of schooling, from grading practices or promotion policies, to dress codes and other rules governing
student behavior, or the role of elected school boards, can come to
symbolize a larger debate between opposing conceptions of what is
appropriate for the young to learn. At the height of the alternative
school movement in the early 1970s, for example, large numbers of
predominantly upper middle-class parents, with support from radical
or progressive educators, came to believe that traditional schools undermined the intellectual independence and the natural curiosity of
the child, and surrounded students with unnecessary rules that discouraged initiative and autonomy. "How can we expect our children to
think for themselves and make their own decisions," they asked rhe-
torically, "if schools regiment and control students at every step and if
teaching consists overwhelmingly of lecturing and recitation?"[16] In
many school districts during this time, a clash over such apparently
trivial items as corridor passes, dress codes, and permission to leave
school grounds during lunch hours came to symbolize a larger debate
between opposed visions of American ideals. Those who condemned
schools for teaching unthinking obedience to authority tended also
to call for a critical reexamination of the American dream and a redirection of our foreign policy.[17] Repression in the schools, they claimed,
was part and parcel of a smug, intolerant, and self-righteous society.
Thus the reform of education, and the beginning of new, more "liberated," less authoritarian schools came to symbolize a wider process
of social reconstruction and national redirection.

It is difficult, if not impossible, to separate educational controversy
from larger social and political debates between competing groups
in the society. This is the case not only with such obviously general
issues as prayer in public schools or bussing to achieve racial integration,
it is also true of what might seem, at first glance, merely technical
debates about educational strategies. Issues such as promotion policies,
grading practices, and the number of required and elective courses
have recently come under scrutiny in a debate about the nature of a
"quality education" and the supposed decline of academic standards.
People began to argue in the early 1980s that U.S. schools had abandoned the pursuit of educational excellence and followed the path
of easy mediocrity, allowing students to graduate who are barely literate, failing to insist that students master fundamental skills and permit-
ting students a free choice among a potpourri of undemanding courses.
But many larger issues are involved in this current and still developing
debate.

In part, this controversy reflects the beliefs of elite and middle-
class groups that their children's futures are in jeopardy because educational standards have been lowered to accommodate the demands of

minorities and disadvantaged groups for equality of educational opportunity. And, indeed, the pressure to raise standards seems likely to benefit privileged rather than disadvantaged students. To some extent, the excellence debate also reflects hostility to what many conservatives see as the control of schools by liberal or progressive professional educators. Two decades of educational reform under the leadership of professional educators, this argument maintains, have led to the erosion of discipline and what they see as the appropriate authority of the school to enforce standards of hard and unremitting effort. The controversy about falling test scores also reflects broader worries and concerns about the decline of excellence in our society and our apparently declining status in the race for economic, technological, and even military superiority.[18] Though it would be too much to say that worries about standards in schools are simply a projection of these larger concerns about the decline of excellence and achievement in the wider society, the current educational crisis cannot be understood apart from these broader issues. Today, as in the past, people look to schools to help create or sustain the values they feel are highest on the national agenda.

Just as we can now see, with the perspective of hindsight, that the source of complaints about repressive schooling in the early 1970s lay in broader concerns with personal fulfillment in the society as a whole as much as with real deficiencies in schools themselves, so we should recognize that the current schooling crisis reflects new societal priorities as well as an objective diagnosis of the ills of schooling. Perhaps it is true that students learned less in school in the early 1980s than in the 1960s (this issue will be examined in some detail in this book), but it is also true that a heightened concern with excellence or quality in almost every field, from our scientific research to car manufacturing, has helped define what we see as *the* most urgent educational problem. Schools are simply the most obvious and visible target on which we can project our current worries about the condition of our society.

The Knowledge Revolution

Some 90 percent of all scientists who have ever lived are alive today. That assertion serves as one indication of a profound difference between contemporary education and education in virtually all societies of the past. It is often said ours is a *knowledge* society.[19] This means that not only is the stock of human knowledge, particularly scientific knowledge, much larger than in the past, it also indicates that this knowledge plays a much more important role than ever before both in individual lives and in the society as a whole. Economic growth, for example, depends increasingly on new improved technologies that are in turn dependent on scientific knowledge. Advances in health and medicine and agriculture are intimately connected to recent research in biology. Governments, in their attempts to make rational choices between alternative social policies, rely increasingly on statistics collected by trained social scientists and on studies of the effectiveness of their respective costs and benefits. And individuals, of course, need more knowledge in their daily lives. Far more than ever before individuals have jobs that require advanced training and skills based on scientific and mathematical competence. There are many jobs, previously learned by apprenticeship or on-the-job training, where reliance on tradition and experience is increasingly replaced by new tasks and procedures that require formal instruction.

The knowledge revolution has had profound effects on the importance and character of education. In 1900 most U.S. children left school by the age of ten or eleven years; today over 40 percent of seventeen and eighteen-year-olds continue on to some form of higher education.[20] This enormous expansion of education has been accompanied by increasingly close connections between schooling and adult status. Success in school, to a much greater extent than in the past, affects success in life. Entry to the more desirable and prestigious occupations is increasingly closed to those who do not have the appropriate schooling. Although there has been some suspicion in recent years that not all of this expansion of schooling is absolutely necessary to prepare people for jobs, there is little question that work in modern society is more complex than in the past and that some kinds of elaborate training is therefore needed.

The most dramatic expansion of schooling in recent decades has been in higher education. Since World War II the size of many leading universities has tripled or quadrupled, and the previously overwhelming predominance of undergraduate teaching has given way to more emphasis on research and graduate training. In many of the great research institutions, the concerns of undergraduates probably occupy only a small part of the time and attention of most administrators and some of the faculty. Instead, these institutions see themselves as producing and disseminating the new knowledge upon which economic growth and social betterment ultimately depend. Universities do fundamental research on the frontiers of knowledge, but they also do a great deal of applied research for the specific needs of a variety of clients: the U.S. Department of Defense, the U.S. Department of Agriculture, private businesses and foundations, and even local communities. The role of the university in modern society, therefore, goes far beyond the teaching of undergraduates. Because of its increasing role in producing new knowledge and new kinds of specialized skills, it has become, some theorists maintain, the key institution of our emerging knowledge-based society.[21]

The changing role of the university has altered the character of the education it provides. Universities still educate students in the traditional arts and sciences, but they increasingly see their task as *training* students in highly specialized fields and preparing them for the variety of new occupations created by the knowledge revolution. Before World War II the great majority of undergraduates majored in one of the traditional arts and sciences disciplines, but that is no longer the case today. Since 1945 there has been a dramatic increase in the number of students majoring in the often highly specialized new professional and semi-professional disciplines: food science, resource management, public health, and hotel and travel administration, for example. The explosive growth in these new fields, together with the steady increase in business, marketing, and accounting, means today only a minority of American undergraduates are majoring in the arts and sciences.[22] Thus in 1980, which is the latest date for which we have information, the combined percentage of students majoring in the humanities *and* the natural sciences was only 14.6 percent, compared with 17.9 percent who majored in the single most popular field, business.[23] Increasingly the university has become a place where students are trained for work rather than broadly educated in traditional fields of knowledge.

The knowledge revolution has tended to undermine the dominance of the traditional liberal arts disciplines in other senses as well. In every field of human inquiry the sheer amount of information and ideas that could, in principle, be taught has expanded enormously in the last three or four decades. This is true not only in the obvious case of scientific and technical knowledge, but even in the traditional fields of history or literature. The body of available literature in even the most highly specialized fields has expanded so much that an individual can hardly claim the kind of mastery about whole areas of scholarship some could claim in the not so distant past. Inevitably, therefore, this exponential growth of new knowledge has posed, in acute form, the problem of selecting what should be taught.

Fifty or even thirty years ago, a diverse group of professors or professional educators could perhaps agree on what basic or fundamental knowledge everyone should learn. Today, beyond some consensus that everyone should acquire basic skills of literacy and numeracy, that possibility of agreement is remote. Teachers of English, for example, no doubt agree that everyone should study literature, but they have long been divided about the relative merits of Shakespeare or modern novels as the essential core of that discipline. With similar disagreements characterizing virtually every field, from science and mathematics to social studies or sex education, the authority of schools and colleges to prescribe what students should learn became greatly weakened. Increasingly during the 1960s and 1970s, students themselves began to choose what they wished to study and an almost free choice among dozens or even hundreds of elective courses replaced the traditional prescribed curriculum. Although there has been some reaction against the proliferation of elective courses in the 1980s, it is far from clear that the kind of consensus that used to prevail about what an educated person should know can be restored. The explosion of knowledge in the recent decades, by undermining the taken-for-granted character of the traditional curriculum, has made the task of prescribing a basic curriculum far more difficult.

The Problem of Credentials
and the Knowledge Revolution

Behind these disagreements over curriculum, there are larger and more general issues at stake. How much knowledge and what level of skills do young people need in the emerging "knowledge society"? Is our society seriously hampered by the lack of skills and competence among the population, or do we already have more highly educated and highly trained people than we need in most fields? Until the mid-1970s, there was little disagreement among sociologists or professional educators about this question. They claimed the rapidly increasing complexity of modern society required steadily increasing levels of cognitive skills and competence among the population.[24] Thus the rapid expansion of the educational system during the period from 1950 to 1975, and increasing emphasis on training and the inculcation of specific skills rather than general education, were rational and necessary adaptations to those requirements. However, doubts on this score began to increase in the latter part of the 1970s, fuelled by the spectacle of increasing numbers of underemployed college graduates. Although still a relatively small minority, more and more critics began to argue that *most* work and *most* jobs, even in contemporary society, did not require dramatically higher levels of skills and competence than in the past.[25] Those who had impressive educational credentials, the critics admitted, were likely to get higher status jobs than those without them, but this did not mean that the job they obtained could only be performed adequately by people with a great deal of education. Although none of these critics denied that the knowledge revolution has increased the importance of schooling and the need for higher levels of training in some specialties, they claimed that evidence that most occupations had become radically more complex was conspicuously lacking.[26]

These arguments will be examined in some detail later in this book. For now it is only necessary to point to the significance and some of the ramifications of the debate. According to the still dominant interpretation of the knowledge revolution, steadily increasing levels of formal education are necessary to the welfare of modern society both to prepare people for more complex work and to provide the new knowledge upon which economic growth increasingly depends. To meet these new responsibilities, furthermore, the character of education must be transformed. There is a new emphasis on cognitive skills replacing the old concern with moral instruction and factual memorization, and at the college level an emphasis on training replaces the old stress on educating a well-rounded or cultivated individual. In the alternative view, many of these changes reflect shifts in beliefs and educational fashions rather than objective necessity. Modern societies have *convinced themselves* that training for work is the paramount function of formal education, and because large numbers of people *believe* this, many jobs that used to require a high school diploma thirty years ago now require a college degree. Whereas these beliefs are not wholly false, they are, in this interpretation, only partly founded on real changes in the character and complexity of contemporary life. Most work in modern society is not so complex that it requires 25 percent of the population to obtain college degrees, nor have changes in work *dictated* that the primary purpose of higher education become training rather than liberal education. Thus we have developed a system of largely unnecessary educational credentials, and in the process degraded the educational system in the name of the knowledge revolution.[27]

At issue in this debate is the question of how we should interpret what is by common consent the much greater importance of schooling in modern societies than in the past. Are such changes in the role of formal education to be seen as rational, necessary, and useful adaptations to the needs of the complexity of modern society? Or is a more skeptical or even cynical view appropriate? As one critic phrases it, have modern societies developed a "diploma disease" whereby the true values of education have been perverted in the name of extended training for work that is not really needed?[28]

THE ALLOCATION OF STATUS AND EQUALITY OF OPPORTUNITY

All contemporary societies use formal education as a way of allocating status. The amount of schooling individuals have and the particular credentials or certificates they have acquired have powerful and lasting effects on their subsequent status. An M.B.A. from any Ivy League university does not guarantee a lifetime of financial security or a highly regarded professional job, any more than dropping out of high school closes off all high-status aspirations. Fortunately, individual careers are not entirely predictable by sociological variables, but formal education does greatly affect the *probabilities* of what we usually define as success or failure in adult life. This is far more true in modern society than in the past. In the late Middle Ages, for example, it was possible for a butcher's son, Cardinal Wolsey, to rise through the church schools to achieve close to supreme power in England, but this was wholly exceptional in a society where virtually all occupations were passed from father to son and where schooling was restricted to a tiny fraction of the population. In modern societies, by contrast, we believe status should be *achieved* by an individual's own efforts rather than *ascribed* on the basis of birth, and we use schooling as our main indicator of such achievement. Impressive educational qualifications, as the great German sociologist Max Weber saw early in this century, have become the modern equivalent of noble blood or distinguished ancestry—the litmus test that persuades others that the individual in question is entitled to high prestige and a desirable occupation.[29]

The significance of this change can be appreciated if we recognize that status is, by its very nature, both scarce and desirable. Not everyone wants to be, or wants their children to become, doctors, lawyers, architects, or engineers, but it is safe to say that there are many more parents who hope their children will obtain these jobs than parents who would like to see their children become plumbers, carpenters, or X-ray technicians. Even of those parents who are not especially ambitious for their children, there are few who would not want them to achieve "respectable" occupations and salaries that are above rather than below the national average. Inevitably, therefore, the number of people who want, or want their children to have, high- and middle-status occupations greatly exceeds the number of available positions. Somebody has to do the generally unpleasant and menial jobs that have low prestige, and somebody has to earn wages that are substantially below average. Whereas many people who do these jobs may reconcile themselves to their fate or even enjoy what they do, it is unlikely that their parents wanted their children to work in these kinds of occupations.

The scarcity and desirability of status, therefore, lead to a process of competition for the educational qualifications that have quite powerful effects on an individual's subsequent career. Students compete with each other for the grades, diplomas, and degrees that will help them achieve their occupational goals. Parents try to ensure that the school or college their children attend will give them the best possible start in life, and often spend the equivalent of a year's (or more) salary to send their children to college.

There is also competition between *groups* for educational success, attempts by those who already have high status to preserve it by ensuring that their children go to prestigious schools, and efforts by disadvantaged groups to improve their position to gaining access to better educational opportunities. Conflicts over access to what are seen as desirable educational opportunities can become a major focus of group conflict. Blacks in southern United States, for example, were denied access to predominantly white public schools and universities until the 1960s. Southern public schools were integrated only after enormous and bitter controversy, including, in some cases, the intervention of federal marshals to protect black students from angry white parents. Although the often bitter resistance of southern whites to integration reflected their prejudiced attitudes toward blacks, it was also shaped by straightforward calculations of self-interest. Segregated schools preserved the greater opportunities of white students to obtain better schooling and better jobs. Integrated schools threatened that privileged position because blacks would then be able to compete on more equal terms.

In a slightly different form, this conflict is still with us today. Bussing to achieve school integration in northern cities is highly controversial because, for many white parents, sending their children to integrated schools threatens to reduce the relative advantages they used to enjoy. Part of the reason for opposition to bussing perhaps is that parents want their children to attend neighborhood schools rather than face long journeys every day. Behind affirmations of the principle of neighborhood schools, however, lie calculations of self-interest: Attending schools that are 50 percent or more black will, many white parents feel, reduce *their* children's opportunities.

Because schooling is so closely associated with adult status, it often becomes the focus of conflicts between different groups who seek to improve their relative position. Since these conflicts usually take the form of principled educational debates about such issues as open admissions, or bilingual education, or affirmative action, we need to recognize that the roots of the conflict often lie in struggles for status and power between different groups. Affirmative action, as applied to admissions to graduate or professional schools, for example, is partly a debate about what is a fair and just admissions policy, but it is also a policy from which some groups—notably minorities and women—stand to benefit, and other groups—white males—will lose some of their previous advantages in access to scarce desirable occupations.

Equality of Opportunity

As the major link between status of origin and adult status, schools inevitably become the focus of controversy between groups seeking to improve their status in society. The root of this controversy, that status and power are scarce and that some people have more than others, is most commonly expressed in the form of an argument about *equality of opportunity* in education. Thus most of us expect schools to provide equal opportunities for all students regardless of their social origins, and to enable talented but impoverished students to achieve positions commensurate with their merits. At the same time, although this is less often stressed, we expect untalented or less motivated students, even from privileged origins, will experience some difficulty in obtaining the same status as their parents. Thus, in the broadest sense, equality of opportunity means the competition for status should be fair and just, and that merit rather than privilege should be rewarded in our schools.

Although this general principle is almost universally accepted, ambiguities remain. What sort of a school system provides true equality of opportunity? Does equality of opportunity mean simply that there are formal or legal rights for all students to attend the same school and that all should be treated alike? Or is it a system that quite consciously seeks to remove the barriers or obstacles to the success of low-status groups? Should schools or colleges be expected to compensate for the handicaps that low-status or minority students have experienced, or should they be simply required to demonstrate they have not discriminated against any group? If these questions are not complicated and difficult enough, there are also issues of what *in fact* have been the experiences of different groups in the school system. Have schools in fact worked to reinforce inequalities of class and race, or have they generally facilitated the mobility of talented but less privileged individuals and helped to create a more meritocratic society? Let us now examine, in a preliminary way, how sociologists approach these questions.

In all modern societies, sociologists have pointed out, inequality is legitimated or justified by the principle of equality of opportunity. We believe, in other words, status and income should be earned in fair competition with others, and we do not believe people deserve high-status positions simply because their parents enjoyed high status. Equality of opportunity, therefore, is the belief that such ascribed characteristics of individuals as sex, race, social class, and religion should not affect their chances of upward mobility and that only inequalities resulting from an individual's talents and efforts can be regarded as fair and just. As schooling has become more and more closely related to adult status, modern societies have increasingly looked to schools as the principal avenue through which equality of opportunity could be achieved: to provide avenues for the upward mobility of talented individuals and to compensate for the disadvantages experienced by children from low-status families.[30]

In the last sixty years virtually all modern societies have responded to demands for equality of opportunity by policies that increase educational opportunities for less privileged groups. In Great Britain, for example, before World War II it was financially very difficult for working-class parents to send their children to secondary schools with an academic curriculum. After the war, publicly supported secondary education and higher education became essentially free of charge and open to anyone who could pass the relevant examinations. By the end of the 1960s, the previous distinctions between academic secondary or "grammar" schools and other lower status vocational schools was abolished, and all children, regardless of their academic aptitude, began to attend comprehensive secondary schools. This dramatic and controversial change, still attacked by British conservatives as ruining the schools, was quite explicitly addressed to the problem of ensuring greater opportunities for working-class and disadvantaged groups.[31]

Similar changes have taken place throughout Europe in the last fifty years. Virtually everywhere before World War II, there were separate, often fee paying, schools for the talented minority that led to white-collar occupations and college entrance, and terminal secondary schools stressing vocational preparation for blue-collar occupations for the majority. Lower class children enjoyed some formal opportunities, of course, and a small number of talented working-class youth were able to gain admission to elite secondary schools and even to universities, but these numbers were miniscule. Overwhelmingly, those who entered colleges and universities, and therefore those who entered the most prestigious professions, were from highly privileged origins.[32] After World War II, however, and particularly after 1960, educational opportunities greatly increased. The number of university places available was vastly expanded and scholarships were provided for those who could not afford tuition. The previously exclusive secondary schools were opened to working-class students, and in many cases the traditional separation between academic and vocational secondary schools was abolished in favor of comprehensive high schools that all students would attend. In essentially every European country, therefore, we can speak of a dramatic and quite deliberate expansion of educational opportunities in the last forty years.[33]

Although the United States has not shared the European pattern of separate schools for different classes of students, there has been a similar revolution in equality of opportunity. After the 1954 Supreme Court decision in the case of *Brown* v. *Board of Education*, black students, previously prevented from entering white schools in the South, began attending these schools in increasing numbers, although progress was slow until after 1960. Around that time the federal government began to give substantial financial aid to local schools, with the explicit objective of equalizing educational opportunities and reducing some of the differences between well-to-do suburban schools and schools attended by poor students. In response to demands from low-status groups and their supporters for "real" rather than merely formal educational opportunities, federal and state governments began to target schools in blighted urban areas for assistance. Such programs, it was believed, were not only fair and just; they would also actually help increase the chances of talented low-status children to experience upward mobility.[34]

The massive expansion of higher education also began in the early 1960s. New junior colleges were created to provide higher education opportunities for those who could not afford college expenses or gain admission to universities because of their educational handicaps. The federal government began a program of grants and loans to students, making it possible for thousands of working-class students to attend four-year institutions for the first time. At many colleges and universities admission standards were revised so that students who were previously excluded because of their inadequate preparation could now be admitted. By 1980, for example, there were few large colleges that lacked a special office whose task it was to meet the problems of students from minority or disadvantaged origins. In 1960 such special concern was virtually unknown.

A great deal of educational change in recent decades, therefore, has had as its objective the creation of greater equality of opportunity. Partly because they have thought this ideal worthwhile and just, and partly because they have been prodded or pushed by low-status groups and their supporters, elites in every modern society have attempted to reform the educational system to help create more opportunities for the poor and the disadvantaged. In other words, a major program of educational expansion and educational reform has been seen as the key to a wider social reform: the creation of a society where inherited inequalities no longer play a major role. By some criteria, at least, these educational changes have been a striking success. The number of black women attending American colleges, for example, increased more than six times between 1960 and 1980.[35] Also, in country after country the barriers that effectively excluded working-class or minority students from prestigious educational institutions, and hence from the most desirable occupations, have disappeared. In every society, low-status groups have much greater educational opportunities today than three or four decades ago.

As many sociologists have pointed out, this success is far from unambiguous, however. In formal terms, educational opportunities for low-status groups have enormously increased, but there still remain very large differences between groups in their rates of success in school.

Black students are now much more likely to attend integrated schools in southern United States, but their test scores and dropout rates are still below those of white students.[36] The number of working-class students enrolled in college has dramatically increased since 1960, but the great majority of college students are still middle class rather than working class, and this disproportion is greater in the more prestigious colleges than in the two-year institutions.[37] Furthermore, in every country for which we have data, disadvantaged students continue to fare less well in school than more privileged students, whether we use test scores, IQ tests, grades, or years of school completed as our criterion of success. Therefore, increasing educational opportunities have not resulted in the disappearance of inequalities between individuals of different social origins in their success in school.

What is perhaps most disappointing, however, is the relative absence of evidence that increasing educational opportunities have helped reduce the more glaring inequalities between groups in terms of income and access to desirable occupations. For example, despite a very rapid increase in the number of women in colleges and in graduate school in the last two decades, working women's average salaries in 1980 remained at about 60 percent of men's salaries, virtually the same percentage as in 1960.[38] Black salaries for 1960, again approximately 60 percent of white salaries at that time, improved relative to whites during the 1960s, but were back at approximately that level by 1980.[39] Large numbers of blacks and women made great gains over the twenty-year period, of course, in considerable part because of greater educational opportunities, but *most* blacks and *most* working women have not made similar gains in income. Also, as we shall see in Chapter 4, there is little evidence that the relative chances of upward mobility of low-status children is now much higher than it was earlier this century. Low-status or working-class groups have more chances of going to college than in the past, but they have not apparently been able to translate these increased educational opportunities into an increased share of high-status jobs for their children.

All these generalizations, of course, need to be qualified and spelled out in much greater detail (as they will be in subsequent chapters). My purpose here is simply to show that the problem of equality of opportunity has in no way been solved and remains highly controversial. In a formal or legal sense, virtually all modern societies now provide equality of educational opportunity for all their citizens. Few if any students today are excluded from colleges or universities because they cannot pay the tuition, as was the case several decades ago. Also, students are no longer excluded from publicly financed schools simply because of their race, sex, religion, or social class. These changes have not always had the effects their proponents envisaged, however. Despite several decades of educational reform designed to improve their opportunities, children of low-status parents continue to be at a considerable disadvantage in the competition for educational success and high-status jobs compared with children of high-status parents. Although some groups, notably Japanese Americans and Chinese Americans, have been able to use the school system to make large gains in their relative status, most groups have been less successful in this regard.

These disappointing findings have led to several kinds of responses. Many members of minority groups and those who consider themselves politically on the left have called for more radical educational initiatives to overcome the obstacles disadvantaged children face. Calls have been made for preferential admissions to colleges and graduate schools for minority students, a new curriculum more sensitive to the needs of disadvantaged students, the abolition of biased IQ tests, and new methods of evaluation and assessment. For many of those who oppose these policies, such initiatives move us further away from a society of equal opportunity because they require reverse discrimination. Instead of assessing merit as measured by individual performance in school, these policies mean that students will be treated differently because of their social origins.

Behind this often rancorous political debate are larger questions regarding the school's role in helping to create a society of equal opportunity. Increasingly in recent years questions have been raised concerning the long-standing faith in schools as an instrument of social reform. Perhaps our convictions that schools can compensate for or overcome the handicaps suffered by disadvantaged children have been misplaced and only more modest objectives are appropriate. If we try to use schools as a way to achieve equality, this argument continues, it may well interfere with such other valued educational objectives as excellence or the maintenance of high academic standards.

In part, of course, these are philosophical and ideological disputes between people who hold different values that cannot be resolved by sociological theory or research. However, sociological knowledge can greatly clarify the issues involved. Sociologists have learned much in the last twenty years about the obstacles children from disadvantaged backgrounds face in school. Some of this knowledge has great relevance for policies designed to reduce these obstacles, and suggests why we have not been more successful in this regard. Research on trends in equality of opportunity cannot tell us which policies we *should* adopt, but it can tell us a great deal about how effective school reforms have been in the past and what the likely effect of similar policies will be in the future. Most important of all, sociological research can give us a sense of the complexity of such apparently simply questions as: Do schools reinforce inequalities of class or race? or Can schools create equality of opportunity? Our political and ideological views encourage many of us to give unequivocal answers to these questions, but much of what I shall say in this book implies that no straightforward answer can do justice to what we have discovered in two decades of research.

THE SOCIAL ORGANIZATION OF SCHOOLING

In our daily thoughts about education we often pay little attention to the distinctive character of those formal organizations we call schools. We expect schools to achieve equality of opportunity, develop cognitive skills in students, teach our cherished values to the young, and train students for work, yet we rarely reflect that the very organization of schooling may make any or all of these tasks quite difficult, and that it may be asking too much to expect the same institution to achieve all these objectives. Let us consider first some basic features common to virtually all primary and secondary schools in every modern society and then examine how the distinctive organization of schooling in the United States influences achieving these objectives.

To the sociologist, schools are first and foremost *work organizations.*[40] Like factories or offices, they are places where people are supposed to engage in productive tasks. Schools are expected to make students do things they might not otherwise choose to do: to work steadily and consistently at a variety of tasks that result in learning, such as listening to teachers, writing exercises or essays, and reading textbooks. Like adult work organizations, schools must find ways of motivating people to engage in these often onerous and difficult tasks—ensuring, for at least a fair proportion of the time, they are, for example, paying attention, not engaging in disruptive activity, and following teachers' instructions. However, there are good reasons for believing that this is rather difficult to do with any consistency, especially for older students who are rather bored with school work. Schools cannot depend on the obvious and powerful motivation of money, which is probably the single most important motivator of adult work. Since students are unpaid, schools must resort to other and perhaps less effective means of encouraging students to work hard. Teachers use different combinations of praise, appeals, and threats to enforce their often fragile authority, and, most obvious of all, they attempt to motivate students by holding out the prospect of high grades for good work and low grades for bad work. Students are told grades will have important consequences for their future career, as well as for how their parents, friends, and other teachers will think of them. No doubt for many students and in many schools, grades and other teacher evaluations work reasonably well. After all, most students do care intensely about what teachers think of them. However, if grades, as one sociologist phrased it, are thus the currency of academic life, they also have weaknesses.[41] Schools must motivate students to work hard today or this week for the sake of grades and other evaluations that follow *next* week or *next* term. Students are told that if they do not work hard today then some unpleasant consequences, like denial of college admission, menial jobs, or unemployment, will follow many years in the future. In other words, the effectiveness of grades partly depends on the ability of students to postpone gratification for a considerable period of time. Just as the fear of contracting lung cancer at age fifty or sixty does not always deter young people from smoking, grades are not always effective motivators for elementary and secondary school students.

All this would be of less importance if it were not for the fact that schools must make demands that run counter to students' natural inclinations. Unlike college students, children cannot choose whether to attend school or not, nor are they generally permitted to skip a class to which they have a particular aversion. Furthermore, unlike adults in offices or factories, students within the classroom must ignore tempting opportunities to interact with their neighbors and must instead concentrate on their own solitary work. Students are expected to remain silent unless called on by the teacher, sit relatively motionless in their seats for extended periods, and listen to what must be, for them, often tedious monologues. Paradoxically, therefore, we ask immature students to do things we do not routinely expect adults at work to do: ignore their neighbors, remain silent and close to motionless unless given explicit permission, and comply immediately and without protest with such orders as "Stop daydreaming," or "Stop gazing out of the windows." Students' lives in school are controlled and regimented in ways we would believe to be quite inappropriate in adult work organizations.

It should be no surprise, therefore, that sociologists have characterized schools as inherently conflict-prone institutions.[42] Schools are vulnerable to conflict because one or two disruptive students in the classroom can make it impossible for teachers to teach and children to learn. Conflict is also highly likely because of the demands schools make, and to some extent must make, on their students. Even if most students thoroughly enjoy the challenges of school work, some will not, and the behavior of these students must be prevented from interfering with the work of others. Even if most students do not find it intolerably onerous to sit still in their seats and pay attention, teachers will almost inevitably run into students who find the demands impossible to fulfill with any consistency. The effort to control disruptive or inattentive students can often create a vicious circle whereby disruption leads to increased controls and more rules, which in turn lead to more resentment and further disruption. Skillful teachers can isolate disruptive students and mobilize the other students against them, but less adept teachers often purchase their freedom from disruption only at the expense of the sullen resentment of the majority who may find that even their facial expressions are subject to teacher's control.

Two conclusions follow from these preliminary observations, and they will be developed in greater detail in Chapter 8. First, schools face difficult problems in getting students to work steadily and consistently at assigned tasks. A good proportion of teachers' time and energy, and some put this as high as 50 percent, is spent in managing student attention, in getting students organized to work, and in disciplining disruptive students. Much less time is actually spent in formal instruction than most of us imagine.[43] Thus if students learn less in school than we would hope, we must pay attention to how the organization of schooling creates problems of motivation and control that undermine its effectiveness. Second, and hardly less important, the organization of classroom life tends to militate against the active, inquiring, self-directed kind of learning that many believe should be the ideal of schooling. In most schools, the preoccupation with order and control results in the student role being relatively passive. Not only do teachers find it necessary to control student behavior with highly detailed rules and regulations, but they spend much of their formal teaching time in lecturing and in question-and-answer activities with the class as a whole.[44] Students in schools are not generally treated as autonomous and responsible individuals, nor are they usually taught in ways that suggest *their* ideas or opinions carry much weight. Although this state of affairs may partly be a function of teachers' lack of imagination and fear of the unknown, it is also a result of the very real problems teachers have in managing the activities of twenty-five or more students in a confined space, who are there regardless of their interests or desires. The social organization of the classroom, in other words, places constraints on the educational process that encourage teachers to treat students as passive recipients of information rather than, as many would prefer, as active, inquiring, autonomous individuals.

The Organization of U.S. Education

The organization of U.S. education differs in three important and related respects from the organization of education in much of the rest of the industrialized world. American education is highly *de-*

centralized in comparison with the central state control of education in countries like Japan, France, or Sweden.[45] In contrast to the system of *national examinations* that evaluate and control students' progress in much of the rest of the world, U.S. schools and colleges employ a course credit system that tends to treat courses and grades at one school as equivalent to work at virtually any other school. Also, compared with education in most other countries, American education is relatively *unselective.* Our schools and colleges tend to not make hard and fast distinctions between a gifted minority of students and the remainder, and to reserve separate schools and curricula for these two groups.[46] The effect of these differences in organization is to reinforce some long-standing differences between the priorities of American education and education in most other industrialized countries: a stress on the production of useful and relevant knowledge rather than the transmitting of "high culture," and an emphasis on equality of opportunity and educational equity rather than the maintenance of a set of jealously guarded high standards of excellence. In an important sense (and this point has clear relevance to the current debate on excellence in education and the alleged decline in educational standards), the organization of U.S. education militates against the maintenance of rigorous standards of academic achievement. It tends rather to encourage very diverse kinds of achievements from the majority of students rather than one kind of traditional academic excellence on the part of a few.

Decentralization

Although the role of federal and state governments has increased in recent decades, elementary and secondary education in the United States remains locally controlled to a high degree, compared to much of Europe, Japan, and the Soviet Union. Local school boards and administrators hire teachers and set their salaries and conditions of employment. Local public opinion often has a decisive impact on the curriculum—for example in deciding whether sex education, a foreign language, or art is taught. Principals and school superintendents who are unresponsive to local views as to appropriate educational priorities are likely to have brief careers. More than any other factor, local control accounts for the extraordinary diversity of American education, a diversity that is reflected in large differences between communities in what schools teach, how students are evaluated, and the status and qualifications of teachers. In countries such as France or Japan, all children of the same age study a uniform curriculum throughout the country, are evaluated by the same or similar national examinations, and are taught by teachers who, as employees of the state, have uniform salaries and conditions of work across the entire country.[47]

Despite this diversity, some broad generalizations are possible concerning the effects of this (by European standards) extreme decentralization. First, local control has meant the status of teachers has tended to be lower in U.S. education than elsewhere.[48] In part this results from the greater importance of national culture, and the authority of the teacher as representative of that culture, in societies such as France, West Germany, or Great Britain. However, it is also in part a reflection of relative power and control. Teachers in most of Europe are not at the beck and call of local community opinion because teachers are not paid by the local community. As employees of the state, they are insulated from local community politics and much less subject to the kind of moral and political scrutiny U.S. teachers have experienced in many communities. Until quite recently, it was common in many American small towns for the sexual conduct and the political orthodoxy of teachers to be thought an appropriate area of community concern.[49] It was believed U.S. teachers should set an example for the young, and those who deviated from this norm did so at the peril of their jobs. In France, Japan, or Sweden, teachers who find themselves unpopular with local community opinion can often transfer elsewhere to another school in a different part of the country. Since the local community does not pay the bills, its moral, political, and educational prejudices are of much less consequence. Such teachers may not be paid any more than their U.S. counterparts—though even here there is evidence that American teachers fare rather poorly in relative terms—but their professional careers are not subject to community control to anything like the same extent.[50]

Decentralization has also shaped the distinctive character of the American curriculum. U.S. high school students have long studied subjects that would be scarcely conceivable in most European secondary schools, for example, business English, bookkeeping, typing, or driver training. And as a number of critical reports on high school education have recently reminded us, U.S. students study foreign languages, calculus, and such scientific disciplines as physics, chemistry, and biology rather less than most European or Japanese students.[51] To be sure, some of these comparisons can be misleading because they compare unselective U.S. schools with what are often more selective schools in other countries. Even if we make allowances for these differences in selectivity and differences in school retention rates, significant contrasts remain. Most U.S. high schools have long placed relatively more emphasis on what are thought to be useful or vocational subjects of study and relatively less emphasis on rigorous education in the traditional arts and sciences than the academically oriented secondary schools of Europe. Thus students who enter European universities for the first time are unlikely to know how to type or how to drive a car, but they are more likely to know more advanced mathematics, to have read more classic literature, and to have studied more history than their American counterparts. Furthermore, once American students are in college, they are more likely to study subjects that are at least partly vocational or practical in character. Very few European students study subjects like accounting or business (long the most popular major in American universities); they are much more likely to concentrate intensively on one or more of the traditional arts and sciences.

These differences parallel and are partly explained by the long-standing contrast between central and local control of the educational curriculum. In much of Europe and in Japan national elites have played a dominant, even an exclusive, role in determining the curriculum at all levels of the educational system.[52] National elites, seeing themselves as guardians of a tradition of high culture, have worked to ensure that achievement in the traditional arts and sciences should be the main or even the sole criterion of educational excellence and educational prestige. More practical subjects or nontraditional subjects have been accorded much less prestige; they have been traditionally reserved only for those students who, it was believed, could not handle the more important subjects of the curriculum. The curriculum of the U.S. high school, by contrast, has long reflected what local communities and national elites have thought most worth studying. All U.S. high schools teach foreign languages, mathematics, literature, and science, of course, but these subjects have not had the same exclusive and unquestioned prestige they have enjoyed elsewhere. Local chambers of commerce, local businesses, and the concerns of parents that their children acquire useful and practical skills have had a decisive impact on the curriculum. Although in the largest cities this has not prevented the traditional arts and sciences from occupying the central core of the curriculum, there are many U.S. high schools where vocational and practical subjects have long enjoyed far more support (even to the extent of differential pay for vocational teachers) than what are often seen as the dry or abstract subject matters of the traditional disciplines.[53]

Examinations and Selectivity

The course credit system and the lack of national examinations also help explain some of the most distinctive features of U.S. education. American students, unlike most of their European counterparts, do not take nationally administered examinations that largely determine their educational fate and strongly affect their future careers. British students who fail the General Certificate of Education Examination at age sixteen, for example, are effectively excluded from any opportunities for higher education, as are French students who fail to pass the quite rigorous Baccalaureate examination. In the United States, by contrast, success and failure are gradual or cumulative in character. Students graduate from high school and college on the basis of the accumulation of courses and grades from a variety of individual teachers, without the sudden punctuation of rigorous and demanding examinations over which their own teachers and schools have little if any control. However, to European or Japanese students success in individual courses with individual teachers matters little if it is not accompanied by success in nationally administered examinations taken by thousands of students from many different schools.[54]

Because examinations are the most important event in students' careers, preparing for them dominates the life of the school in much of Europe, imposing a high degree of uniformity in the curriculum and in teaching methods from one school to another. Only at the elementary level do French or British teachers enjoy the kind of discretion over curriculum materials and teaching methods that American teachers routinely exercise. Those who teach teenage students must adhere closely to the prescribed syllabus and to teaching methods that produced examination success in the past. Teachers who stray from this narrow path—teachers, for example, who emphasize social history rather than diplomatic history when the latter is the subject of the examination—endanger not only their own but the school's reputation. Even at the college level, teachers must gear their lectures and course materials toward the examinations at the end of the year. It is on these examinations, graded by anonymous examiners often from other universities, that the students' fate depends, and it is therefore the job of faculty to prepare students for these examinations rather than to teach material they believe is of more interest or significance.

As with central control, examination-based systems therefore create what is by American standards a great deal of uniformity in the curriculum. Although there has been some increased flexibility in recent decades, examinations tend to be offered only in relatively traditional arts and sciences disciplines, in political and diplomatic history rather than social history or sociology, in classical music rather than in jazz, and in physics or chemistry rather than in general science. Thus European students typically study fewer different subjects than American students, and the subjects they do study are more likely to be one of the traditional disciplines taught in a relatively traditional manner. In addition, the United States has no equivalent system of national examinations that imply a set of relatively uniform nationwide standards of excellence. Students who wish to enter British or French universities, for example, must first pass demanding nationally administered examinations in several different fields. Thus, unlike American college students, all university entrants have met certain uniform criteria of academic achievement. Employers frequently use examination success at age fifteen or sixteen as their principal criterion for distinguishing between promising and less promising candidates for a job. Employers and the public at large believe examination results are significant in terms of minimal competence and probable aptitudes.

In contrast, the lack of national examinations in the United States makes it extremely difficult to compare students with one another or graduates of one school with graduates of another school. This is not to say standards of evaluation are therefore necessarily lower in the United States than in much of Europe, but the practical effect of leaving evaluation to individual teachers and schools is that many students, particularly those in schools outside the wealthier communities, are able to obtain grades of A or B without demonstrating the kind of achievement that would be necessary to pass European-style examinations. In some schools and some highly selective universities, U.S. students are evaluated every bit as rigorously as their French or British counterparts, but the gap between those standards and the standards prevailing in the majority of institutions is considerably larger than in most of Europe. Examination systems, by their very nature, mean that large numbers of students experience failure in a dramatic fashion—and one thinks here of the tragic cases of suicide among Japanese youth who fail the examination for entrance to the best universities[55]— but they also set relatively clear and rigorous standards of achievement throughout the *whole* educational system, of which there is no counterpart in U.S. education.

Finally, U.S. education differs from education in most other societies in the degree of its selectivity. Academic secondary schools and colleges in Europe have long been far more selective than American high schools and colleges. As recently as 1960, for example, only 3 percent of British students aged eighteen or nineteen were admitted to colleges or universities, compared with more than 25 percent in the United States, and less than 15 percent were successful in passing the "11 plus" examination that allowed them to enter secondary schools with a predominantly academic curriculum.[56] Until very recently, most European societies maintained essentially separate systems of education for the small minority who were deemed academically talented, and the majority who were thought incapable of serious academic work. In practice, though not in theory, this distinction coincided with a deep cleavage between terminal schools stressing vocational skills attended by mostly working-class students and rigorous academic schools attended by overwhelmingly middle- and upper-class students. Although this difference between Europe and America is not as sharp today as in the past, the percentage of students attending college in the United States remains more than double the percentage for any Western European country.

American schools, therefore, to a much greater degree than in much of the rest of the world, have attempted not to make hard and fast distinctions between different kinds of students, to keep all students together in the same institution, and to permit second or third chances for students who do not make the grade. With the exception of black students in the southern states, U.S. high schools have long enrolled virtually all students of a given age in that community, and although these schools have been internally divided into tracks, the distinctions between them have never been as sharp and impermeable as those between the separate schools attended by European secondary students. Students in the United States have also traditionally remained much longer in schools than their European counterparts. If this has meant, as some national commissions now complain, that students graduate without minimal skills in literacy or numeracy, most Americans have long believed that all students, even those without academic talents, can benefit by extensive formal education. Higher education has also been very unselective, by European standards. Almost all European students apply and gain admission to a particular college or university and remain there until graduation. In the United States not only are standards of admission for most colleges rather less rigorous, but students can routinely transfer credits from one institution to other institutions of very different academic standards. Thus U.S. students who fare poorly in high school can attend a community college, and on the basis of their record at that institution, transfer to a major state university. Few would argue that a literature course in a high-caliber university is the same thing as a literature course at a community college, yet the system of credit equivalence treats them as though they were identical.

In all these respects, the distinctive organization of U.S. schooling shapes its educational outcomes. The decentralization of U.S. education, the absence of a system of national examinations, and its relative lack of selectivity are partly responsible for what are generally considered to be both its strengths and weaknesses. Historically one of the great strengths of the U.S. system has been its unparalleled opportunities for all students, including those from less privileged origins. Unlike most students elsewhere, American students have not been subject to the kind of invidious distinctions at an early age between the talented minority and the less talented majority that effectively closed off educational opportunities for most European students. In addition, American education has never made the sharp distinction between patrician or serious and plebian or unserious subject matter that is common in other schools. Because of the weakness of national elites and the decentralization of control, the range of subject matter considered worth studying, from agriculture to business or from the problems of the environment to sex education has always been much wider than in

Europe. Students have more choice at almost every level of the system and, one suspects, they have rather more interesting choices than are provided in most European schools and colleges. Teachers and schools are freer to teach what they want and what local communities deem important than is possible in centralized, examination-based systems.

However, if these strengths flow from the organization of U.S. education, many of the most criticized features of the U.S. schooling can be attributed to the same source. Some highly selective U.S. universities and high schools encourage their students to achieve levels of excellence in science, mathematics, literature, or history that equal or surpass the best European schools. Also, some individual teachers at virtually every institution encourage high standards of achievement. The organization of American education cannot be said to be conducive to the maintenance of rigorous academic standards as a primary goal, however. The absence of national examinations means that grading and promotion standards differ greatly from one school to another and between teachers within the same school. In many cases, demands for equal or open access or demands that students should be given another chance will conflict with attempts to enforce the rule that work below a certain minimum standard is unacceptable. Faced with a relatively unselected group of students, many of whom have real difficulty with the subject matter, college instructors cannot very well fail over half the class because they do not meet the standards of excellence they themselves would like to maintain. Almost inevitably, therefore, in the absence of agreed upon and external criteria of excellence, evaluation tends to be shaped by the *actual* achievements of the majority of the student body.[57]

If diversity and relevance are considered strengths of the U.S. curriculum, the other side of this coin is that U.S. students spend less time studying the traditional and basic subjects of the liberal arts and sciences and more time in what some conservatives are fond of calling frills. However, if mathematics and science education and foreign language instruction are both less extensive and less rigorous than in France and Great Britain, this is a predictable outcome of decentralization and the lack of a system of national examinations that would effectively prescribe such curricula. Local communities and state legislators, until recently at least, have not uniformly insisted that these subjects are of such importance that courses such as driver training, business English, or home economics should be dropped to make room for them. Also, if national elites are convinced that some change in educational priorities is called for and that weaknesses in science and mathematics education need to be remedied,[58] as seemed to be the case in the early and mid–1980s, it is far from clear that most local communities share this sense of urgency and are willing to scrap their long-standing preferences for utilitarian and vocational subject matter in favor of single-minded concentration in these fundamental disciplines. Nor is it obvious that if such a change in priorities did take place, highly trained mathematics, science, or foreign language teachers could be attracted into what remains, by European standards, a low-status profession.

All these considerations have substantial relevance to recent debates on excellence in education, to claims that the American educational system is thoroughly mediocre in its lack of emphasis on rigorous standards, and to calls for an abandonment of frills and return to basics. Nothing I have said implies that reform along these lines is impossible, of course, and indeed there are a number of signs in the mid–1980s— tightening admission standards to universities, minimal competency examinations for high school seniors, and more emphasis on required courses—that may indicate a reversal of many of the trends of the 1960s and 1970s. However, the unique structural and organizational features of the U.S. system of education, which, of course, are highly resistant to change, would seem to set limits to how much educational priorities can be shifted in any fundamental way. To ask that U.S. high schools concentrate on rigorous achievement in the traditional disciplines to the same degree as highly selective French schools, for example, would seem unrealistic, given the absence of national examinations, the decentralized control of education, and the unselective character of U.S. education. Similarly, it is unlikely that the achievement of most U.S. high school students in science and mathematics could soon parallel the standards achieved by many of their Soviet counterparts. There are no national or regional examining bodies that could maintain and insist on these standards in each and every school, and the relatively low status of teachers makes it unlikely that massive numbers of highly qualified people could be lured away from lucrative jobs elsewhere to teach these subjects. Nor is it clear that large numbers of American parents would be willing for their children to experience the kind of repeated failure that new and rigorous standards would, initially at least, imply.

Finally, as I will make clear later in this book, not all educational objectives are compatible with one another. To place more stress on basic disciplines means there will be *less* time for and emphasis on other subjects that are in the curriculum because some groups and some communities regard them as of great importance (even though some may regard them as frills). Raising admission standards for universities and tightening requirements for promotion from grade to grade may encourage many students to work harder and achieve more, but it will almost certainly increase the sense of failure and discouragement of other students. Furthermore, much evidence shows that those who will become discouraged and drop out of school in these circumstances will be disproportionately drawn from disadvantaged and minority backgrounds.[59] In other words, the cost of remedying the weaknesses of U.S. education may be in the risk of undermining what have been historically regarded as its greatest strengths: its emphasis on equality as well as excellence, and its stress on acquiring useful or relevant knowledge as well as achievement in the arts and sciences.

SOCIOLOGICAL RESEARCH AND THE STUDY OF SCHOOLS

Sociology is often seen as a scientific subject whose task is to discover objective knowledge about social phenomena. The job of the sociologist is to construct theories and hypotheses and then to test these ideas by subjecting them to the scrutiny of empirical evidence. Such scientific procedures are often contrasted with reliance on opinion, illustration, or examples characteristic of everyday discourse. Laypersons have opinions they support with illustrations, whereas social scientists make generalizations supported with data or facts. Such a stereotype is not entirely misleading. Sociologists, whatever their differences may be, are concerned with theory and evidence; the search for data that enables them to test their ideas and respect for what that evidence shows is fundamental to the sociological enterprise. Although such a simple distinction between common sense thought and scientific or sociological research is not wholly false, it can lead to a number of misconceptions about the nature of sociological research and the contribution it can make to an understanding of schooling. I will attempt to correct some of the possible misconceptions and, in so doing, indicate the kind of analysis I shall pursue in this book.

The trappings of large-scale sociological research—the esoteric and specialized language, the technical methodology—may lead many to conclude that this research is more definitive than is in fact the case, and that the knowledge produced has a relatively high degree of certainty. However, the sheer complexity of the process of schooling and the difficulties sociologists encounter in obtaining evidence about what schools do and do not do make any definitive or certain knowledge unlikely. Sociological knowledge of schools is greatly superior to that of common sense, but it is hardly certain knowledge. Those who cannot tolerate uncertainty are advised to look to the popular educational panaceas found in any bookstore. There we can find certainty and definitive conclusions but not, I suspect, a great deal of reliable or objective knowledge.

If the complex nature of schooling makes conclusions about what schools do very difficult, the task of the sociologist is further complicated by the fact that schooling is a subject about which virtually everybody has strong convictions. The controversies surrounding schooling make the kind of dispassionate inquiry that we think of as the hallmark of the scientific method a great deal more difficult. Let me now discuss in some detail why it is a difficult and uncertain process to obtain reliable knowledge about schooling and its effects.

Methodological Difficulties in the Study of Schooling

Some of the most frequently asked questions in the study of education concern the effects of different schooling experiences on students. Thus we can ask specific questions about the effects of a specific elementary curriculum on the reading skills of young children, questions about the relationships between teaching styles and student learning, and questions about the effects of small and large class sizes on the speed with which students acquire cognitive skills. We can also ask very general questions about what schools teach: Does a liberal arts college promote liberal values? Do high schools teach patriotism and punctuality? Do open schools teach or promote different values than traditional schools? These questions are all basically similar. They require that we identify and measure those characteristics of schooling in whose effects we are interested and then measure these effects by observing differences in outcomes among students who have been exposed to this kind of schooling and those who have been exposed to some different educational experience. The difficulties involved in answering even the simplest of these questions are formidable. I shall illustrate some of the difficulties with a brief discussion of the problems in assessing the impact of integrated and segregated schools on student learning.

Assessing School Effects

The first problem confronting all such studies of school effects is measuring and identifying the independent variable necessary for scientific research. It is not difficult, of course, to identify which schools are integrated and which are segregated and devise some scale or degree of integration. The difficulties arise when we recognize that integrated schools are likely to differ from segregated schools in a number of respects besides their racial composition. Integrated schools, for example, may spend more money on the average pupil, hire better teachers, or have different curricula. Quite simply, integrated schools may also be schools that we regard commonsensically as better than segregated schools. To study the effects of racial composition in schools, therefore, sociologists must find a way of controlling for these other potential differences between integrated and segregated schools. Similar problems, of course, confront virtually any study of the effects of any school characteristic. Sociologists can, for example, measure the degree to which the classrooms in a particular school are open or closed, but they must be extremely cautious before concluding that any differences in student performance in the two types of classrooms is not due to other differences between these classrooms. Open classrooms may employ teacher aides and recruit unusually enthusiastic teachers; traditional classrooms may not.

A second difficulty in researching the effects of schooling is that different schools attract different kinds of students. Integrated and segregated schools, for example, may contain students who differ in initial ability and motivation. If there is one universally accepted finding in the study of schooling and its effects, it is that student characteristics have a powerful effect on student performance and test scores, independent of the characteristics of the school they attend. Teachers and principals understandably tend to argue that high test scores or other evidence of student performance are results of their teaching or of the quality of the educational program their institution offers. Without substantial evidence of student characteristics, however, sociologists cannot know if these claims are justified. What they do know is that the ability, motivation, and socioeconomic status of students vary from school to school, and that in any one school these characteristics may change a great deal over a number of years. At the very least, therefore, control for the influence of these possibly contaminating variables is necessary before concluding anything about effects of schools.

Although research has become a great deal more sophisticated in recent years in ferreting out the mutual impact of student and school characteristics, it is important to recognize that these controls are necessarily imperfect. IQ tests, for example, do not capture everything that we mean when we talk about ability, especially when administered to groups of students rather than to individual students. Measures of socioeconomic status reveal only approximately the large differences among individuals from the widely differing environments that help to shape success or failure in school. Nor can sociologists expect to measure *all* characteristics of students that may influence their performance in school or to isolate these characteristics from those of the schools. Social scientists cannot do, of course, what is commonplace in the physical sciences—they cannot conduct an experimental manipulation of all the relative variables. Social scientists cannot conduct a large-scale experiment, randomly assigning students to integrated and segregated schools or to open and traditional classrooms by a toss of the coin, even though with such a method they could have considerable confidence that any observed differences between schools are not attributable to differences in the characteristics of the student body.

Finally, all research on the effects of schooling is plagued by a dilemma that resists solution. On the one hand, if the problems I have described of making valid inferences from the data are to be even partly resolved, the social scientist must use quite elaborate statistical techniques to control for the influence of possibly contaminating variables. This suggests that they must study hundreds of schools at one time, or better still, that they study many schools over a number of years, measuring the test scores or other indicators of student learning at perhaps six-month intervals. The statistical controls needed to make valid inferences from data simply require large numbers of cases. At the same time, the larger the study the more difficult it is to use any but the crudest indicators of school and student characteristics and learning outcomes. In a large-scale study, social scientists may have to use students' estimates of their parents' income as the measure of socioeconomic status. They may have to rely on group-administered IQ tests as the sole measure of ability. They may have no recourse but to use crude summary measures of cognitive skills that can be compared across all schools.

The larger the study, therefore, the more difficult it is to do justice to the subtlety and complexity of schooling and its effects on students. Case studies of individual schools, again preferably over an extended time period, can move us much closer to this reality. A study of several classrooms within one school or a comparison between two schools can satisfy the desire for measures and indicators that reflect the observed complexity. A well-executed, small-scale study can be intellectually satisfying in a way that is difficult, if not impossible, for a study of thousands of schools with a few crudely measured variables to be. In generating fruitful ideas about what schools teach and how students learn, there are few substitutes for the day-to-day observations of the participant observer. However, small-scale studies clearly have serious disadvantages unless the observations of the studies are made over a substantial time period on a substantial number of students. With such a small sample, it is particularly difficult to determine whether any observed learning effects are indeed the result of a particular independent variable—class size, teacher styles, curricula, or track assignment—rather than a result of initial differences in student characteristics. The results of such a study, furthermore, cannot be generalized to other schools and other students without further information. What may appear to be quite general and positive about school effects may turn out to be idiosyncratic effects unique to a particular school.

None of these problems means that sociologists know nothing

about the effects of schools on students, nor that research on this question is confronted with difficulties of such magnitude as to render it impossible. Existing evidence on what schools do and do not do, however imperfect, is a great deal better than common sense guesses. Many theories and hypotheses about the effects of schools are made more or less plausible by this evidence, but knowledge of the effects of schooling is, for the reasons I have suggested, both limited and uncertain. Instead of the polarized certainties that characterize much popular discussion of schooling and its effects, sociology offers a painstaking and difficult search for evidence, an awareness of the pitfalls and errors that can characterize any conclusions about the effects of schools, and recognition that whatever answers do derive from this search are necessarily tentative.

Ideological Barriers to Clear Thought about Schools

If sociological research on schools is subject to formidable methodological difficulties, sociological theories of schools and their role in society are often inextricably involved with the kinds of ideological controversies described earlier in this chapter. Theories of schooling, in principle at least, purport to describe what is the case, rather than what should be the case. They are attempts to explain why schools have one set of effects instead of other effects, and to provide a general interpretation of what schools do rather than a set of assertions about what schools ought to do. However, in practice it is often difficult to separate the general interpretative and explanatory statements we call theories from the mixture of arguments, values, and assumptions we call ideologies. Sociologists, like everyone else, have political opinions about such issues as the nature of power and inequality in our society, assumptions about the nature of human motivation and the distribution of human abilities, and opinions about how schools should be changed to realize their ideals. Inevitably these assumptions and premises shape the kind of theories they find most plausible as professional sociologists as well as the beliefs they hold as private citizens. Consider, for example, the problem of theories of inequality in schooling.

Until the late 1960s the dominant interpretation of the effects of schooling on inequality was what we shall term the *functional theory.* In this basically optimistic and liberal interpretation, schools were agencies that helped create a more meritocratic society: a society of equal opportunity where status would increasingly depend on ability and effort rather than inherited privilege. The steady expansion of educational opportunities, this theory claimed, would gradually result in the improvement of the position of disadvantaged groups as more and more talented lower-class individuals achieved upward mobility through the educational system. From this theory's perspective, these developments were not only humane, they were also *functional* or rational for the welfare of the society. Schools provided the indispensable function of sorting and selecting the most talented people for the most important high-status positions. In that regard, they contributed to the welfare of the society by helping to ensure that only the most competent filled the most important jobs and by enabling all groups to participate in this competition on equal terms.

Beginning about 1970, however, this theory began to be challenged by quite a different interpretation. In this more radical and pessimistic account, schools have tended to solidify and reinforce existing inequalities rather than create a more meritocratic society. In this view, schools have long worked to consolidate the advantaged position of high-status groups and to convince the poor and disadvantaged that they have only themselves to blame for their failure. To accomplish this task, schools used supposedly objective measures of intelligence to demonstrate that, by and large, poor students have less intellectual abilities than privileged students. In reality, these tests are heavily biased against lower-class groups, and (in some versions of this argument) deliberately designed to measure only those skills that are prominently displayed by middle-class students. Behind the facade of the rhetoric of an increasingly meritocratic society, therefore, schools continue to do what they have always done: convince the poor and disadvantaged that they do not have the skills to obtain high-status positions and to reinforce the dominant position of privileged groups.

In this debate, questions of ideology and questions of theory and evidence are almost inextricably intertwined. In principle, most of the issues involved are empirical questions that could be resolved by a patient search for the relevant evidence. In practice, however, opinions on any one of these questions are often closely related to opinions on the remainder of the issues, and these in turn are related to commitment to a particular ideology. Those who are highly critical of the extent of inequality in contemporary society, for example, are likely to believe both that schools perpetuate existing inequalities and that IQ tests systematically load the dice against the poor and the disadvantaged. To many political radicals, indeed, it is entirely *obvious* that schools cause lower-class failure by a combination of biased testing procedures, tracking them into vocational courses, and by lower teacher expectations.

For those with opposed ideological preconceptions, quite different interpretations are obvious and in need of little or no evidence. For many who see our society as increasingly meritocratic and more dependent on competence and expertise it is obvious that intelligence, whether acquired early in life or genetically determined, is an extremely powerful determinant of success in school and in life. If lower-class students fail in school, therefore, this is not because, except in unusual circumstances, schools discriminate against lower-class students, but because such students are either culturally deprived or lack native ability.

If we knew a great deal more about human abilities, school success, and inequality than we do, much of this ideological controversy would be far less significant. If we knew more about mental ability, for example, we might be able to say that X percent of intelligence is inherited, Y percent is acquired in the first three years of life, and Z percent can be modified in later life. With more knowledge about the determinants of success in school, sociologists could say, whatever individuals with different ideological views would like to believe, that success in school performance is largely determined by a particular combination of types of ability in association with particular kinds of teaching styles. In fact, of course, they do not have this kind of reliable knowledge, either about the determinants of success in school or about the effects of school on students, and still less about such global questions as the relationship between schooling and the wider society. Sociology does have a great deal more knowledge than fifteen or twenty years ago, and a major purpose of this book will be to present this knowledge as fairly and clearly as possible. However, the relative paucity of knowledge in relation to the questions needing answers still permits widely different interpretations.

Disentangling Ideology and Theory

These considerations explain why clear thought about schools is so difficult, even more difficult perhaps than on most subjects of sociological concern. On the one hand, most of us have theories about schools, about what schools teach, how children learn, and why some children succeed and others fail—theories heavily shaped by ideological convictions about the character of the social world and human nature. On the other hand, sociology's knowledge of schooling, in a scientific sense, is highly imperfect. The temptation to fill in those large knowledge gaps by reference to ideological convictions is powerful: to say, for example, that of course students learn more in open classrooms than in traditional classrooms or of course traditional classrooms are more effective in teaching punctuation, spelling, and other basic skills. The search for reliable and valid knowledge about schools and their effects, knowledge that might be a basis for policies to create schools to work in the way intended, is not only inherently difficult, but is also greatly complicated by the ideological assumptions shaping the kinds of questions asked and the answers expected.

meritocratic

The solution to this problem does not lie in abandoning all ideological preconceptions and pursuing objective, value-free social science. Such a strategy ignores the fact that the obstacles to clear and rational thought about schools come from taken-for-granted assumptions that are unconscious rather than conscious ideological prejudices. A great deal of the older research on inequality in schooling, for example, now strikes most people as profoundly limited and misleading, but this is not primarily because such work was motivated by conscious political bias to blame the poor for failing to create a stimulating environment for their children. That earlier work was limited because it took for granted a series of assumptions—an increasingly meritocratic society, an undifferentiated concept of intelligence, the obvious relationship between intelligence and success in school—leading almost inevitably to a particular interpretation of inequality in school performance. These assumptions in turn were part of an optimistic, liberal ideology that stressed the increased importance of ability in contemporary industrial society and the school's role in searching out that ability. If growing numbers of intellectuals and social scientists now reject these assumptions for a less sanguine and more skeptical view of the nature of the achievement in modern society, it is by no means clear that increasingly popular contemporary explanations of that inequality—as a product of self-fulfilling prophecies and teacher expectations or of middle-class curricula—do not also contain taken-for-granted assumptions of their own that, in the future, we will come to see as equally problematic.

The role of sociologists of education, therefore, should be broader than the task of weighing evidence against competing theories. They must also examine the intellectual assumptions underlying particular theories that prevail in the field: theories of the determinants of success in school, theories of what schools teach, and theories of the role of schooling in contemporary society. If these assumptions cannot always be subject to empirical test (assumptions about the character of human nature can probably never be falsified or confirmed in any scientific sense), there is great merit in simply explicating these assumptions and laying bare what is often taken for granted in a particular theory or research study. Such a process of explication will not free sociologists entirely from the preconceptions of their own time, but to ignore this task will probably guarantee that their work will, at some future time, either be ignored or held up as an example of some dead tradition of research that made assumptions or posed questions now seen as invalid or no longer significant. Sociologists, like everyone else, are to a substantial degree prisoners of the intellectual fashions and assumptions of their time; but if they cannot escape from these constraints entirely, they can at least make efforts to become aware of the nature of these fashions and assumptions.

CONCLUSION

In this chapter I have given reasons why people who are interested in schools should also be interested in sociology by illustrating some of the distinctive insights and ideas that the sociological approach to schooling offers. The most important conclusion of that discussion is that what might seem at first sight to be strictly educational issues are on closer examination inextricably involved with larger social and political questions in the wider society. As agencies of cultural transmission, schools are charged with reproducing in the minds of the young the central ideals, values, and cultural emphases of the society. Because consensus on which of many values and ideals should be taught is often fragile or nonexistent, what schools teach (or perhaps what schools *appear* to teach) is almost inevitably controversial. Although these controversies are often phrased in strictly educational terms—implying that some educational expert has an answer to them—they almost always involve some larger debate about what kind of individuals we want our children to become and what kind of society we want in the future. This is as true of the current controversy over "quality education" and declining achievement as it was of the criticisms of overregimented and authoritarian schooling that were so much a feature of the early 1970s.

Schools are also inevitably the subject of controversy because they are, particularly in contemporary societies, so closely tied to the allocation of scarce and desirable high-status positions. Here again, popular discussion of education tends to minimize the extent of conflict that results from this development. However, the hard sociological fact is that since formal education now constitutes the major avenue of upward mobility, and since not everyone can enjoy such mobility, different groups in society will come to focus on schools as a major way either to preserve their advantaged position or to improve their disadvantaged status. Behind the philosophical and educational debates about the true meaning of equality of opportunity or the merits of affirmative action, in other words, is a struggle between individuals and groups for higher status for their children. While future schools can perhaps provide greater opportunities for the children of disadvantaged groups than they do now, and certainly more than they have in the past, there is a sense in which, like the debate over cultural transmission, the issue can never be resolved to everyone's satisfaction. In a diverse and unequal society no schools can satisfy everyone's ideals of a good education: policies that help one group of students succeed may well hurt the relative chances of other groups; new rigorous curricula stressing science and mathematics will almost inevitably mean that other subjects, of deep concern to some, will receive less emphasis.

If, for these reasons, schools are often at the center of social and political controversies, the social organization of schooling places constraints on the kinds of outcomes that the parties to this debate can reasonably expect. On the one hand, virtually all classrooms everywhere are organized in a way that tends to encourage passive compliance rather than active engagement on the part of the student. Imaginative and resourceful teachers, of course, can overcome the problems of motivating a captive audience without recourse to the kinds of detailed control that often breed sullen resistance among many students, but many teachers cannot. In many schools the problems of coordinating and controlling the activities of a large number of students tend to interfere with the task many contemporary educators see as supremely important: promoting active rather than passive learning styles, encouraging independent thought, and meeting the needs of each individual student. Furthermore, the organization of U.S. education tends to create a bias in favor of one set of educational outcomes, equality and equity, relevance and usefulness, at the expense of other and more currently fashionable outcomes: achievement in the basic disciplines or maintenance of high standards of excellence. Because schools in the United States have long been locally rather than centrally controlled and because of the relative weakness of national educational elites and the relative absence of examinations, U.S. schools have long been less concerned than their counterparts in Europe with maintaining high achievement in the traditional arts and sciences. Other concerns—the promotion of more equal opportunity, the reluctance to label students as incapable of benefitting from formal education, and the provision of relevant and useful knowledge—have long had relatively more importance in the United States than a single-minded concentration on excellence in the traditional disciplines. Although these concerns partly reflect differences between U.S. values and European values, they are, to some extent, built into the organization of U.S. schooling. The distinctive organization of education in the United States is designed to produce great diversity in the curriculum rather than a concentration on the traditional arts and sciences, and an emphasis on equality and equity rather than the outstanding achievements of a few.

In the first part of the chapter I have showed how a sociological perspective on schooling raises issues and questions that are often ignored in popular discussions about the problems of schooling. Popular discussion usually takes the social organization of schooling for granted. It tends to see schools simply as instruments for carrying out society's bidding without regard to the very real difficulties of shaping these often refractory institutions to achieve goals different from those they have traditionally achieved. Popular discussion is also sometimes naive about the nature of these goals, confusing the fashions of the moment with long-standing values, and minimizing the extent to which different groups in society have different goals for schooling. However, as my discussion of sociological research in schooling implies, that naivete applies to ways in which we often view the role of sociological and scientific research on schools as well. Research can provide much better answers to many of the most commonly asked questions about schooling than seat-of-the-pants guesses or answers based on the received conventional wisdom. But two considerations make it likely that these answers will be partial rather than complete and tentative rather than definitive. First, it is very difficult, for methodological reasons, to answer questions like: What kinds of schools are most effective? If we are interested in the effects of different kinds of schools on students, for example, it is extremely difficult to separate the school's effects from the effects that can be attributed to the fact that different schools attract different kinds of students. Second, and equally important, sociological research is conducted by individuals with particular ideological and political assumptions, and these assumptions continually threaten to get in the way of the quest for objective or scientific knowledge. Sociologists are committed to different theories of what schools in fact do and to different cultural and political ideals about what they *should* do. These assumptions shape the kinds of questions sociologists ask and the way in which they report the evidence despite conscious attempts to be fair and objective. It is important to note that the implication of this fact is not that all research is equally biased or that one person's opinion is as good as any other's. Sociologists have discovered real knowledge about schools and it would be foolish for the layperson or the policy maker to ignore this knowledge. My argument does imply, however, that we should look to sociology for the *clarification* of the questions we ask about schooling and seek tentative rather than definitive answers to our educational problems. Only through such painstaking and wide-ranging inquiry are we likely to achieve the kind of knowledge upon which effective educational policy can be based.

Endnotes

1. Charles Silberman's *Crisis in the Classroom* (New York: Random House, 1969) is the most representative account of the mood of this period. For a detailed, retrospective, and critical account, see Diane Ravitch, *The Troubled Crusade: American Education 1945–80* (New York: Basic Books, 1983), Chapters 5 and 7.

2. Silberman, *Crisis in the Classroom.* See also Lawrence Kohlberg and Rochelle Mayer, "Development as the Aim of Education," *Harvard Educational Review* 42 (1972): 449–496.

3. The most influential of the many reports of 1983 was National Commission on Excellence in Education, *A Nation at Risk: The Imperative for Educational Reform* (Washington, D.C.: U.S. Government, 1983).

4. Ravitch, *The Troubled Crusade,* Chapter 2.

5. For the earlier excellence movement, see John W. Gardner, *Excellence* (New York: Harper, 1961).

6. Arthur Bestor, *Educational Wastelands* (Urbana, Ill.: University of Illinois Press, 1953); and Hyman Rickover, *Education and Freedom* (New York: Dutton, 1959).

7. Ravitch, *The Troubled Crusade.*

8. There are also a few educators who have, to their credit, managed to remain immune to whatever crisis is currently fashionable. See John I. Goodlad, *A Place Called School* (New York: McGraw Hill, 1983).

9. Consider, for example, how dated the diagnosis now seems in Silberman, *Crisis in the Classroom.* See especially Chapter 4, "Education for docility."

10. Philip K. Bock, *Modern Cultural Anthropology* (New York: Knopf, 1969); and Raymond Firth, *We, The Tikopia* (Boston: Beacon Press, 1957).

11. Urie Bronfennbrenner, *Two Worlds of Childhood: U.S. and U.S.S.R.* (New York: Russell Sage, 1970).

12. Robert Dreeben, *On What Is Learned in School* (Reading, Mass.: Addison-Wesley, 1968).

13. Remi Clignet, *Liberty and Equality in the Educational Process* (New York: Wiley, 1974); and Ronald S. Anderson, *Education in Japan* (Washington, D.C.: U.S. Government, 1975).

14. Jacqueline Kasun, "Turning Children into Sex Experts," *The Public Interest* No. 55 (Spring 1979): 3–14.

15. Martin Eger, "The Conflict in Moral Education: An Informal Case Study," *The Public Interest* 63 (Spring 1981): 62–80.

16. See Silberman, *Crisis in the Classroom,* Chapter 4; and John Holt, *How Children Fail* (New York: Pitman, 1964).

17. Paul Goodman, "The Present Moment in Education," *New York Review of Books,* April 10, 1969.

18. National Commission on Excellence in Education, *A Nation at Risk;* and National Science Board Commission on Precollege Education in Mathematics, Science and Technology, *Educating Americans for the 21st Century* (Washington, D.C.: National Science Foundation, 1983).

19. Daniel Bell, *The Coming of Post-Industrial Society* (New York: Basic Books, 1973).

20. Christopher Jencks, et al., *Inequality* (New York: Basic Books, 1972), pp. 19 and 21.

21. Bell, *The Coming of Post-Industrial Society,* p. 246.

22. Charles Anderson (ed.), *Fact Book for Academic Administrators, 1981–2* (New York: American Council of Educators, 1982), pp. 140–180.

23. Ibid., pp. 140–180.

24. Burton Clark, *Educating the Expert Society* (San Francisco: Chandler, 1961).

25. Ivar Berg, *Education and Jobs: The Great Training Robbery* (New York: Praeger, 1970).

26. James O'Toole, *Work, Learning and the American Future* (San Francisco: Jossey Bass, 1977).

27. Randell Collins, *The Credential Society* (New York: Academic Press, 1979).

28. Ronald Dore, *The Diploma Disease* (Berkeley: University of California Press, 1976).

29. He wrote: "Today, the certificate of education becomes what the test for ancestors has been in the past." Hans Gerth and C. Wright Mills (eds.), *From Max Weber: Essays in Sociology* (London: Routledge and Kegan Paul, 1948), pp. 240–241.

30. We shall examine the evidence that schools have had this effect in Chapter 4.

31. A. H. Halsey, A. F. Heath, and J. M. Ridge, *Origins and Destinations: Family, Class and Education in Modern Britain* (New York: Oxford University Press, 1980).

32. Ibid.

33. Raymond Boudon, *Education, Opportunity and Social Inequality* (New York: Wiley, 1974).

34. Ravitch, *The Troubled Crusade.*

35. U.S. Department of Commerce, Bureau of the Census, *Statistical Abstract of the U.S. 1981* (Washington, D.C., 1982), p. 159, Table 267.

36. Jencks, et al., *Inequality,* p. 81.

37. Jerome Karabel, "Community Colleges and Social Stratification," *Harvard Educational Review* 42 (1972): 521–562.

38. U.S. Department of Commerce, Bureau of the Census, *Statistical Abstract of the United States, 1983* (Washington, D.C., 1984), p. 434.

39. Richard Freeman, "Black Economic Progress Since 1964," *The Public Interest* No. 52 (Summer 1978): 52–68; and U.S. Department of Commerce, Bureau of the Census, *Statistical Abstract,* p. 465.

40. Charles Bidwell, "The School as a Social Organization," in John G. March (ed.), *Handbook of Organizations* (Chicago: Rand McNally, 1965).

41. Howard S. Becker, Blanche Geer, and Everett C. Hughes, *Making the Grade* (New York: Wiley, 1968).

42. Willard Waller, *The Sociology of Teaching* (New York: Wiley, 1961) (originally published in 1932).

43. Eleanor Leacock, *Teaching and Learning in City Schools* (New York: Basic Books, 1969).

44. John I. Goodlad, *A Place Called School* (New York: McGraw-Hill, 1983).

45. Harry Passow, et al., *The National Case Study: An Empirical Comparative Study of Education in Twenty-One Countries* (New York: Wiley, 1976).

46. These differences in turn reflect distinctive American values. See Seymour Martin Lipset, *The First New Nation* (New York: Basic Books, 1963); and Robin Williams, *American Society* (New York: Knopf, 1970).

47. Anderson, *Fact Book;* and Passow, *The National Case Study.*

48. For an examination of the status of school teachers in America, see Dan Lortie, *School Teacher: A Sociological Study* (Chicago: University of Chicago Press, 1975).

49. See the examples in Waller, *The Sociology of Teaching.*

50. Lortie, *School Teacher.*

51. National Commission on Excellence in Education, *A Nation at Risk.*

52. Passow, *The National Case Study.*

53. Charles Krug, *The Secondary School Curriculum* (New York: Harper, 1960).

54. Ezra P. Vogel, *Japan as Number One* (New York: Harper, 1980).

55. See "Examination Hell: Japanese Style," *New York Times,* November 16, 1982.

56. Halsey, Heath, and Ridge, *Origins and Destinations.*

57. Becker, Geer, and Hughes, *Making the Grade.*

58. National Science Board Commission on Precollege Education in Mathematics, Science and Technology, *Educating Americans.*

59. This point is conspicuously ignored in recent reports; c.f., National Commission on Excellence in Education, *A Nation at Risk.*

chapter 2

Theories of Schooling and Society: The Functional and Conflict Paradigms

The word *theory* often triggers some degree of anxiety in the reader. Theory suggests to some people a high degree of abstraction and complexity and an intricate structure of logically related propositions. The theories I shall discuss in this chapter, however, need provoke no great anxiety. These ideas are neither highly complex nor particularly esoteric. Sociological theories of schooling, indeed, are closely related to implicit common-sense ideas about education and its function in modern society—a group of more or less coherent ideas, rather than a set of tightly knit theoretical propositions.

Until fifteen years ago discussion of theories of schooling in modern society would have made little sense. The contest between groups of competing ideas, each claiming to offer an explanation of what schools do and why they do it, is fairly recent. Until a decade or so ago one major interpretation of the role of schooling in modern society prevailed almost unchallenged. This theory, which I shall call the *functional paradigm,* offers both an explanation and a justification for the role of educational institutions.

In simplest terms, the functional paradigm argues that the reason why schooling is so much more important in modern society than in previous societies is that it performs two crucial functions. First, schooling represents an efficient and rational way of sorting and selecting talented people so that the most able and motivated attain the highest status positions. In other words, schools help create a society of equal opportunity where effort and ability rather than family background determine a person's status. Second, the functional paradigm sees schools as teaching the kind of cognitive skills and norms essential for the performance of most adult roles in a society increasingly dependent on *knowledge* for economic growth. In the post-industrial society of the future, this argument states, creation and transmission of knowledge become ever more important, and the institutions that are primarily concerned with such knowledge become increasingly vital to the societies' welfare.[1]

Although these beliefs continue to be widely held and still constitute the core of what might be called the liberal orthodoxy in educational thought, they have lost some of the taken-for-granted character they possessed not so long ago. Beginning in the 1970s, disillusionment and skepticism with schooling began to spread and puncture the liberal optimism that lay at the heart of the functional paradigm. By the mid-1970s, the period of extremely rapid growth in higher education appeared to be over and a new era of contraction, with too many colleges chasing too few students, began.[2] The view that the United States needed far more highly trained workers was challenged by the growth of a pool of underemployed and unemployed college graduates. Skeptics began to suggest that we lived in an over-educated society, and that many degrees and diplomas were not so much necessary qualifications for work but rather arbitrary credentials having little relationship to the often modest skills really needed to do a particular job.[3] Such skepticism was not only confined to higher education. Disillusionment with primary and secondary schooling has also increased in the past fifteen years. Educational liberals and radicals were generally disappointed with the apparent failure of the open classroom experiments of the early seventies, and more generally with the apparent failure of any educational reforms to produce demonstrable and unambiguous improvements in learning outcomes.[4] Many educators were also disturbed by the large differences in scholastic achievement between students from different social backgrounds, particularly between black student achievement and white student achievement. Finally, a great deal of attention began to focus on evidence of declining standards of academic achievement, particularly at the high school level. Despite two decades of educational innovations, or, as conservative critics suggested, *because* of these innovations, there is evidence that by all sorts of criteria U.S. high schools were less educationally effective in the early 1980s than in the 1960s. Scholastic Aptitude Test scores have fallen sharply, absenteeism has increased, homework assignments have been reduced, and enrollment in rigorous academic subjects like physics or calculus has declined.[5]

All these developments helped erode the liberal optimism that is implicit in the functional paradigm. It was not merely that public support for and confidence in schooling was lower in the early eighties or late seventies than two decades ago, it was also that there has been increasing disillusionment with the fundamental idea *that schools were gradually improving and that we knew how to improve them.* More and more educators and intellectuals began to question whether the reforms of the sixties and seventies actually improved equality of opportunity and whether more individualized instruction and innovative curricula have any of the effects claimed for them.

The *conflict paradigm* grew out of this disillusionment and began to develop strength as the crisis of the functional paradigm deepened in the late 1970s.[6] At bottom, it is an essentially skeptical or even cynical view of the role of schooling in modern society. Thus if the functional paradigm sees schools as more or less rational instruments for sorting and selecting talented people, the conflict paradigm often depicts them as institutions that perpetuate inequality and convince lower-class groups of their inferiority. While functional theorists stress the usefulness of the cognitive or intellectual skills that schools teach for the demands of a complex economy, conflict theorists often argue that most jobs require few complex cognitive skills. From this skeptical point of view, it is the class-related values and attitudes that schools convey rather than the skills they teach that are most important. In the conflict paradigm, furthermore, instead of an emphasis on how schools teach *consensually* held values or ideals, we find an argument that schools are often instruments of *class domination,* a way in which elites render the mass of the population docile and compliant. The two paradigms, therefore, represent fundamentally different ways of looking at schools and their role in modern society (which is not to say, of course, that one cannot imagine a combination of the best ideas of both). The debate between these models underlies virtually all of the issues I shall discuss in this book: from the study of inequality to the problem of the relationship between schools and jobs and the issue of how to change and reform schools. In this chapter I describe these paradigms in some detail and begin to examine their merits and limitations.

THE FUNCTIONAL PARADIGM OF SCHOOLING

The functional paradigm of schooling is not the work of any one individual theorist, nor does it consist exclusively of the ideas of sociologists. In its most general form the functional paradigm has long been part of the conventional wisdom of liberal intellectuals in Western society and, to a large extent, part of the working assumptions of the great majority of all who have thought and written about schooling in Western societies until quite recently. Many of its assumptions are found in commencement addresses and political speeches on the benefits of education, as well as in textbooks on the sociology of education.[7]

Modern Society—The Functional View

At the heart of the functional paradigm is an analysis of what adherents to the model see as the unique character of the modern Western world and the crucial functions that schooling plays in that world. The paradigm sees modern Western societies differing from most previous societies in at least three crucial respects.

The Meritocratic Society

In modern societies occupational roles are (and should be) achieved rather than ascribed. Contemporary intellectuals have long regarded the inheritance of occupational roles, and more broadly the inheritance of social status, as anathema. People believe high-status positions should be achieved on the basis of merit rather than passed on from parent to child. The children of the poor should have equal opportunity to achieve high status with more privileged children. And in all Western societies, particularly since World War II, governments have responded to this belief by trying to increase equality of opportunity: by expanding higher education, introducing universalistic rules for employment intended to discourage nepotism, and legislating elimination of discrimination on the basis of religion, race, and sex. The functional paradigm, therefore, sees modern society as *meritocratic*: a society where ability and effort count for more than privilege and inherited status. Although there is disagreement about just how far along this road to a perfectly meritocratic social order we have traveled, there is agreement that modern society is at least more meritocratic than most societies of the past.[8]

In part, this contention is a moral argument. It is simply wrong, we believe, that doctors or members of elite groups should enjoy overwhelming advantages in passing on inherited status to their children. Besides the moral argument, however, underlying the meritocratic thesis is a conviction that achievement is a far more rational way of allocating status than ascription. The theory maintains that modern society demands and requires far larger percentages of highly skilled people than ever before. The percentage of professionals in the United

States labor force, for example, has multiplied about ten times since 1900. It is essential, therefore, that the most talented individuals be recruited for these demanding occupations. The health and the economic well-being of a society depends on the degree to which it can find and place its most talented individuals in the most demanding occupations. An increasingly meritocratic society is not only morally justified, but it is also a more rational and efficient society.

The Expert Society

A second distinctive feature of the contemporary social order is closely related to these ideas about talent, efficiency, and rationality. The functional paradigm sees modern society as an expert society:[9] one that depends preeminently on rational knowledge for economic growth, requiring more and more highly trained individuals to fill the majority of occupational positions. Schools perform two crucial functions in this view. First, the research activities of universities and colleges produce the new knowledge that underpins economic growth and social progress. Second, extensive schooling both equips individuals with specialized skills and provides a general foundation of cognitive knowledge and intellectual sophistication to permit the acquisition of more specialized knowledge. Extensive education, therefore, becomes an increasingly necessary feature of any modern society. Skills that were primarily acquired on the job must now be acquired in specialized educational institutions. If schools cannot always teach the highly specific knowledge and skills required by an increasing number of jobs, they do provide a foundation of general cognitive skills that alone permits effective learning of more specialized knowledge. Since occupational skills change or rapidly become obsolete in contemporary society, individuals need an extensive general education as a foundation to learn new skills. They may also require later retooling educational programs long after adolescence. Some progressive accounts of this argument, indeed, see schooling as lifelong learning and the whole society as a learning society. The crucial function of schools is not so much to teach specific useful vocational skills, but to teach people how to learn.

The Democratic Society

The functional paradigm portrays contemporary society as a democratic society moving gradually toward the achievement of humane goals: toward social justice, a more fulfilling life for all citizens, and the acceptance of diversity. Implicit in the functional paradigm, therefore, is a particular kind of political liberalism—a view that does not deny the evils and inequities of the present society, but does believe that progress has been made and will continue to be made. Increasing levels of education are at the core of this conception of progress. An educated citizenry is an informed citizenry, less likely to be manipulated by demagogues, and more likely to make responsible and informed political decisions and be actively involved in the political process. Education reduces intolerance and prejudice, and increases support for civil liberties; it is, in other words, an essential bulwark of a democratic society dedicated to freedom and justice. Finally, a more educated society will be a better society in another sense: a society dedicated not only to economic growth and material wealth, but also to the pursuit of social justice. The educated society is concerned with the quality of life and the conditions that make individual fulfillment possible.

Schooling and Society

The heart of the functional paradigm, therefore, can be seen as an explanation of why schooling is of such crucial importance in modern society. This explanation stresses the multiple functions that schools perform in modern society—the production of cognitive skills, the sorting and selection of talents, the creation of an informed citizenry—and it maintains that these functions could not be adequately performed without extensive and elaborate formal schooling. Thus the functional paradigm views the close relationship between schooling and future status in contemporary society as an essentially rational process of adaptation: a process where the needs of the increasingly complex society for talented and expert personnel are met by outputs from the educational system in the form of cognitive skills and the selection of talented individuals. And if only the most uncritical supporters of the paradigm would assert that such a process of social selection in schools is *perfectly* meritocratic or that disadvantaged groups have *identical* opportunities to those afforded to more privileged students, there is some general confidence that the direction of educational change has been in a meritocratic direction. From this perspective, the net effect of the expansion of schooling has been to increase the percentage of poor but talented students who reach high-status positions, with the assumption that further expansion of schooling will move us closer toward a society of equal opportunity. What schools teach is also, although imperfectly, a functional adaptation to the needs of the social order. As the nature of the modern economy increasingly demands (even in middle- or lower-status occupations) more sophisticated cognitive skills and flexibility and adaptability in the work force, so pedagogical techniques and curricula shift away from rote memorization and moral indoctrination to concern with cognitive development and intellectual flexibility. In this respect, the functional paradigm is by no means necessarily conservative in its implications for school practice, as its critics sometimes allege. Indeed, the argument that the new complex skills needed by modern society in turn require the transformation of traditional pedagogy and the traditional curriculum were virtually an article of faith among many functional theorists during the 1960s and 1970s.[10]

If the functional paradigm is not necessarily politically conservative, it certainly does portray the major features of contemporary society in fundamentally benign terms. Inequality, for example, is often seen as a necessary device for motivating talented individuals to achieve high-status positions. Although it is recognized by most observers that the correlation between ability and high status is far from perfect, they see the problem of inequality in contemporary society as one of erasing barriers to the mobility of talent rather than as a problem of redistributing wealth from high-status positions to low-status positions. That talent in turn tends to be conceived as one dimensional, underlying both success in school and success in life. And while liberals within this tradition argue there are vast reserves of untapped talent among disadvantaged groups, others more pessimistically conclude that such talent is inherently scarce.

HUMAN CAPITAL THEORY

Within the functional paradigm, economists have developed an important body of theory and research known as *human capital theory*. Human capital theorists see education as an investment that, by increasing an individual's human capital, knowledge, or expertise, will pay off in the future in the form of increased earnings. In a simple yet powerful model, these economists see decisions to attend schools or colleges as shaped by essentially the same process of weighting costs and benefits as decisions to buy consumer goods. The *benefits* of attending school are the likelihood of obtaining a higher paying job or a job with greater prestige. The *costs* consist not only of the actual expenses of an education but the income that is foregone by individuals who choose not to work and attend school instead. Human capital theorists recognize, of course, that individuals differ in how they reckon such costs and benefits—for some individuals college is very hard work and for others it is inherently enjoyable—but they insist that most students (or their parents who are footing the bill) behave as the model predicts. Thus, as the return on educational investments increase, and college graduates enjoy much higher salaries than nongraduates, the number of people attending college will increase.

When that relative ratio declines, as it did for males between 1970 and 1980, the number of students entering work directly from high school should increase. Similar reasoning has led economists to attempt to explain the shift away from the liberal arts majors toward business majors during the 1970s and the increasing proportion of college students who were female during that same period.[11]

Human capital theory becomes, for many sociologists, more controversial and more problematic in its explanation of why employers are willing to pay more money for highly educated employees than less educated employees. Employers, human capital theorists say, find that educated employees are more *productive* and contribute more to the profits of the corporation than less educated employees. This increased productivity is explained by the skills and abilities or human capital that the employees have acquired in the course of their education. As Thomas Juster writes:

> Individuals begin life into a certain amount of potential capital in the form of genetic endowment; they add to that capital throughout early childhood, school years, and the early working years; and they suffer deterioration or depreciation of the capital as their learning or training becomes out moded or obsolescent.[12]

The stock of human capital, Juster believes, "explains in considerable part, observed differences in the level, distribution and lifetime profiles of financial earnings realized by individuals in the market."[13]

Many human capital theorists believe that what is true for individuals is also true for whole societies. A societal decision to invest more in education and thus to increase the stock of human capital can be seen as rational because it increases overall productivity and, in the long run at least, economic growth. In support of this assertion, correlations have been observed between rates of economic growth and societal expenditures on education.[14] Popular versions of these arguments have become quite widespread in recent years. In the early 1980s, for example, it was fashionable to maintain that part of the great economic success of Japan might be attributable to the effectiveness of its school system in teaching basic cognitive skills, and, conversely, that the relatively poor performance of the U.S. economy could be partly attributed to declining educational achievement.[15] In a similar vein, much attention has recently focused on the growth of high-technology industries, which will demand much more sophisticated skills in the labor force than the old basic industries that once fuelled economic growth.

Despite some general plausibility, arguments of this kind are hard to evaluate. There is good evidence that schooling does increase cognitive skills, though by how much is difficult to measure. There is also evidence that there is some level of skills below which an individual's performance on the job falls off: Semi-literate workers, for example, cannot read or write memoranda effectively. But it is a big leap from these modest propositions to the argument that economic growth depends on the level of educational investment. Not only is it true that economic growth depends on many factors besides the stock of human capital, but it is also difficult to establish what levels of human capital or cognitive skills constitute the minimum necessary for the effective performance of particular jobs. So great is the uncertainty in this regard that some skeptics have argued that contemporary society, far from facing a shortage of skills among the labor force, is experiencing a large *surplus* of educated and skilled labor in most fields.[16]

Whatever the merits of this particular debate, there are also more general questions that can be raised about human capital theory from a sociological point of view. For the human capital theorists, employers are ultimately rational actors who are concerned with maximizing profits. In the long run, therefore, if overqualified employees were hired whose skills are surplus to the requirements of the job, the employers would lose business to competitors who hired less educated and cheaper employees. It is far from clear, however, whether actual employers behave in the way suggested by this model. For example, employers may prefer to hire college graduates less because of their demonstrably greater productivity but because they find such individuals share their tastes and values more than high school graduates. In addition, employers may wish to raise the status and prestige of their profession by excluding all but college graduates as a way of demonstrating the point that their profession "only employs the best people." In other words, college graduates enjoy a certain prestige, and employers who hire them assimilate some of that prestige for themselves. While human capital theory offers one interpretation of why employers prefer highly educated employees, therefore it should be recognized that competing and equally plausible interpretations are possible.[17]

DIFFICULTIES IN THE FUNCTIONAL PARADIGM

The set of assumptions I have described are still influential among social scientists, policy makers, and educators, but they have lost some of the taken-for-granted character of a decade or more ago. The rate of educational expansion has declined; past projections of the need for college graduates have been confounded by a surplus of unemployed or underemployed degree holders. In the face of these developments it becomes more difficult to argue that industrial societies require ever-increasing percentages of highly educated individuals. But the difficulties of the functional paradigm are more fundamental than those posed by the current (and possibly temporary) imbalance between educational outputs and the supply of high-status jobs. In the past decade a substantial body of research has developed that poses a challenge to almost all the main assertions of the paradigm—to the link between schooling and jobs, the assumption of an increasingly meritocratic society, and arguments about increasing opportunities for the mobility of talented, but underprivileged youth.

Schooling, Skills, and Jobs

In the functional paradigm, cognitive skills provide the crucial link between education and jobs. This is not to say that the major function of schools is to teach vocational skills that are directly relevant to job performance. The functional paradigm does assert, however, that the general cognitive skills and intellectual sophistication that schools develop have positive functions for the performance of adult occupations, and that, indeed, they are indispensable for the performance of growing numbers of middle- and high-status occupations.

To the extent that we can test such very general ideas, recent evidence from United States research does not support them. Consider first the relationship between college grades and occupational status and future earnings. College grades are a rough and ready measure of the success with which an individual has learned the things that colleges attempt to teach. What should happen, therefore, according to the functional paradigm, is that college grades should predict occupational status and relative earnings. Those who do well in college should, other things being equal, obtain better jobs and make more money than those who did less well. Research on the relationship between college grades and occupational status and future earnings, however, has not been able to demonstrate such a relationship. In comparing bachelors degree recipients, grade point average in college does not predict either occupational status or future earnings with any degree of consistency.[18]

Direct measures of cognitive skills provide a second test of the hypothesis. Individuals whose test scores in school indicate high cognitive skills do indeed obtain better jobs and make more money in later life than individuals with lower cognitive skills. However, this relationship largely disappears when researchers control for educational attainment and family background. Christopher Jencks summarizes: "If we compare two men whose test scores differed by 15 points, their occupational status would typically differ by about 12.5 points. If they have the same amount of education and the same family background, their status will differ by only about 2.5 points."[19]

If the effect of cognitive skills on occupational status is problematic, studies of performance on the job provide little support for the functional paradigm. Even among teachers, the correlation between grades in college and observer ratings of job performance average only between 0.2 and 0.3.[20] Among physicians, grades in medical school predict ratings of job performance only weakly in the early years of medical practice and not at all in later years.[21] How well people do in a particular job, as Ivar Berg has shown, can rarely be predicted by measures of how well they have learned what they were taught in school.[22]

These findings pose a challenge to the functional paradigm. If increasing levels of education are somehow necessary for the performance of increasingly complex jobs, then there should be a relationship between cognitive skills (which schools presumably teach) and occupational status, earnings, and job performance. A large part of the explanation for the well-known correlation between educational attainment and occupational status should be that such educational qualifications reflect the possession of cognitive skills necessary or useful for effective role performance. But the evidence we have suggests that it is educational *credentials* as well as cognitive skills that predict future status and earnings. We know that employers prefer to employ college graduates, but there is no solid evidence that they make great efforts to hire people with the highest levels of cognitive skills. Nor is there evidence that once on the job those who have the highest skills perform better than those with lower skills.

These findings, therefore, suggest a different picture of the relationship between schooling and jobs than that provided by the functional paradigm. Instead of saying that educational institutions teach the skills that are necessary for the performance of complex occupations, it can be argued that educational credentials are used to ration access to high-status occupations. Employers who are faced with many potential applicants for a few jobs can use educational credentials as a convenient screening device that appears to be quite impersonal and fair. They can say that only college graduates or only holders of the M.A. degree are qualified to do the job. And, of course, as the percentage of the population with high levels of education credentials rises, so the standards for admission to a particular occupation rise also, not in response to any increasing complexity of the job itself, but as a reflection of the rise in average education levels in the population and the shifting supply and demand for particular jobs.

There is other evidence that supports this interpretation. There are, for example, great differences in the amount of education credentials required for entry into professional occupations in different Western societies. In Great Britain, for example, physicians qualify with three years less formal education than their U.S. counterparts. In much of Europe, only very recently have engineers and lawyers had to obtain college degrees before practicing their professions. In the United States, furthermore, entry requirements for many occupations—pharmacy, police work, physical therapy—have increased dramatically over the last twenty years. There are perhaps some grounds for asserting that new recruits to these jobs must know more than in the past, but it is also plausible that any occupation has much prestige to gain by attempting to raise its admission requirements. Police departments around the country may argue that the complex nature of modern police work demands at least two years of college as a preparation. Such arguments, however, seem self-serving. Raised standards increase the status of people already in the job and are crucial for claiming the high status of the occupation within the community at large. It is entirely understandable that police, pharmacists, physical therapists, and social workers (to name but a few occupations where educational requirements for admission have escalated in recent years) should argue that these occupations now require far more credentials than they did in the past. However, it is dangerous to confuse what may be self-serving justifications for new admission standards with an objective necessity for new recruits to have much higher levels of cognitive skills.

The link between schooling and jobs, therefore, is a good deal more problematic than the simple model implied by the functional paradigm. We cannot see rapidly escalating educational requirements as an obvious reflection of the increasing complexity of contemporary occupations. Do people need a college degree to be efficient secretaries or to sell insurance? The need to ask the question suggests that the functional paradigm does not provide a satisfactory account. Those who have high levels of education do, of course, generally obtain higher-status jobs than those who have less education. But this does not seem to be because of the cognitive skills educated people learned in school. It is the possession of the education credentials, rather than the acquisition of the cognitive skills that those credentials denote, that seems to predict future status. The relationship between education and occupational status, then, is a good deal more complex and perhaps less rational than suggested by the functional paradigm.

Schooling and Equality of Opportunity

A second argument of the functional paradigm is that educational institutions sort and select talented people in a way, however imperfect, that is greatly superior to selection on the basis of such ascribed characteristics as parental social status, religion, or race. To tie occupational status closely to educational attainment, the paradigm suggests, will maximize society's chances of discovering its most talented individuals and placing them in the most important occupations. Implicit in this paradigm, therefore, is the idea that the expansion of education—more and more access to higher education for lower-class and minority students—will have the effect of increasing the chances of those individuals to gain access to high-status occupations. Educational expansion is not only morally justified, it is also a rational policy because it increases the discovery of talented individuals.

Research has challenged these arguments, too. It is true that measures of IQ are quite good predictors of school achievement. It is also true that IQ scores and occupational status and income are positively correlated.[23] But what prevents such findings constituting valid evidence for the meritocratic thesis is the strong relationship between all these variables and socioeconomic status. Samuel Bowles and Herbert Gintis, for example, show that when socioeconomic status is controlled, IQ exerts an only slight effect on earnings.[24] Controlling for IQ, by contrast, still leaves very large associations between socioeconomic status of parents and the incomes of their children. Bowles and Gintis show that those with the lowest socioeconomic status scores, but average IQ scores, have a 6 percent chance of being in the top one-fifth of all wage earners. Those with the same IQ scores, but from the highest decile of socioeconomic background have a 41 percent chance of being in the top one-fifth of all wage earners.[25] Jencks reports evidence supporting this general interpretation. He shows that much of the relationship between IQ and occupational status and future earnings disappears when we control for school attainment and for socioeconomic background.[23]

Our society, then, is far from a pure form of meritocracy where intelligence or talent largely determine success in school, and where employers in turn use schooling as a rational way of sorting out the most talented from the least talented individuals. Socioeconomic status of the parents is a better predictor of future economic success than measured IQ. In part, this is because socioeconomic status predicts school achievement even when IQ is controlled; it is also because socioeconomic status predicts future adult status even after we take schooling and IQ into account.[26]

The evidence also raises questions about the argument that educational expansion increases meritocratic selection. If the expansion of schooling in the last fifty years has increased the relative chances of underprivileged youth to gain access to high-status jobs, we would expect a gradual decline in the relationship between parent's status and that of their children. What should happen, the meritocratic argument implies, is that high-status parents should experience increasing difficulty in passing on their high status to their children, and that more and more low-status children of high intelligence should be able to take their rightful places in prestigious occupations that demand unusual talent. Unless intelligence is inherited to a very high degree, it would follow that increasing educational expansion will increase the mobility chances of the underprivileged. Detailed treatment of this complicated issue will be postponed until Chapter 4, but the evidence for the United States indicates that the relationship between parent and child status has not declined in the last four decades. Parent social status remains about as good a predictor of a child's future status today as it was in the 1920s, despite enormous educational expansion and great efforts to ensure fairness and universality in selection procedures.[27]

Again, we are confronted with empirical evidence that is difficult to reconcile with the functional paradigm. No one would say, of course, that our society is perfectly open to talent or that IQ alone is the main determinant of income and status. But what should happen, according to the functional paradigm, is that we should be able to observe some reduction in the ability of privileged parents to pass on their advantages to their children. The fact that we do not observe this suggests that contemporary U.S. society is not a great deal more meritocratic than several decades ago.

Quality of Schooling and Equality of Opportunity

Implicit in virtually all thought about education in the early 1960s was the theory that the quality of schooling available to different students was crucial to their future chances of occupational mobility. Poor students were severely handicapped by inferior schools, black students by the fact that most of the schools they attended were, quite simply, bad schools. Black students attended, for the most part, segregated institutions. Poor white students went to schools that hardly compared in facilities and resources with the schools attended by more privileged students. Inferior schooling compounded the initial handicaps of these students and led directly to the perpetuation of poverty and inequality in the next generation. In such books as Patricia Sexton's *Education and Income,* a direct line was drawn between inferior schools, reduced opportunities to learn, low prospects for higher education, and the persistence of inequality.[28] This vicious circle could be broken only by equalizing school resources for all students.

A great deal of empirical research has challenged this argument. A series of large-scale studies of schooling and its effects show that student test scores are only weakly associated with measures of school quality, but powerfully associated with measures of student characteristics: socioeconomic background and IQ. Measures of teacher experience, pupil/teacher ratios, and the amounts of money expended per pupil all constituted some indications of what people meant when they talked about school quality. Yet none of these variables has proven to be of much help in predicting how well students will perform on particular tests.[29]

In research on school effects in a number of different countries, indicators of school quality have shown only a very weak or insignificant relationship with student performance on tests designed to measure cognitive learning.[30] And while such research has important shortcomings, which I shall discuss in later chapters, it does show that we can in no sense solve the problem of the unequal school achievement of different groups of students by equalizing school resources. Every study indicates that students from low-status families do less well on tests of cognitive achievement than more well-to-do students, but no study demonstrates that the gap can be substantially closed by providing what amounts to middle-class schooling for lower-class students.[31] Indeed, the history of research on school effects in the last ten years is a history of failure to confirm the proposition that eliminating differences in school quality can significantly close the gap in school achievement between students from different social origins. Results of research on school integration have provided, at best, equivocal positive findings. Most early studies tended to show mildly positive effects on black student performance. Although more recent studies do not necessarily contradict this assertion, a number of them indicate some negative effects of integration on black self-esteem, and even on white achievement in majority-black schools.[32]

No study has demonstrated that integrated schools reduce most of the gap between black and white school achievement. Nor has research on the effects of compensatory preschool education demonstrated the kind of clear-cut and lasting effects on later school achievement that its proponents hoped for. Although evaluation of such programs is exceedingly difficult, the most judicious conclusion is that strong positive effects on later school performance have not yet been demonstrated.[33]

While I shall have a great deal more to say about this research later in this book, this initial examination of the findings of large-scale research on school effects indicates serious difficulties for the orthodox interpretation of school reform and its effects on inequality that prevailed during the 1960s. One assertion of the functional paradigm is that the expansion of schooling in modern society brings about an increasingly meritocratic social order. A closely related assertion is that better or higher quality schooling will reduce the advantages of privileged parents in passing on their high status to the next generation and increase the chances of underprivileged children to close the gap between themselves and more privileged students. Much of what we have learned in the last ten years casts serious doubt on both of these assertions.

THE CONFLICT PARADIGM

I have shown that the model of schooling and society that dominated much thought about education until quite recently is beset with serious difficulties. Schools do undoubtedly teach cognitive skills and increase the intellectual sophistication of their students, but it is not clear that it is these skills that explain the relationship between schooling, occupational status, and earnings. The available evidence does not suggest that U.S. society is substantially more meritocratic than in the past. Nor is there much evidence to indicate that increased resources devoted to schooling have resulted in more favorable opportunities for the talented children of disadvantaged parents to obtain high-status positions. Simply put, the expansion of schooling does not seem to have worked in the way the functional paradigm suggests it should work.

The conflict paradigm offers a very different interpretation of schooling in its relationship to society. Like the functional paradigm, the conflict paradigm sees schools and society as closely linked—and, I shall argue, too closely linked—but it stresses the links between schools and the demands of elites rather than the needs of the whole society. It also stresses the connection between schooling and the learning of docility and compliance rather than the acquisition of cognitive skills. If the functional paradigm sees schools as more or less efficient mechanisms for sorting and selecting talented people and for producing cognitive skills, the conflict paradigm sees schools as serving the interests of elites, as reinforcing existing inequalities, and as producing attitudes that foster acceptance of this status quo.

The Intellectual Background

The functional paradigm took shape at a time when the climate of intellectual opinion was predominantly optimistic about the main features of contemporary society and its likely future evolution. Modern society was viewed as increasingly rational and meritocratic, a society where prejudice, racism, intolerance, and the ignorance that fostered these evils would gradually disappear. Schools taught, sus-

tained, and nurtured essentially modern cosmopolitan values and attitudes. Schools, at least the best schools, worked to emancipate children
from parochialism, from an unreflecting respect for the traditions of
the past, and from ignorance and prejudice. The new mathematics
of the late 1960s, with its stress on understanding the principles of
logic rather than the mere acquisition of immediately useful skills,
and the new English curriculum, with its use of modern novels that
invited frank discussion of contemporary moral issues, both symbolized
a commitment to modern, liberal, and cosmopolitan ideals. The best
schools taught rationality; they developed the ability to handle moral
complexity and to tolerate ambiguity. If the prisons of ignorance, prejudice, and unthinking respect for the past prevented many parents
from entering this new world, schools were agencies of emancipation
for the next generation. In the modern world, schools do not merely
reproduce the values, attitudes, and skills of the past, they are active
agents in creating a more liberal, a more rational, and a more humane
society.[34]

The attack on these ideas in the later 1960s and 1970s reflected
a broader critique of their view of society, a disenchantment with
the liberal vision of the modern world, and a rejection of the optimism
of that world view. The ten years from 1965 to 1975 were a time of
increasing skepticism about the benefits of science and technology
and an increasing cynicism about the good intentions and moral purposes of established authority. The liberal model of modern society—
a world admittedly full of serious imperfection, but nevertheless moving in a fundamentally progressive direction—was replaced, for more
and more intellectuals, by a model of society requiring urgent and
wholesale surgery to avoid disaster. The new, more skeptical vision
saw greedy business corporations intent on destroying the environment, cynical and corrupt politicians concerned with their own power
and privilege, and entrenched racism and sexism in virtually every
social institution. Instead of a model of society where authority was
based on expertise and competence, this radical vision defined a society
where powerful elites manipulate public opinion to preserve their own
entrenched position. Such elites might make symbolic or token conces-
sions to pressures for reform, but such evils as racism, poverty, and
sexism could only be eliminated by changing the distribution of power
in the society.

Such were the new skeptical ideas that began to gain ground on
the older liberal orthodoxy at the end of the 1960s. Although it would
be misleading to claim that ideas like these became more popular
than the liberal and optimistic ideas that underly the functional paradigm, they were hardly confined to those who considered themselves
educational or political radicals. By the mid to late seventies, disillusion-

ment with the liberal interpretations of schooling became quite wide-spread among educators and intellectuals. Large numbers of people were aware, for example, that major differences in school achievement by race and by social class persisted even after educational reforms designed to eliminate them. There was also emerging awareness of the large number of highly educated young people who could not find jobs commensurate with their qualifications. In other words, the system did not seem to work in the way that liberal common sense (and the functional paradigm) said it should work. The climate of opinion was ready for an alternative interpretation.

The conflict paradigm, even less than the functional paradigm, is not a unitary set of unambiguous propositions about the relationship between school and society. Indeed, disputes within the conflict paradigm, between Marxists and non-Marxists, or even between rival Marxists, are often more heated than arguments between functionalists and conflict theorists.[35] But we can nevertheless distinguish a set of broad assumptions to which most conflict theorists would subscribe, whatever their other differences, and with which few functional theorists would agree.

First, conflict theorists assert that we live in a divided and conflict-ridden society where groups compete for the control of the educational system. To argue that schooling reflects societal needs, therefore (as functional theorists maintain), is to miss this essential fact. Groups who compete for control of schooling use the rhetoric of societal needs to conceal the fact that it is *their* interests and *their* demands they are trying to advance. These elites may succeed in manufacturing consensus about the purposes and organization of schooling, but beneath the apparent consensus, conflict theorists believe, is always a struggle for power and status: *whose* values and ideals will be taught to the young, and *whose* children will obtain the most desirable jobs. Second, conflict theorists see this struggle between groups as unequal. Existing elites, though they must make compromises and bargains with other groups, almost always have the upper hand because of their superior resources and their control over the means of communication. Because of this, equality of opportunity has not been and is unlikely to be a reality within the confines of the present social order. The *rhetoric* of equality of opportunity conceals the fact that schools are organized in such a way as to make it inevitable that children of privileged groups will have great advantages over children of disadvantaged groups.

Finally, conflict theorists are skeptical of the view that the schools are linked to jobs in modern society primarily through the cognitive skills they teach. Rejecting the view that most work in modern society is intellectually highly demanding, conflict theorists emphasize instead that employers are more concerned with the attitudes and values of

their future employees, particularly their loyalty, compliance, and docility, rather than their cognitive sophistication. From this perspective,
therefore, while the *manifest* concern of schools is primarily with the
teaching of cognitive skills, their fundamental business is to shore up
the present social order by teaching appropriate attitudes and values.
Again, the rhetoric of the official orthodoxy conceals the real nature
of the relationship between schools and society.

These, then, are the ideas with which most, if not all, conflict
theorists would agree. To understand the conflict paradigm more fully,
however, we need to consider in some detail more specific theories,
one neo-Marxist and the other non-Marxist.

The Neo-Marxist Theories
of Bowles and Gintis

Samuel Bowles and Herbert Gintis's 1977 book *Schooling
in Capitalist America* is probably the best known and most coherently
argued statement of a specifically Marxist interpretation of schooling
in modern society.[36] Published at a time when disillusionment with
the liberal interpretation of schooling was beginning to be widespread,
its radical interpretation of schooling has had a great deal of impact
and stimulated extensive debate. That thesis is supported, furthermore,
by a good deal of empirical evidence and closely reasoned argument—
qualities that have not always characterized radical critiques of the
functional paradigm.

Bowles and Gintis's central thesis is that schools serve the interests
of the capitalist order in modern society. Schools reproduce the values
and personality characteristics necessary in a repressive capitalist society. Although all schools must repress and coerce students to secure
a compliant and efficient adult labor force, different schools accomplish
this function in different ways. The values and qualities required by
an efficient manual worker on the production line are different from
the values and qualities needed by an executive of a large corporation.
While the manual worker must be taught punctuality, the ability to
follow instructions, and some degree of respect for superiors, the executive needs some degree of flexibility, an ability to tolerate ambiguity,
and favorable attitudes toward change and innovation.

Therefore, schools whose graduates enter predominantly low-status occupations stress rule following, provide minimal discretion in
choice of tasks, and teach obedience to constituted authority. Schools
and universities that prepare students for elite positions, by contrast,
encourage students to develop some capacity of sustained independent
work, to make intelligent choices among many alternatives, and to
internalize norms rather than to follow external behavioral rules. If

we compare junior colleges with elite universities, for example, or the college preparatory tracks of a suburban high school with the vocational curriculum, we will find not only differences in curriculum, but also differences in the social organization of instruction. In junior colleges and in the lower tracks of a high school, students will be given more frequent assignments, have less choice in how to carry out those assignments, and will be subject to more detailed supervision by the teaching staff. By contrast, the college preparatory tracks of many suburban high schools and elite universities have a great deal more open and flexible educational environment. Such dissimilarities mirror both different class values (the preference of working-class parents for stricter educational methods and the preference of professional parents for schooling that encourages initiative and independence) and the different kinds of qualities of personality needed for good performance in high- and low-status occupations. The social organization of particular schools—the methods of instruction and evaluation, the amount of choice and discretion permitted the students—reflects the demands of the particular occupations that their graduates will eventually obtain.[37]

Reinforcing Inequality

Bowles and Gintis's major argument is that the educational system reinforces class inequalities in contemporary society. Different social classes in the United States usually attend different neighborhood schools. Both the value preferences of parents and the different financial resources available to different communities mean that schools catering to working-class students will teach different values and different personal qualities than schools serving higher-status populations. These latter schools are not better or freer in any absolute sense, but high-status schools communicate to their students the distinctive values and attitudes required by high-status occupations in modern capitalist societies. The great majority of occupations in contemporary society, Bowles and Gintis believe, require a loyal and compliant work force to perform tasks with little responsibility and discretion. Most schools, therefore, teach their students to follow orders reliably, to take explicit directions, to be punctual, and to respect the authority of the teacher and the school. Such schools, which satisfy the preference of most parents for discipline and good manners in their children, channel students to manual and lower-level white-collar occupations. But schools serving more elite groups are only superficially less repressive. Such schools encourage students to work at their own pace without continuous supervision, to work for the sake of long-term future rewards, and to internalize rules of behavior rather than depend on specific and frequent instructions. These qualities are essential to effective performance in middle- or high-status positions in large organizations. However, work in such organizations permits only limited freedom and autonomy. Workers may question specific procedures, but not the purpose of the organization; employees may be flexible and innovative, but they must be loyal. The capitalist society requires that all schools teach the values of individual achievement, material consumption, and the inevitability of the present social order. Free schools are therefore impossible in a repressive society.[38]

Bowles and Gintis decisively reject the meritocratic hypothesis, with its assumption that schools are efficient ways of selecting talented people. Instead, schools work to *convince* people that selection is meritocratic. It is essential for the legitimacy of the capitalist order that the population be convinced that people in high-status positions do deserve these positions, that they are more talented and harder workers than others. Schools are an essential prop of this legitimacy. Selection for particular tracks within a school must *appear* to be made on the basis of ability and intelligence, and such purportedly objective criteria as IQ and grades serve this function. But these criteria mask the fact that success in schooling, and of course success in later life, is strongly related to social class and shows no indication of becoming less closely related over time. The correlation between college graduation and social class in the last twenty years, they report, has remained unchanged despite the rapid expansion of higher education. Schools remain institutions that reproduce and legitimate existing inequalities between social classes. This state of affairs will continue indefinitely in capitalist societies unless capitalism itself is abolished. Reforms in the educational system alone cannot reduce inequalities in the life chances of different social classes. The premise of liberal educational reform—that educational expansion and improved schooling can create equality of opportunity—is false. Schools that liberate, diminishing rather than reinforcing the handicaps of inequality, can only be achieved after a revolution in the distribution of power and the ownership of the means of production in contemporary capitalist society.

Reinterpreting Educational History

A major part of the Bowles and Gintis book, which I shall describe in some detail in the next chapter, reinterprets U.S. educational history and challenges its liberal interpretation. Schools have never been effective in creating equality of opportunity, nor was the reform of schools in the last fifty years a gradual triumph of progressive and humane ideals over the repressive practices of the past.

From its inception, compulsory schooling was an agency of control. The spread of the factory system of production in New England in the mid-ninteenth century created a demand for a loyal, obedient, and docile labor force. Factory owners advocated compulsory schooling, not because schools taught literacy and literacy was essential to factory work, but because schools encouraged habits of punctuality, hard work, and respect for authority. The development of the comprehensive high school in the interwar years did not so much represent a triumph for the progressive ideals of an educational system geared to the needs of each child, but an adaptation to a capitalist society requiring both vocational skills for the majority and a growing white-collar population who could effectively work in large-scale organizations. The introduction of tracking systems into the new high school and the use of objective tests to confirm the correctness of those tracks did not encourage a meritocratic order. Instead, it provided a legitimate means of channeling the poor and underprivileged into low-status positions.

The relaxation of the barbaric discipline and corporal punishment that was widespread in many schools early in the twentieth century did not so much represent a triumph for humane ideals as an adaptation to a social order that increasingly required more subtle and more effective ways of motivating individuals. The increasing emphasis on group mindedness and life adjustment in the high school curriculum reflected a demand for a labor force engaged more and more in working with people rather than things and in selling services rather than in the production of manufactured goods. In short, the direction of educational change is predominantly shaped by the changing demands of capitalist elites for new values and new skills.

The Limits of School Reform

If the educational ideals of the past had been sabotaged by the demands that schools teach willing and cooperative workers, Bowles and Gintis have little optimism that contemporary movements for school reform will be any more successful. Schools are repressive not because of mindlessness and lack of thought, as Silberman argues, but because they must serve the interests of corporate capitalism. The repressive aspects of schooling "are by no means irrational or perverse but are rather, systematic and pervasive reflections of economic reality."[39] Indeed, the open classroom and other less authoritarian, more informal modes of education may serve the interests of corporate capitalism better than the traditional schools of the past. Such less overtly repressive schools prepare children of predominantly privileged groups for work that requires flexibility, innovation, and some degree of questioning of traditional authority—attitudes functional for life in elite positions in large organizations. However, to imagine that most schools could be genuinely cooperative, democratic, and participatory is illusory. Such a belief rests upon a misunderstanding of the intimate connection between schooling and the nature of work in capitalist society and upon neglect of the fact that much work in such a society is necessarily lacking in discretion and authority. Ultimately the transformation of schooling must, Bowles and Gintis believe, await a transformation in the nature of work in capitalist society.

The Conflict Theory of Randall Collins

Randall Collins is perhaps the leading non-Marxist conflict theorist in the United States, and his book, *The Credential Society,* although it has received nothing like the popular attention paid to the work of Bowles and Gintis, is of equal importance as a statement of the conflict approach to education.[40] Collins's work, unlike the work by Bowles and Gintis, is not aimed at a radical reconstruction of U.S. society, but it is no less scathing in its indictment of conventional thought about education. Collins's work is not a call to arms or even a call for educational reform. Instead, the book attacks virtually all conventional assumptions about schooling, including the assumption that we know how to reform and improve schools.

The central idea in Collins's theory is suggested by its title, *The Credential Society.* Increasingly, he argues, we are becoming a society where largely unnecessary educational credentials determine access to desirable jobs. Collins rejects the arguments of those who claim that most of these credentials are indeed necessary qualifications for effective performance on the job. Instead, he maintains that while such credentials may be necessary for any *individual* to obtain a particular job, from the point of view of the society as a whole, the system is an irrational one. It is irrational because large numbers of individuals are excluded from many occupations they could perform quite adequately solely because they lack appropriate credentials. It is also irrational because many individuals spend a great deal of unnecessary time in educational institutions acquiring credentials that will entitle them to scarce but not generally very complicated jobs. Such an irrational system persists, Collins believes, because employers and educational institutions have vested interests in steadily raising levels of educational qualifications, and because of our beliefs in the "myth of technocracy":[41] the myth that jobs in modern society are rapidly becoming so complex than only people with high levels of sophisticated cognitive skills can perform them adequately. This myth, of course, is none other than a simplified version of the functional paradigm.

Collins presents several arguments to show that the myth of technocracy is false. First, he argues that over the course of this century educational expansion has been much more rapid than the expansion in highly skilled and professional occupations.[42] Thus if the number of college graduates, for example, has increased tenfold in the last fifty years, the number of positions generally considered as professional has expanded less than half as much. Second, Collins cites studies questioning the argument that most contemporary jobs are indeed more complicated than similar jobs several decades ago. The research on job complexity, he reports, shows very modest changes in the skills required to perform the most common occupations, with only a small minority of technical jobs requiring clearly more skills than in the past.[43] Third, Collins argues there is very little evidence that employees who have been trained in school for a job are any more productive than those who have received less formal education and acquired their skills on the job. Most such research, he concludes, is inconclusive in its findings, suggesting that for all but a few highly technical fields, extensive formal educational training has few clear benefits in on-the-job performance and, in some cases, seems to lead to lower ratings by supervisors. Finally, in an attempt to hammer a last nail in the coffin of the technocratic myth, Collins asserts that schools are extremely ineffective institutions for the production of cognitive skills and that schooling "has more to do with teaching conventional standards of sociability and propriety than with instrumental and cognitive skills."[44] In other words, the content of much public education is more concerned with the inculcation of middle-class culture than the teaching of skills that might be useful in some later occupation.

Collins's critique is unrelenting. Most jobs are not of great complexity and the skills they require can usually be learned on the job. Employers and educational spokesmen have vested interests in claiming that work is rapidly becoming more complicated, but these claims should not be taken at face value. And despite their official pronouncements to the contrary, schools are not primarily concerned with teaching cognitive skills. Not only are schools singularly inefficient in this regard—and Collins asserts that much of what schools teach is rapidly forgotten—but their major concerns are better seen as the teaching of middle-class standards of taste and manners, rather than the transmission of intellectual skills.

If the functional paradigm is thus entirely unsatisfactory in its account of schooling, Collins then proceeds to develop an alternative account. Historically, Collins maintains, the major function of schooling has been with the teaching of status cultures rather than useful skills. Most schools in most societies have had the task of teaching the values, ideals, tastes, and standards of a particular group, usually the dominant groups or elite in that society. The content of status cultures varies, of course, from society to society, but the curriculum, social organization, and even the social activities of schools can all be seen as a way of conveying a particular set of admired qualities to the young. Thus the British private boarding schools of the nineteenth century prepared the future elite by teaching a curriculum that stressed Latin, ancient history, and team sports that emphasized fair play and the development of character rather than winning at all costs. These schools attempted to develop the qualities of a gentleman: a person of broad cultivation, moral rectitude, character, and an air of moral superiority that would impress his inferiors with his leadership ability. Boys (and such education was largely an all-male affair) who graduated from these institutions were accepted into elite positions, whereas those with more technical and scientific skills were largely excluded.[45]

Collins believes the content and character of schooling in the United States has been shaped historically by the status culture of the dominant Anglo-Protestant elite. The most prestigious schools, and the private secondary schools that prepared students for these colleges, were those that closely conveyed the qualities most admired by that elite: qualities of character and leadership, a broad and not too specialized education in the liberal arts, and tastes and values that were patrician rather than plebian. To gain status and prestige, furthermore, other schools attempted to emulate these institutions by adopting watered down or simplified versions of this same curriculum. In most societies, Collins believes, what schools teach is not primarily a matter of knowledge in some absolute sense, but the kinds of knowledge and the tastes and values that are deemed valuable by elite groups. What counts as a good education, therefore, has historically been an education that inculcates the status culture of the dominant group.

Although Collins believes this interpretation of education as the teaching of a status culture applies to virtually all past societies, he also claims that education in contemporary United States differs in important respects from this simple model. Because U.S. education is highly decentralized and because the United States is so ethnically heterogeneous, the hold of the dominant elite over the educational system has long been weaker than in most European societies.[46] For example, until quite recent times, elite groups in much of Europe have been able to enforce strict controls on the number of students enrolled in universities and to limit the content of the curriculum to the traditional arts and sciences. In this way, elites have ensured that their children and their values and tastes will remain dominant. In the United States, on the other hand, elite control over the educational system has been more tenuous. While the prestige of the traditional liberal arts institutions remained high, the decentralization of U.S. education and the competition among ethnic groups for status led to much more rapid expansion of education and to a great diversity in curriculum than elsewhere. As a result, Collins argues, U.S. education began to take on the character of a contest for educational credentials at

Credential Inflation

the expense of any particular educational content. As the number of institutions proliferated and the traditional curriculum became abandoned or modified, the sheer number of courses or degrees became increasingly important and the content or character of that education became less significant.

This observation leads Collins to speak of education in modern United States as a "cultural currency,"[47] a term that draws attention to the fact that it is the *quantity* of schooling, summarized by diplomas, certificates, or degrees, that is important rather than *what* one has learned. Such a cultural currency functions rather like money in that it can be exchanged for desirable goods, in particular, desirable occupations. It is also like money in that its value can decline over time as more and more of the currency comes into circulation. Thus the expansion of the educational system has led to inflation in the cultural currency as more and more educational credentials are required to "purchase" a given desirable occupation.

The resulting system, Collins believes, is irrational and wasteful. The struggle between groups for dominance and prestige (which Collins, as a conflict theorist, believes is a permanent feature of any society) takes the form of a contest for the educational credentials that will enable them to impress others and obtain desirable jobs. As the pressure of this competition drives up the quantity of educational credentials needed to purchase desirable jobs, many of the participants privately realize that the qualifications required are out of proportion to the complexity of the job for which they are preparing. However, it is not in their self-interest to make this private skepticism public. Students who wish to obtain high-status jobs must invest in the appropriate educational credentials whether they believe in their relevance or not. Educators, for their part, have vested interests in defending a system that keeps a large proportion of the population in school. And employers can gain prestige and respectability for their particular fields by claiming that work in that occupation is of a sufficiently professional character to require extensive educational preparation. Finally, the whole system is given legitimacy by prevailing beliefs in the myth of technocracy: beliefs that technical and scientific change are radically changing the character of work so that only extensive educational training can adequately equip the future labor force. Invoking these false gods serves to justify a vast waste of labor that otherwise could be productively employed and a corruption of the educational system in the name of preparing people for work.

In the long run, Collins believes, this irrational system may be unworkable. Credential inflation may reach such proportions that individuals may see its irrationality more clearly than they do now. In addition, to the extent that the content of education does become less important than its quantity—and Collins is somewhat ambiguous as to how far this trend has advanced—people may cease to see education as an intrinsically good and worthwhile thing and purely as a means to an end. Cynicism and disillusionment may spread, and the long U.S. romance with education may come to an end.

CONCLUSION

This exposition of some of the major sociological theories of schooling raises a series of questions that will concern us throughout the rest of this book. First, it raises questions about how we should view the relationship between schools and society, and in particular the relationship between education and work. In the modern world, it is agreed by both paradigms, schooling plays a much more important role than in any previous societies: in social mobility, in preparation for work, and in moulding common values and attitudes. But how are we to interpret this transformation? For functional theorists, the key to the explanation of this heightened importance of formal schooling lies in the distinctive needs of modern society. They see the expansion of schooling as an essentially rational adaptation to these needs. Not everything that schools teach is indispensable or even useful, of course, nor are schools ideally efficient in teaching cognitive skills, but the expansion of schooling is nevertheless best viewed as a response to new needs for sophisticated cognitive skills and cultural consensus. The world in general and the world of work in particular are more complex than in the past. It is therefore rational for public opinion to recognize that investments in education will equip the young for effective performance in that world.

For the conflict paradigm, such an interpretation misconstrues the relationship between schools and society and the nature of what schools primarily teach. It is the demands of elites, and not the needs of a society as a whole, that propel changes in schooling, and it is these demands for compliance and control over the mass of the population that shape the character of schools. In the Marxist version of the conflict paradigm, the changing character of capitalism and the struggle between capitalist elites and masses explains both the expansion of schooling and (from this point of view) its repressive character. Certainly employees need some levels of cognitive skills, but they also need a labor force willing to submit to the discipline of the work place, or, in the case of high-status jobs, employees who are willing to make the goals of corporate capitalism their own. Thus the primary link between schools and work is in the compliant and conforming values and attitudes schools convey rather than in the cognitive skills they teach. The hierarchical organization of schools, with their restrictive controls over student behavior, correspond to and reproduce the hierarchical organization of work. And although non-Marxist conflict theorists are less explicit about the correspondence of the organization of schooling with the organization of work, they too share its emphasis on elite control over the content of schooling and the irrational character of the escalation of educational credentials in recent decades.

A second set of issues concerns the relationship between schooling and equality of opportunity. Here the primary question is straightforward (though as we shall see in Chapter 4 it is very difficult to answer): Has the expansion of schooling increased equality of opportunity? The functional paradigm generally answers yes to this question, stressing how access to higher levels of education has been democratized in recent years and how this in turn is part of a shift toward a more meritocratic society where talent and effort rather than social origins determine status. Conflict theorists deny this optimistic account. From this perspective, the belief in equality of opportunity is a smokescreen behind which elites and privileged groups use the school system to perpetuate their superior position. Because of the dominance of this ideology, those who fail in school tend to blame themselves, accepting the official view that the system is meritocratic and that only their lack of intelligence or lack of motivation is responsible for failure. But in fact, argue conflict theorists, the odds of success in school remain heavily rigged against lower-class groups despite the expansion and reform of schooling.

These differing answers to the broad question, Has equality of opportunity increased? lead to varied interpretations of differential success in school. With some exceptions, functional theorists see the persistence of class or ethnic differences in school success as the result of factors largely outside the school's control: differences in class cultures, in early childhood environments, or in intelligence. Conflict theorists, on the other hand, place much more emphasis on processes within schools. Unwilling to accept the results of ability tests as indications of intelligence, they are likely to see the curriculum and teaching procedures and methods as part of a systematic process that helps sustain the myth that lower-class children are not *capable* of school success.

All these questions raised by the clash between the two paradigms are considerably complex. They involve theoretical issues that are often tricky and present pitfalls to the unwary. Answers to these questions require that we rely on empirical evidence that is often inadequate and subject to several possible interpretations. Necessarily, therefore, the detailed discussion of these issues that follows in this book will not result in a clear-cut *resolution* of many of the questions, but in their *clarification,* and in the posing of new questions that require evidence we do not yet possess.

But although it will be necessarily tentative rather than definitive, the discussion that follows will lead us to the conclusion that neither of these paradigms offers an adequate account of the nature and role of schooling in modern society. It is not only that neither paradigm can do justice to the complexity of the empirical evidence, though that is certainly the case, it is also that both paradigms tend to exaggerate the dependence of schooling on the wider society. Both views obscure the fact that a great deal of what happens in schools has little to do with the needs of society *or* the demands of capitalist elites. The limits of schooling, I shall argue, have as much to do with our inability to teach the young what we want them to learn within the constraints of the classroom situations as with outside forces dictating what schools can and cannot do. From this perspective, I shall maintain that while the liberal optimists' claim that schools can transform society is exaggerated, neither is there much justification for the more radical and pessimistic views of conflict theorists who argue that schools inevitably reinforce inequality and teach compliance and docility.

Endnotes

1. Daniel Bell, *The Coming of Post-Industrial Society* (New York: Basic Books, 1973). For a popular treatment, see Alvin Toffler, *Future Shock* (New York: Bantam Books, 1971), Chapter 18. For an early sociological account, see Burton Clark, *Educating the Expert Society* (San Francisco: Chandler, 1962).

2. Richard Freeman, *The Overeducated American* (New York: Academic Press, 1977).

3. James O'Toole, *Work, Learning and the American Future* (San Francisco: Jossey Bass, 1977); Randall Collins, *The Credential Society* (New York: Academic Press, 1979); and Caroline Bird, *The Case against College* (New York: McKay, 1975).

4. John I. Goodlad, *A Place Called School* (New York: McGraw-Hill, 1983).

5. Report of the Advisory Panel on the S.A.T. Score Decline, *On Further Examination* (New York: College Entrance Examination Board, 1977).

6. Samuel Bowles and Herbert Gintis, *Schooling in Capitalist America* (New York: Basic Books, 1976); Martin Carnoy (ed.), *Schooling in a Corporate Society* (New York: McKay, 1975), pp. 1–37; Maurice Levitas, *Marxist Perspectives in the Sociology of Education* (London: Routledge and Kegan Paul, 1974); and Collins, *The Credential Society.*

7. The clearest statement remains in Clark, *Educating the Expert Society.* For an account of the theoretical foundations of these ideas, see Talcott Parsons, *Structure and Process in Modern Societies* (New York: Free Press, 1960).

8. Bell, *The Coming of Post-Industrial Society.*

9. Clark, *Educating the Expert Society.*

10. Talcott Parsons, "The School Class as a Social System," *Harvard Educational Review* 29 (1959): 297–318.

11. Freeman, *The Overeducated American*.

12. Thomas Juster (ed.), *Education, Income and Human Behavior* (New York: McGraw-Hill, 1975), p. 8. See also Gary Becker, *Human Capital* (New York: National Bureau of Economic Research, 1964); and Theodore Schultz, "Investment in Human Capital," *American Economic Review* 51 (March 1961): 1–17.

13. Ibid., p. 8.

14. Fred Harbison and Charles Myers, *Education, Manpower and Economic Growth: Strategies in Human Resource Development* (New York: McGraw-Hill, 1964).

15. See the arguments in National Commission on Excellence in Education, *A Nation at Risk: The Imperative for Educational Reform* (Washington, D.C.: U.S. Department of Education, 1983).

16. For an economist's critique of human capital theory, see Mark Blaug, "The Empirical Status of Human Capital Theory: A Slightly Jaundiced Survey," *Journal of Economic Literature*, Vol. 14, No. 3 (September 1976): 827–855; and O'Toole, *Work, Learning and the American Future*.

17. The current status of the theory is assessed in Irvin Sobel, "The Human Capital Revolution in Economic Development: Its Current History and Status," *Comparative Education Review* (June 1978): 278–308.

18. Christopher Jencks et al., *Inequality* (New York: Basic Books, 1972), p. 187.

19. Ibid., p. 186.

20. Ibid., p. 187.

21. Ivar Berg, *Education and Jobs: The Great Training Robbery* (New York: Praeger, 1970), pp. 85–104.

22. Ibid.

23. See Otis Dudley Duncan, David Featherstone, and Beverly Duncan, *Socioeconomic Background and Achievement* (New York: Academic Press, 1972).

24. Bowles and Gintis, *Schooling in Capitalist America*, pp. 111–113.

25. Ibid. See also Christopher Jencks, *Who Gets Ahead?* (New York: Basic Books, 1979), pp. 115–121.

26. Jencks, *Who Gets Ahead?*, Chapter 3.

27. Peter Blau and Otis Dudley Duncan, *The American Occupational Structure* (New York: Wiley, 1967), pp. 81–113.

28. Patricia Sexton, *Education and Income* (New York: Viking, 1961).

29. The literature on this subject is vast. Perhaps the original Coleman Report itself, *Equality of Educational Opportunity*, and the reanalysis of the data in Jencks are the best sources. For a different interpretation of the evidence, see James Guthrie, et al., *Schools and Inequality* (Cambridge: M.I.T. Press, 1971).

30. Alan Purves, *Literature Education in Ten Countries* (New York: Wiley, 1973); Robert L. Thorndike, *Reading Comprehension in Fifteen Countries* (New York: Wiley, 1973); and L. C. Comber and John P. Keeves, *Science Education in Nineteen Countries* (New York: Wiley, 1973).

31. None of these data implies that if poor students attended schools that spent, for example, four times as much money as present-day schools, they would not do better. In this sense the research is dealing with questions of

practical policy as much as with theory. See Philip Green, "Race and I.Q.: Fallacy of Heritability," *Dissent* (Spring 1976): 181–196.

32. Nancy St. John, *School Desegregation* (New York: Wiley, 1975).

33. Milbrey W. McLaughlin, *Evaluation and Reform: The Elementary and Secondary Education Act of 1965* (Cambridge: Ballinger, 1975).

34. The phrase *active agent* comes from Clark, *Educating the Expert Society.*

35. As the Marxist paradigm has lost popularity in recent years these disputes have assumed an increasingly doctrinal character.

36. Bowles and Gintis, *Schooling in Capitalist America.*

37. Ibid., Chapter 5.

38. Unless that is, the new revolutionary consciousness produced by free schools transforms the society. See their ambivalent comments on free schools, ibid., pp. 254–255.

39. Ibid., p. 252.

40. Collins, *The Credential Society.*

41. Ibid., Chapter 1.

42. Ibid., p. 12.

43. Ibid., p. 13.

44. Ibid., p. 19.

45. I should make it clear that this is my example and not Collins'.

46. Ibid., Chapter 5.

47. Ibid., pp. 60–62.

chapter 3

Explanations
of the Expansion
# of Schooling

Although schools have existed since ancient times and in all the great civilizations of the world, it is hard to realize that it is only within the last one hundred years that schooling has been a shared experience of the mass of the population in any society. At the beginning of the industrial era around 1800, for example, most adults in Western Europe had not attended any kind of school; and even one hundred years later it was unusual for someone to have had more than four or five years of formal education.[1] Thus it is the twentieth century that has seen the real revolution in schooling: the development of mass education in virtually every society in the world, starting in the richer societies of the West in the early decades of this century and spreading to the developing societies of Asia and Africa after the second World War.

The schooling revolution began earlier and developed more rapidly in the United States than in almost any other country.[2] The United States pioneered the development of what used to be called the common school, a publicly supported school attended by lower- and middle-class students alike. Elementary schools of this kind were established in virtually every major city by the mid-nineteenth century. To a considerable extent, the public comprehensive high school is also a U.S. innovation. Starting around World War I, the old private academies with their essentially classical curriculum were replaced by or merged into the comprehensive high schools we know today: schools that taught vocational subjects as well as Latin or Greek, and bookkeeping and business English as well as Shakespeare.[3] In 1910, for example, less than 15 percent of those aged fourteen to seventeen years were enrolled in secondary schools; by 1940 over 75 percent were in school, and high school graduation had become a realistic aspiration for close to half of the population.[4] High school graduation rates continued to increase in the three decades after World War II, and though they have fallen slightly in the last decade, they currently exceed 85 percent of all students.[5]

Finally, of course, the United States pioneered mass higher education. In the early decades of this century the elite private institutions were joined by new land grant universities offering a far wider selection of courses than their European counterparts, and they became accessible to middle class and a few selected working-class students as well as to the children of elite groups. Expanding steadily during the 1920s and 1930s, college and university enrollments exploded after World War II. By 1940 about 15 percent of those aged eighteen to twenty-one years were enrolled in colleges and universities, and this figure grew to 25 percent by 1950. By 1970 about 45 percent of this age group were still enrolled in full-time education.[6] In part, this increase represented a change in the size of existing schools; by the 1970s, for example, some large state universities enrolled more than 40,000 students. In substantial part, as well, the growth took the form of the creation of new institutions in which curriculum and educational emphases differed a great deal from the traditional liberal arts and science university: junior and community colleges offered Associate degrees, and thousands of new two- and four-year technical and vocational schools opened.[7]

Changes in European education were slower and later than in the United States. As late as 1959, for example, only 33 percent of fourteen-year-old Italian children were still in school, and in that same year only 5 percent of those aged eighteen to twenty-one years in Great Britain attended universities.[8] Furthermore, virtually all European countries long maintained separate secondary schools for students who differed in aptitude and ability. In Great Britain, for example, until about 1970, an examination at age ten years determined which child would go to the academic grammar schools or to more vocationally oriented technical or secondary modern schools. But the long-term direction of change in Europe has been essentially the same as in the United States: a steady lengthening of the time that individuals spend in formal education, and a democratization of institutions that previously catered to only a small elite. In the 1960s and 1970s the age of compulsory schooling was raised virtually everywhere to age sixteen or seventeen. In many countries new comprehensive high schools were established which all students attended, regardless of their social origins and academic aptitude.

Beginning in the 1960s, college and university enrollments in most European countries grew, although from a smaller base, even more rapidly than in the United States. Existing universities doubled or tripled in size (the University of Rome, for example, now enrolls about a quarter of a million students) and new technical and vocational institutions were created.[9] Although no country in Europe approached the U.S. level of college and university enrollments, by the 1970s some form of higher education had become a reasonable expectation of most middle-class students and more than a tiny minority of working-class students in many Western European countries.

It makes sense, therefore, to speak of a schooling revolution in the modern world—a revolution that in demographic terms, at least, seems largely complete in the United States and in a few other rich industrialized nations, but that is only now in its early stages in much of the developing world. That revolution represents a fundamental change in how young people are prepared for life in the adult world. In the past, preparation for work and for adult roles involved, in large part, direct observation of and participation in the life of the community. Children received some formal instruction, of course, from their parents and future employers, but most learning was informal and experiential in character. In the modern world, however, we separate young people from the life of the community and from direct experience of adult work and place them in institutions where they spend much of their time in the primarily solitary and intellectual tasks of listening to teachers, reading books, and performing exercises and assignments. And while much can be said in defense of this method of educating the young, it should be obvious that, in terms of the feelings of boredom and irrelevance many young people experience in these institutions, it also involves certain costs.

The schooling revolution also involves a major shift in the character of formal education itself. Institutions that formerly catered almost exclusively to the needs and concerns of a tiny elite faced the problem of educating the mass of the population. Beyond the stage of learning the three Rs, formal education used to mean education in the traditional liberal arts and sciences with heavy emphasis on rote learning and memorization of facts and precepts. Today, fewer than half of all U.S. college graduates major in subjects that could even be loosely placed into this category, and business, which was not even offered as an academic subject in most colleges before the 1930s, is the most common major.[10] What we mean by formal education, therefore, has changed fundamentally in the last one hundred years.

This chapter aims to make intellectual sense of the schooling revolution. It takes the theories we examined in the previous chapter and tests their adequacy as an account of the expansion and transformation of schooling during this century, with particular attention, for this is the weakness of the dominant theory, to the expansion of higher education since World War II. This task, it should be recognized, is no substitute for the full historical account that would be needed to give a sense of the real complexity of this process. But my aim here is interpretation and theoretical analysis rather than detailed chronology. I shall compare functional and neo-Marxist explanations for the major stages of this explanation, and, after assessing the weaknesses of these accounts, provide what I believe is a more satisfactory theory, derived from conflict theory but non-Marxist in character.

FUNCTIONAL EXPLANATIONS FOR THE EXPANSION OF SCHOOLING

Though it has been challenged in recent years by more radical Marxist-inspired theories, the functional paradigm still provides the dominant framework for interpreting the revolution in schooling. The logic of the functional argument, it will be recalled from Chapter 2, is very straightforward. The complexity of modern society requires extensive formal education of the young. The needs of modern industrial society for literacy and more complex cognitive skills, for cultural and moral consensus, and for the efficient sorting and selection of talent, make extensive formal schooling increasingly imperative. Only specialized institutions exclusively devoted to the education of the young can meet their needs. Increasingly, therefore, societies recognize the importance of mass education, remove young people from the labor force, and devote more and more resources to schooling. Let us now see how this explanation works in detail.

The Breakdown of Traditional Socialization

The industrialization and urbanization that spread throughout Western Europe and North America in the nineteenth century undermined traditional socialization arrangements. In the preindustrial West most people lived in the countryside, and most children learned the skills, values, and beliefs of adult society by participating in the adult world from what we today would consider a very early age. The employment of ten-year-old children in the production of goods, for example, was commonplace in preindustrial society. The distinctions between paid employment and education and between work and socialization were much less clear cut 150 years ago than they are today. Children learned to be farmers, blacksmiths, or potters by observing their parents or other adults in the community and by participating in that activity after a short period of apprenticeship. There was some formal instruction for a minority, of course: church-related schools taught literacy, religion, and elementary arithmetic to a small but growing number of children. However, for the majority there were no specialized educational institutions and little, if any, formal instruction by teachers.

Industrialization and urbanization weakened the foundations of this system. They undermined the tradition of passing on occupations from parent to child by destroying many existing occupations and creating new occupations for which parents and communities were ill equipped to prepare their children. The early industrial revolution in textile production, for example, effectively destroyed the livelihood of thousands of spinners and weavers. The huge urban migration meant that a large percentage of children of farmers would not be farmers themselves. This meant not only that parents increasingly could no longer pass on their occupations to their children, but also that parents and indeed communities as a whole were increasingly incompetent to teach the kinds of skills required by new occupations. Farmers could not teach their children about factory work; blacksmiths could not teach their children to be clerks.

The first part of the functional explanation for the rise of schooling, therefore, stresses the needs of the new industrial society for institutions to teach the young the skills underlying the performance of new occupations. As Burton Clark writes,

> *Work itself became complicated and specialized under the advancing techniques of production and distribution, and with this the educational "threshold" of employment was progressively raised. The worker needed longer systematic instruction, although at first this amounted for most only to reading, writing and arithmetic of the simplest kind.*[11]

Schools met this need. They were a response to the growing inability of traditional socialization to teach the young the skills required by the enormous expansion of new occupations in towns and factories during the late nineteenth century.

In the functional argument, therefore, a crisis in traditional socialization occurred toward the middle of the nineteenth century. The apprenticeship system was in decline, and was never as strong in the United States as in much of Europe; new jobs were being created for which traditional informal education was inadequate. New needs could be met only by more universal schooling. One of these needs, though its relative importance is the subject of considerable debate, was for the development of literacy and arithmetical skill among the future labor force. A second need, according to the functional theory, was for new kinds of more general competencies which the traditional socialization system could not supply. The new factories needed workers who could follow simple written instructions; they also needed employees who would be punctual, and workers who could adapt to demands for steady, unremitting effort that the new factory system imposed. The schools of this time, with their clocks, their rows of desks bolted to the floor, and their emphasis upon precise following of instructions, taught these new skills.

From this point of view, therefore, employers in the new factories and business organizations that developed so rapidly in the second half of the nineteenth century supported the causes of universal schooling because it promised to provide a more competent and adaptable labor force. At the same time, of course, it became to the advantage of parents who were ambitious for their children to send them to school as formal education became a preferred or necessary qualification for employment. Thus beliefs that formal education was beneficial coincided with self-interest. As child labor increasingly became illegal or regarded as exploitative, formal education commanded steadily increasing support.

Cognitive Skills and the Expansion of Secondary and Higher Education

If the development of factories and mass migration from farms to work in cities created a need for literacy among the working population, functionalists see the rapid development of secondary education as a response to the huge expansion of white-collar occupations in large organizations in the early decades of this century. Martin Trow, for example, argues that "the growth of the secondary school after 1870 was in large part a response to the pull of the economy for a mass of white collar employees with more than an elementary school education." As the size of business firms and other work organizations expands, Trow explains:

> *Papers replace verbal orders; papers replace rule of thumb calculations of price and profit; papers carry records of workflow and inventory. . . . And as organizations grew, people had to be trained to handle those papers—to prepare them, to type them, to file them, to process them, to assess and use them.* [12]

For preparation for such tasks, furthermore, the classical liberal arts curriculum of the traditional high school academy was unsuitable. Under the leadership of John Dewey and other progressive reformers, the old curriculum appropriate for a homogeneous student body was transformed in favor of a new more relevant curriculum emphasizing business English as well as literature, bookkeeping as well as algebra, and citizenship and social studies as well as history and geography.[13] The new curriculum, with its stress on useful skills as well as abstract knowledge, and its elective courses and division into tracks, was an adaptive response to the need to prepare a new more heterogeneous high school population for the growing complexity of work in large-scale organizations, and for life in a society where the speed of change was making old knowledge obsolescent.

While the period of the high school's most rapid growth coincided with the expansion of white-collar clerical employment, functional theorists maintain that the rapid increase in professional and technical occupations underlay the revolution in higher education after World War II. In the post-war period, writes Martin Trow,

> there was a growth of demand for more highly trained and educated people of all kinds. Between 1940 and 1950, the numbers of engineers in the country doubled; the number of research workers increased by 50 percent. Even more startling, between 1950 and 1960 the total labor force increased by only 8 percent, but the number of professional, technical, and kindred workers grew by 68 percent—and these, of course, are the occupations that call for at least some part of a college education.[14]

With the replacement of routine labor by automation, Burton Clark argued in 1961, "a large proportion of jobs increasingly fell into the upper ranges of skill and expertise, in the range from professional to technician."[15] The largest and fastest growing corporations, he argues, led the way in demanding highly trained and professional employees; so much so that "the number of Ph.D.'s employed in these firms probably exceeds the number employed in liberal arts colleges."[16] As higher education became more important for the economy, its character was transformed. Higher education, Clark argues, became more specialized and more vocational. The role of the traditional four-year liberal arts curriculum declined in relative importance under the twin pressures of demands for useful, occupational skills and demands for specialized preparation for graduate school.[17] Thus the most rapid growth in higher education was in the large research-oriented universities that turned out Ph.D.'s, on the one hand, and in the community or junior colleges offering occupationally relevant training on the other. As higher education expanded, therefore, its traditional emphasis on a general and humane education was replaced with more stress on the preparation of *specialists,* from research scientists to x-ray technicians.

Finally in this regard, the leading functional theorist, Talcott Parsons, sees the development of higher education as the culmination of a long-term trend toward cognitive rationality in U.S. society. Placing less emphasis than Clark and Trow on the demand for preparation for complex jobs, Parsons sees the expansion of the U.S. university as part of an evolutionary trend toward the greater importance of *knowledge* in ordering and organizing human society.[18] Universities produce new knowledge that makes it possible for societies to increase their control over their long-term fate, and hence their adaptive capacity. Thus Parsons, and his collaborator, Gerald Platt, stress that the importance of the university does not lie solely or even primarily in its development of knowledge that will further economic growth, but in its development of *new* knowledge in all fields, in the social and behavioral sciences as well as in the natural sciences and engineering. Nor do they see that the major task of university education is in preparation for work and the development of job skills. What universities do, Parsons and Platt maintain, is to develop *cognitive competence* among their students: a general approach to problem solving that replaces concern with custom or tradition with reliance on reason, expertise, and an ability to separate objective facts from values and emotions.[19] The central importance of the university, therefore, goes beyond the particular knowledge that it generates or transmits, to the role of instilling a commitment to rationality as a way of solving problems. Although Parsons and Platt stress the difficulty of this task (it is worth noting that they were writing at the height of the countercultural movement in U.S. society in 1972), they are confident that, in the long run, the experience of higher education will prove a decisive step forward in the ability of U.S. society to gain control of its destiny and to shape its future in a rational way.[20]

Moral and Cultural Consensus

A second component of the functional explanation of the expansion of schooling stresses the requirements of industrial society for some minimal moral consensus and cultural homogeneity. Durkheim, for example, writing at the turn of the century in France, saw schools as crucial institutions in restoring some degree of cohesion and moral unity to a society torn apart by industrialization.[21] Schools provided a uniform moral education for all children whatever their social origins; they were crucial agencies in creating a truly national society. Schools, argued Durkheim, emancipated individuals from the limited parochial world of the family and local community. Through the teaching of history and instruction in values and morality, schools tied students to the ideas and purposes of the nation-state. Schools and only schools could make citizens.

Durkheim's theme has characterized much discussion of the common school in the United States and the role of that school in creating Americans from generations of immigrants of diverse origins.[22] The U.S. common school, in this view, was essentially a response to the need for some degree of cultural homogeneity in the face of ethnic and class diversity. Almost all students, no matter what their social origins, attended public elementary schools, and later the comprehensive high schools that developed in the early decades of this century. In these schools all students were taught English, United States history, the virtues of free enterprise, and the importance of individual achievement and hard work.

This interpretation, therefore, stresses the importance of schooling in forging a sense of nationhood and a commitment to common values. Because the United States was so much more heterogeneous than most of Europe, it can help illuminate some of the reasons why schooling developed more rapidly in this country than elsewhere. Although the societies of Western Europe faced essentially similar problems of the effects of industrialization and urbanization, they were not confronted with the task of socializing successive generations of immigrants with different customs, languages, and cultural traditions. This extreme heterogeneity in the United States created a danger of rancorous conflict between groups and challenges to the dominance of the Anglo-Saxon Protestant tradition.[23] Schools by no means erased the cultural differences between Irish and Italians, or Scandinavians and Greeks, but they did ensure that in the next generation there would be a common framework of language and shared understandings, and a recognition of a common history that guarded against some of the more extreme manifestations of conflict between these groups. As Durkheim stated almost one hundred years ago: "Society can survive only if there exists among its members a sufficient degree of homogeneity; education perpetuates and reinforces this homogeneity by fixing in children, from the beginning, the essential similarities that collective life demands."[24]

Contemporary functional sociologists have extended Durkheim's general argument in an interesting way. In addition to teaching common values and a sense of nationhood, schools teach general *norms* that are necessary for effective performance of adult roles in *any* modern society. Robert Dreeben, for example, notes that in modern societies "individuals must distinguish the person from the position he occupies [and] must accept the fact that everyone in the same circumstances will or should be treated the same way. . . ."[25] In modern societies, in other words, a great deal of behavior is governed by the norm of *universalism*, a rule that implies, for example, that teachers should fail students who do bad work regardless of whether they like them as individuals, and that employees should hire people on the basis of their qualifications rather than on the basis of their personal relationship to them. Schools, Dreeben believes, teach a number of general rules of behavior that families are quite ill-equipped to teach.[26] Thus families treat their members personally rather than impersonally, and in terms of their relationship to each other rather than in terms of what they can do. Schools help bridge the gap between the world of the family and the world of adult work by teaching children that their good performance in school work is more important than being friendly or affectionate, and that teachers treat or should treat everyone the same regardless of their personal likes or dislikes. In schools, Dreeben continues, students learn appropriate ways of relating to individuals with whom they have no personal affective ties, of working under the constraint of common externally imposed impersonal rules, and such traits as the ability to defer gratification until the future and the ability to be punctual. In all these respects, he argues, schools are functional for modern society. These norms and traits are much more important in modern society than in the more personal small-scale communities of the past, and it is schools rather than families that have the main task of teaching them.

Equality and Talent Sorting

The last major component of the functional explanation of the schooling revolution stresses the connection between support for schooling and demands for equality and equality of opportunity. Mass formal education expanded rapidly, this argument maintains, because it was seen as a way of achieving a society of full equality of opportunity and of minimizing some of the disadvantages suffered by the children of poor and minority parents. Particularly in the United States, schools were seen, almost from the inception of compulsory schooling, as perhaps *the* major way to achieve equality of opportunity. Public schools charged no tuition and, with the major exception of black Americans, were open to all. Ability rather than social background determined a student's course of study, and although many of the most prestigious colleges charged stiff tuition and admitted only a tiny number of scholarship students, many state universities and colleges as early as the 1920s made considerable efforts to recruit working-class students and charge minimal tuition. Again, this explanation throws more light on the issue of why schooling expanded more rapidly in the United States than elsewhere. From the founding of the Republic to the present, people in the United States have placed more stress on equality of opportunity than virtually any other society.[27] Schools were seen as the main way in which this central value could be implemented and brought closer to reality. Schools could create avenues of mobility previously closed to the poor and disadvantaged. And, particularly if virtually all students from different backgrounds attended the same kind of schools, they would work to erase class distinctions between rich and poor, and privileged and underprivileged.

In contrast, these themes were much less in evidence in much of Europe. Until quite recently, Europeans were less optimistic than Americans that most children, particularly working and lower-class children, could benefit from extensive schooling.[28] Nor were Europeans as committed to the idea that all children, regardless of their origins, should attend the same schools and study the same curriculum. Instead, the emphasis was on maintaining traditional academic standards, safeguarding the cultural traditions of elites, and selecting a few outstandingly talented poor students to be admitted to the prestigious schools. As late as 1960, only tiny percentages of working-class students in France, West Germany, Great Britain, and Italy received any kind of higher education, and the great majority left school at ages fourteen or fifteen.[29] In the United States, on the other hand, much greater educational opportunities created and sustained higher demands for schooling among all groups in the population.

The same argument can be applied to post-World War II developments as well. To fully achieve equality of opportunity, functional theorists argued, required a massive expansion of *higher* education, as well as the creation of universal secondary education.[30] The creation of the new community colleges, for example, enabled disadvantaged students with minimal financial resources and grades too low to gain admission to universities to prove they were capable of college-level work.[31] The provision of extensive financial aid to college students by the federal government, a program dating from the 1960s, greatly improved the prospects of poor and minority students who had been excluded by their inability to afford the tuition or by the need to help support their families. Last, but by no means least, the integration of schools and universities in the 1960s and 1970s, although hardly fully achieved, can be seen as an attempt to break down the last and greatest barrier to equality of opportunity: the exclusion of blacks from the mainstream educational system. That momentous change, the functional argument maintains, was the most recent step toward implementing the egalitarian and democratic ideal that Americans have always shared and that schools have played the major role in fulfilling.

Finally, functional theorists argue that, in the last analysis, such ideals and values are rational and functional for modern society. As we saw in the last chapter, the functional paradigm argues that modern society, far more than previous societies, needs an efficient mechanism for the sorting and selecting of talented people because it is particularly dependent on expert knowledge for its effective administration. A society that neglects to provide educational opportunities for a sizable fraction of its youth is, in the long run, behaving in an irrational manner since it is depriving itself of large numbers of potentially talented people. Over the long haul, though, functional theorists believe all modern societies tend to develop strong beliefs both in equality of opportunity and in schooling as the most effective way to realize that ideal.[32]

NEO-MARXIST THEORIES OF EDUCATIONAL EXPANSION

In the last twenty years the dominant functional interpretation of educational expansion has been challenged by a group of revisionist historians who, despite important differences of emphasis among them, are perhaps fairly described as neo-Marxist. The titles of some of their books (Colin Greer's *The Great School Legend* and Joel Spring's *Education and the Rise of the Corporate State*) suggest the difference between the revisionist interpretation of educational history and the liberal and functional orthodoxy.[33] Educational expansion is not a march of progress toward ever greater equality of opportunity, but a story of betrayals and false promises. Educational reform movements for humane schooling and creation of schools that provide more opportunities for the poor have been undermined or subverted by the power of corporate elites. Schools have served and continue to serve as "channeling colonies": channeling the poor into careers appropriate to their abilities as defined by officially sanctioned tests. In Bowles and Gintis's version of this argument, a major source of educational change lies in the changing demands of capitalist production and in the power of elites who own these means of production to shape educational institutions to their ends. Demands for a loyal, compliant, and disciplined labor force shape both the social organization and the curriculum of schools. Changes in those demands, reflecting changes in the nature of capitalist production, in turn lead to the expansion and change of schooling.

Rise of Compulsory Schooling

The most interesting and, I believe, the most convincing application of neo-Marxist theory is in the explanation of the rise of compulsory schooling in the nineteenth century. Revisionist school historians have pointed out that orthodox educational history provides only a highly selective account of the motives and objectives of the advocates of compulsory schooling. Many such orthodox accounts portray U.S. reformers Horace Mann and Henry Barnard as progressives, whose concern was primarily with opening channels of mobility for the poor and arguing against unthinking obedience and punishment as the watchwords of elementary education. What the critics and others have shown, however, is that other more authoritarian and controlling impulses lay behind the success of the movement for compulsory schooling in the nineteenth century.[34] Mann, for example, argued that conscience and affection should predominate in schools rather than fear and punishment. He also wrote that his objective was "the removal of vile and rotten parts from the structure of society as fast as sound ones can be prepared to take their place."[35] And in case there should be some doubt as to who Mann means when he refers to the "vile and rotten parts," another key figure in the public school movement, Henry Barnard, is even more explicit about some of the goals of compulsory schooling:

> *No one at all familiar with the deficient household arrangements and deranged machinery of domestic life, of the extreme poor and ignorant, to say nothing of the intemperate—of the examples of rude manners, impure and profane language, and all the vicious habits of low bred idleness, which abound in certain sections of populous districts—can doubt, that it is better for children to be removed as early and as long as possible from such scenes and examples.*[36]

The revisionist critics argue that the movement for compulsory schooling in nineteenth-century United States took on the character of a moral crusade to reform the character of the poor. Schools were seen as a way of abolishing "open and abandoned profligacy," of breaking up the "moral jungles," and of purifying "the infected and waste districts of society." In their important book, *Schooling in Capitalist America,* Bowles and Gintis extend this interpretation along specifically Marxist lines.[37] They provide substantial evidence for the proposition that compulsory schooling was directly related not to urbanization or even to economic growth, but to the factory mode of production. They report studies of New England, for example, that show school boards pressed for educational expansion not in the largest or richest towns, but in communities where a high percentage of the labor force was engaged in manufacturing, particularly in large factories. They show that factory owners and managers figured prominently on school boards in towns with a large factory population. Factory owners, they argue, were especially concerned to see compulsory schooling because they believed that only schools could guarantee them the kind of stable, industrious, and compliant work force on which their prosperity depended.

Employer Motives and Compulsory Schooling

What is most interesting about this interpretation, however, are the qualities that were most demanded by the early factory owners from schools. Factory owners made little reference to literacy or to arithmetical skills as important qualities for their potential employees to acquire. Overwhelmingly, rather, they referred to the moral qualities that schools were thought to produce. An educated worker, they thought, would be a worker who was less likely to be unreliable, rebellious, or disrespectful of authority; less inclined to drunkenness and disorderly behavior, and more inclined to be a stable and industrious worker. And if schools did teach specific cognitive skills, these were valued less for themselves than for the moral qualities they were thought to imply. A literate employee, they believed, was less likely to be a criminal, a potential troublemaker, to join a strike, or to attempt to unionize.[38]

The demands for such qualities, Bowles and Gintis believe, are directly related to the social organization of instruction in early schools in factory towns. In comparison with schools of the past, the new schools contained relatively small classrooms that permitted detailed teacher supervision of each student, the school day was broken up into periods, and school clocks regulated the daily sequence of activities. Such schools were, by contrast with the voluntary schools of the past, far more efficient in securing disciplined and orderly work from students and in inculcating an appropriate respect for the authority of both the school and the wider society. And while Bowles and Gintis do not deny that lower-class groups demanded access to such schools for their children, the particular form that schools took was largely dictated not by lower-class demands, but by the demands of the new factory system of production. In a very real sense, they argue, compulsory public schooling was *imposed* on the poor.

The Expansion of Secondary Schooling

A change in the character of capitalist production, Bowles and Gintis believe, helps account for the expansion of secondary schooling in the early decades of this century. For the increasing number of white-collar jobs created after the turn of the century, obedience, punctuality, and deference to authority were not enough. Schools were needed to create some degree of internalized motivation in their students to make them want to do what they had to do. New impersonal and social skills that would permit people to interact smoothly with each other and in large organizations were required. At the same time, the years after the turn of the century were years of unprecedented labor unrest. Militant unionism was growing in strength; increasing numbers of European immigrants raised fears that socialist and radical ideas would come to dominate the attitudes of the labor force. Elites faced the problem of devising a school system that would simultaneously provide the skills needed by the new white-collar jobs and solve the problem of pacifying and controlling a potentially militant lower-class group.

The comprehensive high school was a solution to these two problems. For the lower class, vocational education provided a way of teaching technically useful skills and isolating the youthful lower-class populations from radical ideas. The reform of the classically dominated curriculum of the past, the introduction of electives, and the progressive emphasis on interpersonal skills and relevant subject matter served to prepare middle-class youth for white-collar occupations. Schoolwide sports and athletic events forged a sense of loyalty on the part of all students to the school and to the wider social order. The diversity of the curriculum and the introduction of separate academic and vocational tracks made it possible to efficiently train people in the various required occupational skills and qualities.[39]

In the new comprehensive high schools, therefore, the progressive emphasis on tailoring education to the students' needs was used to support the strategy of channeling lower-class students into vocational education and middle-class students into the academic curriculum. Such a process of tracking was justified by the extensive use of IQ tests after World War I. These tests, financed substantially by such foundations as Carnegie and Rockefeller, were not, Bowles and Gintis argue, instruments for discovering unsuspected talent among the poor and the lower class. The results of these tests, rather, tended to confirm existing elite prejudices against such groups and to scientifically support the existing social hierarchy. The eminent psychologist, Lewis Terman, speaking of Indians, Mexicans, and Negroes in 1911, wrote, "Their dullness seems to be racial. Children of these groups should be segregated into special classes . . . they cannot master abstractions, but they can often be made efficient workers."[40]

In Bowles and Gintis's interpretation, then, the humanistic and egalitarian objectives of the progressive movement were undermined by the subservience of schools to the demands of corporate capitalism. And they believe this is likely to be no less the case with the radical and humanistic school reform movements of the present day. They write:

The new corporate organization itself requires a shift in the social relationship of education. Direct discipline and emphasis upon external rewards, characteristics of the assembly line and the factory system, have given way for a huge segment of the work force to motivation by internalized norms characteristic of the service and office worker. Cooperation rather than individually competitive work relationships are increasingly emphasized. Entrepreneurial capitalism, which brought us the chair-nailed-to-the-floor classroom has given way to corporate capitalism. It may belatedly usher in the era of the open classroom, minimization of grading, and internalized behavior norms contemplated for at least a century by so many educational reformists. [But] as in the case of the progressive movement, the ideology of educational liberation can become a tool of domination.[41]

The Expansion of Higher Education

Bowles and Gintis interpret the rapid expansion of higher education in the last few decades as an adaptation both to popular demands for equality and mobility and the further evolution of capitalism.[42] Although corporate capitalism now requires a larger percentage of employees capable of sustained work without direct supervision, it does not require such qualities in close to half of the population. In fact, the organization of higher education today closely parallels the division between vocational and academic tracks in the high school. Junior colleges are primarily vocational institutions that supervise and monitor the work of their students in close detail. They are institutions that give many poor students the illusion of upward mobility, but in fact they channel students to lower-level white-collar occupations that permit little autonomy or discretion. Only in universities preparing students for elite status, Bowles and Gintis argue, do we find a great deal of choice and discretion and long-range work without supervision. But even here, they pessimistically conclude, the fragmentation of subject matter with emphasis on specialized technical competence rather than on grasping the whole meaning of the particular subject makes it unlikely that significant numbers of students will raise serious questions about the legitimacy of the social order.[43]

FUNCTIONALIST AND NEO-MARXIST EXPLANATIONS COMPARED

There are obvious differences between these two approaches to understanding the expansion of schooling. The functional theory places great emphasis on the role of schools in providing cognitive skills essential to the performance of the increasingly complex jobs in modern society. The neo-Marxist model rejects this as a primary explanation and places much more stress on how schools have taught future workers to be docile and compliant workers who can accept the industrial discipline of the workplace. Functionalists stress how schools transmitted common values and forged a sense of nationhood in an ethnically diverse society. Neo-Marxists emphasize that these values were the values of capitalist elites and were imposed on the mass of the population. The functional argument sees schools as the major vehicle through which increasing equality of opportunity was achieved. Neo-Marxists see this belief in equality of opportunity as a smokescreen behind which schools worked to perpetuate inequality and convince the poor that their failure was their own fault.

The two theories are also different in the basic character of their explanations and in the models of society they imply. The functional theory refers to the needs or requirements of the society as a whole: for cognitive skills and for the transmission of core values. The expansion of schooling is explained by postulating certain changing needs and how schools meet these needs. The underlying metaphor is that of a society as a self-regulating organism that, in ways that are not always clear, recognizes its changing needs and whose values and priorities adjust accordingly. In its cruder formulations, at least, it is teleological in character. People in societies recognize that institutions are not meeting new needs, they recognize that schools would correct some of these deficiencies, *therefore,* they give more support to schools. The neo-Marxist account, by contrast, is clear that it is capitalist elites rather than impersonal needs that shape the character and developing of schooling. As the character of capitalism changes, from small-scale family firms to larger corporations, and from factory to office work, the kind of schooling that meets the interests of capitalist elites in maximizing profits changes. A stress on obedience and rule following gives way to emphasis on getting along with others, and mere obedience to external authority is replaced by an emphasis on the internalization of rules.

The two explanations also differ in whether they regard the expansion of schooling as a good or progressive development. The functional explanation tends to see the schooling revolution as the triumph of liberal values over ignorance and prejudice. Schools are not only a more *efficient* way of preparing people for life in a complex society than traditional methods of socialization, they also foster the development of liberal and humane values: rationality, tolerance, and equality of opportunity. Certainly none of these values has been, by any means, completely achieved, but there is, according to this view, nonetheless clear progress in recent decades. Neo-Marxists, on the other hand, distinguish between the liberating potential of *education* and the repressive character of *schooling* as it exists in capitalist society. In some unspecified post-capitalist societies, schools could promote the full human intellectual and moral potential, and could help achieve true equality of opportunity. However, within the constraints of capitalist society, all reform efforts will inevitably be sabotaged and the original promise of schooling betrayed.

At the same time, if we set aside these obvious ideological differences, there is also considerable common ground between the two approaches. Both functional and neo-Marxist theories see the development of schooling as intimately connected with the changing character of work and the larger process of industrialization in modern society. Both theories see the expansion of schooling, and the development of mass secondary education in particular, as a way of socializing and unifying a heterogeneous population and of thereby reducing the extent of ethnic and class conflicts. Also, both the neo-Marxists and functionalists stress how demands for equality and equality of opportunity have shaped the schooling revolution. Neo-Marxists deny that the development of mass education has created equality of opportunity, but they place hardly less stress than the functional argument upon how demands for equality of opportunity, whether realized or not, have shaped the expansion of schooling.[44] Finally, and most important of all for the argument I shall now develop, functional and neo-Marxist theories both stress what they see as the very close connection between societal changes and the development of schooling. Both accounts concede very little autonomy to schooling. Schools, they imply, *need* to develop in the very way they did because they must necessarily reflect the impact of such powerful societal forces as the demands of industrialization and the ideology of equality of opportunity. Before evaluating the respective merits of the two explanations, therefore, I want to present a third theory of educational expansion that implies a rather looser integration between school and society than either the functional or neo-Marxist account. This theory, I will suggest, is strongest where the other theories are weakest: in the explanation of the expansion of higher education and the current credential crisis.

Status Competition and the Credential Crisis

The functional theory of educational expansion was developed primarily in the first two decades after World War II during the period of the greatest expansion of higher education. That theory expected and predicted a continuing expansion of higher education until the end of this century, powered by rapid increases in demand for highly skilled labor as technological change further increased the complexity of work. It has been clear since the mid-1970s, however, that this prediction was incorrect. The boom period of higher education seems now to be over, and while there remain shortages of skilled workers in a number of fields, the general picture in the United States and Western Europe is a surplus of college graduates, and M.A.'s and Ph.D.'s as well, and a scramble among these highly qualified people for scarce desirable jobs.[45] While part of this crisis in the "purchasing

power" of educational credentials may be due to such possibly temporary factors as the slowing down of economic growth, it is not clear
that the functional theory, in particular, can readily explain these recent developments.

The work of Randall Collins and Raymond Bondon suggests that
we can see this credential crisis, and educational expansion in general,
as an outcome of a process of *status competition* between groups.[46]
From this perspective, it is the competition among groups for status
and prestige rather than the needs of the society as a whole for more
elaborate training that explains educational expansion. Because education is closely linked to power and status, Collins argues, different
groups will seek to improve their position by obtaining more education
for their children than they themselves had in the past. Disadvantaged
groups, for example, will try to improve their position by seeking more
education for their children. Ironically, however, the success of disadvantaged groups in this respect will stimulate middle- and upper-class
groups to maintain their relative positions in the hierarchy by increasing their own levels of education as well. This in turn will mean that
disadvantaged groups must seek even more extensive schooling for
their children if they are to have a chance for success in this contest.
Over time, therefore, the educational "ante" tends to increase, almost
regardless of whether a particular level of qualifications is in fact appropriate for a particular job. High-status groups, for example, who had
been traditionally able to secure professional jobs for their children
by having them complete college, found this security disappearing
as more and more middle-class students attended universities after
World War II. Increasingly, therefore, this elite group aspired to *graduate* education for their children as a way of maintaining their relative
advantage. In turn, this triggered a further cycle of educational expansion, when completion of two years of college began to become a
prerequisite for the same kind of lower middle-class jobs that could
have been obtained by high school graduates twenty years before.

Collins argues that this process of status competition through the
educational system has been more important in the United States than
in other societies. Because of its ethnic diversity, he maintains, the
conflict between groups was more intense in the United States than
elsewhere.[47] Also because of the decentralized character of the U.S.
educational system and relative lack of control by a traditional elite,
status competition tended to result in a more rapid and earlier educational expansion. In Europe, elites could effectively monopolize control
over the most prestigious institutions longer than in the United States.
How much schooling an individual had was less important than *what
kind* of school a student attended. Thus British upper-class families
whose children attended elite secondary boarding schools did not fear

competition from middle-class students who graduated from less prestigious colleges. However, as elite monopolies over prestigious education have gradually declined everywhere, it became necessary for all groups to seek more schooling for their children if they wished to maintain or improve their relative positions.[48] In Europe, Japan, and the United States, the struggle between groups for power and status increasingly took the form of a contest for educational credentials which, in recent decades at least, has steadily raised the level of educational qualifications required for admission to moderately good jobs.

The importance of status competition theory is that it can offer an explanation of educational expansion without making reference to the needs of society or to the demands of capitalist elites. No sensible person would suggest that educational expansion can be seen solely as a process of status competition. But even if it be granted only a modest role in such an explanation, the theory is important because it draws attention to the possibility that the expansion of schooling may be, from the point of view of society as a whole, a partly irrational process.

EVALUATION AND INTERPRETATION OF THE THEORIES

Frustrating as it may be for those who prefer unambiguous either/or solutions, I think we need all three theories to understand the basic processes that underlie the schooling revolution. None of the theories, of course, does justice to the historical record—that as always is too many-sided and too complicated to be reduced to a sociological theorem. But even if we restrict ourselves to the task of understanding in schematic fashion the very general processes of change that lie behind the historical narrative, we find that while each of them is illuminating and indeed indispensable, no one of these theories alone offers a satisfactory model of the expansion of schooling. Let us now evaluate the theories against the available evidence.

Education and Work

Perhaps the central assertion of both the functional and neo-Marxist theories is that changes in the character and complexity of work underlay the expansion of schooling. Both these theories argue that schools taught skills, values, and personality characteristics which became increasingly useful or functional as factories and large-scale organizations replaced farm work or traditional crafts. Sticklers for historical detail, however, may point out that one such skill, literacy, was rather widespread *before* the advent of mass elementary education.[49] Nor is there clear evidence that, in the United States at least, compulsory schooling occurred earliest in those states that had experienced the most rapid industrialization.[50] However, if we look at the enormous changes in the character of work that occurred over the long run—between, say, 1850 and 1920—it is difficult to escape the conclusion that some form of formal education was an indispensable preparation. The new workplace, as neo-Marxists point out, required new forms of discipline: punctuality, and the ability to work at a pace dictated by machines or by bosses. Traditional socialization did not stress this discipline nearly as much as the early elementary schools, nor did it teach literacy and arithmetical skills in any systematic way.

The precise mix of skills and values that employers found most useful is difficult to assess. Historians remain divided on whether to characterize employers' demands as primarily cognitive in character— for smart, able, literate employees who could learn new tasks quickly— or on whether the stress was placed on such traits as reliability, regular work habits, and willingness to follow orders.[51] What is clear, however, is that schools were *thought* to teach both sets of characteristics, and that employees who had attended schools were generally regarded as superior to those who had not. Although the functional arguments' stress on the cognitive skills that schools taught is not entirely misplaced, we also need the neo-Marxist emphasis on how the social organization of early schools (the desks bolted to the floor, the clocks on the wall, the emphasis on repetitive tasks) paralleled the organization of work, and may have inculcated values and personality traits that employees found desirable.

As we move toward the present era, however, the connection between schooling and the transformation of work becomes rather more problematic. We can agree with both functional and neo-Marxist theories that *some* further expansion of schooling was made necessary or demanded by the rapid development of white-collar work in large-scale organizations and by the growing technical or professional character of work in recent decades. It seems implausible, however, to explain most of the educational expansion in these terms.

Between 1950 and 1960, for example, the percentage of professional, technical, and kindred workers grew by 68 percent, while the percentage of semi-skilled and unskilled workers declined sharply.[52] Most of these new occupations demanded that employees be able to read extensive written materials and perhaps write memoranda; many also required a broad foundation of elementary scientific and methodological knowledge upon which more specialized skills could be built. As the labor force increasingly shifted from working with machines to working with people, a new set of interpersonal skills also became desirable: civility, good manners, and learning how to avoid open conflict while getting one's own way. However, it seems a mistake to argue that these changes necessitated four or more years of secondary education, and still less, the development of mass higher education. As we pointed out in Chapter 2, the expansion of education has been considerably more rapid than the expansion of the highly skilled labor force. As a result, educational requirements for *essentially similar* jobs increased steadily. In 1937, for example, 11 percent of employers required high school diplomas for skilled laborers; by 1967, 32 percent required high school graduation for skilled laborers.[53] Similar increases in educational requirements can be noted in virtually every field—x-ray technicians, teachers, police, insurance salespeople, and so on. Since the evidence that educated employees perform consistently better on the job than less educated employees is weak,[54] it seems implausible to argue that the more recent expansion of schooling can be satisfactorily explained by the increasing complexity of work.

The functional account of the relationship between schooling and work is not a satisfactory explanation of the changes in the educational curriculum in recent decades. It is generally true, as the theory asserts, that the high school curriculum shifted over time from its traditional emphasis on the liberal arts toward more directly useful subjects of study. It is also true that community colleges have, in recent decades, offered a greater proportion of directly vocational courses (fashion marketing, refrigerator mechanics, fire science) than they did two decades ago. But if the broad functional interpretation of educational change is correct, we should expect to find a steady trend toward increasing concentration on mathematical, scientific, and technical subjects of study as the pull of an increasingly complex and scientifically based economy exerts pressure on schools and colleges to prepare students for new kinds of more demanding work. Remarkably enough, however, a computation of the percentage of students majoring in the natural sciences and engineering shows very little change between the early years of this century and 1979 (the latest year for which these data are available).[55] Due to the huge expansion in the number of college students the *absolute* number of such majors has increased, but there is no obvious trend toward increasing concentration in the fields which, according to the theory, should expand most rapidly. Table 3–1, which reports more detailed changes in major fields of study between 1955 and 1979, also offers little support to a straightforward functional interpretation of the changing nature of the college curriculum. The table shows that the percentage of students majoring in engineering fluctuated considerably over the period, but it shows no clear overall trend. And while it is true, as the theory would predict, that the percentage of humanities majors has fallen, the percentage of students majoring

Table 3-1 *Bachelor's and Master's Degrees by Selected Major Fields of Study, 1955, 1965, 1970, 1975, and 1979, Percentage Distribution*

	Natural Sciences and Mathematics*		Humanities†		Business‡		Engineering	
	% of all Bachel.'s degrees	% of all Mast.'s degrees	% of all Bachel.'s degrees	% of all Mast.'s degrees	% of all Bachel.'s degrees	% of all Mast.'s degrees	% of all Bachel.'s degrees	% of all Mast.'s degrees
1955	6.2	9.3	11.7	11.6	14.2	5.7	6.2	5.8
1965	11.2	10.1	20.3	7.5	14.9	7.7	6.1	8.1
1970	8.4	7.4	16.7	10.9	13.9	11.3	4.3	5.5
1975	7.0	4.9	10.6	7.1	15.0	13.1	3.3	3.7
1979	6.4	4.2	8.2	5.2	17.9	17.3	4.4	3.6

Computed from U.S. Department of Education, National Center for Educational Statistics, *Earned Degree Series*, Washington, D.C., 1982.
Note: Because of noncomparable categories, social science enrollments are not shown.
* Includes statistics, computer science, and biological sciences.
† Includes foreign languages.
‡ Includes accounting and marketing.

in science and mathematics has not increased; indeed, since 1970 it has also fallen.[56] The only consistent trend revealed by the table is the steady increase in the proportion of students majoring in business, both at the bachelor's and the master's level.

There are dangers in reading too much into data of this kind, which, after all, refer not to course enrollments as a whole but only to major fields of concentration. In absolute terms, of course, there are far more scientifically and mathematically trained students than ever before. However, these trends in majors do serve as a cautionary note to those who claim that the character of higher education must inevitably be transformed by a scientific and technological revolution. If higher education appears to be more vocational in character than it was in the past, as evidenced by the increase in the percentage of business majors, there is little evidence here that students are spending more of their time in what are, presumably, the key subjects of the new scientific age: mathematics, statistics, or the fundamental scientific disciplines. The claim of Parsons and Platt that there is a long-run trend toward cognitive rationality in U.S. society, in particular, receives little support from these data. If anything, the trend is away from the core subjects that presumably provide cognitive rationality, and toward more applied and vocational courses of study.

It seems plausible to argue, therefore, that the fit between the changing character of work and changes in education is a good deal looser than the functional argument and the neo-Marxist theory imply. Formal education does become more closely linked to jobs over time, and some part of the expansion of education and its changing curriculum can be seen as an adaptation to the changing demands of work. It seems likely, however, that functional theorists have exaggerated how much work has been changed by scientific and technological developments and how closely educational change has reflected these changes. The mere fact that employers prefer to hire educated employees (that businesses prefer M.B.A.'s over B.A.'s, for example) does not mean that they could not manage well with less qualified employees.

Consensus Building and Educational Expansion

The functional and neo-Marxist theories give very different accounts of how educational expansion was related to demands for cultural consensus and the transmission of common values. Functional theorists, and historians working in this tradition, have stressed how support for public schooling reflected widespread beliefs that these institutions could forge a sense of nationhood in the American Republic: teaching distinctively American rather than European values, and a national rather than a purely regional or ethnic culture. Neo-Marxists, on the other hand, have emphasized how in many respects schooling was *imposed* on a more or less reluctant working-class population, and how the values and ideals that schools taught reflected the interests of capitalist elites rather than consensually held beliefs. Consistent with this emphasis, neo-Marxists place great stress on what they see as the repressive character of schooling—the emphasis on deference to authority, regimentation of student behavior and deportment, and rote memorization, and the emphasis on the transmission of specifically pro-business values and attitudes.

In large part, these differences in interpretation reflect differences in ideology that cannot be resolved by any empirical evidence. The argument that schools are repressive, for example, is not a factual assertion but a statement that reflects particular values about the desirability of "liberation" and untestable ideas about how schools would be different in a non-capitalist or post-revolutionary United States. Neo-Marxists, with their hostility to capitalism and their faith in the revolutionary potential of the working class, will tend to see values and attitudes that schools convey to the mass of the population as a process of indoctrination into business values. Functionalists, for their part, because of their premise that societies are indeed held together by common values and their commitment to the idea that the expansion of schooling was for profoundly humane and progressive development, tend to minimize what the neo-Marxists most emphasize: the greater power of elites to shape schools to suit their own interests, and the transmission of a culture that reflects the values of a relatively small group.

Some recent research on the expansion of schooling, interestingly enough, does not give much support to either the functionalist or the neo-Marxist interpretation.[57] According to the neo-Marxist argument, for example, rapid immigration should have caused an expansion of public schooling because it posed threats to elite control. Potentially refractory and troublesome groups needed to be civilized and indoctrinated with the dominant ideology. The functionalist theory, though for different reasons, makes the same prediction. The need for social and cultural consensus posed by rapid waves of immigration should have increased support for public schooling. However, the evidence indicates that the rapid immigration of southern and eastern European populations from 1890 to 1924 was associated with a *slowing* down in the rate of public schooling and increases in the growth of private schooling. The dominant Protestant groups, Ralph and Rubison argue, reacted to the massive immigration of these culturally very different groups by excluding them from the public school system and confining them to private schools.[58] Only when the character of the immigrants changed after the 1924 Immigration Act, which effectively restricted immigration to northern and western Europeans, did the growth of public schools resume. Ralph and Rubison's interpretation emphasizes that neither functionalist nor a neo-Marxist approach can explain these findings. Instead, they suggest the evidence best fits the status competition theory, where groups support the public school system to the extent that it enables *their own* children to gain an advantage in the struggle for status and prestige. It is worth noting that similar processes may have been at work in the 1970s, where a fall in support for public schooling by middle-class groups coincided with a sharp increase in the numbers of lower-class blacks and Hispanics attending what were previously segregated schools.

The Expansion of Schooling and Equality of Opportunity

All theories of educational expansion agree that there was a close connection between equality of opportunity and the expansion of schooling. Whether or not schools *did* indeed help create a society of equality of opportunity (the debate on this question will be examined in the next chapter), there is no doubt that citizens of the United States *believed* that schools would create equality of opportunity, nor that these beliefs provided an important source of support for the expansion of public schooling. Both functionalist and neo-Marxist theories stress how beliefs of this kind helped justify the development of public schools. In the first period of expansion, for example, the early school reformers argued that schools could help erase the advantages enjoyed by the children of the rich, and create avenues of mobility for the deserving poor. Those same justifications were employed, Bowles and Gintis point out, in the development and use of IQ tests in the high schools of the 1920s and 1930s.[59] Tests were seen as instruments that could read through the overlay of social and cultural differences to the natural talent possessed by many poor and disadvantaged students. And if we now know that this was a naive view of the testing process, there is little question that these arguments were widely believed at the time, and helped develop widespread legitimacy for the system of tracking that began in the high schools of this period.

The expansion of higher education after World War II was also closely linked to beliefs in and demands for equality of opportunity. It was almost universally believed that the development of mass higher education would greatly increase the mobility opportunities of working class and disadvantaged groups. As the influential Carnegie Commission pointed out,[60] while increased scholarships and financial aid could help these groups attend universities, a really decisive expansion of opportunity required the expansion of the whole system of higher education: the creation of thousands of new junior colleges which any high school graduate could attend, and the quadrupling or quintupling in size of places at four-year institutions with many of them reserved specifically for disadvantaged or minority students.

At the same time, however, it is important to make a clear distinction between *beliefs*, on the part of elites or masses, that the expansion of education would have certain consequences for equality of opportunity, and the actual *effects* of such expansion. There is no question that people's beliefs that educational expansion would have important effects on equality of opportunity are an important explanation of why they were willing to support additional expenditures on schools. And, in this limited sense, both the functional theory which stresses the role of general public opinion, and the neo-Marxist theory which emphasizes the importance of elite demands, are correct. But, as we shall see in the next chapter, there are important questions as to whether the expansion of schooling has had the effects on equality of opportunity claimed for it. Those effects, to the extent that we can assess them, do not support the functional view that the expansion of schooling is a preeminently rational way of sorting and selecting talented people and creating a more meriotcratic society. Nor do they clearly support the argument that schools were a major instrument in perpetuating elite control during the period of educational expansion. In this sense, therefore, both theories overstate the rationality and intentional character of the expansion of schooling.

CONCLUSION

Twenty years ago there was little controversy among sociologists about the causes of the schooling revolution in this century. The basic explanation of the development of mass education was assumed to be self-evident: Modern industrial societies *needed* extensive formal education to prepare the young for increasingly complicated and demanding work, to forge cultural consensus, and to create equal opportunity. Where these arguments were spelled out in detail, furthermore, they were often couched in language that suggested a celebration of the expansion of schooling rather than a dispassionate analysis of its causes. The expansion of schooling was seen as a crucial part of an inevitable march of progress toward a more rational enlightened and equal society. Some, it is true, deplored the trend toward the increasing connection between education and work, because it appeared to devalue the traditional liberal arts curriculum. Others pointed out that schools were still in many ways atavistic institutions, encouraging passive and rote learning, and ill-adapted to the emerging knowledge-based society. But the basic thrust of the argument was overwhelmingly optimistic. If equality of opportunity had not been achieved, it would be brought closer by the next wave of expansion. If schools contained survivals of past practices no longer relevant, these would eventually disappear. And if the increasingly close connection between school and work weakened the position of the humanities, it would, in the long run, lead to more emphasis on the development of cognitive skills and cognitive rationality.

By the mid-1970s, a different argument, in some ways a mirror image of the first, began to be popular among sociologists though not yet among the general public. The development of mass education was the story of promises betrayed. The potential of schools to create equality of opportunity, to develop rational and critical thought, and to realize the human potential had been subverted by elite control. Compulsory schooling was imposed on reluctant masses to civilize them and to create a docile, obedient work force who were willing to submit to industrial discipline. And while this interpretation, every bit as much as the functionalist, stressed that the expansion of education was necessary for the maintenance of the present social order, it saw every step of that expansion through jaundiced, cynical eyes: from the progressive reforms of the 1920s and 1930s that democratized the curriculum, to the creation of junior colleges in the 1960s.

With the advantage of hindsight, we can see the weakness of both of these explanations. In their desire to celebrate or condemn schooling, they both tend to exaggerate how closely the development of schooling reflected the needs of society as the demands of elites. Both provide an *overdetermined* account of the expansion of schooling in which what happened had to happen for rather deep and profound structural reasons. In part, of course, the schooling revolution *was* a product of long-term shifts in the character of industrial society—changes that made it difficult to prepare people for work, to build cultural consensus, or to achieve societal ideals like equality of opportunity without extensive formal education. And in the working out of the process of change, both functional and neo-Marxist accounts are necessary, and indeed complementary. In important respects, as the functionalist argument claims, the expansion of schooling did reflect generally, if not universally, held values—that schooling was a profoundly good thing, that it would create a more equal or more just society, and that extensive formal education was a necessary or useful preparation for work in the modern era. At the same time, as neo-Marxists claim, much of the history of schooling can be seen as the outcome of conflicts and struggles between groups for control of what was taught and how it was taught. While capitalist elites did not win these struggles perhaps as often as neo-Marxists argue, any adequate analysis must recognize that the interests of elites in domination and control often lay behind the liberal rhetoric of educational change. Schools did not simply reproduce the values and ideals of a ruling elite, nor were leading educators simply proxies for capitalist interests, but neither should we be so naive as to accept the view that schools merely conveyed, in some automatic fashion, consensually held values and ideas. The expansion of schooling was supported by elites in part because it enabled them to channel demands for upward mobility and improved status into avenues in which they and their children held a superior hand. The belief in equality of opportunity through the school system undoubtedly reduced the intensity of conflict and challenges to elite control. However, that expansion was also genuinely popular with the mass of the population, and that popularity cannot be adequately characterized as false consciousness or elite manipulation.

Although both accounts are necessary, both are also seriously flawed. Neither theory, for example, can provide a satisfactory account of the current credential crisis in the United States. Higher education, it now seems obvious, expanded far more rapidly in the later 1960s and 1970s than the supply of skilled and higher-status jobs. This also seems to be true in Western Europe and many developing countries. The resulting credential crisis—in which rapidly rising levels of educational qualifications are required for the same or similar jobs—poses a problem for both theories. To explain it, we have to concede a greater autonomy to developments in education than either the functional or neo-Marxist accounts allow. As the status competition theory suggests, the educational system can expand quite independently of the needs for skilled labor or demands of elites. Given that education is closely tied to career prospects, pressure from competing groups anxious to secure respectable or high-status jobs for their children will keep demand for educational credentials high, even at a time when the actual number of skilled or high-status jobs is static. In recent years these competitive pressures have led to increasingly vocational attitudes toward higher education and a moving away from both the arts and sciences toward business and other vocational subjects. But it is surely a mistake to argue that these trends represent rational or necessary adaptations, and to take at face value employers' justifications of their preference for employees with very high levels of educational credentials. Employers who offer jobs that are in high demand, after all, must find *some* criteria for selecting applicants, and educational qualifications offer the advantage that they are generally regarded as fair and legitimate criteria.

This point can be made more general. Modern societies, it seems increasingly clear, do not have or have not been able to find a great deal for young people in their teens or early twenties to do.[61] A combination of technological change, slowing economic growth, and the vested interests of people already in the labor force combined in the 1970s and early 1980s to make a great deal of the labor of young people surplus to the economy's requirements. In part, therefore, mass higher education can be seen as a way of accommodating a large population that would otherwise remain idle. That education, no doubt, has many benefits for those who receive it, though there are signs of increasing cynicism among young people who have had their high expectations dashed; but it is important to note that these benefits cannot be seen as an adequate explanation of why these young people are in schools rather than in the labor force. To argue that would be to fall into the teleological trap that the functionalist paradigm sets for us: that things happen because society needs them.

Modern societies are highly committed to a self-image of rationality and expertise, and mass higher education plays a crucial part in sustaining that self-image. To admit that in part mass higher education serves a baby-sitting function—and perhaps diverts attention from the difficult task of finding employment for young people—is therefore inconsistent with that self-image. As is so often the case in thinking about schooling, therefore, what we want to believe, and what it serves our interests to believe, interferes with our ability to sustain a more complex and truthful vision.

Endnotes

1. Raymond Williams, *The Long Revolution* (New York: Columbia University Press, 1960). Williams notes that there was widespread literacy before universal schooling.

2. For an explanation of this, see Randall Collins, *The Credential Society* (New York: Academic Press, 1979), Chapter 5.

3. Charles Krug, *The Shaping of the American High School, 1880–1920* (Madison: University of Wisconsin Press, 1969).

4. Martin Trow, "The Second Transformation of American Secondary Education," *International Journal of Comparative Sociology*, Vol. 2 (1961): 144–166; and U.S. Department of Health, Education and Welfare, *Progress of Public Education in the United States* (Washington, D.C., 1960), p. 11, Table 2.

5. U.S. Department of Commerce, Bureau of the Census, *Statistical Abstract of the United States, 1983* (Washington, D.C.), p. 160.

6. U.S. Department of Commerce, Bureau of the Census, *Historical Statistics of the United States, Colonial Times to 1957* (Washington, D.C.); and American Council of Education, *Fact Book on Higher Education* (annual). See also Trow, "The Second Transformation."

7. Burton Clark, *The Open-Door College* (New York: McGraw-Hill, 1960).

8. Corrado de Francesco, "Myths and Realities of Mass Secondary Schooling in Italy," *European Journal of Education*, Vol. 15 No. 2 (1980): 135–152.

9. Barbara B. Burn, *Higher Education in Nine Countries* (New York: McGraw-Hill, 1971).

10. Christopher Hurn, "The Vocationalization of American Education," *European Journal of Education,* Vol. 18 (1983): 45–64.

11. Ibid., p. 14.

12. Martin Trow, "The Second Transformation of American Secondary Education," in Sam R. Sieber and Daniel E. Wilder (eds.), *The School in Society* (Free Press: New York, 1973), p. 45 (originally published in *International Journal of Comparative Sociology,* Vol. 2 (1961): 144–166).

13. See Krug, *The Shaping of the American High School.*

14. Trow, "The Second Transformation," p. 50.

15. Clark, *The Open-Door College,* p. 48.

16. Ibid.

17. Ibid.

18. Talcott Parsons and Gerald M. Platt, *The American University* (Cambridge, Mass.: Harvard University Press, 1973). See also Daniel Bell, *The Coming of Post Industrial Society* (New York: Basic Books, 1973).

19. Parsons and Platt, *The American University.*

20. Ibid.

21. E. Durkheim, *Moral Education* (Glencoe, Ill.: Free Press, 1961).

22. See, for example, David Tyack, *The One Best System* (Cambridge: Harvard University Press, 1974), Part III.

23. Collins, *The Credential Society,* pp. 90–95.

24. Durkheim, *Moral Education,* p. 275.

25. Robert Dreeben, *On What Is Learned in Schools* (Reading, Mass.: Addison-Wesley, 1967), p. 27.

26. Dreeben also provides a critique of the cognitive skills explanation for educational expansion in "American Schooling: Patterns and Processes of Stability and Change," in Bernard Barber and Alex Inkeles (eds.), *Stability and Social Change* (Boston: Little, Brown, 1971).

27. Tyack, *The One Best System.*

28. This belief, of course, was closely related to different conceptions of the purposes of education: maintaining the highest possible standards for a select few on the one hand, or promoting democratic access to opportunities on the other. See the discussion in Chapter 1.

29. Burn, *Higher Education in Nine Countries.*

30. For this argument, see Clark Kerr (ed.), *A Digest of Reports of the Carnegie Commission on Higher Education* (New York: McGraw-Hill, 1974).

31. For an argument that the community college does not increase educational opportunities, see Jerome Karabel, "Community Colleges and Social Stratification," *Harvard Educational Review* 42 (1972): 521–562.

32. Talcott Parsons, *Structure and Process in Modern Societies* (New York: Free Press, 1960).

33. Colin Greer, *The Great School Legend* (New York: Basic Books, 1972); and Joel Spring, *Education and the Rise of the Corporate State* (Boston: Beacon Press, 1972).

34. Michael Katz (ed.), *School Reform, Past and Present* (Boston: Little, Brown, 1971).

35. Ibid., p. 75.

36. Quoted in Michael Katz, *Class, Bureaucracy and Schools* (New York: Praeger, 1975), p. 31.

37. Samuel Bowles and Herbert Gintis, *Schooling in Capitalist America* (New York: Basic Books, 1976).

38. See the essays collected in Katz, *School Reform.*

39. Bowles and Gintis, *Schooling in Capitalist America,* Chapter 7.

40. Lewis Terman, *Intelligence Tests and School Reorganization* (New York: World Books, 1923), p. 125.

41. Bowles and Gintis, *Schooling in Capitalist America,* p. 254.

42. Ibid, pp. 203–213.

43. Ibid., p. 205.

44. Ibid., Chapter I.

45. Ronald Dore, *The Diploma Disease* (Berkeley: University of California Press, 1976).

46. Collins, *The Credential Society;* and Raymond Boudon, *Education, Opportunity and Social Inequality* (New York: Wiley, 1974).

47. Collins, *The Credential Society,* pp. 95–102.

48. Raymond Boudon, *Education, Opportunity and Social Inequality* (New York: Wiley, 1974).

49. Williams, *The Long Revolution.*

50. John G. Richardson, "Variations in Date of Enactment of Compulsory School Attendance Laws: An Empirical Inquiry," *Sociology of Education,* Vol. 53 (1980): 153–163.

51. See the interesting discussion in Tyack, *The One Best System.*

52. Trow, "The Second Transformation," p. 50.

53. Collins, *The Credential Society,* p. 5.

54. Ibid., pp. 15–16.

55. Christopher Hurn, "The Vocationalization of American Education," *European Journal of Education,* Vol. 18 (1983): 45–64.

56. Ibid.

57. John H. Ralph and Richard Rubison, "Immigration and the Expansion of Schooling in the U.S., 1890–1970," *American Sociological Review,* Vol. 45 (1980): 943–954.

58. Ibid. See also John W. Meyer, et al., "Public Education as Nation Building in America: Enrollments and Bureaucratization in the American States, 1870–1930," *American Journal of Sociology,* Vol. 85 (November 1979): 591–613.

59. Bowles and Gintis, *Schooling in Capitalist America,* Chapter 7; see also Clarence Karier, ed., *Shaping the American Educational State* (New York: Free Press, 1976).

60. Clark Kerr, *Priorities for Action: Carnegie Commission on Higher Education, Final Report* (New York: McGraw-Hill, 1973).

61. For a useful (and more than usually frank) statement of this problem, see James S. Coleman, et al., *Youth: Transition to Adulthood* (Chicago: University of Chicago Press, 1973).

chapter 4

Schooling
and Equality
of Opportunity

The previous chapter explored the causes of the great expansion of schooling in this century. We now turn to an examination of perhaps the most important controversy about the consequences of the schooling revolution: its effects on equality of opportunity. Particularly in the United States, schools have been long seen as a great equalizer, as perhaps the single most important institution that works to erase the handicaps of birth and create a society truly open to the talented.[1] More educational opportunities, it has long been argued, are the key to creating a more meritocratic society: a society where talent and effort rather than privilege and social origins would determine an individual's status. If few have believed that education alone could solve problems of inequality and discrimination, it has been an article of faith among liberals that the expansion of educational opportunities would be translated into improved status for all disadvantaged groups.[2] Those educational opportunities might do little to help the individuals already in the labor force, but they could, it has been widely argued, enable the children of rich and poor and black and white to compete on something like equal terms.[3]

Such arguments, stated in more formal and precise terms, are part of the functional paradigm, and they continue to enjoy wide support, despite mounting evidence that the expansion of educational opportunities in recent decades has not had the dramatically merit-ocratic effects envisaged by the theory.[4] But they received significant challenge during the late 1960s and 1970s from more radical and con-flict-oriented theories.[5] According to the neo-Marxist critique, for exam-ple, it is not only the case that schools have betrayed the promise of equality of opportunity; it is also true that schools, within the confines of capitalist society at least, *can have no other consequence* than the maintenance of existing differences in life chances between privileged and disadvantaged groups. The rhetoric of equal opportunity, from this perspective, serves to conceal a process by which schools today, as in the past, reproduce class divisions and persuade large parts of the population that they lack the skills and aptitudes needed for high-status populations.[6] Other conflict theories, though less deterministic than the neo-Marxist account, are hardly less pessimistic in character. In all modern societies, conflict theorists point out, there is a struggle for a limited number of scarce and desirable high-status positions, a contest in which the children of those who already have such status have great advantages. And since schooling has now largely replaced other more traditional avenues of mobility in modern society, it is naive, conflict theorists suggest, to believe that high-status groups will not use their greater resources to reserve the lion's share of the most valued educational qualifications for their own children.

This chapter evaluates the merits of these rival theories against the available empirical evidence. I shall address the issue of what effects the changes in schooling in this century have had on equality of oppor-tunity, both in the United States and elsewhere, and then assess the adequacy of different theories that claim to account for these findings. This then leads to the problem of the following two chapters—that of explaining why it is so often the case that low-status groups fare less well in school than students from more privileged origins.

CHANGING CONCEPTIONS OF EQUALITY OF EDUCATIONAL OPPORTUNITY

Although a central core meaning has remained, the concept of equality of educational opportunity has undergone important changes over the decades.[7] The heart of the idea has remained the belief that all should have an equal chance to succeed or fail in a common school system. But what an *equal chance* means and to whom those chances should be extended have changed substantially, espe-cially in the decades after World War II. Over time the concept of equality of educational opportunity, like the concept of equality of opportunity in general, has become both more inclusive and more activist in its implications. The scope of who is included has widened to encompass blacks, women, and other minorities, as well as white males. The emphasis has shifted from the provision of *formal* or legal equality of opportunity to the requirement that educational institutions take active or *affirmative* steps to insure equal treatment of different groups. Underlying this shift of emphasis, as James Coleman has argued, is the emergence of a conception of equality of opportunity as "equality of results," where educational institutions begin to be held partly accountable for gross differences in the attendance or success rates of different groups, and are expected to take measures to reduce those differences.[8]

Up until about 1950, equality of educational opportunity had a relatively simple and restricted meaning. It referred to the right, then enjoyed by all except black Americans, to attend the same publicly supported comprehensive schools and to compete on formally equal terms with all other students, regardless of their class or ethnic background. Such rights, American educators were fond of pointing out, were not enjoyed by European students to anywhere near the same degree. In much of Europe separate schools for the academically able were the rule, and in practice this meant a higher concentration of upper middle-class students in the college preparatory schools.[9] To be sure, in Great Britain, West Germany, or France, some outstandingly able working-class students were sponsored by elite secondary schools and groomed for high-status occupations. But in contrast to the U.S. system where rich and poor students often rubbed shoulders in the same schools, the avenues of opportunity seemed much narrower. In this formal and restricted sense, equality of educational opportunity also existed in U.S. higher education. Again, in contrast to much of Europe, publicly supported universities with low tuition were open to the more successful high school graduates who had completed the required high school courses. Competition for admission to higher education was formally equal; universities did not set quotas on admission of students from publicly supported schools, nor were rigorous examinations likely to be taken only by privileged students a prerequisite for admission, as they often were in Europe. And if such a system, as it existed in the late 1940s, for example, largely disregarded the fact that the actual chances of poor students attending college were very small indeed, it did provide avenues of mobility that were *formally* open to all.

The twenty years following the Supreme Court's *Brown* v. *Board of Education* decision in 1954 saw a steadily broadening conception of equality of educational opportunity. The Court ruled that the maintenance of separate school systems for black and white students was unconstitutional because such segregated schools were inherently unequal.[10] It is important to note that this decision did not outlaw *de facto* segregation: schools that were all black because the communities in which they were located were overwhelmingly black.[11] But the decision did nonetheless have momentous consequences. Starting around 1960, the maintenance of separate public school systems for black and white students, widespread in the South and parts of the mid-West for many decades, became effectively illegal. Often with the accompaniment of federal marshals, black students began to enter the previously all white schools and universities of the South.

If *Brown* v. *Board of Education* extended the meaning of equality of opportunity specifically to include black students, the criteria on which the decision was based also broke new ground. The testimony heard by the Court, some of it provided by social scientists, established that segregated schools attended by blacks were inferior in their facilities and resources to schools attended by white students. In ruling that segregated schools were unequal because they were inferior schools, therefore, the Court opened the way to a much broader conception of equality of educational opportunity, one that stressed the communities' or the school's responsibility to provide some rough equivalence of *effective* opportunity for all students and not merely the responsibility to make *some* opportunities available.[12] During the 1960s this new position became explicit. For the first time, the government began to give aid to local school districts in an attempt to reduce some of the large differences in school expenditures per pupil.[13] State governments moved in the same direction. Scholarship and financial aid programs were implemented, enabling more poor and working-class students to attend college. Under the Head Start program, the federal government provided money to communities with substantial numbers of disadvantaged students for pre-school education.[14] The Courts also moved to a more activist conception of equality of educational opportunity during the 1960s. The Courts increasingly began to rule that equality of educational opportunity required that black and other minority students should have real rather than merely formal opportunities to attend the same schools as white students. Northern cities were required to produce plans for school integration that would ensure all schools, in whatever neighborhood they were located, would have roughly balanced representation of black, Hispanic, or white students proportionate to the representation of these groups in the city as a whole.[15] And to enforce these orders, the federal government often threatened to withhold school aid unless an acceptable bussing plan was implemented.

However, it was during the 1970s rather than the 1960s that the most radical changes occurred in the concept of equality of educational opportunity. First, the term became still more inclusive in the groups to which it was thought to apply. Thus new attention was paid to providing equal educational opportunity for the handicapped, and new mainstreaming legislation was passed requiring that if possible the handicapped should be educated in the same schools and classrooms as the rest of the student body.[16] Separate colleges for male students also came under attack, and toward the end of the decade, a majority of previously all-male or all-female colleges had opened their doors to at least some members of the opposite sex. There was also controversy about the denial of equal opportunity implicit in the greater subsidies given to male school sports than to female sports. Prompted by the federal government and court rulings, women's athletics began to receive a larger share of school athletics budgets.

At the same time, a radical shift occurred in the criteria that were used to assess whether equality of educational opportunity existed. During the mid–1970s an increasing number of liberal and radical critics began to define equality of educational opportunity as the existence of roughly proportional educational *outcomes* for all groups, or, as James Coleman put it, as "equality of results."[17] In this new position, schools were held responsible for insuring that blacks, women, or other minorities moved toward parity with white males across a whole range of educational outcomes. Differences in these outcomes, from the underrepresentation of women in the physical sciences to the overrepresentation of blacks among high school dropouts, tended to be taken as evidence of inequality of educational opportunity. Affirmative action programs mandated by the federal government partly reflected this new, more activist conception of equality of opportunity.[18] Large employers, unions, colleges, and universities were all expected to demonstrate that their admission or hiring decisions were consistent with the goal of substantially increasing the proportion of minorities. Such affirmative action plans had to include detailed documentation of how these decisions were made and target figures specifying, for example, how many minorities a professional school would admit by a certain date.[19] If affirmative action did not necessarily invoke either quotas or "reverse discrimination," it did place the burden of proof squarely on institutions to demonstrate that they were *not* discriminating rather than on minority individuals to prove that they were the object of discrimination.

These ideas had consequences for a variety of practices in elementary and secondary schools as well. During the 1970s, both testing and ability tracking came under severe criticism. The fact that ability tracking resulted in the overrepresentation of blacks and Hispanics in the lower tracks was taken as evidence, by some people, that tests of ability discriminated against these groups. The generally higher scores of white middle-class students on IQ tests and aptitude tests was interpreted as a demonstration of the culturally biased character of the tests. For some more radical critics, indeed, any difference between groups in educational outcomes was regarded *ipso facto* as proof of bias or discrimination in educational institutions, curriculum, or testing procedures. Many, if not most, schools reacted to this criticism by changing curricula that were criticized as sexist or racist, abandoning ability testing, and abolishing previously sharp distinctions between fast and slow or college preparatory and general tracks.

It would be misleading to say that this new activist position of equality of educational opportunity as equality of results is now dominant. Since the end of the 1970s, there have been signs of a reaction against some of the trends I have described: Courts have ruled in favor of some complaints by white males of "reverse discrimination,"[20] the term *quotas* invites quite general opprobrium, and bussing is widely unpopular and is no longer supported by a more conservative administration.[21] More generally, the early 1980s saw a replacement of equal educational opportunity as *the* dominant problem of education with a heightened concern for excellence and higher standards of academic achievement in the core subjects of the curriculum. But although it is too soon to characterize the decade as a whole, so far there has not been a reversion to older and more limited conceptions of equality of educational opportunity where schools, for example, can be said to provide equal opportunity if they merely provide *some* avenues of mobility for minority groups. Graduate and professional schools are still expected to increase the representation of minorities over time and to devise special admission procedures to that end. Remedial courses and special counseling services for minority students at four-year colleges remain in place. Despite the new emphasis on excellence and the education of gifted students, high schools have not abandoned the idea that it is partly their responsibility that black students are less successful in school than white students. In other words, the retreat from equality of opportunity has not meant a "hands off" policy on the part of schools—a belief that the schools' responsibilities are limited to the provision of roughly equal resources for all students and the absence of active discrimination.

All of these considerations mean that there is no simple answer to the question: "Do schools provide equality of educational opportunity?" If we were to use as our criterion of equality of educational opportunity the most activist definitions of the 1970s, then the answer would be an unequivocal no. Very large differences still exist between the relative success of different groups in the educational system, even though, as we shall see below, the gap in the number of years of schooling completed between privileged and less privileged students has closed somewhat. Black students, for example, still average between ten to fifteen points lower on tests of academic ability when the average score is standardized at one hundred.[22] Lower-class black students, in particular, are much more likely to drop out of high school and to fail simple tests of literacy than white students. If this is what is meant by equality of educational opportunity, therefore, it is not close to being realized. Adopting the criteria of equality of educational opportunity that prevailed before about 1960, on the other hand, yields quite a different result. There is no question that there are far more formal opportunities available to disadvantaged students now than existed a few decades ago. The extension of scholarships and financial aid and the enormous expansion of community colleges have meant a great increase in the chances available for disadvantaged students to attend college. The end of legally segregated schools in the South meant that black students were no longer denied access to predominantly white public schools on the basis of color. By this criterion, therefore, if schools do not yet provide complete equality of educational opportunity, they have made huge strides in that direction.

For the sociologist, a rather different question is equally important. Instead of asking whether in absolute terms equality of educational opportunity has been achieved, sociologists are interested in the degree to which changes in schooling have changed the *relative* chances of different social classes and ethnic groups. The general issue, in other words, is whether schools continue to reinforce or reproduce existing patterns of inequality among groups, or whether, conversely, schools have helped create a society that is open to individual talent and effort regardless of social background. Have schools helped create a more open society, or have they solidified or added to existing class divisions? As educational opportunities have expanded, has the relationship between educational success and social class declined, as the functional paradigm would predict, or has it remained strong as conflict theorists assert? Let us now examine the evidence that bears on both of these questions.

The Meritocratic Hypothesis
and the Functional Paradigm

A central argument of the functional paradigm is that the development of mass education helps create a more meritocratic society—a society where talent and effort rather than birth or privilege determine status. There are two reasons why this should be so. First, as modern societies have become more complex and more dependent on a highly trained and skilled labor force, educational achievement should have increasingly powerful effects on an individual's adult status. Second, the argument goes, because success in school depends on such universalistic criteria such as performance on tests and examinations, the ability of privileged parents to pass on their status to their children should be reduced when schooling becomes the principal criteria for allocating adult status.[23] In all societies, of course, privileged children enjoy advantages in the struggle for future status over less privileged children, but as adult status increasingly depends on success in school these relative advantages should diminish. In schools, so this argument continues, talented and energetic children from disadvantaged backgrounds will be more successful than untalented or lazy children from more privileged backgrounds. Over the long haul, therefore, the increase of educational opportunities should substantially reduce the advantages that children of high-status groups enjoy in the struggle for desirable occupations and increase the chances of upward mobility for low-status children. Educational expansion, in other words, should have helped create a more meritocratic society: a society where there are few if any barriers to the mobility of talent.

From the functional paradigm, therefore, we can extract three propositions:

1. The correlation between educational and occupational status will increase over time.
2. The correlation between parents' social status and the social status of their children will diminish over time.
3. The correlation between parents' social status and the educational achievements of their children will diminish over time.

If all these propositions are true, but only if *all* are true, we can say that the expansion of educational opportunities has worked as the functional paradigm claims it should have worked, to increase the relative chances of talented but disadvantaged children to obtain high-status jobs. Let us now examine the evidence that bears on these assertions.

The first of these propositions is the most straightforward. As we would expect, the available evidence clearly shows a tightening of the link between educational achievement and occupational status in this century. In their analysis of trends over time in the experience of adult U.S. men, Blau and Duncan report that the correlation between years of school completed and occupational status rose from 0.34 for those born between 1910 and 1920 to 0.55 for those born between 1940 to 1950.[24] A great deal of other evidence confirms the common impression that schooling (as measured by years of schooling completed) is now the single most important determinant of an individual's occupational status—more important, for example, than the person's parents' occupation or parents' education.[25] An individual's career depends on much else besides schooling, of course, and we should not make the mistake of assuming that such factors as class background, race and ethnicity, and personality characteristics play only a minor role. But schooling, more than in the past, now plays a crucial gate-keeper role in entry to desirable jobs. Some evidence even indicates that schooling continues to have effects on a person's career even after entry on the first job.[26]

The Strong Version of the Meritocratic Hypothesis
The remaining two propositions are both more difficult to test and more controversial. Let us first consider the evidence for what may be called the strong version of the meritocratic argument— the claim that the expansion of schooling has helped to create a society where *careers* are progressively more open to talents. An investigation of changing rates of mobility provides one way to test this hypothesis. Since schooling now determines one's future career more than in the past, and since, according to the theory, expanded opportunities should make it easier for lower-class children to succeed in schools, we should expect an increase in rates of mobility over time. Talented lower-class children should experience more upward mobility because of increasing opportunities, and untalented upper-class children should experience more downward mobility as the increasingly meritocratic system increasingly rewards intelligence and effort rather than privilege. Rates of mobility, of course, provide only a rough and approximate indication of the degree to which a society is open to talented individuals. Differential rates of fertility and changing proportions of high- and low-status jobs can both affect the amount of mobility from one generation to the next. But if schooling has had a *dramatic* effect on the relative chances of low-status youth, we should find part of that effect reflected in higher rates of mobility.

The evidence does not generally confirm this prediction. Almost all recent studies of occupational mobility over generations, in Europe as well as the United States, suggest that mobility rates have remained rather *constant* in this century, with minor rather than sharp fluctuations and no clear overall trend of increasing upward or downward mobility.[27] None of these studies is, by common consent, entirely satisfactory. All of them must rely on extremely broad and crude categories of occupations. They cannot tell us, for example, whether the relative chances of a miner's child becoming a doctor have improved or deteriorated, but only whether children of manual workers have improved their chances of becoming nonmanual workers over time. There are also severe problems in research on mobility in distinguishing between changes attributable to shifts in the distribution of the labor force and changes that indicate a more open or closed society.[28] There are proportionately more nonmanual and professional workers now than in the past, and this makes calculations of changing relative chances of different groups quite difficult.

These difficulties noted, however, it is remarkable that virtually all recent research on social mobility between generations reveals very little in the way of trends over time. Among the most recent cohorts in the United States, for example, Hauser and Featherman estimate that about 20 percent of the sons of manual workers reached professional or managerial occupations.[29] Among the earliest cohorts they examined born just after the turn of the century, this percentage is virtually identical. A slight trend toward the declining importance of status origins in the 1940s and 1950s appears to be balanced by a trend toward more status ascription in the most recent cohort. Research from Great Britain and Sweden reports rather similar findings. In neither country is there a clear trend toward decreasing dependence of current status on father's social origins over time; furthermore, what variations in rates of mobility are observed seem to be attributable to changes in the occupational distribution of the labor force rather than to changes in the fluidity of the class structure. The overall picture, it should be emphasized, is not one of extreme status inheritance, either today or earlier in this century, and in this respect comparative data on social mobility do not support a radical view that only tiny proportions of low-status youth are able to overcome the handicaps of their origins. What is most relevant for our purposes, however, is that there is little evidence of *increasing* social fluidity (to use Grusky and Hauser's term).[31] The dramatic expansion of educational opportunities that occurred in virtually every Western society was widely expected to increase the relative mobility prospects of low-status youth, but, so far at least, there is little evidence that this has been the case.

There is a second, more direct way to test the strong version of the meritocratic hypothesis. If it is true that contemporary societies are more meritocratic than previous societies we should expect to find that as the role of ascription declines there should be an increasingly strong relationship between IQ scores and occupational status. Over time, the hypothesis predicts, the expansion of educational opportunities should make it easier for exceptionally talented low-status individuals to gain high status, and, equally important, make it more difficult for untalented high-status children to hold on to their parents' status. If this argument is correct, therefore, we should find that the IQ scores of high-status individuals should become more uniformly high and the IQ scores of low-status individuals more uniformly low. And while IQ scores are hardly an ideal measure of talent, and few observers would predict that increasing educational opportunities can completely erase the barriers to the mobility of such talent, if the hypothesis is correct we should be able to observe some signs of an increasing correlation between IQ and occupational status.

Since intelligence testing began early in this century, psychologists have collected information on the IQ scores of individuals in different occupations in an attempt to establish that the tests are valid predictors of occupational performance and occupational mobility. A review of these studies reveals no trend toward an increasing correlation between IQ tests and occupational status. That correlation, Jencks estimates, is around 0.50, but "when the Army first administered the first group 'intelligence' tests to military recruits in 1917 and 1918, the pattern of occupational differences was very similar to what it is today."[32] Nor, Jencks argues, should we accept this relatively high correlation as evidence that IQ determines occupational status to a substantial degree. Much of the relationship between IQ and occupational status must be attributed to their common relationship to schooling rather than to the impact of mental ability itself. Jencks concludes that "our findings, therefore, do not characterize the United States as a meritocracy, at least where merit is measured by general cognitive skills."[33]

Changes in Social Class Differentials in Educational Success: The Weak Version of the Meritocratic Hypothesis

There is a second and more direct way to test the basic argument of the functional paradigm about the effects of increasing educational opportunities. If educational expansion has not apparently had appreciable effects on rates of intergenerational mobility it may nonetheless have had important consequences for class differences in rates of educational success. The functional paradigm claims that schools are, at bottom, meritocratic institutions. High-status parents can place their children in schools with superior facilities, they can teach their children, and they can impress upon them the great importance of remaining in school. In the last analysis, however, success in school depends on the aptitudes and effort of the individual student. High-status students cannot succeed in school unless they are capable of or willing to do the required work and pass the relevant examinations. To the extent that the children of the poor have increasing educational opportunities, therefore, the theory would predict that the *educational achievements of children of privileged and less privileged parents should become increasingly similar.*

In order to understand the limitations of the available data as an adequate test of these ideas, let us imagine what a close to ideal set of data would look like. In an ideal world constructed for the benefit of the sociologist, we would have a set of historical data from the turn of the century to the present containing a variety of measures of school success and parents' social status. These data would contain information on test scores, grades, and enrollment in different high school tracks; it would also include information about attendance at and completion of college, preferably with a breakdown by the type of institution in which students were enrolled. We could then use these data to estimate just how much, if at all, the relative chances of different groups have changed.

Unfortunately, however, very little of these data are available for the United States. The decentralized school systems of the United States do not, and did not in the past, collect information on the social status of the parents of their students, nor can we estimate with any degree of accuracy what percentage of high school students was enrolled at different periods of time in college preparatory, general, or vocational curricula. In this country, comparable data over a long period of time are restricted to a measure of number of years of schooling completed, an unsatisfactory substitute for more detailed information on grades, tracks, and types of institution attended. In a number of European countries, on the other hand, the available information is richer and more detailed. In Great Britain, Holland, and Sweden, for example, we have information on social class differences in attendance at different kinds of selective secondary schools over a considerable period of time. And in recent decades we also have detailed information on the changing class origins of university students during the period of the most rapid expansion of higher education. Let us begin, therefore, with European rather than U.S. data, and then examine whether the trends we find for European education also apply to the United States.

Perhaps the most important finding of research on inequality of opportunity in European education is that, even in recent times, social class differentials in educated achievement remain very large indeed. In gaining access to the highly selective universities of Great Britain, for example, sons of professional and managerial workers have more than an eight to one advantage over sons of unskilled and semi-skilled workers.[34] Similar or even larger differences have been reported for most countries with highly selective universities.[35] There is a great deal of evidence, furthermore, that these social class differences in educational success are cumulative over a student's career.[36] In countries that have selective secondary schools, for example, the chances of lower-class students gaining admission are much inferior to the chances of upper- or middle-class students. Once in these schools, there are substantial differences in chances of examination success and, even among those formally qualified for university entrance, considerably fewer lower-class students enter universities than middle- or upper-class students.[37] At each major step in a student's career, lower-class students are at a disadvantage, and although this disadvantage may not be very large at any one step, the disadvantages accumulate over time, so that, for example, a two to one disadvantage in admission to a selective secondary school may become an eight or ten to one disadvantage in admission to university.

If there is consensus among European sociologists about both the large size and cumulative nature of class differentials in educational success, there is rather less agreement about the direction of trends over time. The data in Table 4–1 illustrate part of the reason for this difference of opinion. Trends in class differentials in access to the academically selected tracks of Dutch secondary schools show that in the years from 1942 to 1960 lower-class students increased their representation from 4 to 7 percent, while upper-class students increased from 45 to 67 percent. The *relative* chances of lower-class students obtaining a college preparatory curriculum, therefore, increased faster than the upper-class students, but at the same time the *absolute magnitude* of class differences increased over the period. Table 4–2 shows parallel findings for trends in admission to the highly selective British universities. For students born between 1923 and 1932, 15.9 percent of those of Class I or Class II background attended university, compared with only 1.2 percent of the lowest group. The chances of all groups had increased a great deal for those born between 1943 and 1952; the chances of the lowest group had increased from 1.2 to 3.1 percent, while the chances of the top group increased from 15.9 to 26.4 percent. But these data, like the data in Table 4–1, are rather equivocal in their implications for the thesis that class differences in educational opportunity are declining. On the other hand, one could

Table 4–1   *Percentage of Boys Admitted to the Academic Secondary School Curriculum, Holland.*

Social Class	Admission to Academic Curriculum		
	1942	1949	1960
Upper Class	45	50	67
Middle Class	14	15	25
Lower Class	4	4	7
All Classes	10	11	17

Adapted from Organisation for Economic Co-operation and Development, *Group Disparities in Educational Participation*, Report of Group No. 4, Conference on the Politics of the Expansion of Education (Paris: O.E.C.D., 1970). Adapted by permission of the publisher.

Table 4-2   *Attendance at British Universities by Date of Birth*

Father's Social Class	(percentages)			
	1913–22	*1923–32*	*1933–42*	*1943–52*
I, II	7.2	15.9	23.7	26.4
III, IV, V	1.9	4.0	4.1	8.0
VI, VII, VIII	0.9	1.2	2.3	3.1
All	1.8	3.4	5.4	8.5
N	(1846)	(1879)	(1856)	(2246)

Source: A. H. Halsey, A. F. Heath, and J. M. Ridge, *Origins and Destinations: Family, Class and Education in Modern Britain* (New York: Oxford University Press, 1980), p. 188.

claim that the relative chances of lower-class groups have increased— in fact, they more than doubled over the period, while the chances of Class I and II students increased little more than 50 percent. But at the same time the absolute magnitude of class differences increased over the period. In other words, most of the new university students over the period were from relatively privileged origins, and very few new students came from lower-class backgrounds.

In an extensive survey of the European data, Raymond Boudon reports similar findings for many countries.[38] Virtually everywhere, he notes, the effects of the expansion of education have been to improve the relative chances of working-class children to obtain a college preparatory or university education. In France, Holland, and Sweden, Boudon reports, the relative chances increase more rapidly for working-class students than for middle-class students. But because there were so few working-class students in these schools at the beginning of the period of expansion, Boudon argues that it is almost inevitable that most of the new students will be drawn from middle- or upper-class origins. In the short run at least, therefore, increasing educational opportunities may *widen* class differences as more middle- and upper-class than working-class students take advantage of these new opportunities. And while optimists, like Boudon, can argue that in the long run working-class students will catch up because the rate of increase in their numbers is greater than for middle- and upper-class students, there are few signs thus far that in access to higher education at least, class differentials have greatly narrowed. The great majority of the new university students in most European countries in the 1960s and early 1970s were middle or upper class rather than working class in origin.[39]

The more limited data available from the United States is also somewhat equivocal in its support for the meritocratic hypothesis. First, as with the European data, there is strong evidence of both the persistence of class and ethnic differences in educational achievement, and of the cumulative character of these differences. William Sewell, perhaps the leading student of class differences in educational attainment, writes:

> *We estimate that a higher SES student has about 2.5 times as much chance of continuing in some kind of post-high school education. He has an almost 4 to 1 advantage in access to college, a 6 to 1 advantage in college graduation, and a 9 to 1 advantage in graduate or professional education.* [40]

The best evidence on trends over time in school attainment in the United States has been collected by Featherman and Hauser.[41] At first sight their evidence supports the hypothesis of increasingly meritocratic selection. Over time, Featherman and Hauser report, the variation in the number of years of schooling completed by U.S. students has fallen and there has been a substantial reduction in the correlation between parents' social status and years of schooling completed. For those born between 1907 and 1911, for example, the correlation between father's occupation and the number of years of schooling completed was 0.31.[42] For those born between 1947 and 1951, that correlation had fallen to 0.16.[43] Similar reductions can be observed in the strength of the relationship between father's education, regional origins and race, and years of school completed over time. For men born between 1907 and 1911 of southern or farm origins, race and socioeconomic status were all-powerful determinants of how much schooling they would complete. For men who were born thirty or forty years later, all of these variables, although still significant, were much less powerful. This, therefore, is some evidence for increasingly meritocratic selection and the declining importance of ascription in U:S. education.[44]

What makes this evidence rather less than overwhelming, however, is that the data on recruitment into higher education do not show the same clear trends. The strength of the relationship between father's occupation, father's education, and college education has hardly changed over the past thirty years according to the best available data reported by Featherman and Hauser.[45] The importance of farm or southern origins and race has declined significantly, but the relationship between attendance at college and measures of social class remains virtually the same for the cohort born in the immediate post-war years as it was for those born between 1907 and 1913.[46] Since it is now college education rather than high school graduation that serves as the key dividing point in rationalizing access to high-status jobs, the persistence of class differentials in access to higher education is of great significance. Gross statistics on college education, rather than figures on type of college attended, furthermore, tend to underestimate these differences. Community colleges, for example, typically enroll much higher percentages of working-class students than four-year colleges, and the proportion of students from professional and managerial backgrounds is higher in the more prestigious universities than in the public four-year colleges that have no graduate programs.[47] Studies of transfers from two- to four-year institutions, furthermore, have shown that working-class students are less likely to transfer than middle-class students.[48]

These findings provide only equivocal support for the weak version of the meritocratic hypothesis. On the positive side, we find almost everywhere that lower- and working-class groups experience an increase in their relative chances of high educational achievement. The percentage of children of lower-class fathers attending college in Great Britain, for example, almost tripled in the twenty years beginning with 1955, a much higher rate of increase than for middle- or upper-class students.[49] There is also good evidence of a narrowing in class differentials in secondary school attainment. A student's social class used to be a good indicator of how long one would remain in secondary school. In the United States, and for at least some countries in Europe, that is much less true than it was in the past. Both these observations suggest that the expansion of education has worked as the functional paradigm agrees it should work, to reduce the power of ascriptive characteristics to shape educational success and to help create a more meritocratic system.

But the evidence on the other side is no less compelling. Particularly in access to educational credentials that are of most significance today—and this means college rather than high school graduation—there is little sign of a reduction in the size of the very large class differences that have long existed. True, lower-class groups have made the most rapid relative gains in recent decades, but these gains were from a very small base. The great majority of new college students in the 1960s and early 1970s in both Europe and the United States were middle and upper class rather than lower class. At the more prestigious universities from which the most desirable employers recruit, the student population remains highly unrepresentative in terms of class origins of the population as a whole. Bowles and Gintis emphasize that only in the two-year institutions that prepare people predominantly for lower-level white-collar and technical occupations, are disadvantaged students well represented.[50] From this skeptical viewpoint, indeed, one could argue that lower-class groups have caught up with middle- and upper-middle class groups only in those educational credentials whose worth is now of somewhat questionable value in the struggle for high-status positions.

It must be emphasized, however, that these conclusions, both in favor and against the hypothesis, are based on data which are, by common consent, not very satisfactory. The data, to be sure, are a far better guide to trends than the kind of impressionistic judgments and illustrative case studies upon which sociologists had to rely two or three decades ago. But a fully adequate test of the functional argument that education reduces inequalities in social background requires much more extensive data than are available even today.

In addition, it is important to note that the data on which we have to rely are, in important respects, already out of date. The latest period for which data on social mobility are available in the mid-1980s, for example, is 1972. Thus we cannot yet estimate the effects of the considerable expansion of education that took place during the 1970s.

These important caveats aside, we can say that previously widespread confidence that educational expansion would have major meritocratic effects appears to have been misplaced. Educational expansion, and the expansion of higher education in particular, has not resulted in a *dramatic* reduction in the relationship between social status and school success. Nor, it is apparent from the data on social mobility, has it resulted in any substantial reduction in the ability of parents to pass on their status to their children. Education has not proved to be the great equalizer that the proponents of educational expansion from Horace Mann to the Carnegie Commission of the 1960s hoped it would be.[51] Let us now consider the reasons for these rather depressing findings and their implications for social policy.

Discussion and Implications of the Findings

Why has increasing equality of opportunity in education failed to produce, by most measures, increasing equality of opportunity in society? The apparent failure of the expansion of education to reduce the advantages enjoyed by children of privileged parents has led to two simple but very different explanations: Both are seriously misleading, but because of their simplicity and popularity, they warrant treatment before more complex and satisfactory theories are examined. The first of these explanations stresses the importance of intelligence in school achievement and in occupational success. Richard Herrnstein and Arthur Jensen are the best known advocates of this position. For Herrnstein and Jensen, intelligence is primarily an inherited trait, which in turn largely explains differences in school achievement and continues to predict occupational achievement after the school career. As educational opportunities initially expanded, Herrnstein argues, previous barriers to the mobility of talented lower-class children fell.[52] But the process of increasingly meritocratic achievement leads to an increasing concentration of untalented individuals in low-status positions as the most talented children are "creamed off," achieve high-status positions, and pass on their talents to their children. After the initial period of educational expansion is over, therefore (and Herrnstein is not specific about the length of this period), we should not expect any reduction in the relationship between educational success and social status.[53] Some minority groups, and Herrnstein gives blacks as his major example, still face major barriers to the mobility of their talented members, but with these exceptions, we should expect an increasing correlation between intelligence and social status as educational opportunities expand. In the last analysis, therefore, this argument claims that the reason why the children of poor parents tend to inherit their parents' poverty is that educational opportunities in previous generations have sharply reduced the number of highly intelligent individuals in low-status positions.

A full discussion of the vexing issues of intelligence and its measurement will be reserved for Chapter 5. Here it is only necessary to point out that a number of these assertions appear incorrect. Intelligence as measured by IQ tests is a good predictor of school success, but its cumulative effect over the whole career is hardly as powerful as Herrnstein or Jensen argue. Holding measured ability constant, social class and educational aspirations have important effects on school success.[54] Furthermore, the link between school and job success does not appear to be primarily a matter of their mutual dependence on measured ability.[55] Scholarly credentials and parents' social status have independent effects on occupation and earnings, which are more important than the effects of measured ability alone.[56] Even if it is true that intelligence is largely inherited, therefore, virtually all recent research indicates that it is considerably less important an explanation of social mobility than Herrnstein's argument maintains. The inheritance of lower intelligence can conceivably explain some small part of the reason why children of disadvantaged parents do poorly in school, but it is unsatisfactory as the major explanation of that relative failure.

The second straightforward explanation for our findings stems from a radical critique of the educational system and of the society as a whole by neo-Marxist sociologists. This argument claims that the rhetoric of equality of opportunity has concealed a great deal of systematic discrimination by schools and employers against disadvantaged youth. The picture that these theorists present is one of a society where inheritance of status is very high indeed, and of schools that routinely assign lower-class students to slow tracks and discourage them from pursuing educational careers that might lead to upward mobility. In extreme form, at least, this argument does not fit with the evidence either. The data on social mobility, for example, indicate that rates of upward and downward movement were quite high throughout this century and perhaps in the nineteenth century as well.[57] The data tell us that there have been no clear *trends* in the amount of upward or downward movement in a relatively open society; they do not tell us that social status is primarily inherited. As Featherman and Hauser conclude, "There is a great deal of movement among occupational groups between generations. . . . More than two-thirds of adult men moved out their fathers' station to their current occupation."[58]

In addition, as we shall see in the next chapter, there is no persuasive evidence that schools consciously and systematically discriminate against disadvantaged children. Some studies have found some relationship between grades and track assignments and social class, suggesting that school success is not ideally meritocratic.[59] No large-scale study, however, has indicated that grades and tracks are assigned *primarily* on the basis of ascribed characteristics rather than performance in school work. There is considerable agreement that the qualities and aptitudes students bring with them to school as well as the differential treatment of students by schools are important in explaining the difference in school success among students. Although the neo-Marxist argument is important in sensitizing us to the possibility that some part of these differences can be explained by school discrimination against disadvantaged students, it is not plausible that this can be the major explanation for the persistence of class differentials in school success.

A rather better, though still hardly complete, explanation is suggested by the status competition theory.[60] That theory, it will be recalled, places great stress on how the process of competition between groups leads to a rapid expansion of educational credentials that may be only tangentially related to the real skills needed to do a particular job. The expansion of schooling increases the average educational attainment of low-status groups and it provides skills and qualifications that, in the past, would have entitled them to claim desirable jobs. But such expansion also increases *everyone's* educational achievement, and high- and middle-status groups have the resources that enable them to take greater advantage of these new opportunities than low-status groups. What matters in determining the chances of any particular group to obtain desirable jobs, therefore, is not the absolute level of its qualifications, which may, the theory suggests, be more than adequately satisfactory to perform the jobs in question, but its *relative* educational qualifications in comparison with other groups.[61] As our data suggest, therefore, low-status groups have made gains in closing the gap between themselves and others in educational credentials that used to be associated with middle-class jobs in the past; but in access to such qualifications as college graduation, which are now demanded for such occupations, they suffer about the same disadvantage as they suffered in high school graduation rates twenty or thirty years ago. Increasing educational opportunities create the illusion of progress toward more general opportunities for disadvantaged groups, but because high-status groups always have greater resources to obtain more schooling to restore their competitive position, the relative chances of low-status students will remain virtually constant despite rapidly increasing levels of education. The implication of this theory is that educational opportunities will lead to increasing general opportunities only if there are *deliberate* and *conscious* strategies that increase the relative position of a particular group in possession of educational credentials that are currently most significant for desirable occupations. Only through affirmative action, the theory seems to imply (which, of course, has not been followed for lower-class white groups), will low-status students be able to catch up with more privileged students.

BLACKS AND EQUALITY OF OPPORTUNITY

So far in this chapter we have been concerned exclusively with issues of class, status, and equality of opportunity. The problem of changes in the relative position of black Americans and the role of the educational system in those changes deserves separate treatment. This is because blacks have experienced far greater disadvantages, most of which can be traced to explicit and overt discrimination. Historically, more than many other ethnic group, blacks have looked to the educational system as a vehicle for improving their relative status.[62] But it is only in the last two decades that blacks have enjoyed even formally equal educational opportunities, having experienced, for much of this century, exclusion from the public schools that most whites have attended. To what extent has the provision of increased educational opportunities in recent years improved the position of blacks in American society? Here again we encounter a rather mixed bag of evidence, although on balance the picture of change is more optimistic than in the case of lower-class whites.

In terms of both high school graduation and college attendance, blacks made large gains not only in absolute terms but relative to whites between 1960 and 1981. In 1960, for example, only 18.4 percent of black high school graduates went on to college, compared with 24.2 percent of white high school graduates.[63] By 1981, this gap had closed considerably. In that year, 28.0 percent of black high school graduates were enrolled in college, compared with 32.5 percent of white high school graduates.[64] Although black students are still less likely to graduate from high school than white students, they have closed much of the gap between themselves and whites in this respect. In 1968, blacks were almost twice as likely to drop out of high school as white students, but by 1981 only 15.4 percent failed to finish high school, compared with 11.3 percent of whites.[65] Salaries for recent college graduates have begun to close a good part of the income gap that has long existed between black and white degree holders. Initial salaries for female black college graduates, for example, were equal or slightly ahead of salaries for white female graduates in 1981.[66]

These real and important gains must be seen against a context of continuing disadvantages for the great majority of young blacks who do not go on to higher education. Unemployment differentials between black and white teenagers have not altered significantly in the last twenty years, and blacks remain at more than a two to one disadvantage in this regard.[67] Whereas blacks have made great gains in educational achievement, there are as yet few signs that the considerable gap between black and white test scores has narrowed. In tests of academic ability and on scholastic aptitude tests, blacks average approximately 15 percentage points below whites.[68] And although such tests have been, partly for good reasons, much criticized in recent years, there is little doubt that their results reflect real differences in the kind of cognitive skills important for success in school and in adult life. In this crucial respect, therefore, the results of programs to insure full equality of educational opportunity for blacks have been disappointing.

School Integration

In the 1960s it was widely believed that the difference in school achievement between blacks and whites could be substantially narrowed or erased by two kinds of policies. First, it was thought that the racial integration of public schools would reduce the handicaps suffered by black students because of the inferiority of segregated schools in resources and in the quality of their teachers.[69] Second, it was also believed that preschool programs aimed at disadvantaged students would compensate for lack of adequate preparation for school work in the home environment, and as the name of this program implied, give these children a "Head Start."[70] Almost fifteen years of research on both school integration and Head Start, however, has told us that these high hopes were unrealistic. Research on the benefits of Head Start programs has been relatively inconclusive, partly because it did not clearly focus on specifically educational programs rather than general programs to provide a safe and pleasant environment for disadvantaged children.[71] But even the most optimistic evaluations of recent years do not suggest that more than a small fraction of the differences between black and white early school achievement has been reduced by existing Head Start programs.[72] No doubt such small but nontrivial effects are worth the expenditures involved. It has been increasingly clear, however, that faith that such programs would solve the problem was misplaced. The results of research on school integration have also been disappointing to those who saw black and white differences in educational achievement as being largely caused by inferior and inadequate schooling. Of the thirty-seven studies of black student achievement and school racial composition reported by Nancy St. John in her review of integration research, only seven reported clear positive results on all tests of school achievement, while eighteen reported mixed results on different tests, and the remainder showed either no difference or negative results.[73] St. John writes, "Desegregation has rarely lowered and sometimes raised the scores of black children. Improvements have often been reported in the early grades, in arithmetic and in schools over 50 percent white, but even here the gains have usually been mixed, intermittent or significant."[74]

None of this means that school integration is a failure in some absolute sense. After all, integration is justified primarily because we believe it is morally right that black and white children attend the same schools rather than in terms of its effects on learning alone. And those effects, when measurable, are generally positive rather than negative. But, as with the case of Head Start, it seems clear that school integration has not substantially reduced the gap in school achievement between black and white students.

Affirmative Action

The success of affirmative action programs for black students is even harder to evaluate. Beginning in the late 1960s, many colleges and graduate schools began to adopt admissions procedures designed to maximize the number of black students who would be accepted into the program. In part these took the form of explicit or implicit quotas reserved for black or other minority applicants, and in part of admissions procedures that paid relatively less attention to black students' scores on standardized tests and more attention to their background characteristics.[75] In addition, a few colleges (notably the City University of New York) adopted "Open Admissions" policies, under which any high school graduate could be admitted regardless of test scores and grades and where students who could not have qualified under regular admission policies were provided with special remedial instruction.[76] All these policies are and were (the Open Admissions experiment in New York has been abandoned, a victim of budget cuts and faculty opposition) highly controversial, and precisely because the issues of reverse discrimination that are sometimes involved are so sensitive, little research has been done on the effects of these strategies. How many black physicians or lawyers are now practicing because of differential treatments of black and white applicants by professional schools? We simply do not know, although the numbers may be quite substantial. But the results of the Open Admissions policies of the City University of New York have been studied, and they suggest that the policy was generally effective in broadening the socioeconomic composition of the student body in the years in which it was in force. Most of the new admissions, Alba and Lavin report, were from low-status backgrounds and the proportion of black students admitted were close to the proportion of blacks living in New York City.[77] Although the drop-out rate for these open admissions students was substantially higher than for regularly admitted students, over 40 percent of these students had, by ten years after admission, graduated from the university, a figure that is remarkable in view of the lack of conventional qualifications of most students at the time of admission.[78] There seems little question, therefore, that the policy did have some of its intended effects and that substantial proportions of minority students who would otherwise not have attended college were able to graduate.

Even in the absence of such policies, however, it seems probable that the expansion of educational opportunities has been rather more successful in improving black opportunities than is generally the case for nonminority low-status populations. The expansion of higher education has provided channels of mobility for large numbers of academically talented black students that did not previously exist. It has probably been a crucial factor in the growth of a large black middle and upper-middle class whose incomes, job prospects, and style of life have come increasingly to resemble those of whites with similar levels of education.[79] In this sense, schools have worked in the way that the functional paradigm and liberal reformers have said they should work: to reduce the handicaps suffered by talented but disadvantaged youth, and to create a more open society. But the evidence for nonmiddle-class blacks, and particularly for those of the black population that are classified as poor, is more discouraging. Poor black children who lack obvious academic talent have not substantially benefited from the educational changes of the last two decades. Their school performance remains below the performance of whites of similar socioeconomic status in a society where educational credentials are increasingly necessary for steady and secure employment. Although we cannot say that the schools themselves must be held accountable for this lack of improvement (and we take up this issue in the next chapter), there is no question that it was widely believed that policies aimed at creating equality of educational opportunity would work for this group as well.

CONCLUSION

Though equality of educational opportunity remains a slippery concept and many different meanings have been attached to it in the last one hundred years, it has always involved the assumption that schools could help create a society where all could compete on the basis of talent and effort, rather than birth and privilege. Functional theorists and educational reformers have argued that schools could help neutralize the advantages that children of privileged parents enjoyed and provide opportunities that did not exist before for talented lower-class and minority students. Beliefs of this kind were virtually universal in western Europe and the United States until about 1970, and they played a crucial part in mobilizing support for the expansion of education in every country, but particularly in the United States.

There is no question that a number of the assumptions supporting these beliefs are true. Schools have become a more important source of upward mobility than they were in the past. Middle-class and professional jobs are increasingly closed to those who have not been successful in school, and this means, of course, that parents can no longer place their children in desirable jobs as easily as they could; children must earn those jobs by their own performance in school. Nor is there much question that, by most criteria, equality of educational opportunity has greatly increased in recent decades in all Western societies. The expansion of schooling has meant a large increase in formal opportunities for the children of poor parents to complete secondary education and attend college. The provision of extensive scholarships and financial aid has removed many of the obstacles that previously prevented many students from going on to higher education in the United States. In a number of European countries, furthermore, selective secondary schools for the academically most gifted have been replaced by U.S.-style comprehensive schools with the specific objective of improving the chances of working-class students. And in most countries, there have been efforts to equalize the educational resources available to students from different backgrounds—federal and state government have allocated funds specifically earmarked for schools in impacted or disadvantaged areas. No doubt there is more that governments could do in all these respects—from more scholarship aid to American college students to phasing out of exclusive but publically supported secondary schools in France or Germany. But it is not possible to deny that, by any reasonable criterion, real as well as formal educational opportunities have greatly increased in recent decades.

It is against this background that the paradoxical character of the findings of this chapter emerges. Educational opportunities have greatly increased, but the disadvantages suffered by poor and low-status students in the competition for desirable jobs have not proportionately diminished. Education has not been the great equalizer that its proponents expected. Rates of intergenerational mobility have not increased; the well-to-do appear to have about the same advantages in passing on their privileges today that they enjoyed early in the century, both in the United States and in western European countries. These conclusions are tentative, of course, because our data are in many ways inadequate. It may also be true that future research on the consequences of the educated expansion of the 1970s will yield different results. The final verdict is not yet in.

Nonetheless it is clear that the arguments made by educational reformers and functional theorists that educational expansion would sharply reduce the disadvantages of low-status groups were overstated. Educational expansion has increased *everyone's* opportunities for more schooling, those of the upper and middle class as well as the poor. Superior resources, whether financial, cultural, and possibly intellectual, have enabled middle- or upper-class groups to maintain advantaged positions in the contest for educational credentials that will enable their offspring to obtain secure and prestigious jobs. Working-class groups have made some relative gains in closing the gap between themselves and others in secondary school education in the United States, and in substantially increasing their originally tiny representation in European universities; but in the possession of educational credentials that are of most importance for high-status positions, they have made less progress. Only in the case of black U.S. students is there clear evidence that the expansion of higher education has enabled disadvantaged groups substantially to close the gap between themselves and the more privileged majority in the kind of jobs and income they receive, and this applies, of course, only to those young blacks who have recently graduated from college.

The persistence of class and race differences in success in school and on tests of academic ability has also proved surprisingly resistant to educational policies designed to bring about equality of educational opportunity. In every country for which we have data, disadvantaged students do less well on tests of aptitude and achievement, and drop out of school sooner than more privileged students. Noncomparable measures of achievement make it virtually impossible to compare the magnitude of these differences from one society to another; we can say, however, that significant difference in achievement between groups seems to persist after the introduction of a number of reforms designed to minimize them. Thus, marked social class differences in school achievement in Great Britain remain after the replacement of the old selective grammar schools by comprehensive secondary schools;[80] and black–white differences in tests of academic aptitude do not appear to have been substantially reduced by Head Start pre-school programs or by the integration of public schools in the last two decades. These programs have had some positive effect, but they have not had the kinds of dramatic consequences that their proponents hoped for in the 1960s.

Perhaps most disappointing of all is the lack of evidence that the enormous expansion of higher education in the three decades after World War II has had dramatic effects on the chances of lower-class students to gain access to high-status positions. Virtually all observers at the time believed that the removal of many of the barriers that had previously prevented many lower-class students from attending college would greatly increase their relative chances in competing for professional and managerial jobs. In most countries, and particularly in the United States, those barriers *did* fall. During the 1960s and 1970s scholarships, loans, and other forms of financial aid made it much easier for many students who could not previously afford to go to college to attend. Admission policies were changed and became increasingly sensitive to the special difficulties of disadvantaged students.[81] Far more disadvantaged and working-class students did attend college in the 1970s then ever before—in that respect the policies worked as they were supposed to. But what was not anticipated was that middle-class students took advantage of those increased opportunities more than working-class students. With the important exception of blacks, whose relative position did improve, the expansion of higher education benefitted middle-class students as much, if not more, than working-class students. The number of working-class students in college greatly increased, but in the more prestigious four-year institutions, their increasing numbers were dwarfed by the rapid increase in the percentage of middle-class students who now began to regard college completion as a normal expectation. Although we do not yet know very much about the jobs held by those who were in college in the 1970s, the evidence to date suggests that in terms of access to professional and managerial jobs, working-class youth made little if any relative gains during the period of the greatest expansion of higher education.

It seems clear that the functional paradigm cannot provide a satisfactory account of these trends and that we need the more skeptical perspective afforded by the conflict theory to make sense of them. Working-class groups have made great gains in their educational credentials and accomplishments in recent decades, but during the same period there has been a substantial devaluation of the educational currency. The gap between disadvantaged and privileged groups in high school graduation in the United States has been greatly reduced, but the worth of high school graduation as a ticket to desirable jobs has declined a great deal. In access to educational credentials that will now "purchase" desirable occupations, therefore, working-class groups are in a no more favorable position than they were in the past. Such groups may have the illusion of relative progress in that the current generation has far more schooling than past generations, but their position in the competition for desirable high-status occupations remains no better than it was before the expansion of higher education. The gains that disadvantaged groups made are continually erased by a steady devaluation of the educational currency. As Collins and other skeptical critics of educational expansion point out, there is no reason to expect the situation to change in the future. If educational expansion continues, we may expect that graduate or professional school may be a prerequisite for admission to the kinds of jobs that are now open to those with bachelor's degrees. Even if working-class students catch up with others in their rates of college graduation, therefore, they will not necessarily make relative gains in the competition for high-status jobs.

While this needs to be said, there is danger of overstating the pessimistic argument. Is it, after all, entirely reasonable to argue that schools should compensate for social inequalities, that they should erase handicaps of class and race? Does equity and fairness require that the same *percentage* of low-status and high-status groups succeed at every stage of the educational contest? Or are these criteria satisfied when no obvious financial obstacles and no inequalities or resources and no overt discrimination exist? By these latter criteria, a great deal of progress has been made. In virtually every country a large number of the obstacles that used to make it very difficult for low-status, talented children to obtain a university education have been removed. And the effects in a number of countries have been quite dramatic. The number of working-class students at British universities, for example, almost tripled between 1910 and 1975, and the number of black female college students in America increased six times between 1960 and 1981. Far more low-status children have a real chance of developing and realizing their talents than ever before. Nor is it fair to disregard programs that equalize the quality of schooling or programs of school integration because they have not had, so far at least, substantial effects on the relative performance of low-status or black students. The justification for such reforms, after all, does not rest solely, or even primarily, on their ability to equalize educational achievement. It rests rather on our ethical beliefs that it is wrong that, because of their race or social class, children must attend schools with inferior facilities, with inexperienced teachers, and cut off from day-to-day interaction with students of different social backgrounds. In all these respects, important gains have been made. What our findings suggest, therefore, is not that growth of educational opportunities in the last several decades has been insignificant or trivial, but that these increasing educational opportunities have not yet been translated into clear improvements in the relative chances of low-status youth to obtain high-status jobs. Part of the reason for this is that educational credentials alone are not the whole story—working-class youth with college degrees are not as likely to get good jobs as middle- and upper-class youth. But there is little question that a major reason for the continuing difficulties that working-class youth face is also that, on average, they do less well in school than other students. To understand what could be done to reduce these differences, therefore, and to formulate policies that might be more effective than those of the past, we must first consider the reasons why low-status youth so often do poorly in school.

Endnotes

1. Horace Mann, for example, referred to schools as the "great equalizer in the conditions of man"; quoted in Michael Katz (ed.), *School Reform: Past and Present* (Boston: Little, Brown, 1971), p. 141.

2. And not only in America; see, for example, T. H. Halsey, "Equality and Education," *Oxford Review of Education*, Vol. 1, No. 1 (1975): 1–28.

3. The argument that the expansion of schooling can enable disadvantaged groups to compete on equal terms is distinct from the view that schooling can help reduce inequalities of income. For an effective critique of this latter argument, which in my opinion was never as widespread as Jencks and others assumed, see Lester Thurow, "Education and Economic Equality," *The Public Interest*, Vol. 28 (Summer 1972): 66–81.

4. Although it cannot be denied that equality of opportunity has been placed (circa 1985) on the back burner of the national agenda.

5. Samuel Bowles and Herbert Gintis, *Schooling in Capitalist America* (New York: Basic Books, 1976).

6. Ibid., Chapter 4.

7. See Halsey, "Equality and Education"; and James Coleman, "The Concept of Equality of Opportunity," *Harvard Educational Review* 38 (1968): 7–32.

8. Coleman, "The Concept of Equality of Opportunity."

9. Halsey, "Equality and Education."

10. See the useful discussion in Diane Ravitch, *The Troubled Crusade: American Education, 1945–1980* (New York: Basic Books, 1983), Chapter 5.

11. Ibid.

12. Coleman, "The Concept of Equality of Opportunity"; and Ravitch, *The Troubled Crusade.*

13. Ravitch, *The Troubled Crusade,* pp. 148–149.

14. Ibid., pp. 158–160.

15. Ibid., p. 176.

16. Ibid., Chapters 5 and 17.

17. Coleman, "The Concept of Equality of Opportunity," pp. 7–8.

18. Ravitch, *The Troubled Crusade.*

19. Ibid., p. 285.

20. Ibid., pp. 285–290 presents a discussion of the Bakke decision of 1977.

21. The Reagan administration took a clear stand against activist conceptions of affirmative action beginning in 1981.

22. Christopher Jencks, et al., *Inequality* (New York: Basic Books, 1972), p. 142.

23. This hypothesis is implicit in virtually all functionist work; see, for example, Talcott Parsons, "The School Class as a Social System," *Harvard Educational Review* 29 (1959): 297–308. For an explicit statement, see Donald Treiman, "Industrialization and Social Stratification," in Edward Laumann (ed.), *Social Stratification: Research and Theory for the 1970s* (New York: Bobbs-Merrill, 1970), pp. 207–234.

24. David L. Featherman and Robert M. Hauser, *Opportunity and Change* (New York: Academic Press, 1978), pp. 356–364.

25. Peter Blau and Otis Dudley Duncan, *The American Occupational Structure* (New York: Wiley, 1967).

26. Ibid.; and Featherman and Hauser, *Opportunity and Change.*

27. Robert Hauser, "Temporal Change in Occupational Mobility: Evidence for Men in the U.S.," *American Sociological Review* (October 1976): 585–589.

28. See ibid.; and Blau and Duncan, *The American Occupational Structure,* for a discussion of this problem.

29. Featherman and Hauser, *Opportunity and Change,* p. 89.

30. John H. Goldthorpe, *Social Mobility and Class Structure in Modern Britain* (Oxford: Clarendon Press, 1980); and Gosta Carlson, *Social Mobility and Class Structure* (Lund, Sweden: Almqvist, 1958).

31. David B. Grusky and Robert M. Hauser, "Comparative Social Mobility Revisited: Models of Convergence and Divergence in 16 Countries," *American Sociological Review* Vol. 49 (February 1984): 19–38. Grusky and Hauser find considerable differences in rates of mobility between countries but they do not find that such variations can be attributed in any simple way to degrees of industrialization or educational development.

32. Jencks, *Inequality,* p. 186.

33. Jencks, *Who Gets Ahead?* (New York: Basic Books, 1979), p. 121.

34. A. H. Halsey, A. F. Heath, and J. M. Ridge, *Origins and Destinations: Family, Class and Education in Modern Britain* (New York: Oxford University Press, 1980). For the French case, and a general review of the evidence for other countries, see Maurice Garnier and Lawrence Raffalovich, "The Evolution of Equality of Educational Opportunities in France," *Sociology of Education,* Vol. 57 (January 1984): 1–10.

35. Raymond Boudon, *Education, Opportunity and Social Inequality* (New York: Wiley, 1973).

36. Ibid.

37. There is some evidence, however, that in rigorously selective systems those few low-status students who survive the stage of admission to university may have an equal chance of graduation with higher-status students. See A. H. Halsey, A. F. Heath, and J. M. Ridge, *Origins and Destinations* (Oxford: Clarendon Press, 1980).

38. Boudon, *Education, Opportunity and Social Inequality*. See also Garnier and Raffalovich, "The Evolution of Equality."

39. Boudon, *Education, Opportunity and Social Inequality*. See also Halsey, Heath, and Ridge, *Origins and Destinations*. Halsey and his associates, like Boudon, argue that the effect of initial expansion of a particular stage of the educational system will be *wider* inequalities as the new entrants are overwhelmingly from middle-class origins, but that in the long run low-status groups will catch up in college attendance rates just as they have caught up in high school graduation rates. Ibid., pp. 216–219.

40. William H. Sewell and Robert M. Hauser, "Causes and Consequences of Higher Education: Modes of the Status Attainment Process," in William H. Sewell, Robert M. Hauser, and David L. Featherman (eds.), *Schooling and Achievement in American Society* (New York: Academic Press, 1976), pp. 9–28.

41. Featherman and Hauser, *Opportunity and Change*, pp. 238–252.

42. Ibid., p. 242.

43. Ibid., p. 243.

44. See also Robert Hauser and David Featherman, "Equality of Schooling: Trends and Prospects," *Sociology of Education*, Vol. 49 (April 1976): 99–119.

45. Featherman and Hauser, *Opportunity and Change*, pp. 249–251.

46. Ibid., p. 250 (Tables 5 and 12).

47. Jerome Karabel, "Community Colleges and Social Stratification," *Harvard Educational Review*, Vol. 42 (1972): 521–562; and Fred L. Pincus, "The False Promise of Community Colleges," *Harvard Educational Review* Vol. 50 (1980): 332–360.

48. Richard D. Alba and David E. Lavin, "Community Colleges and Tracking in Higher Education," *Sociology of Education*, Vol. 54 (October 1981): 223–227.

49. Halsey, Heath, and Ridge, *Origins and Destinations*.

50. Bowles and Gintis, *Schooling in Capitalist America*, pp. 205–211.

51. For a different approach, see Henry M. Levin, "Assessing the Equalization Potential of Education," *Comparative Education Review*, Vol. 28 (February 1984): 11–27.

52. Richard Herrnstein, *I.Q. in the Meritocracy* (Boston: Little, Brown, 1973); and Arthur Jensen, "How Much Can We Boost I.Q. and Scholastic Achievement?" *Harvard Educational Review* 39 (1969): 1–123.

53. See also Richard Herrnstein, "I.Q.," *Atlantic Monthly* (September 1971): 43–64.

54. See the discussion in Chapter 6.

55. Jencks, *Who Gets Ahead?*, p. 115.

56. Thus much, but not all, of the effect of measured ability upon future status derives from its effect upon scholarly credentials. Ibid., p. 115.

57. For estimates of mobility in nineteenth-century America, see Stephan Thernstrom, *The Other Bostonians* (Cambridge: Harvard University Press, 1973).

58. Featherman and Hauser, *Opportunity and Change*, p. 135.

59. See the discussion in Chapter 6 and references cited there.

60. Randall Collins, *The Credential Society* (New York: Academic Press, 1979).

61. Boudon, *Education, Opportunity and Social Inequality*, makes this point.

62. Colin Greer, *The Great School Legend* (New York: Viking Press, 1973).

63. U.S. Department of Commerce, Bureau of the Census, *Statistical Abstract of the United States, 1983* (Washington, D.C., 1983), p. 160.

64. Ibid.

65. Ibid., p. 160.

66. Richard Freeman, "Black Economic Progress Since 1964," *The Public Interest*, No. 52 (Summer 1978): 52–68; and U.S. Department of Commerce, Bureau of the Census, *Statistical Abstract of the United States.*

67. Freeman, "Black Economic Progress."

68. Jencks, *Inequality*, pp. 81–84.

69. See the discussion in Ravitch, *The Troubled Crusade*, Chapter 5.

70. Ibid., pp. 158–160.

71. Paul Berman and Milbrey W. McLaughlin, *Federal Programs Supporting Educational Change, Vol. VIII: Implementing and Sustaining Innovations* (Santa Monica, Calif.: Rand Corporation, 1978).

72. Ibid.

73. Nancy St. John, *School Desegregation: Outcomes for Children* (New York: Wiley, 1975).

74. Ibid., p. 119.

75. Ravitch, *The Troubled Crusade*, pp. 284–291.

76. David E. Lavin, Richard D. Alba, and Richard A. Silberstein, *Right versus Privilege: The Open Admissions Experiment at the City University of New York* (New York: Free Press, 1981).

77. Ibid.

78. Ibid.

79. William J. Wilson, *The Declining Significance of Race* (Chicago: University of Chicago Press, 1979).

80. Juliette Ford, *Social Class and the Comprehensive School* (London: Routledge and Kegan Paul, 1973).

81. Ravitch, *The Troubled Crusade*, pp. 284–291.

chapter 5

Explaining
Unequal Achievement:
School Quality and
the IQ Controversy

Few subjects in education are more controversial than the question of why students from different social origins differ in their performance in school. The basic facts are straightforward: Social class or socioeconomic status are clearly associated with educational success, both in terms of persistence in school, or what is usually called *educational attainment,* and in terms of grades and test scores, or *educational achievement.*[1] A student's race or ethnicity also affects school success. Black and Hispanic students are less often successful in school than white students, and Jewish and Oriental-American students are more likely to be successful than the majority. And while there are obviously many exceptions to these generalizations—black students, for example, who score higher on tests of mathematical skills than Japanese-American students—it is noteworthy that most of these differences seem to be cumulative over time. Lower-class and disadvantaged students begin their school careers with measurable but not huge differences in skills compared with middle-class students, but by the age of seventeen or eighteen, these differences are consistently larger than they were at age five or six. At the age of high school graduation, the advantage of high-status over low-status students in continuing some form of higher education is about two to one; and three or four years later, high-status students often enjoy a four to one advantage in college graduation over low-status students.[2]

Even though these basic facts are well known, their interpretation is highly controversial. For some, the explanation of these findings lies in differences in ability and motivation between children from different social origins. Crudely stated, poor children are seen as less intelligent than well-to-do children, and their parents as unlikely to encourage them to do well in school. In support of this view, those on the political right can claim correctly that lower-class students usually score lower on tests of intellectual ability and educational aspirations than middle-class children. Some go so far as to claim that the differences in measured ability between advantaged and disadvantaged students are now primarily genetic rather than environmental in origin.[3] The expansion of educational opportunities, this argument explains, means that, over time, those highly intelligent people who were lower class because of lack of opportunity have experienced upward mobility. Those who still remain in lower-class positions, therefore, are likely to be genetically less intelligent than the rest of the population, and their children, because they inherit this low intelligence, are also destined for lower-class positions.[4]

For those on the political left, however, these arguments are close to anathema. Talk of intelligence, they believe, diverts attention away from the evils of a highly unequal and racist society. It is less an explanation of unequal school achievement than a way of blaming the victims of poverty and discrimination for their misfortune.[5] Suspicious of any attempt to explain school success in terms of ability or motivation, this position blames schools themselves for most of the differences in school success between students from different social origins. Lower-class students attend inferior schools, they suffer at the hands of culturally insensitive or racist teachers, and they are evaluated by tests that underestimate their true abilities.[6] Schools *claim* to be meritocratic institutions offering equality of opportunity to all, this argument continues, but in fact schools work to create and reinforce inequalities between students. As Bowles and Gintis phrase this position, schools are the major institutions that legitimize inequality in modern society, convincing the poor that they deserve to be poor because they lack ability and motivation.[7]

In this field of education, the sociological debate between functionalist and conflict paradigms tends to take on the character of political debate between right and left; and questions of politics and ideology become almost inextricably intertwined with questions of theory and evidence. For functional sociologists, for example, almost all the evidence from large-scale studies of school achievement points to factors beyond the schools' control as the major explanation of differential school success. Measures of student ability or intelligence and measures of student aspirations, this research shows, predict how students will do in school far better than measures of characteristics of schools.[8] Research in this tradition leads to the conclusion that home environments are overwhelmingly more important than school characteristics in explaining educational success. For conflict-oriented sociologists, on the other hand, such a conclusion results from an uncritical acceptance of the results of IQ tests, and the inability of large-scale research to do justice to the complexity of what we mean by good or bad schools. Case studies of individual schools, conflict-oriented sociologists argue, yield a quite different picture of systematic bias against lower-class and disadvantaged students: a picture that demonstrates schools rather than home backgrounds are responsible for unequal outcomes.[9]

Because these issues are so complicated and controversial, I will spread their discussion over two separate chapters. In this chapter, I shall present an analysis of the two major controversies that arose in the recent history of research into unequal school achievement: the controversy over the effects of school quality on student achievement, and the controversy over the meaning and measurement of intelligence. With this background, we can then proceed to understand better the implications of the most recent research on unequal achievement for our two basic paradigms in the next chapter.

THE SOURCES OF UNEQUAL ACHIEVEMENT: THE NEGATIVE FINDINGS OF JAMES COLEMAN

The modern era of research into unequal achievement in schools begins with the publication of James Coleman's study, *Equality of Educational Opportunity,* in 1966.[10] The study was designed and lavishly funded by the federal government to demonstrate a simple point: Unequal school achievement by students from different social origins was a function of unequal educational opportunity. In other words, it was expected that the differences in the *quality* of schools attended by black and white and by lower-class and middle-class students would explain a large part of the differences in achievement by these different groups. Disadvantaged students, it was widely believed, attended schools that were inferior in numerous respects in their pupil/teacher ratios, in the qualifications of their teachers, and in the academic atmosphere they provided.[11] The consequence of this inferior schooling was, it was believed, low educational achievement. Coleman's study was expected to document this relationship, and thus confirm that increasing educational expenditures for schools attended by disadvantaged children would reduce the gap in achievement between lower-class and more privileged students.

In fact, however, the study showed quite different and unexpected findings. Coleman's research found that there was almost no relationship between measures of school quality and student achievement. Thus, in one stroke, it undercut much of the liberal rationale for more expenditures on schools. This in turn precipitated a crisis in thought about inequality in schooling which has persisted until almost the present day. Those who accepted these findings began to speculate on differences in intelligence between groups. If schools could do little to overcome disadvantages experienced by lower-class groups, many reasoned, then perhaps that was because such groups had lower intelligence than others. But there were many who refused to accept the negative findings of large-scale research[12] on school quality and the often dark speculation on innate ability that accompanied them. The findings were counter to common-sense beliefs that bad schools hurt student performance; they also seemed to imply that little could be done to close the gap between the performance of disadvantaged and other students except perhaps to intervene in their home environments. In the volatile atmosphere of the late 1960s and early 1970s, charges and countercharges flew back and forth, often becoming *ad hominem* attacks on the leading protagonists. One figure in this controversy, Arthur Jensen, was unable to speak at a number of campuses because of student demonstrations and boycotts against what were thought to be his racist ideas. To understand the reasons for this impassioned controversy, let us now review its development from the publication of Coleman's study in 1966 until the present.

School Quality and Student Performance

Until the mid–1960s, there was considerable agreement among sociologists and educational reformers that a substantial part of the differences in school performance by different students could be attributed to differences in the quality of the schools they attended.[13] Not only did the argument seem intuitively obvious, it also had considerable impressionistic evidence to support it. Students who attended run-down inner-city schools, often with inexperienced or demoralized teachers, did perform worse on tests of educational achievement than students who attended well-run suburban schools with higher morale and more experienced teachers. Although few were so naive as to believe that these differences in school quality explained virtually all differences in achievement, it was agreed that an unknown but significant fraction of this difference could be so explained. Such an argument had especial force in the United States with its tradition of locally financed public schools. Per pupil expenditures varied a great deal from locality to locality, corresponding in a general way to the wealth and social status of a community's inhabitants. The claim that such unequal resources *caused* differential achievement, therefore, was used to justify expenditures by federal and state governments to compensate for inequalities in the local tax base and to provide schools of more equal quality across the whole country.[14]

Perhaps the most eloquent testimony to the influence of this theory of unequal performance is provided by the individual whose work did more than any other to undermine it. James Coleman stated that when he first conceived his research in the early 1960s, he expected it to document how inequality of school resources was a major factor in explaining the low achievement of low-status children.[15] The purpose of the study, he frankly admitted, was political as well as theoretical. It was to build a case for the greater equalization of school resources by showing that low-status and minority students attended inferior schools and performed less well in school because they attended inferior schools.

However, Coleman's findings, and those of most of the investigators who followed him, showed quite different results. First, he showed that the correlation between measures of school quality and the social composition of the neighborhoods in which they were located was weak.[16] While many poor children attended inferior schools, many also attended schools that were at least as adequate as well-to-do suburban schools. Such measures of school quality as per pupil expenditures, teacher experience, and number of books in the library were only loosely associated with measures of the average social status of the student body. Second, and even more controversial, Coleman's research found very little relationship between student learning, as measured by different test scores, and these indicators of school quality.[17] What was far more important in predicting a student's success in school, Coleman found, were measures of a student's intellectual ability and his or her home background. Crudely, but not entirely inaccurately, Coleman found that it was families, not schools, that made the difference.

In the years since the publication of Coleman's initial findings, there has been an enormous controversy about the significance and validity of his findings. Coleman's data have been reanalyzed by many different investigators, and new data have been gathered.[18] With few exceptions, the results of this work have been to reaffirm and even to strengthen the basic findings of Coleman's work, although the interpretations of the meaning of these findings remain controversial.[19] In this vast body of literature, the work of Christopher Jencks is of special importance because it summarizes all the available evidence, analyzes the data in a highly sophisticated way, and presents the results of the analysis in a clear and trenchant manner.

Jencks' Research

Jencks reiterates and reaffirms Coleman's conclusion that only a tiny fraction of the differences between student achievement can be attributed to differences in the quality of the schools they attend. Lower-class students do not do poorly in school, he concludes, because they attend inferior schools. Let us see how he reaches this conclusion.

In an ideal world designed for the convenience of the social scientist, theories of the effects of schools on students could be tested in the following ways: Different kinds of schools would be created, students would be randomly assigned to these different experimental "treatments," and then the students could be followed over the years with numerous measurements made of their relative academic performance. Such a study, of course, is impossible. No one is in possession of such data. Jencks, however, has a collection of data that permits reasonable inferences about the effects of different school resources on student learning—some derived from longitudinal studies of the same students over time, some derived from observations of students at one time period only. These data provide a crude estimate of the quality of the school, as measured by per pupil expenditures, teacher qualifications, class size, and so on. Jencks also has data on a number of measures of school achievement that give an indication of the amount of learning that has occurred in the school. Finally, the Jencks study gives us data about the characteristics of students: their socioeconomic status and, in some cases, their IQ scores. The crucial question then becomes: What is the relative importance of school characteristics compared with student characteristics in predicting student achievement?

A full-bodied answer to this question would require a consideration of rather complex statistical techniques lying beyond the scope of my discussion. But the conceptual method involved may be sketched: Given the fact that schools differ in the test scores of their students, we can attempt to predict these test scores by progressively introducing more and more variables into our prediction equations. Let us say, for example, that we consider only the socioeconomic status of the parents of students in the school. This alone will allow us to account for perhaps 15 percent of the variation between the average test scores of different schools. Then we introduce student IQ scores into the equation, which permits us to account for about a further 25 percent of the variation between schools. Finally, we introduce variables pertaining to the characteristics of schools themselves, also adding to our ability to explain the variations in the average test scores of different schools. But the crucial point is that the effect of these school character- istics is quite dwarfed by the effect of the first two variables. Our knowledge of the different characteristics of schools, in other words, provides almost no understanding of why students have higher test scores in one school rather than in another. The characteristics of stu- dents rather than the characteristics of schools are most significant in understanding such unequal achievement.

The data show, therefore, that measures of school resources are a poor predictor of student performance, a conclusion reached not only by Jencks and his collaborators, but also by many other investiga- tors using different measures of school resources and different data sets. It has also received substantial support from studies of school achievement in many different countries.[20]

But Jencks goes beyond this simple proposition in several ways. First, he attempts to quantify precisely just how much variation in school achievement is attributable to differing school resources:

> *If we could equalize everyone's total environment, test score inequality would fall by 25–40 percent. . . . Equalizing the quality of elementary schools would reduce cognitive inequality by 3 percent or less. Equalizing the quality of high schools would reduce cognitive inequality by 1 percent or less.*[21]

Second, anticipating the criticism that his measures of school re- sources are extremely crude indicators of school quality, Jencks pro- vides a rather different kind of analysis of his data. Rather than consider- ing schools that differ in terms of their resources, he examines differences between two extreme types of schools: those whose pupils do substantially better than would be predicted by the socioeconomic status of their parents and those where pupils do substantially worse than would be predicted by these criteria alone. In these terms, there- fore, high-quality schools are simply those where students do better than would be expected, and low-quality schools are those where stu- dents do worse than expected. What Jencks finds, however, is that a comparison of the top 20 percent with the bottom 20 percent of all elementary schools by this criterion yields a difference of only 10 points in average test scores (an average test score is standardized at 100). And even these small differences, Jencks maintains, would be reduced further were it possible to control for the probable IQ differences among pupils at these different schools. It follows, he believes, that if all schools were as good as the top 20 percent of all schools, national test scores would rise something like 3 percent. If all schools were as bad as the bottom 20 percent of all schools, national test scores would fall by perhaps 3 percent.[22] Such a change would by no means be without significance, yet it is nonetheless very small compared with the much larger differences in test scores between black and white students and between students of differing socioeconomic status.

Finally, Jencks attempts to assess the impact of school quality on persistence in school as well as on student test scores. Here the question is the calculation of how long students stay in school, rather than on how well they perform on tests of cognitive achievement. The available data suggest that measures of school resources have virtually no relationship to the number of years of schooling that students achieve. Jencks concludes, "Qualitative differences between high schools seem to explain about 2 percent of the variation in student's educational attainment."[23]

The finding that different school characteristics have little effect on student performance is by no means confined to the work of a few sociologists. Research by economists that views education as a "production function" and test scores as "outputs" reaches similarly pessimistic conclusions about the likely effect on student performance of increasing expenditures on schooling. Eric Hanushek, for example, in a sophisticated piece of research, finds almost no relationship between school resources and student performance on test scores.[24] He does find, as did Coleman in his 1966 study, a small relationship between test scores and the verbal ability of teachers, but such a relationship hardly suggests an easy strategy that would narrow the differences in achievement between students from different social origins.

CRITICISM OF RESEARCH ON SCHOOL EFFECTS

I have reviewed some research about the effects of school characteristics on students that is generally disturbing to the conventional wisdom of educators. Very few social scientists, I suspect, would have anticipated such findings twenty years ago. Many contemporary educators still have difficulty in reconciling such data with what seems to them to be obvious—that better schools will teach students more than inferior schools, and that if poor children attend better schools, the gap between their performance and that of higher-status students will sharply diminish. Some educators have such difficulties with this research that they simply reject the findings out of hand. The findings are inconsistent with common sense, they undermine a considerable part of the rationale for liberal education reform, and *therefore* they must be wrong. I turn, then, to some of the criticism that can be made of this research in an attempt to clear up the misunderstandings that surround it.

Misunderstandings of the
Research on School Effects

The first, and potentially most serious, misunderstanding is to see this research as support for the view that schooling has either no effects or only trivial effects on student learning. Popular articles with such titles as "Do schools make a difference?" may encourage such misunderstanding. For obvious reasons, there is very little data on children who *do not* go to school to compare with data for children who *do* go to school. There is scattered information on students who, because of extended school closings or school strikes, have not attended institutions for a period of time. We can also assess student performance at the end of the school year and again at the end of summer vacations and examine changes in test scores during this period. If it is true that student test scores fail to rise as much during the three summer months as they do during any given three months of the school year, a reasonable inference is that school attendance produces cognitive learning. The limited evidence that we have does support such a conclusion. Indeed, it suggests, for minority children in particular, that schooling is crucial to cognitive learning. Jencks reports, for example, a study of New York City's school children that indicates that while white children's test scores significantly improved during the summer months when they were not in school, black student test scores did not show any improvement. Black student test scores did improve at much the same rate as white student scores during the school year, but not during the summer months.[25]

A second criticism of research on school characteristics rests on a misunderstanding of what such research can tell us. Critics of the works of Jencks, Coleman, and other investigators have stressed the crudity of the measures that are used as indicators of school characteristics and the equally crude measures of the test scores employed. Different, more sensitive measures that capture subtler dimensions of school characteristics and more precise measures of student learning presumably would show more powerful school effects. There is no doubt that the measures used in much of this research are extremely crude: Variations in per capita expenditures on schools and in pupil-teacher ratios may tell us little about such matters as school morale or the educational quality of day-to-day interaction in schools. Analogously, group-administered achievement tests of verbal and numerical skills are inferior substitutes for careful individual assessment of student progress in a variety of areas. Such tests may also systematically discriminate against lower-class and minority students (an argument to be considered later). In sum, this criticism that maintains such research tells us little because its measures are too crude to do justice to the complexity of learning in schools.

Social scientists are divided on the merits of large-scale survey research. This kind of research necessarily involves a degree of crudity in the measurement of key variables. They simply cannot gather detailed and subtle indicators of school quality and student learning if they are comparing thousands of school systems and hundreds of thousands of students. Such data are not available, and if they were they would probably be prohibitively expensive to gather. But at the same time, the small-scale research that permits such sensitive measures makes any larger generalizations extremely hazardous. A study of two or three schools and their effects on student learning is simply too limited to permit control for the differing characteristics of students that might produce the observed effects. Case studies of this kind can be theoretically suggestive, to be sure, but they can also mislead us profoundly.[26] All work on school effects, therefore, must choose between two evils: Either it strives for maximum generalizability and must rely on gross and crude measures of key variables, or it must attempt to devise more sensitive and subtle indicators of school characteristics and student learning and pay the price that the findings may apply only to a few schools or to the students studied in that particular sample.

Because large-scale research must compromise, does it tell us *nothing* about the effects of different kinds of schooling on the performance of different groups of students? First, part of this research, at least, does not stand or fall on its admittedly crude measures of school quality. Jencks neatly solves the problem of measuring school quality by comparing schools whose students do relatively better than average with schools whose students do worse than average. A high-quality school therefore is simply a school where students perform better than we would predict if we knew only their socioeconomic status. Jencks's generalization that test scores would rise only 3 percent if all schools were as good as the top 20 percent of all schools is not something we can dismiss by pointing to his inadequate measures of school quality.

Second, although some studies that use different measures of school quality have shown more positive effects than those reported by Jencks, their findings have not always held up under critical scrutiny. Rutter's study of twelve British secondary schools, for example, appears to show relatively strong differences in pupil achievement between schools that could not be attributed to differences in the characteristics of their student bodies.[27] But reanalysis of these data has thrown considerable doubt on these conclusions, which are, in any case, based on too small a sample to generalize to wider populations. Future research into better measures of school quality may show different results, but so far the basic conclusions that Jencks drew from his comprehensive review of the literature have not been convincingly refuted.[28]

Finally, the argument that the crudity of its measures of student learning invalidates large-scale research on school effects is also, I believe, largely unfounded. Some critics have pointed out, for example, that it is implausible to rely primarily on tests designed to measure student *aptitudes* as indicators of how much students have *learned* in school. Aptitudes are one thing, the critics have claimed, and achievements are quite another. But in fact, scores on aptitude tests, ability tests, and achievement tests are very highly correlated, and it makes little difference to the results if one measure is used rather than another.[29] In other words, the correlations hold up regardless of how student learning is measured. Nor is it reasonable to argue that culturally biased tests invalidate the findings. Even if the tests systematically underestimate lower-class or black learning, this would not affect the conclusion that lower-class or black students do almost equally well or equally badly in different schools.[30]

The results of large-scale research on the effects of schooling should not, therefore, be dismissed by those who find these results disconcerting or uncomfortable. There is strong evidence from many studies that differences in school characteristics that can most readily be manipulated—classroom size, per pupil expenditures, teacher qualifications, and the like—have little impact on student learning. There is also strong evidence that differences in test scores between lower- and middle-class students and between black and white students have little relationship to such school resources. The negative policy implication of this research is quite clear: If we wish to reduce inequality in school performance, orthodox liberal reform measures are unlikely to be effective. Such a policy implication is important, but this research does not necessarily imply that quite different schools would fail to have different effects on unequal performance, nor does it demonstrate that the major sources of unequal performance necessarily lie outside the schools' control. Let me now indicate my reasons for these potentially optimistic assertions.

The Limitations of Large-Scale Research

First, large-scale survey research on the effects of schooling tells us nothing directly about highly unusual schools that may have profoundly different effects on students than the great majority of schools. If, as Jencks tells us, in the top 20 percent of all schools student test scores average only a few points above the mean of all other schools, what can we say about the top 5 percent, or top 1 percent, of all schools? It is perhaps quite impractical as a policy matter to assume that all schools could in the future be as effective as the top 5 percent of all present-day schools, but the study of such unusual schools could nonetheless be theoretically significant. Perhaps these unusually effective schools produce positive effects because of unusually gifted individuals who teach in those schools, and since those persons are scarce, such a conclusion would suggest that schools of this kind could not be duplicated on a large scale. On the other hand, if these rare schools differed from other schools in their social organization, teaching styles, or methods of evaluation, these features could in principle be adopted by other schools. Research on school effects tells us about the effects of the great majority of schools, but it says nothing about the theoretical limits of schooling—about the potential effects of very different kinds of schools. This, then, is one limitation of the research of Jencks and his collaborators.

Second, the research is not entirely free from ambiguity in its implications about the sources of differences in performance by social class and race. On the surface the argument is straightforward: Only slight differences in student learning can be attributed to school differences, suggesting that if we wish to find the sources of unequal school performance we must look outside the school. But a different interpretation is also consistent with this evidence. Suppose that schools have *powerful* but *similar* effects on the learning of different groups. Imagine, in other words, that virtually all schools treat social class differences and race differences in similar ways. Intentionally or unintentionally schools may respond to class and race differences among students in ways that heighten or reinforce existing inequalities. If this is the case, and I shall examine this proposition in some detail in the next chapter, then much of the research on the effects of schooling on student learning can be interpreted rather differently. Instead of saying the absence of variation between schools is evidence of the impotence of schools to reduce preexisting inequalities, we could take these similarities as evidence of how virtually all schools have powerful but similar effects on inequality of performance. The finding of similarity of effect, therefore, does not itself tell us how powerful that effect is. The finding that schools varying in their resources have similar effects on cognitive learning may mean that no kind of school reform would have measurable outcomes for student learning and for the size of group differences among students. But it may as easily mean that existing school reforms have not yet penetrated to the root of the matter—that some as yet unspecified change would have the effect of reducing inequalities among people from different social origins.

It can be argued, therefore, that the results of this research have ambiguous implications. The evidence is consistent with the conclusion that schools are largely ineffective in the face of group differences in performance, and that there is little that schools can do to reduce the gap between black and white student performance or between the performance of low- and high-status students. The second possibility, also consistent with the evidence, is that virtually all schools reinforce or even accentuate class and racial inequalities in student performance in similar ways. What does seem clear, however, is that such inequalities are not likely to disappear or even to substantially diminish if we adopt conventional liberal strategies of increasing school resources, hiring more qualified teachers, or improving teacher-student ratios. This does not suggest that we should not do these things on other grounds, but it does suggest that such strategies are not likely to be effective in reducing inequality in achievement in schools.

INTELLIGENCE, IQ, AND UNEQUAL SCHOOL PERFORMANCE

The failure of large-scale survey research to demonstrate clear effects of school quality on student performance—a failure evident as early as 1966 when the Coleman Report was published—led many social scientists and policy makers to conclude that the major sources of inequality in school performance lay in the home environment of the child and, therefore, effectively outside the school's control. The findings of that research undercut the liberal optimism that reformed schools could substantially reduce existing inequalities in performance among students from different social origins. That research suggested the more pessimistic conclusion that such inequalities were largely rooted in enduring differences among students of different social backgrounds. Few orthodox social scientists prior to the publication of the Coleman Report denied that there were real differences in academic aptitudes among students from different social origins and denied that a complete explanation of inequality in school performance must include a consideration of the role of the child's home environment. The findings of large-scale survey research on school effects suggest that differences in socialization or even genetic differences are overwhelmingly more significant than any processes within schools in explaining unequal performance. I hope I have made clear that this research does not necessarily imply such a pessimistic conclusion (it may be, for example, that virtually all schools have powerful but similar effects on students that magnify existing inequalities), but that conclusion nevertheless was, and still is, widely drawn from the findings of Coleman, Jencks, and other investigators. Their findings *seem* to lead inexorably to two possible conclusions: On the one hand, differences in the home environments of children have powerful effects on the development of cognitive abilities or intelligence, or alternatively (and this possibility gained some credence after the apparent failure of the compensatory education programs of the 1960s to produce lasting gains in children's IQ scores), there may be genetic differences in intelligence among individuals from different social origins. The results of the research I have described, therefore, led to a great increase in concern with the problem of intelligence and its determinants, a controversy which has shown no sign of abating since the publication of Arthur Jensen's article "How Much Can We Boost I.Q. and Scholastic Achievement?" in the *Harvard Educational Review* in 1969.[31]

The Intelligence Debate

The controversy over intelligence is not one debate but a series of debates about rather different kinds of issues. The best known argument, of course, is about the relative role of heredity and environment in determining intelligence. For both individual and group differences in IQ scores, a key question has concerned the extent to which these differences can be seen as an outcome of the early environments of the child or of hereditary differences between individuals which are largely outside environmental influence. Quite apart from its scientific significance, this question has obvious policy implications. If intelligence is largely determined by heredity, as some believe, then this has pessimistic implications for policies designed to enrich the environment of the preschool child. An environmental view of intelligence, on the other hand, implies that a person's intellectual abilities can, in principle at least, be substantially modified by policies based on knowledge of the environmental determinants of intelligence.

A second and in some ways more fundamental debate concerns the meaning of intelligence and its relationship to IQ tests. Many differential psychologists see intelligence as a highly stable set of general intellectual abilities underlying performance in a variety of tasks that call for reasoning and abstraction.[32] IQ tests, they claim, although hardly perfect measures, can nevertheless fairly assess these general intellectual abilities among individuals of widely different social backgrounds. In support of this argument, they point to the high correlations between scores on IQ tests and success in school among lower-class and middle-class students and among black students and white students. The critics of IQ tests, on the other hand, claim that these tests are inevitably culturally biased and cannot fairly assess the intellectual abilities of any but privileged or middle-class white students. They are also suspicious of the claim that it makes sense to talk about general intellectual abilities almost without regard to a particular culture. What is regarded as intelligent behavior, they claim, varies enormously from society to society, and it is, therefore, a mistake to think of intelligence as akin to a trait like height or weight or even athletic talent.

Are Differences in IQ Scores Inherited?

The history of the use of IQ tests in the United States and the interpretation of the results of these tests by psychologists is not something of which the scientific community can be proud. As late as the 1930s, for example, eminent psychologists were interpreting data on group differences in IQ tests as self-evident demonstrations of the intellectual inferiority of particular immigrant groups.[33] Although such tests frequently contained many items that could hardly be familiar to individuals not part of the dominant English-speaking white culture, IQ tests were used to make judgments about the innate intellectual potential of people outside of this culture—recently arrived European immigrants, American Indians, and blacks. That the work of Arthur Jensen, Richard Herrnstein, and others on group differences in inherited ability follows directly in this rather disreputable tradition does not necessarily mean the conclusions of this more recent research are wrong, but it does suggest that particularly strong evidence is required before we accept the argument that group differences in observed ability are indeed inherited.

Two different propositions must be demonstrated before such an argument can be accepted. First must be shown that *individual* differences in IQ scores can be explained only by postulating genetic differences among these individuals. Second it must also be shown that *group* differences by social class and race are also inherited. The second of these propositions does not necessarily follow, even if the first proposition is correct.

The Heritability of Individual Differences

There is considerable evidence that what IQ tests measure contains a substantial heritability component. Some of the most theoretically crucial research shows that identical twins reared apart differ very little in their measured ability, while siblings or fraternal twins reared apart differ far more in their IQ scores.[34] If IQ tests measured qualities primarily acquired rather than inherited, then we would not expect such differences. Research that indicates the IQs of adopted children correlate less strongly with the IQ of their foster parents than with the IQ of their biological parents also supports the argument that IQ scores contain a substantial heritability component. Again, if the environmental hypothesis is largely or entirely correct, we would expect much stronger correlations between the IQ of adopted children and their foster parents than their biological parents. These findings have led many contemporary differential psychologists to conclude that what IQ tests measure contains a substantial heritability component.

But some research has thrown doubt on this conclusion. In a carefully reasoned and detailed review of most of the major studies of IQ inheritance, Leon Kamin has shown that most of them contain serious methodological errors.[35] In some of the early twin studies, for example, the IQ of parents was not measured directly by a test of intellectual ability, but was inferred from the social status of the household. Kamin argues that similarly flagrant errors, from incorrect computation of correlation coefficients from the raw data to a failure to specify how IQ was measured, characterize much of this early research. Both Kamin and Philip Green, in a recent exploration of the same sources, show that many authors who conclude that IQ has a substantial heritability component have failed to return to the original studies that provided the basic evidence for their assertions.[36] With this almost exclusive reliance on secondary sources, the errors of past research have been ignored and the shakiness of the foundation of the heritability hypothesis has been overlooked.

At the same time, however, recent and more carefully conducted research continues to support the argument that IQ scores have a considerable hereditability component. In a recent study of adoptive and biologically related children in Minnesota, Scarr and Weinberg find generally much stronger relationships between parents and their biological children's IQ than between parents' IQ and their adoptive children's IQ scores.[37] In the adoptive families, these correlations average around 0.1, while in the biologically related families they are around 0.4. In addition, they observe that there is very little difference between the IQs of adoptive children reared in professional and working-class homes, a finding that is difficult for environmental theory to explain. They conclude that "the evidence of *some* genetic differences in IQ is simply overwhelming."[38]

On balance, I believe, we must accept this conclusion for the heritability of individual differences. Whether IQ tests are culturally biased or not, some part of what they measure appears to be genetically inherited. But it is important to recognize that this does not necessarily imply that observed differences between *groups* in IQ scores are also genetically determined. The finding that individual differences in IQ scores have a genetic component makes it *conceivable* that differences between upper- and lower-class groups or between blacks and whites in IQ could be genetically influenced as well, but it does not necessarily imply that such group differences are partly genetic. Let us now consider the arguments for the heritability of these group differences.

The Heritability of Social Class Differences

The argument that social class differences in IQ scores partly or substantially reflect differences in the genetic endowments of different social classes rests, in considerable part, on the assumption that achievement in U.S. society is substantially meritocratic.[39] Thus if it is the case that intelligence as measured by IQ tests substantially determines both school and occupational achievements, individuals tend to marry others of similar intelligence, and individual intelligence is inherited, then we would expect that over time we would find a concentration of people with relatively low intelligence in low-status positions. If all three assumptions were true, we could claim that a significant part of the reason for the relative failure of low-status children in school is that these children are likely to inherit low intelligence. As we saw in Chapter 4, however, those who make this argument have been too ready to accept the first of these assumptions without adequate evidence. It is true, as Richard Herrnstein and other hereditarians argue, that IQ scores are associated with educational success and occupational status.[40] But it is far from clear that intelligence is the major factor in upward or downward mobility, nor does it seem to be the case that IQ scores are more strongly correlated with occupational success today than they were in the past.[41] An equally strong case could be made for the argument that it is educational credentials rather than intellectual abilities *per se* that are of most importance in determining occupational success.

The evidence that individuals marry others of similar intelligence also seems less than overwhelming. Studies of mate selection indicate that similar tastes and interests (strongly related to similar class and ethnic background) are of great importance in selecting a marriage partner. They also show that people tend to marry others with similar amounts of schooling.[42] But what the hereditarians call the "assortative mating" hypothesis does not receive powerful support. The IQ scores of husbands and wives are correlated, but the size of that correlation is not much greater than the correlation between any two random individuals with similar class backgrounds and similar education.[43]

These considerations mean that while it is entirely possible and even probable that *some* of the observed social class differences in IQ scores reflect genetic differences between social class, only a small fraction of those differences could be so explained. To maintain that genetic differences are a major factor, one must demonstrate that individual IQ differences are largely a function of heredity rather than environment, that individuals marry others with very similar IQs, *and* that IQ is the major factor in upward and dominant mobility. None of the links in this chain of reasoning is as strong as the hereditarians claim.

Black-White Differences in IQ

The case of black-white differences in IQ scores deserves more extended consideration because of the enormous controversy that surrounds this issue, which largely began with the publication of Arthur Jensen's article, "How Much Can We Boost I.Q. and School Performance?" in 1969.[44] In that article, Jensen reviews a great deal of research that showed puzzling and disturbing findings on the persistence of significant differences between black and white IQ scores. Those differences persist even after controlling for socioeconomic status, and they also persist after black students have been enrolled in preschool Head Start programs. If the environmental explanation of black-white differences were the whole story, Jensen argues, we would not expect these findings of continuing differences in IQ scores among samples of black and white students matched on their parents' status.

The case for the genetic explanation of black-white differences in IQ scores is, it should be recognized at the outset, *prima facie* less plausible than the case for social class differences. The heritage of slavery in the South and overt discrimination and prejudice in the North have meant that few blacks enjoyed more than token opportunities for mobility until quite recently. No one could seriously maintain, therefore, that the failure of blacks to achieve higher-status positions *in the past* is attributable to lower intelligence. Because of the concentration of blacks in low-status positions and their denial of educational opportunities, furthermore, we would expect, on purely environmental grounds, lower black IQ scores. Just as none except the foolish or the prejudiced would maintain that the underrepresentation of blacks in the numbers of swimming champions reflects genetic factors rather than simply the absence of swimming pools in black neighborhoods, so it seems implausible to argue for genetic source of IQ differences when overwhelming environmental differences are present. But while I think Jensen's agreement is ultimately implausible, he does nevertheless present some evidence that is not so easy to explain away.

Jensen's first argument is to attack the view that IQ tests are systematically biased against black students. Some of these tests, he admits, do contain items that call for information and draw on experience that poor black students are unlikely to have. But he notes that more "culture fair" tests that minimize the information content show no reduction in black-white differentials.[45] Indeed, he reports that the relative performance of black students is often better on those questions that call for specific information than on those items that ask for abstract reasoning. In most cases, furthermore, blacks are handicapped more on tests of mathematical and numerical reasoning than on tests of verbal reasoning. If cultural bias is the explanation for black-white differences in IQ, Jensen argues, we would expect quite different findings.

Jensen's second major argument is to show that other disadvantaged groups who have experienced comparable discrimination and comparable economic circumstances have generally higher IQ scores than blacks. For example, the levels of income, education, and infant mortality for American Indians are below the levels of most blacks, yet, Jensen reports, they score on the average five points above black children on IQ tests. The same is true for other disadvantaged groups: rural, impoverished whites, poor Hispanics, and lower-class Oriental-Americans. In each case, Jensen maintains, matched samples of blacks score consistently lower than others with similar social status.[46] Given the consistency of these results, Jensen argues, it is difficult to rule out a genetic explanation for part of the differences between black IQ scores and those of other groups.

A great many arguments have been made against Jensen's position, including a number of *ad hominem* attacks on Jensen and accusations that he has misrepresented his data. To some, Jensen's position is simply immoral, and virtually any argument that undercuts this position is justified even if it is contradicted by the evidence. Among many critics, for example, there has been a conspicuous failure to grapple with the difficulties in establishing that IQ scores underestimate black intellectual skills. Because the tests show that blacks score generally lower, some critics maintain they *must* be biased. Fortunately, however, the case against Jensen's position does not rest upon such shaky foundations. The work of Thomas Sowell, in particular, makes a convincing case that black-white differences in IQ scores are, in historical terms, in no way exceptions to the usual patterns of significantly lower scores of other disadvantaged groups.[47]

I have summarized Jensen's strongest arguments for the position that black-white differences in IQ contain some genetic component. Among the many objections that can be made to these assertions, the historical data on the test scores of immigrant groups are perhaps the most decisive. In some pathbreaking research on the results of IQ tests administered in the early decade of this century, Thomas Sowell has shown that many immigrant groups showed performance patterns on IQ tests similar to those of contemporary black students.[48] A survey of Italian-American mental test scores administered shortly after World War I, for example, showed an average IQ of below 84.[49] Studies summarized by Sowell indicated the following average IQ scores in 1926 for different ethnic groups: 83 for Greek, 85 for Polish, 78 for Spanish, and 84 for Portuguese.[50] A contemporary study in Massachusetts showed a higher percentage of black students with IQ scores over 120 than Portuguese, Italian, Polish, or French Canadian students.[51] Most remarkable perhaps are data indicating that Polish and Russian Jewish children frequently scored substantially lower on IQ tests than other ethnic groups in the early years of IQ testing. In contrast to their consistent superiority on tests of verbal ability in recent times, in a 1921 study that Sowell reports, Jews exceeded all other immigrant groups in the "number of certificates for mental defect" at Ellis Island.[52]

The early research on IQ tests, then, found differences between southern and eastern European immigrants and the majority population similar to differences found today between black and white students. That research also discovered similar patterns of performance on tests of abstract reasoning for immigrants as those that Jensen reports for black students. Early administration of IQ tests to Chinese-Americans, for example, showed that they did most poorly on tests of abstract reasoning ability (which today, of course, is quite definitely not the case). Low-scoring immigrant groups were characterized by contemporary psychologists as unable "to master abstractions."[53] A study of children in isolated mountain communities in 1932 showed that the largest difference between their scores and those of the urban population were on items involving abstract comprehension.[54] Furthermore, more recent research on rural working-class children and urban-born children in England shows a similar pattern of larger differences on items involving abstractions than on others.[55] In this respect, therefore, large black-white differences on tests of abstract reasoning are in no way unique and do not require any special explanation.

Sex differences in IQ scores among immigrant groups also displayed similar patterns to those we find today among the black population. Among contemporary blacks, female students outnumber male students in IQ scores above 120 by a ratio of three or more to one.[56] Traditionally such differences have been explained by postulating a matriarchal pattern in black families, which in turn has been associated with the distinctive experience of the black population in the United States and perhaps with the supposed destruction of the black family by slavery.[57] Research on sex differences among other low-status groups, however, reveal similar patterns of superiority among females on IQ test scores. Such findings have been observed in contemporary research on working-class boys and girls in England and in research on Jewish children earlier in this century.[58] Among middle-class populations and more privileged groups, however, the superiority of female performance on IQ tests disappears. Again, therefore, we must reject the hypothesis of distinctive patterns of performance among the black population.

What this evidence suggests, therefore, is that a hypothesis of cultural assimilation explains the available data better than a genetic difference hypothesis. Other disadvantaged groups have consistently scored well below middle-class whites before they were assimilated into the mainstream of U.S. society, and in virtually every case these differences were interpreted at the time as genetic rather than environmental in origin. After their assimilation, these differences became insignificant and the genetic explanations for their previous supposed inferiority were forgotten. But blacks, of course, are still not close to assimilation. Rates of intermarriage between blacks and whites remain low, blacks remain concentrated in low-status occupations, and differences in cultural styles between blacks and whites remain, even among individuals of similar education and income. While there is much that we do not understand about how these environmental differences produce differing IQ scores, there is no reason to have recourse to a genetic explanation to account for them.

Intelligence, IQ Tests, and the Early Childhood Environment

The results of our inquiry into IQ test score differences can be summarized as follows:

1. Individual IQ scores contain a significant heritability component, although its magnitude remains unknown.
2. Social class differences in IQ scores may have a heritability component, but it is likely to be small.
3. There is no persuasive evidence that black-white differences in IQ scores have a genetic basis.

These conclusions, however, by no means solve the problem of IQ. They imply that almost all the difference in IQ scores between disadvantaged and advantaged students is probably environmental rather than genetic in origin, but both the nature of these environmental differences and the meaning and significance of IQ scores remains to be examined. In turning to the issues, I again follow a roughly chronological approach in tracing the history and social context of the controversy between advocates of a cultural deprivation thesis and a cultural difference perspective.

For most orthodox educational psychologists and many sociologists in the 1960s the major explanation of differences in IQ scores between disadvantaged and advantaged students was eminently straightforward. Disadvantaged students were reared in homes that were deprived of the kind of rich and stimulating environment that well-to-do and highly educated parents provided for their children. Lower-class homes, in other words, were seen not only as materially deprived of money, possessions, and a comfortable living environment, but as culturally deprived. The child growing up in such an environment was deprived of the intellectual stimulation and parental teaching that nurtured the development of intelligence in middle-class homes. Thus,

Charlotte Brooks, in a representative statement of this view, writes that the culturally deprived child can be characterized as:

> *essentially the child who has been isolated from those rich experiences that should be his. This isolation may be brought about by meagerness of intellectual resources in his home surroundings, by the incapacity in literacy or indifference of his elders or by the entire community.*[59]

John Hunt, writing in 1964, makes the contrast between the rich environment of middle-class children and the culturally deprived environment of lower-class children even more explicit:

> *Cultural deprivation may be seen as a failure to provide an opportunity for infants and young children to have the experiences required for adequate development of those semi-autonomous essential processes demanded for adequate skill in the use of linguistic and mathematical symbols and for the analysis of causal relationships.*[60]

Both the popularity of the cultural deprivation theory during the 1960s and the intense controversy that has surrounded this hypothesis in more recent times are understandable. The concept was first propounded to describe the distinctive environment of very poor children and to explain how such an environment retards intellectual and emotional growth. Soon, however, the concept began to be applied to minority students and particularly to black students. It figured importantly, for example, in the 1965 report of the McCone Commission appointed to investigate the causes of the Watts riots in Los Angeles. That report argued:

> *Children in disadvantaged areas are often deprived in the preschool years of the necessary foundations for learning. They have not had the full range of experiences so necessary to the development of language in the preschool years, and hence they are poorly prepared to learn when they enter school. . . . The Commission concludes that this is the basic reason for low achievement in the disadvantaged areas.*[61]

Such arguments not only had substantial plausibility, they also had great appeal to the liberal reform movements of the 1960s. Many social investigations during that period dramatized the great disparities between the environments of rich and poor children and aroused public indignation over conditions in the city ghettos. The theory of cultural deprivation suggested that if such conditions were ameliorated, or if at least children living in such environments could be provided with compensatory or enrichment programs, then the disadvantages that poor and black students suffered in school would be greatly reduced.

In its early formulation by educational psychologists, the concept of cultural deprivation was clearly sociologically inadequate. In everyday social science usage, *culture* refers to a set of beliefs, values, customs, and ideals that characterize *any* human group. To be sure, a particular environment may lack the resources to transmit a particular set of values and beliefs, but no group can meaningfully be said to be *deprived* of culture. Recognizing this limitation, students of cultural deprivation seized upon the ideas Oscar Lewis developed in his studies in the slums of Puerto Rico, Mexico, and New York City. Lewis postulated that in many very poor ghettos a "culture of poverty" exists.[62] He argued that such a culture is characterized by a widespread belief that individuals cannot control their environment, a related belief in fate or luck as determinants of a person's life, a low degree of control over aggressive impulses, a present rather than a future orientation, and low levels of aspiration for educational and occupational achievement.

Lewis's conclusion that a culture of poverty exists, distinguishable from a more general lower-class culture, was tentative and hedged with many qualifications. But as has happened frequently in social research, Lewis's idea was taken from the context where it was originally developed and applied as a general explanatory tool to all lower-class groups throughout the United States, and particularly to the black lower class. Arguments were made that such groups do not so much possess a different culture from the dominant culture, but a "deficit" culture. Lower-class black culture, therefore, came to be seen as a culture of deficiency rather than a set of distinctive cultural patterns at variance with middle-class white culture. It was argued that such cultural deficits provide an inadequate environment for the development of intellectual ability, and that if we are to understand the reasons why poor children do badly in school we must focus on the early childhood environment.

Cultural Differences and Cultural Deficits

Beginning around 1970, this simple theory of inadequate and unstimulating environments began to be vigorously attacked. The critics pointed out that the cultural deprivation theory assumed that IQ tests did indeed measure intelligence and ignored the problems of cultural bias inherent in tests that were devised and standardized in work with middle-class children. Furthermore, the critics charged, the concept of cultural deprivation amounted to little more than blaming the victims of poverty for their misfortune. By characterizing the environment of lower-class children as deprived, disorganized, or pathological, the cultural deprivation argument shifted attention away from the failings of the schools and of biased testing instruments to the supposed failure of poor people to bring up their children correctly.

Characterizations by cultural deprivation theorists of the black family came in for especially forceful criticism. Charles Valentine, in a critique of the culture of poverty argument, and Stephen and Joan Baratz, in a review of the cultural deprivation literature, argued that both implied an ethnocentric and racist conception of black families.[63] Valentine and Baratz and Baratz deny that the frequent absence of the father and the dominant role of the mother in lower-class families can be considered in any way pathological. Instead, they assert that it merely reflects long-standing cultural *differences* between blacks and whites.[64] They also deny that language development of young black children is, in any absolute sense, slow or inadequate. Such a belief, they argue, reflects a fundamentally racist characterization of black dialect as an inferior form of English rather than a different and fully developed form of the language. A black child who says "He be" instead of "He is" is not a victim of an unstimulating or pathological environment that has failed to teach him to speak "correctly." He is speaking grammatically correctly within the *different* rules of black dialect. Such a child may be handicapped in schools that demand standard English, but he is not suffering from inadequate linguistic development. Thus Baratz and Baratz argue: "Speaking standard English is a linguistic disadvantage for the black youth on the streets of Harlem. A disadvantage created by a difference is not the same thing as a deficit."[65]

The critics of cultural deprivation maintain that lower-class families are "functionally adequate" systems that are entirely capable of fostering intellectual development in young children. And while they are different from middle-class families, they are in no way inferior in developing linguistic or reasoning skills. A characterization of these families as deficient or inadequate, and attempts to "improve" those environments that follow such a characterization, reflect insensitivity to the biases inherent in IQ tests, and a patronizing assumption that whatever is different from white middle-class culture is thereby inferior.

It is difficult to separate the ideological and political from the scientific issues in this debate. The critics of cultural deprivation theory are probably correct in arguing that some of the characterizations of lower-class environments as unstimulating or pathological do reflect the preferences of middle- and upper-class observers for a very different style of child rearing to that preferred by many lower-class black families. Thus Brooks, for example, in her characterization refers to "the indifference" of lower-class parents, and to their "incapacity in literacy."[66] These are hardly objective terms. The critics are undoubtedly also correct in asserting that all normal black and lower-class children have, by the age of entry into school, linguistic skills and a substantial mastery of grammatical rules that are often overlooked by those who fail to recognize that rules of English have more than one variant.[67] But the most important assertions of the critics are more problematic. In their enthusiasm to defend the integrity of lower-class culture as culturally different rather than culturally deficient, the critics come close to an entirely relativist view when no family environment can be regarded as inferior from the point of view of fostering intellectual growth to any other family environment. This relativism extends to tests of intellectual ability as well. The proponents of the cultural difference view often deny that IQ tests can reasonably be said to measure any enduring intellectual qualities between individuals from differing cultural backgrounds. Instead, they measure "middle-class conceptions of intelligence" which, the critics allege, reflect the cultural assumptions and prejudices of those who devise and administer the tests.[68]

While these criticisms are not wholly without merit, I believe they are overstated. Proponents of IQ testing are in some ways their own worst enemies by making claims that these tests measure intelligence in some absolute sense and by implying that intelligence is a fixed trait. IQ testing has been often used in culturally insensitive ways to label poor and black children as dull or retarded, but this misuse does not mean that the tests merely measure middle-class styles of reasoning rather than more general intellectual abilities that are important for success in Western industrial societies. Two kinds of evidence suggest that this relativist conception of IQ tests is misleading.

First, as we have already noted, there is little indication that black and lower-class students score significantly higher on tests that are relatively free of specific information derived from middle-class culture than on standard tests. No test, of course, can be entirely culture free, but tests that contain little in the way of verbal information do not reveal different patterns of class and race differences than other tests. Nor, as Arthur Jensen reports, do black students show distinctive patterns in the kinds of verbal items they answer incorrectly as compared with white students.[69] Black students who score one hundred on an IQ test, for example, tend to miss the same kinds of questions as white students who score one hundred. This is not what we would expect if the tests were systematically biased in favor of middle-class white students. Second, while critics of IQ tests focus predominantly on the deficiencies of IQ tests in assessing verbal reasoning skills, test results show that black students tend to score closer to white norms on verbal skills, and further below white norms on numerical reasoning skills.[70]

A study by Stodolsky and Lesser of a number of ethnic groups, further-more, shows quite sharp differences in types of abilities between blacks, Chinese-American, Puerto Ricans, and Jewish children, even after so-cial class was held constant.[71] In verbal ability, Chinese-Americans score relatively low, whereas black students score relatively high, and Jewish students highest of all. In numerical ability, Chinese-American students scored highest and black students lowest. The reasons for these differ-ences are not understood, but since they are paralleled by similar differ-ences between the groups in success in science and mathematics courses and even in occupational preferences, it seems unlikely that they are reflections of biases in IQ tests alone.

The claim that lower-class environments are not deficient in their provision of resources for intellectual growth but reflect differential valuations of ideal family forms is also problematic. While we may grant some of the characterizations of lower-class family life as patho-logical are ethnocentric and insensitive to cultural differences, much research has shown that poverty and unemployment make it extremely difficult for lower-class families to maintain relationships *they define* as satisfactory.[72] Among poor black families, for example, over 40 per-cent of households are headed by women, and illegitimacy rates exceed 50 percent.[73] There is little evidence that blacks regard such families as desirable, and indeed there is increasing evidence that in the 1980s the black community began to define this situation as a crisis in the black family.[74] The causes of that crisis undoubtedly lie in the legacy of discrimination and in poverty and unemployment. But it is hard to deny that the instability of family life in many lower-class black households makes for an unpropitious environment for the develop-ment of intellectual skills.

In crucial respects, therefore, the cultural difference view repre-sents a denial of the problem of intellectual differences between chil-dren from different backgrounds rather than a solution of that problem. Black children and lower-class children, these critics argue, are not less intelligent than middle-class white children, nor are they reared in unstimulating or deprived environments. Instead, they are the vic-tims of racist or biased tests and of schools that reward only middle-class styles of behavior. But it is not necessary to believe that IQ tests measure intelligence in some pure form or to accept simplistic descrip-tions of lower-class environments as unstimulating to recognize that this view is misleading. Whatever the limitations of IQ tests as indica-tors of some general property we call intelligence, they do assess the skills and aptitudes required to do well in school with considerable predictive power. There is a great deal of evidence that disadvantaged children enter school with fewer of those skills and aptitudes than advantaged children. Only if this problem is faced squarely rather than denied can we move toward an understanding of why children from disadvantaged backgrounds often do poorly in school.

I have been critical of the cultural difference argument, but as an explanation of why lower-class children score less well on IQ tests, the cultural deprivation argument fares little better. Certainly it is inadequate to argue that there is a close parallel between a deprived physical environment and an unstimulating cultural environment. As Labov, among others, has pointed out, lower-class children are bathed in a constant glow of verbal stimulation from peers as well as from family members.[75] In the black and urban lower class, in particular, verbal facility in games and contests is an important source of prestige and esteem among children. Lower-class children may be deprived of explicit teaching by their parents, as some research suggests, but they are clearly not deprived of verbal stimulation in general.[76] Remarkably enough, however, there has been very little research and no satisfactory theory that goes beyond this simplistic view. We know that lower-class children enter schools with fewer skills required for success in school, and we know that much of these differences are environmental in origin. But we know very little about which *particular features* of the environment led to the development of these skills and aptitudes. The controversy over IQ scores and their meaning and significance has, by its almost obsessive quality, diverted attention from our real ignorance in this regard.

CONCLUSION

Our preliminary investigation of the sources of unequal performance in school has yielded three major findings. First, research on school quality and student performance has failed to uncover the clear relationships that were initially expected. Such obvious and admittedly crude indicators of school quality as per pupil expenditures, pupil-teacher ratios, and teacher qualifications cannot explain more than a very small part of the differences in school performance between advantaged and disadvantaged students. Although this leaves open the possibility that dramatically different schools could reduce or even eliminate such differences, the predominant interpretation of these findings has been that differences in school performance must be sought primarily in the skills and aptitudes that students bring with them to school rather than in the differences between schools attended by advantaged and disadvantaged students.

If it seemed that schools were not the major source of inequality, investigators turned their attention to the problem of assessing the relative importance of heredity and environment in differences in IQ scores between advantaged and disadvantaged groups. This volatile issue was compounded by the equally controversial question of whether IQ tests fairly assessed intelligence. Out of this tangle of conflicting evidence and political and ideological debate, several tentative conclusions emerged. Although the heredity environment debate is in no sense settled, it seems clear that the hereditarian argument is much stronger in the case of individual differences in IQ scores than as an explanation of differences in average scores between social classes or between blacks and whites. Thus it is very difficult to explain why individuals of similar social background differ in their IQ without recourse to a partially genetic explanation. Recent studies of adopted and biological children make the argument for some hereditary component in IQ almost inescapable.[77] The case for genetic factors in the social class differences in IQ is weaker, and the case for hereditary determination of black-white differences weaker still. It *may be* that as highly intelligent members of lower-class groups experience upward mobility and less intelligent members of middle-class groups experience downward mobility, lower-class groups increasingly contain individuals who are, for genetic reasons, less intelligent. But both the absence of any clear trend toward increasingly meritocratic selection and the availability of plausible environmental explanations make it unlikely that a large part of these IQ differences can be explained by this simple model. Certainly genetic factors are less important in the case of social class differences than in the explanation of individual differences between people of similar social background.

The case of black-white differences in IQ is more clear cut. Here there is virtually no credible evidence for genetic factors, and powerful evidence that, given the absence of assimilation of blacks into U.S. society, we should expect generally lower IQ scores for the group on these grounds alone. Historically, many groups of immigrant populations have had similar or lower IQ scores than blacks; as these groups became assimilated into the mainstream of U.S. society, these differences disappeared. Since the barriers to full black assimilation have been much greater than for other groups, there is no reason to suppose that, if such assimilation finally takes place, black IQ scores will remain distinctive.

Finally, although IQ tests are by common consent very unsatisfactory instruments and have been used in insensitive and disreputable ways, the charge that they tell us nothing of importance about the intellectual skills and aptitudes of disadvantaged groups cannot be sustained. Both sides in the IQ controversy are guilty of overstatement and of ignoring important evidence. Neither the claims that IQ tests can "read through" cultural differences to some pure quality of intelligence, nor the argument that they measure merely middle-class skills can be accepted. There is little question that disadvantaged children enter school without a number of the intellectual skills and aptitudes that most advantaged children possess. Whether we call these differences "deficiencies" and these skills and aptitudes "intelligence" makes virtually no difference from a scientific point of view. But these terms have had such political and ideological resonance that it has been difficult to think clearly about the theoretical and empirical problems to which they refer. Differences in early childhood environments undoubtedly explain part, perhaps a large part, of the reason why disadvantaged children often do poorly in school, and this, in turn, helps to explain why the children of disadvantaged parents tend to inherit their parents' low status. But the controversy over IQ and the popular beliefs that IQ scores measure "intelligence," understood as a primarily genetic phenomenon, has greatly retarded our understanding of why lower-class environments tend to lead to lower IQ scores.

Fortunately, there are signs that some of this intense controversy is beginning to abate and that the entrenched and dogmatic positions of the 1960s and 1970s on all these issues are becoming somewhat more fluid and open to new evidence and new theoretical ideas. Large-scale researchers whose studies appeared to show that schools had no effects on reinforcing inequality are reconsidering their positions and beginning to examine processes within schools that might help explain the cumulative disadvantages poor children experience. Opponents of IQ tests who claimed that all talk of IQ diverts attention from the racist or inferior schooling that disadvantaged children suffer, are beginning to recognize that research on test scores cannot be so easily dismissed. In the next chapter, I turn to a discussion of these more recent and promising developments.

Endnotes

1. Christopher Jencks, et al., *Inequality* (New York: Basic Books, 1972). Attainment, as Jencks points out, is often more important in predicting future status than measures of achievement.

2. William H. Sewell and Robert M. Hauser, "Causes and Consequences of Higher Education: Modes of the Status Attainment Process," in William H. Sewell, Robert M. Hauser, and David L. Featherman (eds.), *Schooling and Achievement in American Society* (New York: Academic Press, 1976), p. 13.

3. This view was perhaps the orthodox interpretation until after World War II. See Clarence Karier (ed.), *Shaping the American Educational State* (New York: Free Press, 1976).

4. Richard Herrnstein, *I.Q. in the Meritocracy* (Boston: Little, Brown, 1973).

5. William Ryan, *Blaming the Victim* (New York: Pantheon, 1971).

6. See the articles collected in "Challenging the Myths: The Schools, the Blacks and the Poor," *Harvard Educational Review*, Reprint Series, No. 5, 1975.

7. Samuel Bowles and Herbert Gintis, *Schooling in Capitalist America* (New York: Basic Books, 1976).

8. Jencks, et al., *Inequality.*

9. Ray Rist, "Social Class and Teacher Expectations: The Self-Fulfilling Prophecy in Ghetto Education," *Harvard Education Review* 40 (1970): 411–451.

10. James Coleman, et al., *Equality of Educational Opportunity* (Washington, D.C.: U.S. Government, 1966).

11. See Geoffrey Hodgson, "Do Schools Make a Difference?" *Atlantic* (March 1973): 35–46, for a discussion of the assumptions and preconceptions of social scientists prior to the findings of the Coleman Report.

12. See, for example, James Guthrie, et al., *Schools and Inequality* (Cambridge: M.I.T. Press, 1971).

13. Hodgson, "Do Schools Make a Difference?"

14. I think it is reasonable to say that most policy makers felt that what was fair and equitable (equalizing expenditures across school districts) was also a strategy that would narrow performance differentials between students from different social origins. I think most policy makers still believe this, despite evidence to the contrary. The persistence of such beliefs perhaps indicates the strength of convictions that good causes good and evil causes evil.

15. Hodgson, "Do Schools Make a Difference?"

16. Coleman, et al., *Equality of Educational Opportunity.* See also Jencks, et al., *Inequality.*

17. Coleman, et al., *Equality of Educational Opportunity.*

18. Jencks, et al., *Inequality.*

19. Thus Jencks concludes that the original Coleman findings overestimated the strength of the relationships between social quality and student test scores.

20. There is some evidence, however, that in poor countries the effects of school quality on test scores are more substantial. See Stephen P. Heyneman and William A. Loxley, "Influences on Academic Achievement across High and Low Income Countries: A Reanalysis of IEA Data," *Sociology of Education,* Vol. 55 (January 1982): 13–21.

21. Jencks, et al., *Inequality,* p. 109.

22. Ibid., p. 91.

23. Ibid., p. 159.

24. Eric Hanushek, *Education and Race* (Lexington, Mass.: D.C. Heath, 1972).

25. Jencks, et al., *Inequality,* p. 87. A study of summer learning in Atlanta confirms this conclusion. See Barbara Heyns, *Summer Learning: The Effects of Schooling on Social Inequality Reconsidered* (New York: Academic Press, 1978). Barbara Heyns concludes, "The gap between black and white children, and between high and low income children widens disproportionately when schools are not in session" (Chapter 9).

26. There is first the problem of attempting to control for student background effects in a small-scale study, and hardly less serious, the problem that most observers, we may assume, are looking for evidence that differential treatment by schools produces differences in student performance.

27. Michael Rutter, et al., *Fifteen Thousand Hours* (London: Open Books, 1979). I should note that my evaluation of Rutter's work is not shared by many educators who, understandably enough, look to research for factors "that make a difference." But even if Rutter's finding that positive school climates

increase student achievement are true, it is not clear what combination of school characteristics produce that climate.

28. For criticisms of Jencks, see Donald M. Levine and Mary Jo Bane (eds.), *The Inequality Controversy: Schooling and Distributive Justice* (New York: Basic Books, 1975).

29. Jencks, et al., *Inequality*, pp. 53–58.

30. This is not to say that the tests do estimate the true ability of disadvantaged students (see the following discussion on intelligence), but simply that this issue is a separate question from the effects of school quality on test scores.

31. Arthur Jensen, "How Much Can We Boost I.Q. and Scholastic Achievement?" *Harvard Educational Review* 39 (1969): 1–123.

32. For a dissenting view, see Howard Gardner, *Frames of Mind: The Theory of Multiple Intelligences* (New York: Basic Books, 1983).

33. For accounts of this rather disreputable tradition, see Clarence Karier (ed.), *Shaping the American Educational State* (New York: Free Press, 1976); and N. J. Block and Gerald Dworkin (eds.), *The I.Q. Controversy* (New York: Random House, 1976).

34. Jensen, "How Much Can We Boost I.Q.?"

35. Leon Kamin, *The Science and Politics of I.Q.* (Potomac, Maryland: Erlbaum Associates, 1974).

36. Philip Green, "Race and I.Q.: Fallacy of Heritability," *Dissent* (Spring 1976): 181–196.

37. Sandra Scarr and Richard A. Weinberg, "The Influence of 'Family Background' on Intellectual Attainment," *American Sociological Review*, Vol. 43 (October 1978): 674–692.

38. Ibid., p. 688.

39. Herrnstein, *I.Q. in the Meritocracy*.

40. Ibid.

41. Jencks, et al., *Inequality*, p. 186.

42. Bruce K. Eckland, "Genetics and Sociology: A Reconsideration," *American Sociological Review*, Vol. 32 (1967): 173–194.

43. Jencks, et al., *Inequality*.

44. Jensen, "How Much Can We Boost I.Q.?"

45. Ibid., p. 81.

46. Ibid., p. 85.

47. Thomas Sowell, "New Light on the Black I.Q. Controversy," *New York Times Magazine* (March 27, 1977): 56–63; and Thomas Sowell, "Race and I.Q. Reconsidered" (unpublished manuscript). This manuscript contains the full documentation for the assertions made in the *New York Times* article.

48. Sowell, "New Light."

49. Rudof Pintner, *Intelligence Testing: Methods and Results* (New York: Henry Holt, 1923).

50. Sowell, "Race," p. 6.

51. Ibid.

52. Bertha Body, *A Psychological Study of Immigrant Children at Ellis Island* (Baltimore: Williams and Wilkins, 1926), quoted in Sowell, "Race."

53. Kamin, *The Science and Politics of I.Q.*, p. 6.

54. Mandel Sherman and Cora B. Key, "The Intelligence of Isolated Mountain Children," *Child Development*, Vol. 3, No. 4 (1932): 284, cited in Sowell, "Race," p. 23.

55. Philip Vernon, *Intelligence and Cultural Environment* (London: Methuen, 1970), pp. 66–67.

56. Jensen, "How Much Can We Boost I.Q.?" p. 32.

57. See, for example, Daniel P. Moynihan, *The Negro Family* (Washington, D.C.: U.S. Department of Labor, 1965), pp. 31–34.

58. Vernon, *Intelligence and Cultural Environment*; and Sowell, "Race."

59. Charlotte Brooks, "Some Approaches to Teaching English as a Second Language," in S. W. Webster (ed.), *The Disadvantaged Learner* (San Francisco: Chandler, 1966), pp. 516–517.

60. John Hunt, "The Psychological Basis for Using Pre-School Environment as an Antidote for Cultural Deprivation," *Merrill-Palmer Quarterly* 10 (1964): 236.

61. Governor's Commission on the Los Angeles Riots, *Report of the Commission* (Sacramento, Calif., 1965), pp. 57–58.

62. Oscar Lewis, "The Culture of Poverty," *Scientific American*, Vol. 215 (October 1966): 19–25.

63. Charles Valentine, "Deficit, Difference and Bicultural Models of Afro-American Behavior," in "Challenging the Myth: The Schools, the Blacks, and the Poor," *Harvard Educational Review* (Reprint Series No. 5, 1975): 1–21; and Stephen S. Baratz and Joan C. Baratz, "Early Childhood Intervention: The Social Science Basis of Institutional Racism," pp. 111–132 of the same source.

64. Ibid.

65. Baratz and Baratz, "Early Childhood Intervention," p. 118.

66. Brooks, "Some Approaches," p. 516.

67. Baratz and Baratz, "Early Childhood Intervention," p. 119.

68. Valentine, "Deficit, Difference and Bicultural Models."

69. Arthur Jensen, "Arthur Jensen Defends His Heresy," *Psychology Today* (October 1969): 24.

70. See ibid.; and Susan Stodolsky and Gerald Lesser, "Learning Patterns in the Disadvantaged," *Harvard Educational Review*, Vol. 37 (1967): 546–593.

71. Stodolsky and Lesser, "Learning Patterns."

72. Martin Kilson, "Black Social Classes and Intergenerational Poverty," *The Public Interest*, No. 64 (Summer 1981): 58–78.

73. Ibid.

74. See the series on the "Crisis in the Black Family" in the *New York Times* beginning November 21, 1983.

75. William Labov, "The Logic of Non-Standard English," in F. Williams (ed.), *Language and Poverty* (Chicago: Markham, 1970).

76. Martha C. Ward, " 'Teaching' Them Children to Talk" in Joan I. Roberts and Sherrie K. Akinsanya (eds.), *Schooling in Cultural Context* (New York: McKay, 1976), pp. 386–400.

77. Scarr and Weinberg, "The Influence of Family Background.' "

chapter 6

Do Schools
Reinforce Inequality?

Are schools meritocratic institutions when student performance depends primarily on ability and motivation? Or is it more accurate to see schools as actively reinforcing inequalities of class and race and overtly or covertly discriminating against students from disadvantaged backgrounds? Do schools merely respond in neutral or objective fashion to the differences that students bring with them to school, or do they play a part in magnifying or even creating these differences? These are the questions that will be addressed in this chapter.

The opposed interpretations implied in these questions stem from the two paradigms discussed in Chapter 2. The functionalist perspective, although it is not entirely insensitive to the possibility that processes within schools may handicap disadvantaged students, generally emphasizes that extra-school influences are the predominant reason why disadvantaged students have generally lower levels of educational achievement and attainment.[1] Students come to school with different levels of academic ability and experience different amounts of parental encouragement. They tend to make friends among students with similar ability and of similar socioeconomic status; and in turn these friends influence their achievements and educational plans. All these factors help explain why disadvantaged students are more likely to experience educational failure. But in the functionalist model neither teachers, nor ability tracking, nor the nature of the curriculum have a decisive impact on the relative chances of disadvantaged students.[2] Teachers are not generally unfair to lower-class students either in the grades they assign or in their day-to-day classroom interaction. Ability tracks are assigned on the basis of ability rather than on the basis of social class. And the curriculum is seen as essentially neutral in character, rather than reflecting elite or middle-class knowledge to which lower-class students have great difficulty gaining access.

In the conflict paradigm, on the other hand, we find a challenge to all these assertions. There is a suspicion of the concept of academic ability and its measurement, and an argument that the nature of the academic curriculum is essentially alien to lower-class youth.[3] Conflict theorists often maintain that teachers tend, consciously or unconsciously, to give disadvantaged students lower grades than they deserve, that they expect such students to fail, and that they act differently toward those students because of these lower expectations. Ability tracking also works to the disadvantage of lower-class students. Counselors and school authorities, conflict theorists maintain, regularly assign students to lower or vocational tracks largely on the basis of their social background.[4] Once in those tracks, disadvantaged students receive further discouragement and inferior teaching. They begin to define themselves as failures and lose motivation to continue schooling. Thus what began as relatively minor differences between students at age five or six become, largely because of processes within schools, very large differences in educational outcomes by the age of seventeen or eighteen.

What makes this debate particularly difficult to assess is that these conflicting interpretations tend to rely on different kinds of evidence and use different criteria for assessing the validity of that evidence. In recent years, the functionalist view has been supported by evidence from very large samples of students and schools and by the relatively crude measures of key concepts that are almost inevitable in such research. Thus both parental and teacher expectations are measured by asking *students* their opinions of what these expectations are rather than by direct inquiries of the individuals concerned.[5] Such studies often use reports by students of their grades and the tracks to which they have been assigned rather than inspecting school records.[6] Unsatisfactory measurements of this kind are a price that large-scale research is willing to pay for the advantages that very large samples provide in reliability and generalizability of the results. Frequently, but by no means always, the conflict paradigm has been represented by much smaller scale ethnographic studies of one or two schools.[7] Such studies enable subtler processes to be observed but run the risk of researcher bias and lack of generalizability. Lacking any objective checks on their often impressionistic measurements of key variables, those who conduct small-scale observational studies may confuse what they want and expect to find with what they have in fact found, and what is true in the schools *they* studied with what is true in *all* or most schools.

Potentially even more insidious is the fact that different styles of research, by the very nature of their respective designs, may tend to give different results on the relative importance of school and extra-school factors in student achievement. Because of the small number of cases involved, small-scale research cannot adequately control for such background characteristics as student ability and socioeconomic status. What appears to be discrimination against lower-class students from the standpoint of the observer, therefore, may actually be little more than differential but fair treatment of students of differing ability and past performance. At the same time, large-scale research, because so much of it is based on questionnaires administered to students and because school processes of any complexity are so difficult to measure, may overestimate the effects of differences in student characteristics on student performance and underestimate the importance of schools and teachers. Therefore, despite strenuous efforts on all sides to be objective and conscious of their preconceptions, initial decisions as to how the research should be conducted may tend to shape findings.

In what follows I shall try to be both catholic and eclectic in my summaries and evaluation of the evidence and to strike a balance between excessive reliance on the "hard" data generated by large-scale research and uncritical acceptance of the "soft" data of more ethnographic accounts.

THE RESULTS OF LARGE-SCALE SURVEY RESEARCH

Status Attainment Research

The most important evidence for the functionalist and meritocratic argument is provided by a tradition of research known as *status attainment*.[8] Status attainment research attempts to explain why students from different social backgrounds differ in school achievement and in the length of time they remain in school and college. To explain this dependent variable of "years of school completed," this research tradition has devised techniques for assessing the relative importance of a number of independent and intervening variables: socioeconomic status and academic ability as the primary independent variables; and high school grades, measures of student aspirations, parental encouragement, and friends' plans as intervening variables. The basic model of how these variables interrelate was derived from longitudinal studies of a very large number of students in Wisconsin followed over more than a ten-year period.[9] In later research the same model, with some modifications of detail, has been replicated for other samples and by other investigators.[10]

Status attainment research, like virtually all research in this field, finds very large differences in eventual educational attainment between individuals from different social backgrounds. Sewell and Hauser report, for example, that high-status students have a four to one advantage in entering college over students in the lowest-status category, and a nine to one advantage in entry to graduate or professional school.[11]

To account for these large differences in educational attainment, status attainment researchers construct a statistical model that allows them to estimate not only the relative importance of each variable considered separately but the importance of their mutual effects and their causal order. This model, derived from a technique called *path analysis,* leads to a surprisingly meritocratic picture of educational attainment—meritocratic, in the sense that it is ability and motivation that shape educational attainment rather than any discrimination on the part of schools or teachers. The first finding of status attainment research is that ability, usually measured by IQ tests administered at about age fourteen, is the single best predictor of both grades and educational attainment. Furthermore, when mental ability is controlled the relationship between socioeconomic status and grades virtually disappears. This result obviously contradicts the conflict theory argument that schools award grades on the basis of ascription or social background factors rather than in terms of the performance of the student.[12]

Status attainment research then attempts to explain why students from different social origins differ in their school attainment. The research concludes that two basic processes are involved. Students from high-status origins tend to have higher aspirations for educational achievement and they tend to have friends who have similarly high aspirations, whereas students from low-status origins receive less encouragement from parents and friends. And at the same time, students who have low-status origins have generally lower ability than high-status students. Measures of ability and these different measures of aspirations together account for the great bulk of differences between high- and low-status students in school attainment. High-status students enjoy advantages in initial ability and these advantages are compounded because their parents and their friends encourage them more to do well in school.[13]

The third major finding of status attainment research is that teachers appear to play a basically meritocratic role in this process of educational attainment.[14] Teachers' encouragement does affect educational attainment, though somewhat less powerfully than either parents or friends, but teachers appear to base their encouragement almost entirely on student grades and student ability rather than student social status. Low-status students with high grades and high ability, in other words, do not receive less encouragement to continue in school than high-status students with similar grades and ability scores. As Sewell and Hauser put it: "Far from reflecting overt or covert discrimination, on the whole, teachers' expectations appear to be based on ability and performance and, as such, make a fundamental though modest contribution to the equalization of educational opportunities."[15]

These basic findings have been reexamined by a number of other investigators using national rather than regional samples and using different measures of such key variables as socioeconomic status, ability, and aspirations. The results of this subsequent research have been generally to confirm the original findings, although there is evidence that the Wisconsin study underestimated the effects of ability and socioeconomic status.[16] But no subsequent research in this tradition substantially modifies the basic conclusion that a combination of differing ability and aspirations is by far the most important reason why students from different socioeconomic backgrounds do differentially well in school. Schools themselves, this research tradition finds, bring little influence to bear upon student attainment that is independent of these aspirations and differing abilities.

There are, by common consent, two major weaknesses in status attainment research. First, because it relies on large samples for its generalizations it has proven difficult to obtain enough black students to construct reliable estimates of the degree to which the same basic processes apply to black students as well as white students. What evidence exists suggests that the model does not work as well for black students but there are no clear leads as to why this is the case.[17] Black students score, on average, substantially lower on tests of ability than white students, but have educational attainment that is rather *higher* than white students of similar test scores. It appears probable that other factors, besides aspirations and friends' influence, are needed to explain this result, but there is no clear evidence that these other factors include discrimination against these students by the school. The basic meritocratic model, in other words, does not predict black student attainment as well as white student attainment, but there is as yet no evidence that a conflict model can explain the data any better.

A second weakness of status attainment research is that it is almost entirely atheoretical in character.[18] The research tells us that social status affects ability and aspirations and that these in turn affect achievement and attainment, but it tells us nothing about why social status has these effects. By continually referring to the results of aptitude tests administered at age fourteen as "intelligence," furthermore, the research may create the impression that early environmental or genetic differences between social classes are the sole cause of performance on these tests.[19] But status attainment research has no such information, and it is entirely possible that these differences in "intelligence" at age fourteen are the result of prior school experience as well as differences in preschool environments.

Despite these weaknesses, however, status attainment research presents strong evidence against a simple conflict interpretation of school attainment and in favor of a functional or meritocratic interpretation. Characteristics of students, this research strongly suggests, are much more important than characteristics of schools in explaining school success. High schools cannot be said to cause much of the difference in achievement between high- and low-status students. Instead, schools and teachers appear to respond quite meritocratically to differences between students in aspirations and ability.

Tracking in the Secondary School

Research on tracking provides a second way of examining the merits of our two rival hypotheses. If the functionalist or meritocratic account is basically correct we should expect to find that high schools assign tracks on the basis of student performance and course preferences regardless of social class background. For the conflict theorist, track assignments should be substantially nonmeritocratic. Guidance counselors and teachers will, of course, take ability and past performance into account, but in their judgments of who is and who is not college material, they will be influenced by such extra-academic considerations as good manners, speech styles, values, and other class-related factors.

The consequences of tracking assignments are also important for evaluating both theories. If students assigned to college preparatory tracks learn more, develop higher aspirations, and stay in school longer, then that demonstrates that organizational features of schools themselves, as well as characteristics of students, play an important role in the process of differential achievement and attainment. Combined with evidence of ascription placement of lower-class students into the noncollege track, this would be powerful evidence for the conflict theory. But if students in college tracks do only as well as would be expected from their records prior to teacher assignments and tracking has no independent effects, then this would support the basic findings of status attainment research that characteristics of students rather than characteristics of schools are decisive.

The evidence on both of these issues is decidedly mixed, but it generally offers more support for the functionalist than the conflict theory. In track assignments, all the data suggest that academic ability and past school record play the major role and that a student's social status is of less importance than either of these variables. Thus the correlation between track assignment and father's education in Alexander and Cook's research is only 0.14, yet that between aptitude scores and track assignments is 0.36.[20] Furthermore, a good part of the effects of family background on track assignments seems to be due to the generally higher aspirations and greater academic orientation of high-status students rather than to any measurable bias on the part of counselors or teachers.[21] And although not all large-scale research finds that the effects of social class on track assignments are trivial, it is noteworthy that the research having the best controls for prior academic performance and prior aspirations tends to find the weakest effects for the social class variable. Thus Alexander and Cook conclude, "We find little evidence of appreciable bias, involving SES background, race or gender, in the assignment of students to track high school programs of study."[22]

Research on the *effects* of track assignments on student achievement and attainment is particularly difficult because students in college preparatory tracks are different from other students *before* track assignments in their ability, aspirations, and course work. College track students have higher ability, higher aspirations, and are more likely to go to college. But a considerable part of these differences is undoubtedly due to the fact that such students were different to begin with.

The problem of research on tracking's effects, therefore, is to devise adequate controls for these preexisting differences among students so that we can be reasonably sure that what we are measuring in the twelfth grade is not merely a reflection of differences that already existed in the eighth or ninth grade. Early research on tracking, which generally lacked these controls, showed quite powerful effects on student *learning* as well as on aspirations and the likelihood of entering college. It seemed that the exposure of students to superior teachers, to highly motivated peers, and to an academic college preparatory curriculum made a substantial difference in learning even after IQ and social class background were controlled. More recent research, however, with better controls, casts doubt on this conclusion. Jencks, for example, reports that students' test scores in the twelfth grade can be quite well explained by test scores in the ninth grade without any knowledge of the track to which they were assigned.[23] In the most sophisticated study to date, Alexander and Cook find that the introduction of controls for prior test scores and grades makes it necessary to revise earlier conclusions that track assignments have powerful effects on learning.[24] In tests of both verbal and mathematical skills they report college track students showed only slight superiority over noncollege track students after past performance was controlled.[25]

In contrast, the effects of track assignment on aspirations and college entry seem quite powerful. College track students are considerably more likely to plan to attend college than noncollege track students of the same ability and similar grades. Exposure to peers who for the most part plan to attend college increases educational aspirations. Also, guidance counselors and teachers are more likely to encourage college track students to define themselves as "college material." In these respects, therefore, students become more different from each other because of the tracks to which they are assigned, and these differences are consequential for their future careers. Students who are assigned to noncollege tracks have less chance of going to college than college track students with the same previous academic records.[26]

Although this finding is important in its own right, its implications for our rival theories depends in considerable part on the degree to which initial track assignments are meritocratic. Most recent large-scale research, as we have seen, in contrast to earlier work and some ethnographic research, suggests that this is substantially the case.[27] Tracking has important consequences for future careers and significant effects on self-conceptions. In these respects, internal differentiation within schools can be said to contribute to inequality. But unless it is the case that social class or race affects track assignments *independent* of measured academic ability, we cannot conclude that tracking itself heightens the differences between individuals of different social origins. Some earlier studies of track assignments suggest that teachers and schools were systematically stereotyping students from disadvantaged origins.[28] The latest and most sophisticated research, however, does not generally support this conclusion. Grades and measured ability are substantially better predictors of track assignments for white students than social class origins. Paradoxically enough, black students are slightly more likely to be in college tracks than would be expected by their grades and measured ability alone.

School Contexts and School Climates

Large-scale research provides one more major category of evidence that enables us to test the relative merits of our two major theories. Here, instead of looking at track assignments within schools, we examine differences between schools in the social composition of the student body. Thus we are interested in the extent to which students who attend schools with large numbers of high-achieving and/or middle or upper middle-class students do better than students who go to schools whose population is drawn largely from disadvantaged backgrounds. There are *a priori* reasons for thinking that this should be the case. We know, for example, that student aspirations affect achievements and attainment, and we also know that aspirations are shaped by peers. One reason that lower-class students may generally do poorly in school, therefore, is that they usually attend schools with other lower-class students.

The findings of most research in this field show a now familiar pattern. Early research suggested that the presence of high-status, high-achieving peers did boost achievement and attainment for most students and particularly for disadvantaged students.[29] This research implied that part of the reason for the lower achievement of disadvantaged students was that they often attended schools with low-status populations. But recent research, with better measurements of key variables, has not always supported these conclusions, at least as far as white students are concerned.[30] In the recent literature there is some consensus that two approximately equal but opposite effects are at work. First, as we might expect, the presence of large numbers of high-status peers tends to raise aspirations and achievement because more role models of high achievement are available. Similarly, enrollment in predominantly low-status schools tends to depress aspirations and achievement because the dominant group of peers exercises pressure for conformity to lower standards. At the same time, however, students who attend schools with high-achieving students find themselves in an *inferior competitive* situation to those who go to school with low-achieving students. Meyer argues, "The higher the academic worth of the other students in the school, the lower will be the academic worth of any given student; and consequently, the less likely he will derive or feel encouraged to go to college."[31] Being in school with other high-achieving students appears to lower self-esteem and to have a *discouraging* effect on educational aspirations and educational achievement.

The net result of these opposite effects, most recent research has found, is close to zero for white students. The encouraging effects of being with high-status students or aspirations are cancelled out by the discouraging effects of being a small fish in a big pond. The outcome is that students who attend schools with large numbers of high-status students are no more likely to have higher aspirations or to attend college than students who go to schools with predominantly low-status students. For black students, however, the effects of high-status schools seem to be more positive, although not large.[32] In the case of black students, for reasons that are not fully understood, the positive effects of associating with high-status students or aspirations appear to outweigh the negative effects of being in a relatively more competitive situation. Black students who attend high-status schools seem to do rather better than black students who attend low-status schools.[33]

THE IMPLICATIONS OF LARGE-SCALE RESEARCH

Readers who were hoping for findings that could enable us decisively to reject the functional or meritocratic interpretation of differences in school achievement will have been disappointed by the preceding discussion. The balance of the evidence so far does not favor an interpretation stressing that schools reinforce inequalities of class and race between students. Status attainment research, for example, presents a generally meritocratic view of school achievement and attainment. Class differentials in final attainment are considerable, but they can be largely explained by factors outside the schools' control: differences in ability and differences in parental encouragement and student aspirations that are shaped by peers and social background. Teacher expectations for students have an impact on achievement and attainment, but they are largely shaped by prior student performance rather than by class background. Studies of tracking in secondary schools also generally support this meritocratic picture. Track assignments have significant although generally modest effects on students' subsequent careers, but those assignments appear to be solidly based on ability and prior school achievement and to be modestly affected by student social backgrounds. As we also saw in the last chapter, studies of school quality and school climates show significant effects for black students, yet they offer only weak support for the argument that differences in school characteristics can explain much of the differential achievement between students from different social origins. Perhaps better studies with more adequate measures of the school characteristics that matter most would yield different findings, but existing evidence does not warrant the conclusion that a more equitable distribution of desirable school characteristics would greatly change class differentials in school achievement and college attendance. Finally, we have evidence that the social composition of the student body has negligible effects on the achievement of white students and small but positive effects on the achievement of black students. Counterintuitive though it may be, most students do not appear to benefit from going to school with students who have excellent academic records. The balance of the evidence so far does not support a conflict

interpretation of the role of schools in generating inequality. The best
that can be said for this interpretation is that low-status students appear
to experience a steady cumulation of disadvantages during the course
of their school careers. Such students begin school with fewer skills
required for success in courses and they receive less encouragement
from parents and friends. Once in high schools, low-status students
are slightly more likely to be assigned to noncollege tracks than other
students with the same test scores, and these track assignments, though
hardly decisive for future careers, affect the likelihood of college attendance. But if in these respects initial inequalities become magnified
over the course of the school career, we have so far found little evidence
that schools contribute in a major way to such magnification. By and
large, this research tradition says that schools respond relatively meritocratically to enduring differences between students which, in very
large part, have their origin outside school.

However, another interpretation is also possible. Granted that the
die is largely cast by the time students are in high school, it may be
that *school experiences prior* to high school may account for much
of the observed differences between students that large-scale research
measures at around the age of fourteen or fifteen. Measured differences
in ability, grades, and aspirations at this age, in other words, may be
a function of earlier school experiences as well as home background
factors. Although tracking and teacher expectations in secondary
schools appear to be solidly based on prior student achievements rather
than on social class backgrounds, this may not be the case in elementary
school.

ABILITY GROUPING IN PRIMARY SCHOOLS

As we turn our attention from high schools to elementary
schools, the character of the research upon which we rely changes.
Almost all recent research on high schools relies on very large samples
of students and gains the bulk of its information from questionnaires
administered to these students in the classroom. This methodology
necessarily limits the depth and richness of materials that researchers
can gather about day-to-day interaction between teachers and students.
Large-scale researchers do not routinely observe classroom life from
a seat in the back of the room, they often simply visit schools to administer their questionnaires and collect information on grades and test
scores from school records. Critics of large-scale research have pointed
out, therefore, that in this work the school is treated very much as a
"black box," something that has certain effects on student attitudes
or student behavior, but whose nature is left unexamined.[34] The very

nature of large-scale research makes it difficult if not impossible to give detailed attention to the behavior of students and teachers in the classroom.

For a very obvious reason research on primary schools has assumed a different character. It is difficult or impossible to administer questionnaires to eight- or nine-year-old children asking them to report on their parents' social status, their grades, or their friends' aspirations. Such research must rely to a much greater degree on the observations of the researcher rather than on administered questionnaires. This does not necessarily mean that only one school or one classroom can be studied, but it clearly places a severe limit on the number of cases that one or even a team of researchers can examine in a given research project. Although much research on primary schools thus lacks the kind of ready generalizability to all other schools that large-scale research on high schools enjoys, there are important compensatory advantages that flow from its detailed focus on behavior in the classroom. Observational studies of classroom interaction, often supplemented by videotaped records, provide a richness of data that enables the researcher to begin to understand not only *what* effects schools have, but *why* they have these effects.

Self-Fulfilling Prophecies and Grouping Practices in Primary Schools

Two related ideas underlie a great deal of recent research on primary schools. First, almost all research is in one way or another concerned with exploring how teacher expectations for student performance tend to help produce that expected performance. Because teachers respond to and treat students of whom they expect good performance differently than those students of whom they expect little, this hypothesis suggests teachers' expectations become self-fulfilling prophecies. Closely related to this idea is the argument that ability grouping in elementary classrooms helps create inequalities between students. Research on primary schools attempts to describe how teacher-student interaction varies between different ability groups and to assess the nature of the disadvantage that students placed in low-ability groups suffer. Some of this research shows, for example, that students in low-ability groups receive substantially less instruction than students in high-ability groups in the same classroom.[35] In this way, ability grouping itself can become a self-fulfilling prophecy. Predictions about how well students will perform come true not so much because students are different in ability to begin with, but because students who are assigned to different groups are taught in different ways.

The self-fulfilling prophecy hypothesis is a very old one, part of the working assumptions of most sociologists for sixty years. W. I. Thomas, writing in the 1920s, argued that "if men define situations as real, they are real in their consequences."[36] The meaning of a particular action or behavior, Thomas suggested, is not inherent in that action or behavior. Rather, people must attribute meaning to particular acts and their meanings that have consequences for their own actions in the future. From this point of view, therefore, terms like "stupid" or "clever" are not so much qualities that are inherent in particular behaviors or particular individuals, but labels that are commonly applied to certain kinds of acts. Once these labels are applied, certain consequences follow, according to Thomas's theorem. Teachers who label a child as stupid tend to regard a great deal of that child's future behavior as evidence of stupidity and to act toward that child in accordance with that perception despite conscious efforts to be fair and objective.

If labels applied by individual teachers to students are consequential for future behavior and future evaluations, the same should be true of the official labels that schools apply when students are grouped into tracks or streams on the basis of ability. Thus when a teacher is confronted with a class described by other teachers as "slow learners" we should expect that this official label will also shape that teacher's expectations and future behavior.

Rosenthal and Jacobsen's Research

The first and still the best known attempt to apply these ideas to the elementary school classroom was the research of Richard Rosenthal and Lenore Jacobsen in a single primary school in San Francisco.[37] It was their ingenious idea to create different teacher expectations for student progress by telling teachers a number of "white lies" about the ability of the students they were assigned to teach. At the beginning of the school year all students in grades one through six were given a nonverbal IQ test and for most of the students the results of this test were accurately conveyed to the teachers. However, for the purposes of the experiment a random sample of 20 percent of all students in each grade was selected and deliberately misidentified as children of unusual intellectual promise. Rosenthal and Jacobsen's hypothesis was that teachers would act on this false information and proceed to make it "true": Teachers would treat these students differently and in turn they would learn more.

The original experiment was quite successful in producing higher IQ scores by the end of the year among students who had been falsely identified as promising than the students who were not so identified. The gains in IQ scores, especially among the youngest age groups, were more than double for the experimental group than the control group at the end of the school year. Although Rosenthal and Jacobsen did not include the social class background of students in their analysis, it is noteworthy that they found the effects of differential expectations seemed to be particularly powerful for students who looked like minority students.

> *For total I.Q. and reasoning I.Q. those Mexican boys who looked more Mexican benefited more from teacher expectations than did the Mexican boys who looked less Mexican. There is no clear explanation for these findings, but we can speculate that the teacher's pre-experimental expectations of the more Mexican looking boys' intellectual performance was probably lowest of all. These children may have had the most to gain by the introduction of a more favorable expectation into the minds of their teachers.* [38]

Subsequent attempts to replicate the Rosenthal and Jacobsen study, however, have not generally yielded the same dramatic results. Some of these studies did show that teachers' expectations did result in differential treatment of students, but none have been able to show that the IQ scores of those children of whom much was expected dramatically increased. We do not know the reasons for these inconsistent findings. In part it may be that subsequent research was not effective in convincing teachers that the experimental group of students really were different; ironically the very publicity given to the original study may have made teachers more alert to the possibility that they were being deceived. It is also possible that subsequent studies, most of which measured IQ changes at the end of a term rather than a full year, did not allow sufficient time for expectancy effects to work. [39] But whatever the merits of these arguments, it seems clear that the initial excitement that surrounded the findings of the Rosenthal and Jacobsen experiment have given way to a recognition that expectation effects are neither as simple nor perhaps as dramatic as this initial study implied.

Observational Studies of the Self-Fulfilling Prophecy
The great advantage of observational studies of primary school classrooms is that they reveal how teachers form expectations of students in the classroom and how these expectations then become translated into differential treatment over a considerable time. In contrast to experimental studies that rely almost exclusively on before-and-after measurements of the key variables, detailed observation of classroom interaction enables us to understand the processes that lead teachers to form judgments of different students' capabilities, to act on these differential expectations, and student reactions to this treatment.

Ray Rist's study of several all-black elementary schools in St. Louis in the late 1960s was the first major attempt by a sociologist to explore self-fulfilling prophecies in the classroom.[40]

Rist observed the progress of a group of children from the first day of kindergarten throughout the school year and then continued to visit the classroom regularly until the end of the first grade. Perhaps Rist's most striking findings occurred within a few days of the beginning of his study. He found that the (black) teacher assigned her students to three groups within the classroom only a few days after the beginning of the year. The highest, most promising, group was placed at the front of the classroom and the least promising group at the back. Rist found that assignments of these three groups was largely based on class-linked characteristics of students. Darkness of skin color, hair characteristics, dress style, and even smell were used to determine which students should be placed in the three groups. Within this all-black class, the teacher made judgments of academic promise (and likely future behavior) on the basis of characteristics that were strongly related to socioeconomic status. Rist showed that children whose parents were on welfare, those from one-parent households, and children with one or both parents unemployed were much more likely to be assigned to the lowest group placed at the back of the classroom.

During the course of the school year Rist observed sharp differences in the treatment of the three groups. Those who were placed in the front of the classroom received more praise from the teacher, while those who were at the back received more criticism of their work and their general behavior; but most significantly, those in the front of the class received a great deal more *instruction.* "Those designated as 'slow learners' were taught infrequently, subjected to more frequent control-oriented behavior, and received little if any supportive behavior from the teacher."[41] Such initial placements into three ability groups, Rist observes, soon took on a caste-like character. Not only was there virtually no mobility from one group to another during the course of the school year, academic differentials between the groups increased as the year progressed. This was not, Rist believes, because the children in the lowest group were not able to learn; indeed, in visits to the homes of these children Rist was able to ascertain that they did grasp the material that was taught in class. Rather, these children failed because the "patterns of classroom instruction initiated by the teacher inhibited the low status children from verbalizing what knowledge they had accumulated."[42]

By the end of the kindergarten year objective data about the academic performance of these different students were used to make assignments to ability tracks in the first grade. Rist reported a strong relationship between such assignments to groups in the first grade and the original group assignments in the beginning of the kindergarten year. All the students in the original top grouping in kindergarten who remained in the school were assigned to the top group in the first grade. None of the remaining students were assigned to that top group. Even a year later, by the beginning of the second grade, there was virtually no mobility from the original low group in the kindergarten to the top group. "The distribution of social and economic factors from the kindergarten year remained essentially unchanged in the second grade."[43]

Rist's findings are noteworthy in several respects. First, Rist found that teacher expectations of student performance were shaped largely by ascribed and class-related characteristics of the children. If the children looked and acted like middle-class children and if school records indicated that their parents were not on welfare, they were likely to be assigned to the fast group placed in the front of the classroom. Second, he concluded that once initial ability group assignments had been made they were likely to be relatively permanent with little or no mobility between groups. Third, and potentially most important, Rist observed sharply different patterns of interaction between teachers and students in the three ability groups. Students in the lower groups received less praise and more negative evaluations from teachers. They also received considerably less instruction and had fewer opportunities to answer substantive questions from the teacher. Although Rist has no data indicating that students in the low-ability groups did objectively learn less during the year, there is in the findings the strong implication that ability grouping is a major mechanism by which teachers' expectations become self-fulfilling prophecies.

Subsequent research has not always confirmed Rist's specific charges of teacher bias in the treatment of lower-ability tracks, but a number of studies have provided support for the major thrust of his findings. In a study of kindergarten classrooms in Harlem, Machler found that assignment to ability groups was heavily influenced by such traits as politeness and willingness to follow teacher directions, and, like Rist, he also found that once track assignments had been made there was very little movement of students from one group to another over the course of the school year.[44] There is also good evidence from longitudinal studies of British children that ability grouping in elementary schools has important effects on subsequent test scores. By age eleven, Douglas reports, students who were assigned to high-ability tracks at age eight showed substantially greater gains in achievement than students assigned to low-ability tracks.[45]

The Research of Eder and McDermott

Two recent studies of grouping within elementary school classrooms extend Rist's conclusions in important ways. Both Eder, in a study of a Wisconsin kindergarten class, and McDermott, in research on black elementary school children in New York, used detailed classroom observations and video-tape recordings to study how ability grouping in the classroom affects learning to read.[46] In all the classrooms studied teachers taught children to read by having each child take a turn at reading aloud to the rest of the group. For a child to be successful, therefore, it is crucially important for him or her to have a chance to take a turn at reading and to receive the teacher's undivided attention while doing so. At first sight the ability groups into which the class was divided aid this process because they avoid the problem of large discrepancies in reading readiness between children in the same reading circle. But both investigators report that *low-ability group children were much less likely to get a chance to read to the group than those in the high-ability group.* Eder reports that reading turns were disrupted twice as often in the low-ability group as in the high group, and that students in the low group were much less likely to listen attentively while another student was reading than in the high-ability group.[47] Furthermore, in the low-ability group a much higher percentage of the teacher's time was spent on managing the activities of inattentive students, which made it difficult for her to concentrate her attention on the child whose turn it was to read.

Over the course of the school year, Eder reports, a different set of norms developed in the two groups.[48] In the high-ability group it was expected that there would be a smooth progression around the reading circle, with each student taking his or her turn to read and the others waiting for their turn. In the low-ability group other children would not wait their turn and would supply words at the first sign of hesitation of the child whose turn it was. Teachers were less likely to reprimand children who interrupted in the low-ability group and, partly as a result, the number of reading turn violations more than doubled over the course of the year. McDermott reports almost identical findings. In the low-ability group he studied the teacher abandoned the regular turn-taking procedure that was used for the top group, and children spent much of their time attempting to attract the teacher's attention to get a turn to read rather than concentrating or listening to the child who was reading.[49] Thus in McDermott's as in Eder's classroom a vicious circle was created. Because of lack of trust and confidence that they would get a turn to read, children spent a considerable amount of time attempting to interrupt the child who was reading and to attract the teacher's attention. This made it less likely that when their turn came they would be able to read without interruption and to enjoy the teacher's individual attention.

Neither investigator blames the teacher for this unsatisfactory state of affairs, as Rist tended to do in his study. Instead, teachers are seen as victims of organizational and management problems that are inherently difficult to resolve. Teaching reading in these classrooms involves managing the attention of listeners while simultaneously instructing the one child who is reading aloud. In high-ability groups that task is manageable because the child in question can usually read in comprehensible fashion and because the other children are reasonably attentive. But in low-ability groups neither of these conditions is likely to be present. Because these children are less likely to be attentive they require more management activities on the part of the teacher, which undercuts her effort to teach the individual student who is reading. And because the student who is reading is less likely to learn to read in such a way that the other students can follow along, these other students have less reason to be attentive. Thus initial differences in attentiveness and reading ability which led to ability group assignments at the beginning of the year are likely to become larger over time. McDermott summarizes:

> . . . *For every day in the classroom, the children who are considered less able fall further behind their contemporaries and give the teacher further reasons to handle them differently. Thus, the small differences between children in the early years of school expand quickly to the drastic forms of differential performance which becomes obvious in later years. At the root of these differences is not so much the extreme complexity of the school tasks, nor the differences of the learning potential of the different children, but the differential environments we offer the children for getting organized and on task so that learning can take place.*[50]

EVALUATION AND IMPLICATIONS OF PRIMARY SCHOOL RESEARCH

Considerable caution is needed in interpreting these potentially exciting findings about the effects of self-fulfilling prophecies and ability grouping in elementary schools. Observational studies alone, no matter how carefully conceived and executed, cannot yield the kind of relatively precise estimates of the magnitude of these effects that large-scale research on many schools can provide. Nor are case studies of two classrooms sufficient evidence that students are sorted into ability groups largely on the basis of their social class background rather than on the basis of their ability. One recent large-scale study of precisely this issue suggests that by these criteria, ability tracking in the elementary school, like tracking in secondary schools, is primarily meritocratic in character.[51] At the same time, however, there are some good theoretical and empirical reasons for believing it is to elementary rather than high school education that we must look if we are to find ways in which schools work to magnify and reinforce inequalities among students.

First, what little large-scale research there is on elementary schools consistently shows more powerful effects of differences in schools on inequalities among students than research on high schools. The research on the effects of school quality we reviewed in the previous chapter, for example, shows that while such indicators as teacher qualifications and school expenditures have almost no effects on student learning at the *high school level* they do have some measurable and significant effects on the performance of elementary school children. This seems to imply, therefore, that improving the quality of elementary schools will help low-achieving students more than improving the quality of high schools.

Research on tracking also shows more consistently positive effects at the elementary school level. Assignment to a college track in high school has relatively powerful effects on expectations but, after controls are made for test scores before track assignments, relatively minor effects remain on achievement. At the elementary level, on the other hand, there is a developing body of evidence that ability grouping is indeed a self-fulfilling prophecy. As early as kindergarten, and certainly by first grade, most elementary school students are divided into reading groups. It is becoming increasingly clear that these assignments are highly consequential for future achievement. Students in the low-ability groups, perhaps because they are simply taught less, learn less quickly than other students. And it seems likely that both their expectations of their own future performance and teachers' expectations for that performance diminish. Also, once children are assigned to a particular ability group they tend to remain there for at least a year and perhaps for their elementary school career. Whereas this caste-like character of ability grouping may be partly a result of indolence or prejudice on the part of teachers, it also reflects real differences in student performance partly created by the grouping process itself. No doubt students assigned to different groups are somewhat different to begin with, but there is good evidence that these initial predictions of future performance are generally accurate because the effects of the groups themselves help make these predictions come true.

All this evidence allows us to give a more affirmative answer to the question posed by the title of this chapter for elementary schools than for high schools. For the latter, we have to conclude that although high school tracks have some effects on subsequent performance and track assignments are not perfectly meritocratic, the data generally support the functionalist rather than the conflict interpretation of unequal performance in school. High schools by and large seem to respond to existing differences between students in ability, motivation, and aspirations, rather than to create such differences. Although middle- and upper-class students enjoy advantages in high schools in the form of parental and peer encouragement that disadvantaged students do not have, these advantages do not seem to be the result of discrimination by the school. But observational research on elementary schools suggests that it is a mistake to generalize from these negative findings at the high school level to schools in general and to conclude, as many large-scale researchers have done, that inequality in school achievement is almost entirely a product of differences in home environments or other factors outside the school's control.

By around age fourteen, aptitude and ability scores of students are quite stable and allow us to predict future achievement with some accuracy. But this is not true of aptitude and ability scores at age six or seven, nor of academic expectations.[52] For young children, there is a great deal of malleability in the aptitudes, habits, and skills that produce success in school and there is, therefore, much more "room" for schools, teachers, parents, and peers to have quite powerful effects on these characteristics. Elementary schools, when asked to defend these grouping practices, can point to what they take to be objective differences between students in aptitude and skills. The terms "aptitude," "ability," and "intelligence," as they are commonly understood in our society, suggest the influence of genetic and early environmental influences rather than skills that are learned in schools. But the evidence from observational studies of elementary schools implies that part, and perhaps a large part, of these differences on objective tests may reflect the results of grouping practices in schools and the impact of differential treatments of students in these different groups. What are slight differences in reading readiness at age five may become, by age six or seven, quite large differences in scores on objective tests.

HOME ENVIRONMENTS AND SCHOOL SUCCESS

As we saw in the last chapter, a largely ideological debate between proponents of cultural deficits and cultural differences has obscured how little we really know about the impact of home environments on school performance. The cultural deficit theory sees the failure of lower-class children in school as a result of the absence of the kind of stimulating environments conducive to the development of intelligence. It has been justly criticized on the grounds that it is both too simple in its assertion that intelligence is indeed the main factor in school success and misleading in its account of how intelligence develops. But the cultural difference model is hardly satisfactory either.

In its rejection of the results of IQ tests and its refusal to characterize lower-class environments as in any way inferior for the development of intellectual skills, the cultural differences model merely asserts without evidence that in other kinds of (presumably nonmiddle class or nonracist) schools lower-class children would do better. There are some signs, however, that research is beginning to move away from this relatively sterile controversy toward an emphasis on the kinds of skills and attributes that lead to success in school and the fit between those skills and what is taught to young children in different kinds of home environments. Thus the appropriate question is not "Why are disadvantaged children less intelligent than privileged children?" nor even "Why do schools consciously or unconsciously discriminate against lower class children?" but rather "In what ways do the cultural emphases of middle-class environments match the particular skills and attitudes that schools demand of their students?"

One piece of pioneering research that helps illuminate this question is Bernstein's research on the differing *communication codes* of lower- and middle-class children in England.[53] Bernstein argues that schools require students to use language "universalistically," to make meaning explicit rather than to leave it implicit, and to use language in such a way that speech and writing are freed from a particular context and made understandable to all. This rather complicated assertion can best be illustrated by an example of lower-class and middle-class responses to a particular task. In one experiment, five-year-old children were asked to tell a story represented in four pictures: some boys playing football, the ball going through a window, a man making a threatening gesture, and a woman looking out of the window and the boys moving away. The middle-class child told the following story:

> *Three boys are playing football and one boy kicks the ball and it goes through the window the ball breaks the window and the boys are looking at it and a man comes out and shouts at them because they had broken the window so they run away and then that lady looks out of her window and she tells the boys off. (Number of nouns: 13. Number of pronouns: 6.)*

The lower-class child told the following story based on the same pictures:

> *They're playing football and he kicks it and it goes through there it breaks the window and they're looking at it and he comes out and he shouts at them because they'd broken it so they run away and then she looks out and she tells them off. (Number of nouns: 2. Number of pronouns: 14.)[54]*

The lower-class child tells the story without freeing it from the context that generated it. Indeed, the child's story would be incomprehensible to the listener without knowledge of the pictures. The middle-class child, on the other hand, spells out the meanings of the story in universalistic fashion so that they are accessible even to those who are not aware of the initial context. Using these and similar examples, Bernstein argues that lower-class children are not verbally deprived, but that they are oriented toward particularistic orders of meaning that are context-specific. Lower-class children often do not understand that the school requires abandonment of this mode of language use, and teachers, insensitive or unaware of the translation problems that lower-class children face, tend to assume that such children lack verbal ability. Bernstein concludes that the teachers

> *must be able to understand the child's dialect, rather than deliberately attempting to change it. Much of the context of our schools is unwittingly drawn from aspects of a symbolic world of the middle class, and so when the child steps into school he is stepping into a symbolic system that does not provide for him a linkage with his life outside.*[55]

Bernstein's work is difficult and obscure and has been misunderstood by many who claim that he is talking about differences in "verbal skills" and "verbal sophistication" between lower- and middle-class populations.[56] But Bernstein denies that lower-class populations lack verbal facility. Instead he asserts that differences in early socialization lead to different linguistic codes that govern the ways in which language will be used in particular situations. Lower-class children, he argues, learn a restricted code which dictates that in most, but not all, situations the meanings of what is said are left implicit and the context that generated what is said is not spelled out. Middle-class children, on the other hand, while their speech with their peers may be similarly implicit, acquire an elaborated code that dictates explicit and universalistic meanings when they are in the company of adults. Lower-class children in school, therefore, face the problem of switching codes: not so much learning to speak in standard middle-class English, but using language in a different and more explicit way than that generally prevailing in their home environment. Whereas Bernstein himself draws few direct policy implications from his work, it would appear that the problem of lower-class failure in schools must be addressed by finding ways of making it easier for these children to shift between these two linguistic codes.

Very different from Bernstein's research but complementary in its implications is work on class-related values and attitudes that stress how working-class and middle-class parents differ in how they prepare their children to play the role of the student. Hess, Shipman, and Jackson, for example, studied what they termed the "socialization styles" of 160 black middle- and working-class mothers of four-year-old children and observed each mother teaching her child in the laboratory.[57]

Although there was little difference among the mothers in the amount of affection given their children, there were sharp differences by social status in how effectively mothers communicated to their children the way in which particular tasks should be carried out. The high-status mothers helped their children plan the task and communicated each of the steps that had to be followed for successful performance. When asked how they would prepare their children to go to school, "working class mothers appeared to be socializing impassive learning styles on the part of the child, teaching him to be docile in such learning situations, in contrast to the more active initiatory behavior of a child from a middle class home." Lower-income mothers stressed the importance of good behavior and following the instructions of the teacher; middle-class parents stressed that their children must be active learners who seek information from the teacher rather than passively following instructions.

Melvin Kohn, in an important study of child-rearing practices, reaches parallel conclusions.[58] What distinguishes lower- from higher-status parents in their child-rearing attitudes, Kohn concludes, is the greater emphasis of low-status parents on good manners, obedience, and conformity to external rules. Middle-class parents, in contrast, stress self-control and the development of their children's ability to shape the environment through their own efforts. Whereas middle-class parents encourage exploration, curiosity, and control over aggressive impulses in the children, lower-class parents emphasize conformity to external rules, obedience, and respectability.

There is some support for the argument that part of the relatively greater success of middle-class children in school can be attributed to acquisition of these differential values. For example, Virginia Crandall reports that, among young children, high-achieving students were able to work without immediate rewards, displaying substantial self-reliance and greater emotional control.[59] Many lower-class children, in contrast, lacked this emotional control and the ability to work for future rewards; many of them are, Harry Miller reports, excessively dependent on the approval of teachers and unwilling or unable to act without specific instructions from the teacher.[60]

Research on class-linked values and attitudes, therefore, shifts attention away from a purely cognitive approach to school success toward a concern with how well students from different social backgrounds are equipped to play the role of the student successfully. There is mounting evidence that, at least as far as elementary school is concerned, teacher judgments of students' behavior and deportment, in addition to sheer intellectual competence, are of great importance in their evaluations and their future treatment of students. Entwisle's research on first grade students, for example, reports that there is a high correlation between teachers' assessment of students' conduct during the year, and grades for academic performance.[61] In the fluid environment of the first grade, Entwisle suggests, where there is as yet little objective evidence of academic competence, teachers use a child's deportment and conduct as indicators of whether that child is likely to be a good student. As in much other research on elementary school achievement, Entwisle finds that once students are typecast as good or bad students on the basis of conduct that evaluation seems to predict future performance very well.

CONCLUSION

There is no simple answer to the question posed at the beginning of this chapter. In the crude and obvious sense of the term, schools do not discriminate against students from disadvantaged backgrounds. At the high school level at least, grades assigned to students seem to reflect performance rather than teacher bias. Although some teachers are undoubtedly prejudiced, they generally base their expectations and encouragement on what students have done in school rather than students' social origins. There is some evidence that track assignments slightly favor middle-class students even after student performance is taken into account, but against this should be set the finding that black students are rather more likely to be in college preparatory tracks than their test scores would predict.

Furthermore, the research is virtually unanimous in its finding that the most easily measured aspects of school quality have little to do with differentials in school success between advantaged and disadvantaged students. The characteristics of schools that one can most easily change, pupil-teacher ratios, teacher qualifications, the level of resources available to students, have very little measurable effect on student learning and cannot serve as an explanation of why, over time, disadvantaged students seem to fall further and further behind.

The evidence on tracking in the high school and on the impact of student cultures is more equivocal in its implications. On the one hand, most research does not support the view that teachers and counselors, in the United States at least, regularly discriminate against students from low-status origins. Track assignments appear to be solidly based on past academic records and test scores and only small correlations between social class and track assignments remain after these factors are controlled for. At the same time, track assignments have relatively modest effects on test scores. The major reason why students in different tracks differ in their school performance is because these students differed *before* track assignments rather than because of any effect of superior teaching or more advanced curriculum. Nevertheless, track assignments do seem to have significant effects on aspirations and future educational attainment, and in this respect we can say that high school tracking magnifies or compounds existing inequalities between students. Since educational attainment, and college attendance in particular, appears to be at least as important as test scores in predicting future occupations, this is a significant finding. If tracks did not exist, we might surmise, relatively more lower-class students might attend college than is presently the case.

The role of student cultures is even more difficult to assess. Some evidence from ethnographic studies of high school classrooms in Great Britain, for example, suggests that in many schools a hostile predominantly lower-class student subculture develops and this plays a major role in inhibiting student effort and depresses student achievement.[62] There is little evidence from large-scale research that such subcultures have important effects in the United States (at least for white students), perhaps because of the inherent limitations of large-scale research in measuring such effects, or perhaps because such rebellious and class-based subcultures are less common in this country. For black students, by contrast, there is evidence that exposure to peers who hold either strongly favorable or strongly unfavorable attitudes toward academic work does have significant effects—a finding that certainly fits with impressionistic observations of life in some inner-city predominantly black schools. Although the tracking evidence for black high school students does not support a conflict interpretation, there is some evidence that the academic achievement of black students is depressed by attending schools with predominantly low-achieving peers.

Perhaps the most important findings in this chapter, however, concern elementary rather than high schools. Whereas an interpretation that stresses the role of the home environment in shaping ability and aspirations and the relatively neutral role of the school fits the data on high schools rather well, it does not square with recent research on elementary schools. With five- or six-year-old children the school appears to be far from a neutral arena in which preexisting differences in talent or motivation become manifest. Some studies show that ability grouping and teacher expectations in elementary schools may have decisive effects on student careers. At this young age, abilities and aptitudes are neither well formed nor easy to assess. For their organizational purposes, nonetheless, most schools find it necessary to assess them and divide students into ability groups. No doubt most schools and teachers try to avoid employing ascriptive criteria when they make judgments about such matters as reading readiness or future "promise." But there is considerable evidence that class-linked behavior plays an important part in such judgments. Schools justify grouping by reference to such presumably universalistic and meritocratic criteria as ability and academic aptitude, but at this young age, it may be extremely difficult to distinguish these characteristics from behavior that simply represents lack of familiarity with the classroom setting, lack of knowledge of the alphabet, or ignorance of appropriate behavior toward teachers.

What makes these speculative conclusions important is that there is good evidence that decisions made by teachers at the beginning of students' careers are of great importance for subsequent achievement. Relatively few students who are assigned to low-ability groups in the first grade are successful in climbing to higher-ability groups a year or two later.[62] And by this time the results of objective tests are available to confirm the school's initial judgment. Probably by the age of eight or nine, and almost certainly by the age of twelve or thirteen, differences in scores on objective tests of ability do reflect enduring differences among students that are difficult to modify. Many schools undoubtedly congratulate themselves that their initial predictions at age five or six forecast these later scores so well. But these predictions in the first year of elementary school seem in considerable part to be accurate because differential treatment *makes them true.* Elementary schools, unlike high schools, appear to help create the differences among students to which they claim merely to react, and while the mechanisms by which these self-fulfilling prophecies work are not well understood, it appears that children in low-ability groups within the classroom do not get as many opportunities to demonstrate their knowledge and skills and receive less instruction than other students.

Thus there is a growing body of evidence that it is in the very first years of school that the educational process most often works to the disadvantage of lower-class students. It is particularly frustrating, therefore, that we really understand very little about precisely how home environments, class, and early school experiences interact with one another. We do not know very much about the kinds of intellectual skills that are most critical for success in the first years of schooling nor how those skills are modified by experiences of success or failure at the tasks children must perform, although we know that "intelligence" is far too general a rubric to describe them. Nor do we know very much about how children from different social origins learn to play the role of students, to pay attention to teachers, to sit quietly for long periods of time, and to begin to conceive of themselves as good or bad students. Research on these questions is a great deal more difficult than the large-scale research on high school achievement that has dominated the field for the last fifteen years. Such research requires that sociologists must give up some of their reliance on questionnaires and traditional objective measures of student achievement. Without time-consuming observational studies, however, it is difficult to see how further progress can be made.

Endnotes

1. At least this has been the case since the findings of research on school quality and school resources became widely known.

2. Of course not all researchers working within the broad tradition believe this, but the functionalist perspective generally subscribes to this model. For similar usage, see Karl L. Alexander and Martha A. Cook, "Curricula and Coursework: A Surprise Ending to a Familiar Story," *American Sociological Review* 47, No. 5 (October 1982): 636.

3. Nell Keddie, "Classroom Knowledge," in M. F. D. Young (ed.), *Knowledge and Control* (London: Collier, 1971).

4. For a sensitive early account of this ascription process, see Aaron V. Cicourel and John I. Kitsuse, *The Educational Decision-Makers* (New York: Bobbs-Merrill, 1963).

5. Assessing parental and teacher expectations by a direct inquiry is, of course, very expensive and time consuming in a large-scale survey.

6. For an account of the biases introduced by using student track perceptions instead of relying on school records, see James E. Rosenbaum, "Track Misperceptions and Frustrated College Plans: An Analysis of the Effects of Tracks and Track Perceptions in the National Longitudinal Survey," *Sociology of Education*, Vol. 53, No. 2 (April 1980): 74–88.

7. The most famous example is Ray Rist, "Social Class and Teacher Expectations: The Self-Fulfilling Prophecy in Ghetto Education," *Harvard Educational Review*, Vol. 40 (1976): 411–451.

8. For a useful summary of the findings of work in this tradition, see William H. Sewell and Robert M. Hauser, "Causes and Consequences of Higher Education: Modes of the Status Attainment Process," in William H. Sewell, Robert M. Hauser, and David L. Featherman (eds.), *Schooling and Achievement in American Society* (New York: Academic Press, 1976), pp. 9–28.

9. Status attainment research is as concerned with the relationship between school attainment and occupational attainment as with the determinants of success in school; here, however, our concern is exclusively with the latter.

10. Karl L. Alexander, Bruce K. Eckland, and Larry J. Griffin, "The Wisconsin Model of Socio-Economic Achievement: A Replication," *American Journal of Sociology*, Vol. 81 (1975): 324–342; and Christopher Jencks, *Who Gets Ahead?* (New York: Basic Books, 1979).

11. Sewell and Hauser, "Causes and Consequences," p. 13.

12. See Bowles and Gintis's discussion of grades in Samuel Bowles and Herbert Gintis, *Schooling in Capitalist America* (New York: Basic Books, 1976), pp.

135–138. Contrast this with Christopher Jencks, et al., *Inequality* (New York: Basic Books, 1972): "When we compare economically advantaged students to disadvantaged students with the same test scores, for example, we find that they get the same average high school grades" p. 139. See also Paul Di Maggio, "Cultural Capital and School Success: The Impact of Status Culture Participation on the Grades of U.S. High School Students," *American Sociological Review,* Vol. 47 (April 1982): 189–201. Di Maggio reports no relationship between grades and social class when test scores are held constant, but he finds evidence that interest in and knowledge of high culture shapes grades when test scores are controlled.

13. Sewell and Hauser, "Causes and Consequences."

14. Ibid., p. 22.

15. Ibid., p. 22.

16. Christopher Jencks, *Who Gets Ahead?* (New York: Basic Books, 1979). This also seems true for Jencks's own earlier work.

17. Denise C. Gottfredson, "Black-White Differences in the Educational Attainment Process: What Have We Learned?" *American Sociological Review,* Vol. 46 (October 1981): 542–557.

18. Lewis Coser, "Presidential Address: Two Methods in Search of Substance," *American Sociological Review,* Vol. 40 (1978): 691–700; and Patrick Horan, "Is Status Attainment Research Atheoretical?" *American Sociological Review,* Vol. 43 (1978): 534–541. Horan argues, I think correctly, that the research contains an implicit functionalist model despite its atheoretical appearance.

19. With the conspicuous exception of Jencks, *Inequality,* researchers in this tradition seem either uncritical of, or not curious about, the concept of "ability" or "intelligence," as their omission of quotation marks around these concepts suggests. Implicitly, therefore, they tend to assume that tests administered at about the age of fourteen years are measuring enduring intellectual characteristics that have their origin prior to the beginning of schooling, rather than skills that are modified by experiences in schools.

20. Alexander and Cook, op. cit. Jencks reports that among northern urban students with the same test scores, those with white collar parents were only 3% more likely to be in the college curriculum than those with blue-collar parents. Jencks, *Inequality,* op. cit., p. 35.

21. Alexander and Cook, "Curricula and Coursework."

22. Ibid., p. 633.

23. Jencks, *Inequality,* p. 108.

24. Alexander and Cook, "Curricula and Coursework."

25. Ibid.

26. Karl Alexander and Edward McDill, "Selection and Allocation within Schools," *American Sociological Review,* Vol. 41 (December 1976): 963–980.

27. In addition to the above citations, see Richard A. Rehberg and Evelyn R. Rosenthal, *Class and Merit in the American High School* (New York: Longman, 1978).

28. Walter E. Schafer and Carol Blexa, *Tracking and Opportunity: The Locking-out Process and Beyond* (Scranton, Penn.: Chandler, 1971).

29. Edward L. McDill, Leo C. Rigsby, and Edmund D. Meyers, Jr., "Educational Climates of High Schools: Their Effects and Sources," *American Journal of Sociology,* Vol. 74 (1969): 567–568.

30. Robert M. Hauser, "Contextual Analysis Revisited," *Sociological Methods and Research*, Vol. 2 (February 1974): 365–375; Duane F. Alvin and Luther B. Otto, "High School Context Effects and Aspirations," *Sociology of Education*, Vol. 50 (October 1977): 259–273; John W. Meyer, "High School Effects on College Intentions," *American Journal of Sociology*, Vol. 76 (July 1970): 59–70; and Christopher Jencks and Marsha Brown, "The Effects of High Schools on Their Students," *Harvard Educational Review*, Vol. 45 (1975): 273–324.

31. Meyer, "High School Effects," p. 63.

32. Clarence Thornton and Bruce K. Eckland, "High School Contextual Effects for Black and White Students: A Research Note," *Sociology of Education*, Vol. 53 (October 1980): 247–252.

33. But these effects seem to be very small. Ibid.

34. Rebecca Barr and Robert Dreeben, *How Schools Work* (Chicago: University of Chicago Press, 1983).

35. Ray Rist, "Social Class and Teacher Expectations: The Self-Fulfilling Prophecy in Ghetto Education," *Harvard Educational Review*, Vol. 40 (1970): 411–451.

36. W. I. Thomas, *The Child in America* (New York: Knopf, 1928).

37. Robert Rosenthal and Lenore Jacobsen, *Pygmalion in the Classroom* (New York: Holt, Rinehart and Winston, 1968).

38. Ibid., p. 82.

39. Jere Brophy and Thomas Good, *Teacher-Student Relationships* (New York: Holt, Rinehart and Winston, 1974).

40. Rist, "Social Class."

41. Ibid., p. 73.

42. Ibid., p. 86.

43. Ibid., p. 92.

44. B. Mackler, "Grouping in the Ghetto," *Education and Urban Society*, Vol. 2 (1969): 80–96.

45. J. Douglas, *The Home and the School* (London: McGibbon and Kee, 1964).

46. Donna Eder, "Ability Grouping as a Self-Fulfilling Prophecy: A Micro-Analysis of Teacher-Student Interaction," *Sociology of Education*, Vol. 54 (July 1981): 151–162; Diane Felmlee and Donna Eder, "Contextual Effects in the Classroom: The Impact of Ability Groups on Student Attention," *Sociology of Education*, Vol. 56 (April 1983): 77–78; R. P. McDermott, "Social Relations as Contexts for Learning," *Harvard Educational Review*, Vol. 47 (1977): 198–213; and R. P. McDermott, "Kids Make Sense," unpublished Ph.D. dissertation, Stanford University, Stanford, Calif. See also Barr and Dreeben, *How Schools Work*.

47. Eder, "Ability Grouping as a Self-Fulfilling Prophecy."

48. Ibid.

49. McDermott, "Kids Make Sense."

50. Ibid., p. 179. See also Brian Rowan and Andrew W. Miracle, Jr., "Systems of Ability Grouping and the Stratification of Achievement in Elementary Schools," *Sociology of Education*, Vol. 56 (July 1983): 133–144.

51. Emil J. Haller and Sharon A. Davis, "Teacher Perceptions, Parental Social Status and Grouping for Reading Instruction," *Sociology of Education*, Vol. 54 (July 1981): 162–173.

52. Dorris Entwisle and Leslie Hayduk, "Academic Expectations and the School Attainment of Young Children," *Sociology of Education,* Vol. 54 (January 1981): 34–50.

53. Basil Bernstein (ed.), *Class, Codes and Control,* three volumes (London: Routledge and Kegan Paul, 1973, 1974, 1976).

54. Basil Bernstein, "Education Cannot Compensate for Society," *New Society,* Vol. 26 (February 1970): 345.

55. Ibid., p. 347.

56. Even in Sarane Boocock's excellent book, for example, we find that Bernstein is interpreted as saying that "middle class children are exposed to a richer, more varied and more grammatically correct verbal communication, which gives them a head start in school." Boocock, *An Introduction to the Sociology of Education* (Boston: Houghton Mifflin, 1972), p. 36.

57. R. Hess, V. Shipman, and D. Jackson, "Some New Dimensions in Providing Equal Educational Opportunity," *Journal of Negro Education,* Vol. 34 (1965): 220–231.

58. Melvin Kohn, "Social Class and Parent-Child Relationships: An Interpretation," *American Journal of Sociology* (1968): 471–480.

59. Virginia Crandall, "Achievement Behavior in Young Children," *Young Children* 20 (1964): 77–90.

60. Harry Miller, *Education for the Disadvantaged* (New York. Free Press, 1967).

61. Entwisle and Hayduk, "Academic Expectations."

62. Paul Willis, *Learning to Labor* (New York: Columbia University Press, 1981). See also Arthur Stinchcombe, *Rebellion in a High School* (New York: Quadrangle Books, 1964).

chapter 7

What Schools Teach:
Problems of
Cultural Transmission

Psychologists often use projective tests to reveal a subject's innermost feelings and anxieties. The subject is presented with a fundamentally ambiguous picture—perhaps a picture of a woman, a child, and a weapon—and the psychologist then asks the respondent to tell a story about what these individuals are thinking, feeling, and doing. The idea, of course, is not that there is one correct interpretation of the picture, but that one can use such an ambiguous stimulus to elicit the true state of mind of the actor.

I suggest that this rather unconventional analogy is useful in understanding recent assertions about what schools teach and fail to teach. Statements about the failings of schools appear to be assertions about what is objectively true: Schools are failing to teach basic skills, they are engulfed by a rising tide of mediocrity, or, as radical critics often argue, they repress students' natural creativity and reinforce the hegemony of the capitalist order. But I think it is useful to think of these kinds of statements not only as empirical assertions that are true or false but as reflections of the values and state of mind of the observer as well. Fashions in school criticism have changed enormously over time; the changing character of these criticisms *may* provide clues to changes in what schools actually teach or fail to teach, but they may tell us even more about our changing societal preoccupations: from a concern with growth and development of the individual in the 1960s and early 1970s, to increasing worries about excellence and declining standards in the 1980s.

I do not mean to suggest that we should abandon efforts to discover, in some objective sense, what schools actually teach to their students. A substantial section of this chapter will be concerned with research that specifically addresses that question. I do suggest, however, that a rather different task is equally important: to understand how schools in modern society have become a lightning rod attracting an almost bewildering variety of criticisms, united only by the common conviction that they are failing to do what they ought to be doing and that the need for reform is urgent.

Schools have always been the object of political and cultural controversy. In almost every society some adults have complained that the young did not respect their elders as they did "in their day" and that the hard-won knowledge and skills of one generation were inadequately taught to the next. In Roman and Victorian times, for example, one can find complaints that schools are failing to teach literacy, respect for authority, and that standards of discipline have declined.[1] Schools were also attacked, although less frequently, by such critics as Rousseau, Pestalozzi, and Comenius for quite different failings: Discipline was too harsh, the needs and desires of the child were not considered, and the curriculum was out of step with the changing times.[2]

There is little doubt, however, that the volume of school criticism has greatly increased in recent decades. Since World War II, U.S. schools have been the object of a prodigious volume of criticism.[3] In the early and mid 1980s, as well as in the 1960s, schools were attacked for what seem at first sight classically conservative reasons: Standards of intellectual achievement were falling, standards of achievement and discipline were abysmally low, and excellence and quality were nowhere to be found. In the late 1960s, and for much of the 1970s, quite different criticisms were more popular: Schools failed to create equality of opportunity, they discriminated against students from lower-status backgrounds, their teaching methods and curricula were out of date and largely irrelevant to the needs of students, and they fostered conformity rather than creativity. Fashions in educational criticism have changed; however, the volume of that criticism has remained high almost throughout the post–World War II period. Why, then, have people of the United States been so chronically dissatisfied with schools for the last three decades?

THE EROSION OF AN AUTHORITATIVE CULTURAL HERITAGE

To understand this dissatisfaction, and the bewildering variety of complaints that are leveled against schools, we need to grasp the impact of the knowledge revolution and increasing cultural diversity on the nature of the educational process. Although formal education was never as simple and noncontroversial a process as we may sometimes imagine, it has become enormously more complicated and controversial because of the erosion of the authoritative cultural heritage that used to form its foundation. Schools used to teach an authoritative body of truth and wisdom and a set of unquestioned values and ideals to their students. But the knowledge revolution and increasing cultural diversity have destroyed much of the consensus that used to exist about that task. What schools *in fact* teach is much more difficult to describe than it was in the past. And equally important, there has been steadily increasing controversy about what schools *should* teach, in other words, what principles or objectives should replace the old and no longer viable traditional conception of what education should do. Our increasing dissatisfaction with schools is a result of these conflicting objectives and rising expectations.

The Knowledge Revolution

The first step in understanding recent dissatisfactions with schooling is to comprehend how the knowledge revolution affects the traditional curriculum and traditional conceptions of education. The vast explosion of knowledge in the modern world has irrevocably undermined the authoritative character of the cultural heritage of modern societies.[4] Schools used to be seen as places where children learned the seemingly permanent wisdom of the past, where they were told what was true and what was false in quite unambiguous fashion, and where teaching techniques like rote learning and memorization reflected this authoritative conception of education.[5] For some decades now, modern Western societies have lost this conviction of a body of enduring truth and wisdom that justified the traditional school of the past. Because of the explosion of knowledge in this century we are less sure than our ancestors about what particular things children should be taught, and because we have lost this certainty we tend also to see the traditional teaching methods of the past as insufferably authoritarian.

In the not so distant past, schools used to teach a curriculum that was a direct descendant of, and bore many similarities to, a course of study first formulated in the Renaissance.[6] And that curriculum, it is sometimes forgotten, was in many respects a revival of the curriculum employed in schools in Roman times.[7] Even today, most schools teach three subjects—grammar, arithmetic, and geometry—that would have been recognized by students in ancient Rome over 2,000 years ago. Nor has it been many decades since Latin and Rhetoric, two equally ancient disciplines, were required courses in almost every high school and college.[8] Thus the core subjects of the curriculum, with the exception of the scientific disciplines, are of very ancient origin.

Even in the United States, where the tradition of high culture has long been weaker than in Europe, schools continued to teach a curriculum originally designed for the education of a leisured elite until well into this century. The emphasis in such a curriculum, furthermore, was on memorizing rules and facts rather than on understanding and discovery. Students were expected to learn the rules of English grammar, memorize certain mathematical formulae by heart, and know the names of the principal actors and the dates of major events in Western history.

Although vestiges of this curriculum still persist, the revolution in human knowledge in this century has destroyed its intellectual justification. The traditional curriculum implied a conception of knowledge as a set of eternal and authoritative truths accumulated over many centuries. Knowledge was the result of the wisdom of great individuals and the moral truths and lessons that could be drawn from the success and failure of past civilizations. Most knowledge was not seen as primarily contemporary in character.

Today, however, most knowledge is recent knowledge. About four out of five scientists who have ever lived are alive now; the scientific knowledge accumulated in this century far exceeds the knowledge of all previous centuries.[9] Even in such fields as history or philosophy, the number of people now active as professionals is far greater than at any time in the past. Thus a large part of our knowledge in these fields is also recent in origin. The scientific study of human behavior is largely a twentieth-century phenomenon, and in terms of reliable, cumulative, empirically based knowledge, very much a product of the last four or five decades. In fields like linguistics, developmental psychology, and physical anthropology, more has been learned in the last twenty or thirty years than in all the centuries of previous scholarship.

If the sheer amount of knowledge is vastly greater than in the past, we no longer see that knowledge as authoritative and absolute in the way our ancestors did. In part, this is because the methods and attitudes of science have become the paradigms for all human knowledge in the modern world. Science, it has justly been said, involves organized skepticism.[10] It does not take the received wisdom on faith but requires substantial and convincing evidence before it is accepted. Scientists are trained to challenge existing theories and to recognize that their own work, no matter how brilliant or creative, will eventually be superseded by others. Although the great scientists of the past may be greatly revered, this is not because what they discovered was true for all time, but because they made discoveries that allow us, standing on their shoulders, to surpass their knowledge.

Finally, and most obviously, modern society is more dependent on knowledge than any previous society. This is true in a double sense. Industrialized societies need new scientific and technological discoveries to produce the economic growth and rising living standards demanded by their populations. At the same time, the contemporary labor force requires more sophisticated skills and cognitive competence than ever before. As I suggested in Chapter 3, it is possible to overstate this increasing complexity of work argument, but there is little question that for the increasing number of white-collar and professional jobs in our society, something more than simple literacy and numeracy is required.

The knowledge revolution, therefore, tends to transform traditional schooling and to foster new ideas of what education should or might be. Rote learning and memorization are less emphasized than they used to be seventy or one hundred years ago, elective courses are now far more common, and a number of the traditional disciplines have lost their unquestioned place at the center of the curriculum. What is equally important, however, is that conceptions of what schools *should* do have changed, and perhaps even more dramatically than schools have actually changed. The knowledge revolution has undermined the notion that education is a body of truths, principles, and wisdom that must be conveyed to everyone in authoritative fashion. We now believe schools should teach students general cognitive skills: to think and understand rather than merely to memorize, and to learn how to learn rather than to regurgitate facts. As committees, commissions, and official reports have emphasized, the education our parents and grandparents received is quite inadequate for the learning and knowledge-based society of the future; to meet that challenge, both the traditional curriculum and traditional teaching methods must be thoroughly transformed.

Increasing Cultural Diversity

The United States has long been a more culturally diverse society than countries like France, Japan, or Great Britain, but it is only in the last few decades that education has come to reflect something of the competing ideals, values, and ideological controversies that have perhaps always existed but not always been recognized. It was not until the 1960s, for example, that many schools began to offer courses in jazz as well as classical music, recent fiction as well as the great classics, or subjects like problems of the environment, war and peace, values clarification, or creative writing.[11] Courses and curricula aimed specifically at minority groups are also a recent innovation. Black studies departments, special programs of feminist studies, and Spanish language instruction for Hispanic students are all developments of the late 1960s and early 1970s. Although courses in human biology or health are hardly new, sex education and especially the discussion of changing standards of sexual conduct are also relatively recent innovations.[12]

The development of new courses is only a small part of what is meant by increasing cultural diversity in the schools. In traditional history texts, for example, as Francis Fitzgerald has shown, U.S. history was portrayed as a triumphal story of increasing freedom and justice, achieved in considerable part by the actions of a small number of "great" individuals.[13] In more recent texts, a decidedly mixed message appears. The faults and shortcomings of the heroes of the past are emphasized and there is a stress on the continuing problems of U.S. society, which in some texts appears to be of at least equal significance with the record of increasing justice.[14] Analogous trends are apparent in the teaching of literature. The teaching of Shakespeare, Dickens, and the inspirational stories of Horatio Alger has by no means disappeared from the English curriculum, but these writers have been joined in recent decades (in some schools at least) by such authors as J. D. Salinger, Judy Blume, and even the lyrics of Bob Dylan or Simon and Garfunkel.[15] Such literature hardly celebrates the importance of moral character and hard work, nor does it always permit easy distinctions between good and evil or virtue and vice.

Contemporary schools, therefore, probably convey rather more complicated and ambiguous moral messages than the schools of the past. At the turn of the century, most schools taught a relatively homogeneous culture to their students—in large part, as Collins has pointed out, the values and ideals of the white Anglo-Saxon Protestant elite.[16] Textbooks like the McGuffey Readers emphasized the importance of morality, self-denial, hard work, and strength of character, as did the biographies of such heroes as Washington, Lincoln, Carnegie, and Rockefeller. Students were not encouraged to debate the merits of these particular values and ideals; instead, to a degree that would be almost inconceivable in many schools today, they were simply *told* that these were the ideals for which they should strive and these were the individuals whose lives they should emulate.

It is conceivable that our society may again recapture that assurance and confidence, with or without the smug self-righteousness that often accompanied it and that denigrated all values and ideals save those of the Protestant elite. But in the 1960s and 1970s this assurance of moral rectitude was substantially undermined. A substantial fraction of the population were perhaps never convinced that the old virtues were in any way imperfect, yet a growing number of educators and intellectuals began to redefine the traditional task of education in quite fundamental ways. What schools should do, they argued, was to expose students to the full range of contemporary controversies, values, ideals, and moral beliefs, and to enable students to make informed choices among them. The traditional concept of moral education, from this point of view, was little more than moral indoctrination. Education for a culturally diverse society, they argued, must involve full and open discussion of such issues as feminism, racism, sexuality, and U.S. foreign policy. Students should not be simply told what is the correct or moral position on every issue, but they should learn to arrive at their own considered moral choices and values.

In the 1960s and 1970s, therefore, the values and ideals schools actually taught and the cultural messages people believed they should teach became far more problematic and controversial. Some conservatives, for example, generally lament these changes and would prefer that schools return to their traditional task of teaching what they still believe to be the eternal virtues: the superiority of the American way of life, and the traditional Anglo-Protestant values. And from this perspective they probably overestimate the changes that have taken place in schools. What schools actually do, some claim, is to undermine patriotism and punctuality, thought and self-denial, and the virtues of family life.[17] For many radicals, by contrast, schools have changed relatively little. What schools should do, they believe, is teach students to challenge and question the traditional values and ideals.[18] Radical critics argue that what schools actually teach is almost precisely what conservatives allege they no longer teach: the hegemony of the Anglo-Protestant virtues, obedience to authority, and the celebration of business values.

What is important, however, is not which of these purportedly empirical descriptions is correct, but the character of the controversy itself. As disagreement has increased over what precisely are American values and virtues, schools, as the major agencies charged with the responsibility of conveying these values and virtues, have become far more controversial as well. As schools have begun to reflect, perhaps for the first time, some of the real cultural diversity of U.S. society, education has become increasingly controversial and politicized. In a pluralistic society, with competing values and ideals rather than one homogeneous set of principles to which all subscribe, agreement about what schools should teach becomes elusive. In almost every community different groups, each claiming to represent *the* American values and virtues, clash over such issues as sex education, the banning of books in the school library, school prayer, promotion practices, and grading policies.[19] Each group tends to believe that the schools have been largely captured by the opposition: They are effective in conveying the values and ideals with which they disagree, and are ineffective in teaching the beliefs and principles to which they subscribe. Thus, to exaggerate only a little, we have a situation of almost universal dissatisfaction with schooling, combined with quite contradictory assertions about what schools in fact teach to their students. If virtually everyone agrees that schools do not provide "quality education" (the modern catchphrase), behind that apparent consensus are very different diagnoses of what that ambiguous phrase implies.

SOCIOLOGICAL THEORIES OF WHAT SCHOOLS TEACH

There is a great deal of overlap between sociological theories of what schools teach and the kinds of assertions that have just been described. Sociologists, like everyone else, have political and ideological convictions; and these beliefs about what schools *should* do tend to shape arguments about what schools *in fact* teach to their students. The "should" statements in sociological theories are not usually explicit—they are often concealed beneath assertions of what schools *need* to do, or arguments about how the changing demands of the new society require different kinds of schooling. But in both functional and conflict interpretations of what schools teach, it is not difficult to discern respectively a broadly liberal and a broadly radical ideology that underlies much of the sociological argument. Interestingly enough, however, there is as yet no sociological theory of what schools teach that could be described as conservative. This omission, I shall argue, is unfortunate because such a conservative perspective illuminates a great deal of the change that has taken place in schools in recent decades.

The Functional Interpretation

As suggested in Chapter 2, the functional theory has become very much a part of the conventional wisdom about the changing character of schooling in modern society. Developed in the 1950s and early 1960s by such writers as Burton Clark, Clark Kerr, and Talcott Parsons, it claims that schools in modern society perform the function of teaching broad-based skills that are needed for effective performance of roles in an increasingly complex world.[20] Thus the important thing about what schools teach from this perspective is not the formal subject matter of the curriculum—the study of history or literature, or the teaching of algebra or geometry receives very little attention in this tradition—but the general cognitive skills that all this specific subject matter presumably develops. Implicit in the functional theory, therefore, is a critique of the traditional school, and an explanation of why both curriculum and teaching methods are changing. Schools *were* primarily concerned with the teaching of specific information and particular moral precepts, but the imperatives of the emerging knowledge-based society mean that they must shift to a greater concentration on broader kinds of cognitive and moral development. Whereas some writers, like Parsons and Clark, believe this shift in the character of schooling is already far advanced, others characterize existing schools as anachronistic and out of step with the changing needs of the time.[21] Boocock and Coleman, for example, generally subscribe to the functional argument and see existing schools as quite inefficient in developing students' ability to reason and think.[22] This view, with its condemnation of passive roles in the classroom that fail to involve the student, or of peer groups that favor athletic rather than academic achievement, was widely endorsed by great numbers of professional educators in the 1960s and 1970s. The imperatives of work and citizenship in modern society dictate that schools *must* change in fundamental ways; however, schools have moved only a small part of the way toward the changes in curriculum and teaching methods that need to be made.

Despite these disagreements, there is virtually no argument among functional theorists as to the general direction of change in schools and the positive results of such changes. New curricula and new teaching methods, better adapted to the task of producing general cognitive skills, will gradually replace the old emphasis on the memorization of specific facts and precepts. The result of this change, virtually all theorists and liberal educators believed until the late 1970s, would be a steady improvement in the cognitive skills of students. The apparent failure of this prediction and the evidence of falling rather than rising test scores in the 1970s, pose as we shall see serious problems for the theory.

Although assertions about the need for increasing cognitive skills are the best known and most influential part of the functional theory, claims that schools produce what can be broadly defined as *modern* attitudes and values are hardly less important. Here the argument is that schools teach very general qualities and attitudes that underlie effective role performance in a modern society. In the work of Parsons and Dreeben, for example, schools are seen as agencies of *moral socialization* mediating between the very different worlds of the family and work in large-scale organizations.[23] Familial relationships are personal, affective, and particularistic. Unlike large-scale organizations, families evaluate people in terms of who they are rather than by set rules of achievement universally applied to all. Whereas it would be inappropriate for a boss to evaluate an employee on the basis of personal likes or dislikes, such behavior is expected of family members. One function of schooling in modern society, therefore, is to teach children the very different norms that apply in the modern world of work in large organizations and to wean them gradually away from the affective, personal relationships of the family. Schools teach children that their performance will be the basis of their evaluation rather than their personal affective relationships to teachers. Students learn that teachers, whatever their personal feelings might be, attempt to treat all students alike, to judge them not as "whole human beings," but as students who display different degrees of competence in the performance of tasks. Thus schools teach the norm of universalism, which underlies adult role performance in virtually every large organization: People should be treated and evaluated according to general rules of competence and performance, and not according to the particular likes or dislikes of those doing the evaluation.[24]

In more general terms, functional theorists see schools in almost every society as a fundamentally modernizing force, teaching norms and attitudes that would be inappropriate in traditional societies and in the personal relationships of family life but that are indispensable or functional for adult work in modern societies. Inkeles has argued that schools in developing societies help develop attitudes that promote innovation rather than tradition and reliance on knowledge and expertise rather than custom.[25] Educated individuals in these societies, he argues, are more likely to be tolerant of different and new ideas, to be far more conscious of the importance of time and punctuality, and subscribe to modern attitudes about human rights and the equality of women. These generalizations about the effects of education in developing societies are similar to claims that western schools promote cosmopolitan and liberal attitudes: They teach tolerance for diverse opinions rather than authoritarianism, and intellectual flexibility and open-mindedness rather than disdain for new ideas.[26]

Radical and Conflict Theories

The extraordinary optimism of the functional theory about the beneficial effects of schooling was shaped by the intellectual climate of the early 1960s, and the pessimism of the radical and neo-Marxist theories also bears the marks of their origins in the late 1960s and 1970s. Today, of course, the key assumptions of the radical theory are no longer in vogue. In the more conservative climate of the 1980s, it is no longer fashionable to argue that schools repress students' natural creativity, that they teach conformity to the status quo, or that the key to more "liberated" schooling lies in wholesale social reconstruction. The rhetoric about the ends of capitalist society and human liberation now seems dated to many if not all students of schooling, but we can nonetheless discern important substantive assertions about what schools teach beneath the often extravagant language that radical theorists employ.

There are essentially two kinds of radical theories about the effects of schooling on their students. The Bowles and Gintis argument, already discussed in Chapters 2 and 3, focuses on how the hidden curriculum reproduces the attitudes and personality traits upon which work in capitalist society depends.[27] The works of Illich, Apple, and Bourdieu and Passerow, by contrast, stress the importance of the explicit curriculum in the reproduction of consciousness in capitalist societies.[28] There is some overlap between these two approaches, particularly in the claim that schools everywhere convince people that success and failure are deserved, but it is important to keep this distinction between the hidden curriculum and the explicit curriculum in mind.

Bowles and Gintis's central assertion is that there is, and must be in any capitalist society, a correspondence between the attitudes and personality traits that are useful in different kinds of work and the attitudes and traits schools teach. Thus the *correspondence principle* states that social organization of the classroom mirrors the social organization of work.[29] Both kinds of organization tend to reward and penalize the same kinds of personality traits. The hierarchical organization of work and the hierarchical organization of the classroom tend to penalize individuals who are creative, aggressive, and independent, and reward individuals who are dependable, persevering, and able to follow rules and identify with authority. These characteristics, Bowles and Gintis show, predict grades in school when test scores are held constant; and these same traits show significant correlations with supervisor ratings of employees in a number of work settings.[30] Furthermore, although less evidence is produced for this assertion, Bowles and Gintis claim that schools serving high-status populations and preparing students for higher-status jobs employ rather "softer" (though no less effective) socialization techniques.[31] Thus elite private colleges often encourage students to work without direct supervision, to undertake long-term independent projects rather than to follow specific directions to the letter. And these qualities closely mirror the kinds of traits that are demanded in upper-level management occupations: Such jobs require that employees be loyal to and identify with the goals of the organization, but they also require that employees display some degree of independence and initiative rather than simply following orders.

What is not clear about Bowles and Gintis's argument, however, is whether parallels between the organization of work and the organization of schooling indicate a causal relationship. Schools, no doubt, do tend to reward students who persevere, who are punctual, and who respect the teacher's authority. But it is not obvious that they reward these characteristics *because* similar traits are valued in the workplace, as the neo-Marxist argument claims, or because, as I shall argue in the next chapter, the problem of organizing student work in almost *any conceivable* society tends to lead to positive valuation of these characteristics rather than creativity or independence. A correspondence has been established, but Bowles and Gintis do not provide persuasive evidence for a causal connection. What is also striking about the correspondence argument is its similarity to the functional argument that schools teach general attitudes and values that are necessary for the effective performance of roles in modern society. There are differences in nomenclature and differences in the attitude of the theorist toward the desirability of such traits, but both arguments claim that schools teach students to defer gratification, to adhere to standardized rules and procedures, and to internalize norms that are useful in the workplace. Thus both theories, despite their very great surface differences, are basically *functional* theories, arguing that schools teach these particular qualities because they are useful or functional in the workplace, and both theories can be criticized because they simply assume, without evidence, that changes in the workplace cause changes in the schools.

The works of Ivan Illich, Michael Apple, and Pierre Bourdieu and J. C. Passerow focus on what radical theorists term the *reproduction of consciousness* rather than the teaching of specific attitudes or values. The curriculum is not merely a collection of particular disciplines, nor, as functional theorists claim, a body of knowledge; rather, it conveys a particular kind of consciousness. Thus, Illich argues that students in school learn to devalue their own vernacular culture and to believe that the only real knowledge is contained in the disciplines and subjects that schools teach.[32] What "school knowledge" conveys is the belief that only experts and large-scale organizations can solve social problems, and that the scientific and objective knowledge that is so valued by elite groups is the only rational knowledge that exists.[33] Thus the consciousness that schools reproduce is, Illich claims, almost totalitarian in character. Not only does it devalue feeling, personal intuitive knowledge, and traditional popular culture, it also denies that any other kind of consciousness is rational. The reproduction of consciousness also legitimates what some theorists call the *structures of domination* in capitalist societies. Elite groups, Illich and Apple argue, are able to conceal their domination of the society by pointing to the objective knowledge and expertise they have acquired.[34] They can claim their power arises not from their own privilege or desire to dominate others but from the very nature of advanced and knowledge-based industrial societies. In the consciousness that schools teach, therefore, such domination is not real domination, but arises from rational necessity. Schools teach that what is, must be.

Bourdieu offers an interesting variant on this general argument. Speaking primarily about France, he claims that schools teach the superiority of a particular form of high culture—a culture that pays lip service to the importance of art, literature, and the free play of ideas. As embodied in the school, such a culture stresses the importance of elegance in written language and emphasizes the cultivation of a graceful and witty style of conversation.[35] Students who lack familiarity with this style, who lack what Bourdieu calls "cultural capital," will appear dull, plodding, and (at best) merely earnest, and they will be consistently typed as worthy members of the middle or lower class but as unsuitable for elite positions.[36] Those who display verbal brilliance and a lively interest in the arts will, almost regardless of their real intellectual abilities, be promoted into elite schools. Although Bourdieu's characterization of the particular culture that schools teach is different from the other radical theorists, he arrives at an essentially similar conclusion about the role of schools in reproducing the domination of one particular kind of consciousness. Schools work to conceal the real character of domination by teaching that there is only one legitimate culture and one form of approved consciousness—that of the highly educated elite.

One's response to these ideas depends preeminently on one's basic ideological convictions. If we basically dislike the dominant culture of industrialized societies or, in Bourdieu's case, the culture of the French elite, we are likely to be sympathetic and receptive to the proposition that this consciousness and this culture are "structures of domination" and that they work to conceal real power relations in the society. Those who are more convinced that our contemporary culture is based on what is, *in fact,* more rational or more objective knowledge than most previous societies are likely to reject these arguments as romantic cries in the wilderness. Suffice it to say that while I regard the functional argument that modern societies are preeminently more rational than previous societies with some skepticism, I am not entirely persuaded by the radical characterization of contemporary culture.

A second difficulty with the reproduction of consciousness argument is that very little empirical evidence is provided. All the writers

I have mentioned, with the possible exception of Bourdieu, base their case on the plausibility of their logic rather than on evidence that students in fact acquire this rather unidimensional consciousness. Those arguments, moreover, are curiously static for theorists who claim as neo-Marxists to be concerned with how schools change as the character of capitalism changes. Thus there is little reference in this literature to how the curriculum has changed in recent decades or to how arguments about cultural reproduction can be reconciled with what appears to other observers to be a period of unprecedented dissent from the core values of industrialized societies among young people during the late 1960s and 1970s. No doubt radical theorists would maintain that the curriculum changes during the last twenty years do not represent, as conservatives claim, the disintegration of a common culture; they would also surely maintain that apparently radical dissent during this period was both superficial in character and temporary in nature. But the fact remains that these rather obvious objections have not been answered.

The Theories of Collins and Meyer

All the theories examined so far in this section can be described as radical. They leave no doubt that the writer thoroughly disapproves of much of what schools teach, and they point the way to some future ideal society in which education would be more humane and truly democratic. The work of Collins and Meyer is much more skeptical and even cynical in its implications. Like all conflict theorists, they take the functional theory as their main target, but they are almost as skeptical of radical assertions about what schools teach as they are of the functional arguments. As we saw in Chapter 2, Collins believes that traditional schools *did* have important effects in teaching the status culture of the Protestant elite.[37] In recent decades, however, Collins maintains, this culture has been greatly weakened. Beyond middle-class standards of propriety and sociability, Collins believes, schools teach little in the way of a consistent culture. Instead, education functions as a kind of cultural currency that enables the holder to purchase certain kinds of adult status but that has little or no definable content.

Meyer takes this argument a step further.[38] Education affects society, Meyer argues, not primarily through socialization—the communication of skills and attitudes and values—but in the way it classifies people into particular categories: college graduates, high school dropouts, M.B.A.'s, and, more broadly, people who have expert knowledge and are thus entitled to elite positions and those who are not so defined. Schools receive a charter from the society to define and classify people in this way, and this charter reflects the conviction that education is the principal way in which status ought to be allocated in modern society. Classifications like college graduate or high school dropout, Meyer argues, may or may not correspond to actual differences in skills and attitudes between these two groups; what is more significant, however, is that people believe such differences are real.[39] On ritual and ceremonial occasions like graduation day, schools and colleges convince students and the public that graduates have rights and entitlements to further high-status positions that nongraduates do not have.

Such social definitions help create the very differences that graduation ceremonies officially certify. Thus college graduates come to believe that they are entitled to high-status occupations and to adopt the attitudes and values associated with those positions, while high school dropouts, defined by society as fit only for low-status jobs, will be influenced by those definitions also. The most important effects of education, therefore, lie in its power to legitimate differences between groups and to create new categories of status rather than its presumed but somewhat questionable effects on actual skills and values.[40] Employers believe that those holding M.B.A. degrees are different from students with no background in business, and both students and the general public become convinced that this is so. Because of this, and because of similar beliefs about differences between trained specialists in every field and untrained individuals, it is seen as entirely rational and just that people who do not have impressive educational qualifications should be excluded from desirable positions.

Meyer extends this argument to the long-term effects of education on culture and political participation as well.[41] Functional theorists argue that the expansion of education helped forge, and was partly explained by, the need for a national and unified culture. It has also been widely argued that educational expansion makes for rising expectations for political participation in almost every society. Meyer argues that these effects have been misinterpreted. Education does not so much forge a unified culture as create widespread *beliefs* that there is a national culture. It does not produce rising expectations through its effects on literacy or modern attitudes, but creates the belief that an educated citizenry have rights to levels of political participation to which uneducated people are not entitled. More generally, the importance of education in modern society lies in the beliefs and attitudes that people have about schooling and its effects rather than in the presumed effects of schools upon skills, attitudes, and values. "Schools," Meyer argues, "*may teach useful skills and values, but whether they do or not,*" they certainly allocate people to particular statuses, and provide what are almost universally believed to be legitimate bases for such allocation.[42]

WHAT SCHOOLS TEACH:
THE EMPIRICAL EVIDENCE

Few subjects in the sociology of education are as important as the effects of schools on their students, but there is probably no issue so difficult to resolve. Indeed, it is in large part because hard evidence of the effects of schooling on students is so difficult to come by that both popular and sociological theories of what schools teach are so various. Thus a skeptical theorist like Randall Collins can maintain that students learn very little in school, that much of what they are taught is rapidly forgotten, and that employer preferences for educated students reflect the prestige of educational credentials rather than anything that students have actually learned as a result of that schooling. Many of those who argue for increasing educational expenditures, on the other hand, justify those expenditures by stressing how investments in human capital will result in a more skilled and productive labor force. Whereas radical critics are convinced that schools teach unthinking obedience to authority and sustain the hegemony of bourgeois values, conservatives are persuaded that schools undermine the traditional virtues. All these views are probably too simple, but such contradictory accounts persist because it is so difficult to obtain firm evidence about the effects of education on their students.

There are three kinds of difficulties in conducting research on the effects of schooling on cognitive skills, values, and attitudes. First, there is the difficulty of separating the effects of schooling from effects attributable to maturation and the impact of growing up in the wider environment that exists outside the school. As they grow older, all children are better able to solve the kinds of intellectual puzzles we call intelligence tests. Their cognitive skills increase and their ability to handle abstractions grows quite steadily until the age of fifteen or sixteen, and then more slowly until their early twenties. Clearly, then, we cannot presume that high scores on tests of intellectual ability are attributable to schooling alone. To test how much of that increase is a schooling effect would seem to require a virtually impossible experiment: We would need to find children who do not go to school and to compare their intellectual progress with those of in-school students. The effects of the wider nonschool environment are equally difficult to separate from the effects of schooling. Parents, peers, and the mass media are only the most obvious examples of a whole range of influences that may well be more important than schools in shaping values and attitudes and in affording propitious or unpropitious environments for the development of intellectual skills. Again, it is very difficult to partial out these diverse kinds of influences. A consistent finding of research on international student achievement, for example, is that test scores in poor countries like India or Chile are substantially lower than scores in richer industrialized societies.[43] But is this because schools are inferior in these societies or because the total environment provided by poor countries is less favorable for the development of intellectual skills? We do not know.

A second set of difficulties lies in the problem of controlling for such characteristics of students as ability, socioeconomic status, and prior attitudes, and separating the effects of these variables from effects that can be properly attributed to schooling. It is easy to show, for example, that college students score considerably higher on tests of intellectual achievement and information, are more tolerant of diverse opinions, and are more politically liberal than their noncollege peers of the same age. What is much more difficult to demonstrate, however, is that this effect is attributable to the effects of *college,* and is not the result of the obvious fact that college students were different from noncollege students *before* they entered college. Not only are college-bound students likely to have higher test scores than others, they may also score higher on measures of open-mindedness than students who do not go to college.[44]

Finally, the problem of assessing the effects of what school teaches raises different issues of measurement. To control for preexisting characteristics of students we must perforce rely on very large samples indeed. And if the expense of the research is not to be altogether insupportable, we must devise relatively short and straightforward measurements of what students have learned. To compare a large number of schools, we cannot confine ourselves to specific questions that ask for information that may not be part of the curriculum at some schools. Inevitably, therefore, our measures of the effects of schooling must be both general and rather crude. Research on school effects has focused almost exclusively on measures of general cognitive skills rather than the organization of the more specific knowledge that the curriculum conveys. These skills are assessed by short group-administered objective tests rather than by longer and individually administered assessments of a variety of learning outcomes. Understandable though these strategies may be, given the difficulties of drawing any conclusions in this field, such measurements may underestimate the effects of schooling by neglecting the obvious fact that students, for a while at least, learn a great deal of specific information and specific skills that the particular subjects of the curriculum teach.

The Cognitive Effects of Schooling

In the short term, of course, it is entirely obvious that schooling has one very clear effect: the transmission of the knowledge, information, and specific skills that are involved in the particular subjects of the curriculum. Most students who study U.S. history, French, or algebra, for example, are likely to learn enough about these subjects to pass an examination that tests their knowledge of such matters as the causes of the Civil War, the formula for solving quadratic equations, or the conjugation of certain French irregular verbs. It also seems safe to say they will learn these things considerably better than students who have not studied these subjects.[45] But there are important questions about the generality and duration of this learning. Do the specific skills of solving quadratic or simultaneous equations lead to the development of *general* mathematical skills that can then be applied to a whole host of problems not specifically addressed in school? Does the information or skills that schools teach stay with students for a long period of time or are they quickly forgotten after they leave formal education? Let us address these questions in turn.

Almost all research on the development of cognitive skills shows a strong correlation between formal schooling and scores on tests of vocabulary, reasoning, and the ability to solve mathematical problems.[46] The longer students stay in school the more likely they are to score higher on these tests; and adults who have received extensive formal education score higher than adults who have received less schooling. The consistency of these results, using a wide variety of measures of cognitive skills, including tests designed to measure intelligence and aptitudes as well as achievement, makes for a strong *prima facie* case that schooling does indeed develop general intellectual skills. What prevents this evidence from being decisive, however, is that virtually everyone in modern society attends school. Thus we cannot readily separate the effects of schooling from the effects of motivation and the wider social environment. For this reason, studies of Western children who do not attend school for extensive periods of time and studies of children in developing societies where schooling is by no means universal are of crucial importance.

During World War II, many elementary schools in Holland were closed because of the German occupation.[47] A study of test scores of Dutch children at the end of the war showed an approximate 7 percent drop in IQ scores compared with the beginning of the war, suggesting that the absence of schooling significantly slowed the intellectual development of Dutch children.[48] Research in the early 1960s on black children who were prevented from attending any school because of the refusal of the local school board to provide integrated schooling showed similar results: These children scored substantially below their in-school black peers on all tests of achievement.[49] An ingenious study of summer learning in Atlanta demonstrated that students who attended summer school continued to make steady gains in test scores over the summer while those who did not attend summer school made much slower progress or had scores that were actually lower in the early fall than at the end of the school year.[50] For black children, in particular, summer schools appeared especially beneficial. The gap between the achievements of black and white children who did not attend summer school widened, but it closed substantially for black children who experienced year-round schooling.

Quite different kinds of evidence from studies of education in developing societies suggests similar conclusions about the effectiveness of schooling. In some developing societies it is easy to locate large groups of children who have no opportunity to attend school, and to be reasonably sure that these children do not differ in initial intelligence from their peers who go to school. Studies of the Wolof of Senegal by Patricia Greenfield and Jerome Bruner show that uneducated children were much slower in attaining the developmental stages made famous by Piaget than educated children.[51] The principle of conservation, for example, which states that the amount of water in a container does not grow when the dimensions of the container are altered, was generally grasped by Western children at age seven or eight. But Wolof children who did not attend school could rarely grasp this principle, nor could they readily understand that a coiled necklace does not grow when straightened out. Children who were in school did much better in these tasks.

Research by Michael Cole in the Yucatan showed large differences between educated and uneducated students in the classification of objects and in their ability to recall those objects.[52] The subjects were presented with twenty photographs of four kinds of objects in common use: food, animals, tools, and clothing. They were then asked to sort these pictures into four categories of their own choosing. Uneducated respondents were less likely than educated children to group the objects into these four categories. Instead, they classified them by the way they were used (for example, grouping "knife" with "bread" or "onions," rather than with "spoon"). They were also far less likely to do well on a test of recalling these objects than educated respondents, and to recall them in what seemed like random order rather than using the categories as an aid to memory. Only respondents who had some secondary schooling, Cole reports, used the four categories as an aid to remembering the objects. Educated respondents also did much better on tests of verbal syllogisms of the form: "The houses in Mexico City are large. My friend has a house in Mexico City. Is my friend's house large?" To this question those who had attended school were likely to respond that it was obviously true by definition (or words to that effect). Uneducated respondents tended to treat the question as a matter of fact rather than of logic. Thus they might say, "Yes, I have heard that houses are large in Mexico City."[53]

This research suggests that education develops abilities to solve problems that are detached from the immediate content of everyday life. Educated respondents have learned to work with abstract categories and with general principles of logic that have no direct relevance to their day-to-day practical reasoning activities. Although this in no way implies that uneducated people in poor countries are less intelligent in some absolute sense, it suggests that schools develop quite general skills that, while they may be of little significance to most people in pre-industrial societies, are of much greater importance in modern industrial societies: the ability to think logically and hypothetically about events removed from one's day-to-day experience, and the ability to organize information into general and abstract categories.[54]

Schooling does seem to have quite powerful effects on general cognitive skills, yet there remains the question of whether these effects should be considered permanent or temporary in character. Does schooling have long-term effects on cognitive skills and the ability to gain new information, or do these effects tend to decline as the experience of schooling recedes into the past? The research of Herbert Hyman and his colleagues suggests that at least some of these effects are long lasting.[55] Highly educated respondents, Hyman reports, are much more likely to be able to answer questions about vocabulary and current events, and to read books, magazines, and newspapers regularly than less educated respondents. These differences are no less marked in samples of respondents over fifty years of age than among younger respondents. Part of these differences, of course, are due to the fact that educated respondents generally have occupations that require or encourage them to engage in more of this kind of activity. But much of the large differences between educated and less educated respondents remains after controls are introduced for current occupation and for class of origin.[56] The effects of education on knowledge appear to be quite general and reach considerably beyond the specific kinds of academic information that are taught in school. Thus highly educated respondents of all ages are not only more likely to recognize the significance of Bunker Hill or to know the name of Aristotle, but they have more knowledge about public affairs, foreign countries, and recent scientific discoveries than less educated respondents. Formal education, therefore, appears to develop interests in, and aptitudes for obtaining, new knowledge over the course of a person's lifetime rather than merely conveying specific information that is rapidly forgotten.

The Effects of Schooling on Attitudes and Values

We know far less about the effects of schooling on noncognitive characteristics of students than on the development of cognitive skills. No doubt schools attempt to convey a whole series of values and attitudes to their students, from the importance of deferring gratification, perseverance, and punctuality to the teaching of patriotism and the virtues of the free enterprise system, but it is extraordinarily difficult to assess how effective they are in conveying these messages. Not only is it less easy to measure these qualities reliably than it is to measure cognitive skills, it is almost impossible to measure these attitudes and values in students before they enter a particular school. Do schools give students who are punctual and who demonstrate perseverance higher grades and thus develop these qualities in their students? Or are punctual and persevering students different from their peers before they even enter school?

In the present state of our knowledge we cannot answer this question because there are few if any studies that reliably measure the attitudes and values of a group of students over a substantial period of time. Even if more research were available it still would be difficult to give a clear answer to the question of the source of any change in attitudes. Students, after all, spend far more time out of school than in school, and are exposed to a multiplicity of influences from peers, parents, and media that may undermine or support the messages that schools are trying to convey. Although schools are, for most students, the most important source of instruction in formal cognitive skills, for attitudes and values the case is much less clear; it is at least arguable that in today's media-saturated world, other sources of influence on such attitudes as patriotism or respect for authority are far more pervasive. For all these reasons it is appropriate to be skeptical about the confident assertions that are made by both radical and conservative critics, and by some sociological theorists as well, about the effects of particular kinds of schooling on attitudes, values, and beliefs. As conservative critics argue, perhaps schools tend to undermine respect for traditional values and subvert established authority. Or perhaps, as many neo-Marxist or radical sociologists have claimed, schools reinforce the hegemony of the capitalist order, teaching students that they live in a preeminently rational and humane society and that success and failure are generally deserved. But one suspects that many of these assertions tell us as much about the opinions of the critic as to what is wrong with our society as about the effects of schooling. School critics and sociologists are by no means exempt from this tendency. They are inclined to see the school as highly effective in conveying attitudes and values they do not like, and much less effective in teaching attitudes and values of which they approve. In the absence of clear evidence on virtually any of these presumed effects that might guide such speculation, these all too human tendencies have full rein.

The research cannot resolve these ideological controversies, but there is a small body of evidence that meets the methodological criteria described above and enables us to make some tentative generalizations about the effects of schooling on some very general attitudes and values: openness to new ideas, tolerance of diverse opinions, and authoritarianism. Trent and Medsker, in a longitudinal study of 10,000 high school graduates, explored how these characteristics changed among those students who attended college compared with students who entered the labor force.[57] Unlike most studies of the effects of college on students, Trent and Medsker were able to administer their attitude questionnaires both at age eighteen and at age twenty-two, and to control for the fact that college students had higher scores on tests of ability. The authors found that college students clearly shifted in the direction of greater tolerance for diverse opinions, greater intellectual openness, and less authoritarianism over the course of their college careers, whereas students who did not attend college either did not change or displayed rather less openness and tolerance than they had four years earlier.[58] These generalizations held regardless of levels of ability and socioeconomic status. Thus not only were college students more tolerant and more intellectually open than noncollege students, a finding that has been documented by literally hundreds of studies, but there is evidence that it was the experience of attending college that produced changes in these attitudes rather than the self-selection of students who already had tendencies in this direction.

Evidence from other sources also supports the conclusion that education increases tolerance for divergent opinions and promotes intellectual flexibility and openness to new experience. Research on support for civil liberties, for example, shows that while large proportions of U.S. citizens would *not* support the rights of individuals to demonstrate against the government if there was a threat of violence and *would* support the firing of communists who teach in schools and colleges, more educated respondents were considerably more libertarian in these responses than less educated respondents.[59] College graduates, including those who were politically conservative, were much more likely to believe that tolerance should be extended to those with very different views than less educated respondents. Although it is not possible to rule out the possibility that college tends to attract more tolerant people or that more intelligent people are more tolerant, this suggests that education may have enduring effects on openmindedness and flexibility. Research by Inkeles indicates that education may have rather similar effects in developing countries as well. In *Becoming Modern,* Inkeles argues that education is the single most important determinant of distinctively modern attitudes and values in all the developing societies he studied.[60] Educated respondents were more likely to be receptive to new ideas rather than relying on custom and tradition, to score low on measures of authoritarianism, and to be able to empathize with the situation of individuals of whom they had no personal knowledge.

Although these findings may be encouraging for all those who believe in tolerance, civil liberties, and openmindedness, I think we need to exercise caution in talking about the effects of education in general rather than the effects of Western or U.S. education or Western-influenced education. One can point to a number of cases where educated populations appear to be rather less tolerant and rather more fanatical in their opinions. University students in Nazi Germany, for example, seem to have been more active in denouncing Jews and in advocating the suppression of civil liberties than the general population.[61] And the Nazi elite contained a disproportionate number of Ph.D.'s and intellectuals among its members. Furthermore, the revival of Islamic fundamentalism appears to be at least as strong among university students in Iran and other Moslem countries as among the general population, so that, according to recent reports, female college students almost universally wear the chador or veil, symbolizing the traditional subordinate role of women.[62] Finally, in many communist societies there is very little evidence that highly educated individuals are more tolerant of diverse opinions than others.[63] In these countries, indeed, educational success may partially depend on acceptance of prevailing ruling orthodoxy that does not brook dissent. Thus the research we have reviewed may not tell us about the effects of schooling in general, but about the effects of a particular and perhaps *historically unusual* kind of schooling—one which explicitly encourages students to question the received orthodoxy, to experiment with different ideas, and to tolerate the views of those who do not share their values.

COMPARING THE EFFECTS OF SCHOOLING: DIFFERENT SCHOOLS, DIFFERENT COUNTRIES, AND COMPARISONS OVER TIME

If schooling has, with the important qualification just noted, rather general and positive effects on both cognitive development and tolerance of diversity, there remain important questions concerning the effects of one kind of school compared with another, the comparative effectiveness of schooling in different countries on cognitive skills, and the recent controversy over the possible decline in these skills in U.S. schools in the last twenty years.

Different Schools: Similar Effects

As indicated in Chapter 5, there is a large body of evidence that shows once student background characteristics are controlled, different schools have very similar effects on the cognitive skills of their students. There is virtually no credible evidence, for example, that schools with smaller classes, better trained teachers, or higher per capita expenditures have substantially better measurable outcomes than schools that are inferior in these respects. Gross differences in school resources make some difference, of course, and it is possible to argue that if all schools were to have teachers and class sizes that were as good as the top 10 percent of all schools, then test scores would rise significantly. But there is little reason to believe that the kinds of increments that are politically feasible would make major differences in measurable outcomes. In terms of their implication for school policy, therefore, the results of research on the effects of different schools on their students are pessimistic.

These conclusions have recently been challenged from an unexpected source.[64] James Coleman, whose earlier research did much to discredit the argument that school resources bear a close relationship to student outcomes, has recently collected evidence that, he believes, shows private and parochial schools have consistently superior learning outcomes to public schools. On the basis of this evidence, Coleman has advocated policies that would channel public funds in the form of educational vouchers to private institutions to provide greater competition between public and private schools.

In a large-scale study of achievement in public, private, and Catholic schools, Coleman and his colleagues found strikingly superior test scores in the private sector even after controlling for the socioeconomic differences in the students who attend different kinds of schools. Scores for high school sophomores and seniors in mathematics, reading, and vocabulary tests were found to be between 15 to 20 percent higher in private and parochial schools than in public schools. Although controls for socioeconomic status remove between one-half to two-thirds of this advantage, the remaining differences are still equivalent to more than a half-year's typical gain in achievement. To account for these differences, Coleman, Hoffer, and Kilgore examined variations in school policies in the different sectors. They found that Catholic and private school students do more homework, are more likely to be enrolled in the college preparatory curriculum, and are less likely to be absent from school and to cut class when they are in school. Each of these variables, the authors note, shows a significant relationship to achievement scores in both the public and the private sector. In part, therefore, Coleman and his colleagues believe private and Catholic schools produce superior outcomes because these schools are more effective in getting students to take more advanced courses, and because they make higher demands on students and translate these demands into actual differences in student effort.

Other nonacademic factors are, in Coleman's view, equally important. Students in Catholic and private schools report fewer disciplinary problems, fewer threats against teachers, and fewer student fights than students in public schools. They also perceive that disciplinary procedures are fairer and more equitable than do students in public schools. Here again, although the results are not as clear cut, Coleman and his colleagues find positive relationships between these disciplinary and behavioral variables and student achievement. In general, though not always consistently, students in schools where disciplinary and behavior problems were severe score less well on tests in both public and private schools.

Almost all of these conclusions have been subjected to exceptionally vigorous and even impassioned criticism.[65] First, and most important, the critics have pointed out that Coleman and his colleagues were not able to control for differences in the ability of the students who attended public and private schools. Most probably, they claim, the observed differences between outcomes in schools in the public and private sectors must be attributed, as in previous research, to differences in the characteristics of students rather than differences in school characteristics. Whereas Coleman, Hoffer, and Kilgore were able to control for the socioeconomic status of the student body, using such measures as parent education and the number of books present in the home, they were unable to rule out the obvious possibility that Catholic and private schools attracted more talented, ambitious, and well-behaved students than public schools. Such a conclusion is not only intuitively plausible, the critics contend, it is also supported by evidence from other large-scale research on differences between public and private schools. Thus Alexander and Pallas, in an analysis of data collected by the National Longitudinal Survey, find that with more adequate controls for student characteristics, differences in learning outcomes between public and nonpublic schools are virtually insignificant.[66]

A second related criticism concerns the interpretation of the findings on achievement in different tracks within public and private schools. Nonpublic schools, all observers are agreed, have higher percentages of students in college preparatory tracks, and of course these students score higher on tests than students in general or vocational tracks. But while Coleman and his colleagues interpret these findings as evidence for the superiority of the policy of encouraging most students to take demanding courses in Catholic and private schools, their critics see these differences as a reflection of the differing characteristics of students. Private and Catholic schools are able to place more students in the college track, the critics maintain, because they have more talented and ambitious students who wish to take and are more capable of taking demanding courses. Greater enrollment in college tracks, therefore, is not a *cause* of the higher achievement in Catholic or private schools but an *effect* of the differing and more selective composition of the student body. Were Catholic and private schools to enroll vastly more students than they do at present, the critics maintain, they could not maintain their current policy of enrolling most students in the college preparatory track.

The critics make essentially the same point about the supposed effects of disciplinary practices and behavior problems in the two kinds of schools. While Coleman and his colleagues see a causal connection between policies in private schools and Catholic schools that ensure good discipline and superior academic outcomes, their critics argue that these policies are possible because of the selective character of their student body. If private and Catholic schools were required to admit all comers, the critics contend, they would not be able to maintain such high standards of behavior and strict discipline. Therefore, the effect of particular school policies has not been demonstrated by the research of Coleman and his colleagues.

On balance, I believe, the critics have the best of this argument. In the absence of longitudinal data that allow us to follow students over the course of their careers in public and nonpublic schools, there is no convincing evidence that the superior outcomes of students in private and parochial schools are attributable to the effects of differences in schools rather than differences in the kinds of students that nonpublic schools attract. Although Coleman and his colleagues make a good case that homework assignments, absenteeism, and disciplinary problems bear a relationship to academic outcomes—an argument we will advance in the next chapter as a partial explanation of falling test scores from 1960 to 1980—they fail to substantiate the claim that private schools score higher on these measures *because* of the distinctive policies they follow. Equally plausible, I believe, is the contention that the characteristics of the student body shape the kind of academic expectations and disciplinary policies different schools follow, and that accordingly if nonpublic schools were no longer selective they too would find no less difficulty in maintaining high academic expectations and avoiding discipline problems than many public schools currently experience. Therefore it seems rather premature to advocate policies favoring greater enrollments in private and parochial schools on the basis of what is, by common consent, such weak evidence.

If this conclusion is accepted, how are we to reconcile these findings of trivial or insignificant effects of school characteristics with common everyday observation and ethnographic accounts of good and bad schools? Such a reconciliation is not easy. In part the discrepancy arises because large-scale research, although it has made considerable progress in recent years, is not yet able to employ measures of key variables that are sensitive to what is perhaps most important about school effectiveness. Large-scale surveys can measure teacher qualifications, for example, but they are not usually able to develop more sensitive measures of the quality of a teacher's interaction with students; they can measure classroom size and type of curriculum, but they still leave us a long way from an adequate account of the character of student-teacher interaction and the precise nature of curriculum materials. Outcome measures in large-scale research are also crude and perhaps insensitive to variations in the quality of the learning experience in different schools. Short paper-and-pencil tests of very general skills are employed, in part because of economy and in part because more specific tests cannot be used in a wide variety of schools with different curricula. But the results of these tests give only an inadequate sampling of the kinds of information and skills that schools teach. In sum, therefore, it could be maintained that the findings of large-scale research are based on an inadequate conceptualization and measurement of what really differentiates good schools from bad schools.

Although this argument has some plausibility, the characteristics that define the good school or the effective school appear to be somewhat elusive. A great deal of observational research on individual schools suggests that effective schools have high morale among faculty, a positive school climate, and an absence of serious student disruption.[67] What is much less clear, however, is what kinds of policies and what kinds of school characteristics are associated with these desirable traits. Recent research by Lightfoot, for example, suggests that there is great variability in the role of the principal, in teaching styles, in curriculum, and in grouping practices from one effective school to another.[68] Some schools rated as highly effective stress basic skills and old-fashioned pedagogical techniques, and some encourage student choice among a wide variety of relevant subjects and classroom participation. In some effective schools the principal's leadership style is highly directive and even authoritarian, in other's the principal works behind the scenes and by consensus. Although there is evidence from observational studies that leadership and faculty morale are very important to school effectiveness, it is possible that this arises from the presence of unusually charismatic or talented individuals or a particularly happy mix of people with complementary talents rather than from the distinctive educational policies that the individuals followed.[69] To the extent that such is the case, the conclusions for school reform are somewhat pessimistic. Effective schools cannot be obtained by following any one set of policies but only by finding those rare individuals who can create an effective learning environment by their ability to inspire others.

It is important to stress that we do not know the answer to these questions in the present state of our knowledge. It would be a mistake to claim that there are no policies that, if consistently followed, would result in more effective schools. It is rather the case that a particular kind of limited research has not yet discovered those policies. It would also be a mistake to argue that because most research reaches conclusions that are contrary to common sense it is thereby wrong. The history of educational reform is filled with examples of particular school policies that inspired, at a particular time, quite extraordinary confidence in their efficacy. At different periods in recent history large numbers of educators and a considerable fraction of the public have been convinced of the benefits of quite different kinds of teaching, curriculum, classroom organization, and disciplinary techniques. Each of these proposals was justified by illustrations of their efficacy in individual classrooms, and documented in most cases by research that showed that the policy in question had at least some of the effects claimed for it.[70] The failure of subsequent more carefully controlled studies to replicate these findings suggests that the burden of proof is on those who would claim that the most recent suggested policies will have the dramatic effects that previous policies lacked. We shall return to these perplexing problems in Chapter 9.

International Comparisons of School Achievement

A full discussion of the problems and difficulties in conducting research on international comparisons in school achievement is beyond the scope of this book. It can only be pointed out that such comparisons are extremely hazardous, given both the difference in selectivity between U.S. schools and schools in most other countries and the differing aims and objectives of schools in different societies.[71] As discussed in Chapter 1, U.S. schools have long placed more emphasis on the importance of educating all students, regardless of their academic aptitude and social origins, than schools in most other societies. This doctrine has shaped the curriculum, the way the students are evaluated, and promotion policies. U.S. schools have also placed less stress on high culture and the traditional arts and science curriculum, and more stress on practical or vocational learning than most other countries. For all these reasons, selective illustrations of the supposed superiority of foreign school systems, citing for example, the superior achievement of Soviet or British students in science and mathematics, are likely to be quite misleading. Soviet or British eighteen-year-olds who study science and mathematics, for example, are likely to be a selected group of all eighteen-year-old students, and to have specialized quite intensively in these subjects for four or five years.[72] Most U.S.

high school students spend more of their time in elective courses like driver training, health, problems of the environment, or creative writing, than their European or Japanese counterparts. Thus it is inappropriate to expect that the levels of achievement in the traditional disciplines of U.S. students should be as high as those of students who have studied little else.

Research on international comparisons of test scores is still in its infancy. It faces very serious methodological problems in devising comparable test items, obtaining representative samples of students, and administering the tests in identical ways in each country. In tests of skills and language and literature, many have argued, the problems of translation and obtaining comparable questions in as many as a dozen different languages are almost insuperable. But even in tests of mathematical and scientific achievement, where translation is less of a problem, the results should be viewed with great caution. Schools in different countries have different curricula, spend differential amounts of time on these subjects, and employ widely varying teaching methods.

The data in Table 7–1 are derived from international studies of mathematics and scientific achievement among ten-, thirteen-, and fourteen-year-olds (that is, before the age of selection into more specialized curricula) in fourteen countries.[73] The data suggest two broad generalizations. First, with the exception of the high scores for Japan, there are relatively small differences between the scores on scientific or mathematical achievement among industrialized countries for this age group. The United States fares rather poorly in mathematics achievement among thirteen-year-olds, scoring only above Sweden, but ranks relatively higher in science test scores for both ten- and fourteen-year-olds. With the exception of Japan, there are few dramatic or consistent differences among industrialized societies. Countries that rank high on science test scores do not always score well on mathematics achievement, and science test scores at age ten are only moderately associated with a country's science test scores at age fourteen. Within these industrialized countries, as Inkeles has suggested, "one would be hard pressed to guess successfully what a student's score will be from knowing his national citizenship."[74]

Very large differences are apparent between science test scores in industrialized societies and the three developing societies of Chile, Iran, and Thailand. With the exception of fourteen-year-olds in Thailand, no developing country's score comes close to any of the scores for any industrialized society. Cognitive skills, as assessed by Western-style standardized tests, appear to be similarly high across all industrialized societies but much lower in developing countries.

We do not yet have an adequate explanation for these findings.

Table 7–1   *Science and Mathematics Achievement Scores for 10-, 13-, and 14-Year-Olds in Fourteen Countries*

	Science Test Scores 10-year-olds		Science Test Scores 14-year-olds		Mathematics Test Scores 13-year-olds	
Country	*Mean*	*S.D.*	*Mean*	*S.D.*	*Mean*	*S.D.*
Australia	—	—	24.6	13.4	20.2	14.0
Belgium	15.9	7.2	18.6	9.0	27.7	15.0
England	15.7	8.5	21.3	14.1	19.3	17.0
Finland	17.5	8.2	20.5	10.6	24.1	9.9
France	—	—	—	—	18.3	12.4
West Germany	14.9	7.4	23.7	11.5	—	—
Japan	21.7	7.7	31.2	14.8	31.2	16.9
Netherlands	15.3	7.6	17.8	10.0	23.9	15.9
Scotland	14.0	8.4	21.4	14.2	19.1	14.6
Sweden	18.3	7.3	21.7	11.7	15.7	10.8
United States	17.7	9.3	21.6	11.6	16.2	13.3
Mean	*16.7*	*7.9*	*22.3*	*11.8*	—	—
Chile	9.1	8.6	9.2	8.9	—	—
Iran	4.1	5.4	7.8	6.1	—	—
Thailand	9.9	6.5	15.6	8.1	—	—

Source: Adapted from Alex Inkeles, "National Differences in Scholastic Performance," *Comparative Education Review*, Vol. 23 (October 1979): 389; and T. Husen (ed.), *International Study of Achievement in Mathematics: A Comparison of Twelve Countries* (New York: Wiley, 1967).

In part, as Inkeles argues, such results may reflect the fact that school children in developing societies have not had much experience in taking standardized tests, though this explanation alone would seem insufficient to explain all of the differences observed. But we do not know whether these results mean that schools in developing countries are less effective in teaching cognitive skills or whether the overall environment in these societies is less propitious for the development of such skills. Inkeles makes a plausible case for the proposition that both factors are involved. In Western societies, he claims, schools have reached a certain minimum threshold of effectiveness, and beyond this threshold increased expenditures and different school policies make little difference. Hence we find that test scores among students in different industrialized countries are very similar. In poor countries, on the other hand, school resources are well below that threshold, with classes of eighty or more students, untrained teachers, and scanty classroom materials. In these countries, therefore, we would expect to find both lower test scores and more variability from school to school and from country to country. There is also some evidence that school effects in developing countries are more powerful compared with the effects of family background than in industrialized societies.

At the same time, Inkeles argues, it seems clear that industrialized and developing countries also differ in the wider environment they provide for the development of cognitive skills. Thus the international study of science achievement shows huge variations in the proportion of children who grow up in homes with books and magazines, ranging from above 90 percent in most Western countries with at least ten books in their household to 31 percent of all students in Chile and 21 percent in Iran.[75] Given these findings, it seems likely that only part of these test score differences can be attributed to the lesser effectiveness of schools themselves.

Changing Test Scores

Do American students learn less than they used to? In the early and mid–1980s, there were confident assertions that the functional literacy, mathematical and reasoning skills, and scientific knowledge of contemporary students had declined sharply from earlier levels. Universities and employers complained that their new entrants could not write coherent paragraphs or even simple declarative sentences without major grammatical errors. National commissions argued ominously that deteriorating schools threatened our national survival in competition with other countries, and called for crash programs to attract new highly trained teachers into the profession and to reconstruct the curricula.[76]

As we might expect, the evidence is more complicated than any of these popular assertions suggest. In the first place, there is good evidence that, by most measures, high school achievement declined significantly between the mid–1960s and 1981 or 1982.[77] There is also evidence that during this same period test scores of older elementary students also fell, though less sharply than the scores of high school students.[78] But test scores of the youngest elementary school students rose slightly during the 1970s, providing little evidence that the basic literacy that is taught in these grades has declined.[79] Although test scores of most students declined during the late 1960s and 1970s, this must be seen in the context of what appears to be a general increase in most scores from the early decades of this century until the 1960s.[80] What follows is a selective (but I hope fair-minded) review of the evidence for these assertions.

The best known evidence for the claim that high school achievement has declined is the trend of Scholastic Aptitude Test scores.[81]

In the early 1960s those tests were taken by only a very small proportion of high school students, primarily those who were planning to attend highly selective colleges and universities. As the proportion of students taking these tests has increased, therefore, one would expect some decline as the *average* ability of students taking the test moves closer to the average ability of all high school students. The decline displayed in Figure 7–1 cannot be so easily explained away, however. Since 1970 the percentage of all students taking the test has remained relatively steady, yet the rate of decline has accelerated. Furthermore, the *absolute number* of high-scoring students declined between 1970 and 1980.[82] A study of valedictorians and salutatorians, for example,

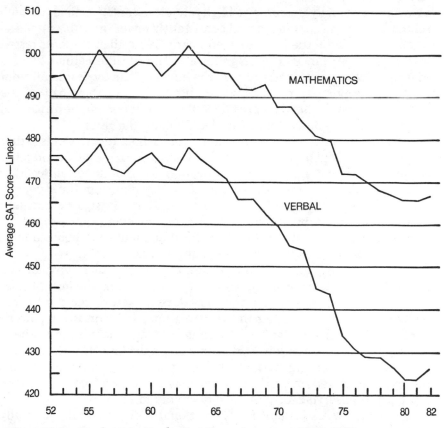

Figure 7–1   *Student Aptitude Test Score Averages, 1952–1982*

Source: Data for 1952–1977, College Entrance Examination Board, *On Further Examination: Report of the Advisory Panel on the Scholastic Aptitude Test Score Decline* (New York: College Board, 1977), p. 6. For 1978–1981, National Center for Education Statistics, *Digest of Education Statistics: 1982* (Washington, D.C.: Government Printing Office, 1982), p. 68. For 1982, National Center for Education Statistics, unpublished data.

showed that the scores of these exceptional students also fell over this period.[83] Research on the changing content of the items on the tests indicates that, if the difficulty of tests has changed over time, they have become slightly easier rather than harder.[84] The decline cannot be explained, therefore, by arguing that standards for what constitutes adequate achievement have risen.

The evidence for declining achievement in high schools is not only confined to the results of S.A.T. scores. Other more specialized tests of subject matter achievement also generally show declines over the same period, as do most of the studies conducted by the National Assessment of Educational Progress of reasoning and comprehension skills of representative samples of seventeen-year-old students.[85] On the question of the direction of the change, therefore, the research evidence is virtually unanimous. High school students, particularly high school juniors and seniors, scored consistently lower on tests of general intellectual skills in the late 1970s and early 1980s than students tested in the 1960s. Although the magnitude of the decline cannot be estimated with any precision, studies of the effects of the increased number of students taking the tests suggest that not more than half of the total decline on the S.A.T. scores since the mid–1960s can be attributed to the changing ability pool of students taking the tests.

The evidence of changes in elementary school test scores is rather less clear cut. Much of that evidence comes from studies conducted by different state departments of education and is of uncertain validity and reliability. The samples surveyed at the different time periods are not always comparable, nor are the test items always of equivalent difficulty. The majority of these state studies, however, show a tendency toward declining scores for only the oldest elementary school students and generally rising scores for the youngest students.[86]

For first- and second-grade students, in particular, virtually all over-time studies show an increase in reading skills during the late 1960s and 1970s, a conclusion that is endorsed even by the most pessimistic observers.[87] In the fourth and fifth grades an inconsistent pattern is observed, with some states reporting increased scores, and others, notably California and New York, reporting a decline.[88] Studies of seventh- and eighth-grade students, however, show a clear trend toward declining achievement, which in its magnitude may come close to the decline observed for juniors and seniors in high school. Research by the National Assessment for Educational Progress, while generally showing fewer cases of decline and more cases of improvement than other sources of data, also indicates that the trend is more favorable for the youngest students and least favorable for the oldest students.[89]

Paradoxically, however, in view of these rather discouraging findings, evidence of earlier trends in test scores has shown a rather consistent pattern of improvement. In 1969, for example, the Educational

Testing Service examined 186 instances in which comparable tests had been administered to representative samples at two different time periods since 1945.[90] In all but 10 of these comparisons, test scores at the later period were higher than at the earlier period, exceeding the earlier scores, the Testing Service reported, by an average of 20 percent. Research on changes in test scores over longer periods, though inevitably highly tentative and based on fragmentary data, also shows a tendency toward higher scores in more recent decades. Jencks, for example, reports that scores on tests of general intellectual ability have risen since they were first administered early in this century and that the tests have had to be renormed several times so that average scores would remain at around 100.[91] Studies of reading achievement generally show rising reading skills for the school-age population from the 1920s and 1930s until the 1960s.[92]

These findings of rising achievement over the long haul fit well with functional theories that schools promote the development of cognitive skills and that increasingly effective schooling has increased the skills of the successive cohorts of students. But, of course, the declining achievement of high school achievement in the last twenty years is not consistent with this view. Perhaps, as some liberal critics maintain, schools are not to blame for this decline, and its explanation must be sought in the increasing turbulence in the wider society during the 1970s. Thus the functional argument may be salvaged. But it is also possible that conservative critics are correct in drawing attention to massive and, from their point of view, disturbing changes in the schools themselves during this period: changes in absenteeism rates, homework assignments, violence and vandalism, and the authority of schools to get students to work steadily at their prescribed tasks. Whatever the merits of these arguments, however (and I will explore them in the next chapter), we are confronted with a paradox: Steadily rising levels of expenditures on schooling and increasing concern that schools should teach more complex cognitive skills in the last two decades have been accompanied by falling test scores.

CONCLUSION

There are three difficulties in assessing the merits of the bewildering variety of statements about what schools teach to their students. First, because of the great methodological problems in measuring the effects of schools, the evidence we possess is fragmentary and of uncertain validity. Because there is no simple and reliable way of separating the effects of schooling from the effects of the wider environment, or the effects of being in school from changes attributable to maturation, and because many of the most important outcomes of schools are so difficult to measure, there is a large gap between our empirical knowledge of what in fact schools teach and the kinds of confident and usually very general assertions that are made in this regard. At the same time, most of these assertions about the effects of schooling may tell us as much about the ideological preconceptions of the critic or observer as about what schools convey to their students. Conservatives believe, and have always believed, that schools ought to teach enduring moral truths and to foster loyalty to the established order. Radicals believe that schools ought to liberate students from blind obedience to tradition and promote the questioning of authority. It comes as no surprise, therefore, that conservative critics believe that existing schools promote moral relativism and disrespect for authority, and radical critics maintain that these same institutions reinforce the hegemony of the existing order. These different claims are, in principle at least, empirical statements that can be tested by evidence, but they also can be seen as differences stemming from radically divergent conceptions of what schools ought to be doing.

A second difficulty concerns the effects of the knowledge revolution and cultural diversity on what schools teach and on our conceptions of the role of schooling in the modern world. On the one hand, both the curriculum and teaching methods have changed in the last forty or fifty years. Because the curriculum is more diverse than it used to be, and because teaching methods are probably less authoritarian, the particular values, attitudes, and knowledge that schools teach are more difficult to specify than was the case in the past. But at the same time, the effects of the knowledge revolution and cultural change on our *conceptions* of what schools *should* teach are as significant as their effects on actual school practice. Teaching methods may or may not have changed fundamentally in the last fifty years, but there is no question that many more observers *believe* that education for life in the modern age requires that the old authoritarian pedagogy be radically transformed. It may be true that schools today, compared with schools in the past, promote intellectual understanding rather than memorization of facts; it is clearly true, however, that most educators in the 1960s and 1970s came to believe that the complexities of work and citizenship required that they shift rapidly from the latter to the former task. Schools have undoubtedly changed in the last four or five decades, but our conceptions of the role of schooling have changed even more rapidly.

All these considerations apply with almost equal force to sociological theories of the effects of schooling as well as to popular criticisms of schools. The functional interpretation of what schools teach, for example, is only partly a theory of what contemporary schools actually teach to their students. It is also an account of how the increasingly vital role of education in the modern world has made it necessary for schools to shift away from their traditional task of moral indoctrination and memorization of a fixed body of knowledge toward the modern imperatives of moral development, tolerance for divergent opinions, and general cognitive skills. And, of course, functional theorists prefer these latter outcomes to the more traditional tasks of schooling. Their statements about what schools convey to their students, therefore, no less than the statements of radical or conservative theorists, will be colored by these preferences.

What, then, can we say about what schools actually teach to their students, bearing in mind that our generalizations, like those of other observers, may be shaped by our views of what schools ought to be teaching, or by general theories as to the appropriate role of schooling in the modern world? The evidence we have is quite sketchy and incomplete, but it suggests that almost all of the arguments and theories we have reviewed are partly misleading. Consider first the problem of the effects of schooling on values and attitudes and the confident assertions that radical theorists make in this regard. We have some evidence that grades in school reflect particular attitudes and personality tests as well as cognitive achievement. But does this mean that schools effectively teach such traits as perseverance, dependability, and conformity to authority? It is equally plausible to argue that students who already have these characteristics tend to get higher grades and stay longer in school than other students. Nor is it obvious that it is only schools and work organizations in *capitalist societies* that reward such traits and penalize people who are aggressive or rebellious. One could also plausibly argue that most organizations in *any* modern society tend to reward and punish these kinds of qualities.[93] Even if schools do encourage such traits, therefore, it is by no means clear that, as Bowles and Gintis claim, this is made necessary by the demands of work in a hierarchically organized capitalist social order. At the same time there is quite good evidence that schooling, at least Western-style schooling, tends to promote a set of attitudes and personality traits not entirely consistent with the radical claim that schools inhibit independent thought and foster conformity to traditional values. Studies in developing societies and in the United States, for example, suggest that education is associated with tolerance for diverse opinions, intellectual flexibility, and open-mindedness, even after differences in ability and socioeconomic status are held constant. No doubt there are limits to such toleration and open-mindedness, and there is no reason to suppose that college education in Mao's China, Hitler's Germany, or contemporary Iran would have the same beneficient effects as college in the United States. Nonetheless, it is hard to reconcile this evidence with the radical and neo-Marxist claims that education in capitalist society is peculiarly repressive of the development of original and independent thought as well as a major bulwark of established values.

Beyond this observation, however, there is virtually no evidence that would enable us to evaluate the merits of the claims and counter-claims about the effects of schooling on attitudes and values. One inter-pretation of this lack of evidence, which I prefer, is that such effects are relatively small: Students in contemporary society are exposed to a wide variety of *competing values and ideals* both within the school and in the wider environment, and many of these implicit and explicit messages cancel each other out. Thus although *particular* and *unusual* schools may have quite powerful effects on some students, schooling *in general* cannot be said to have enduring or important effects on one set of attitudes and values rather than another.[94] But, it should be recalled, lack of evidence does not necessarily mean there is none that could be obtained. If the burden of proof would seem to be on those who claim that most schools do teach a coherent set of ideals and foster one particular set of personality traits, it is conceivable that with better techniques of measurement and more imaginative research such evidence could be produced.

The research on the effects of schooling on *cognitive* skills does not give clear support to any of the theories we have considered. First, there appears to be sufficient evidence of enduring cognitive effects to refute the cynical view that schools merely certify existing compe-tence rather than produce real development in skills and aptitudes. Evidence from studies of young children not enrolled in school, from comparisons of uneducated and educated individuals in developing countries, and from college-age populations in the United States sup-ports the conclusion that schooling has quite powerful and consistent effects on reasoning and analytical skills. Schools may not make people more intelligent in any absolute sense, but they seem to have clear effects on the development of the kinds of intelligence that are particu-larly called upon in modern industrialized societies. In the develop-ment of these skills, the wider environment is also important, as re-search in developing countries suggests, but it is highly probable that if schools did not exist, general cognitive skills, as well as the particular information that the curriculum conveys, would be less effectively learned.

In view of this conclusion, it is paradoxical that there is very little evidence that one kind of schooling or higher-quality schooling has clearly superior efforts than any other. To be sure, there is no doubt that some individual schools are very effective and that others teach very little, but no research to date has produced persuasive evidence that one set of school characteristics has clearly different effects. Most practicing educators and educational critics, of course, are convinced that the particular methods they espouse have better outcomes— whether these be individualized learning, more homework, more relevant courses, or more required basic courses. But the history of educational research, which is, in considerable part, the history of failure to demonstrate measurable differences in outcomes between different methods and curricula, suggests we should be cautious in accepting these claims. Rather, it may be that unusual effects depend preeminently on unusual people rather than unusual school characteristics. While unusual people can produce extraordinary effects with a variety of teaching methods, ordinary people may produce ordinary effects no matter what techniques are employed.

When we examine trends in school achievement over time, the paradox of effective schooling roughly equal effects of different schools is further compounded. Though the evidence is sketchy, it suggests that for most decades of this century cognitive skills have been rising, a finding that supports the functional view that as schooling has become more widespread and perhaps more effective the general intellectual skills of the population will increase. At least until 1960, therefore, one could argue that increasing societal investments in schooling had paid off in the form of higher cognitive skills. Since that time, however, particularly from 1970 to 1980, there is good evidence that the trend has been reversed, and that, as conservative critics have not been slow to point out, increasing school expenditures have been associated with steadily falling test scores (at least at the high school level). Such a trend is inconsistent with the predictions of human capital theory and the broader functional paradigm.

But falling test scores also pose difficulties for the view that different schools have similar effects. If test scores of young children have remained stable or risen, yet the scores of older students have fallen sharply, this at least suggests that we are dealing with a school effect as well as or instead of a societal effect. Thus high schools may have been less effective institutions in producing cognitive skills in 1980 than they were in 1970 or 1965. Although this in no way implies that a conservative diagnosis of declining standards and increased discipline is correct, it does suggest that there may be identifiable changes in schools that are partly responsible for the decline. In a curious way, therefore, the best evidence against the now sociologically orthodox view that different school characteristics have almost identical effects may be that the test scores of high school students have fallen in the last twenty years.

That decline, however, must be placed in appropriate context. Contrary to recent charges by prophets of doom and despair, there is little evidence that U.S. students learn less in school than their counterparts in most other industrialized countries. Such comparisons are extremely hazardous because of huge variations in selectivity and differing aims and objectives of schooling in different countries. But those

international comparisons that are feasible show a quite small difference between most industrialized societies in the scores of students
in their early teens. Nor is there good evidence that a society's ranking
in this international competition over cognitive skills has effects on
economic growth. As we saw in Chapter 2, arguments about the "learning society" of the future and the close connection between cognitive
skills and societal productivity are not persuasively supported by the
data. No doubt it is a bad thing that high school students' cognitive
skills have declined, but there is as yet no credible evidence that this
will have demonstrable effects on future economic growth or national
survival, despite strident claims to the contrary in the media and in
reports of national commissions.

This aside, it must be admitted that the evidence of declining
test scores is a disturbing development for all those concerned with
education and disconcerting to most of our received sociological theory
about the direction of educational change and the effects of schooling
on students. To begin to understand the puzzling development and
the other paradoxical findings of research on school effects, we need
to shift our focus away from the very general issues of cultural transmission examined in this chapter to the structure and organization of
the school itself.

Endnotes

1. Stanley F. Bonner, *Education in Ancient Rome* (London: Methuen, 1977).
2. Charles Silberman, *Crisis in the Classroom* (New York: Random House, 1969), p. 121.
3. Diane Ravitch, *The Troubled Crusade: American Education, 1945–1980* (New York: Basic Books, 1983).
4. Daniel Bell, *The Coming of Post-Industrial Society* (New York: Basic Books, 1973).
5. Thus to the extent that one believes something is absolutely true and eternally important, it makes sense to require students learn it by heart.
6. Emile Durkheim, *The Evolution of Educational Thought* (London: Routledge and Kegan Paul, 1977).
7. Bonner, *Education in Ancient Rome.*
8. Edward A. Krug, *The Secondary School Curriculum* (New York: Harper, 1960).
9. Bell, *The Coming of Post-Industrial Society.*
10. Ibid., pp. 382–383.
11. It is almost impossible to estimate how many schools experimented with such courses at any particular time because of the absence of any national school census, though as Ravitch points out (*The Troubled Crusade*, p. 360) the school surveys conducted by some schools of education provide one untapped source of such data for the period before 1970.
12. For sex education, see Jacqueline Kasun, "Turning Children into Sex Experts," *The Public Interest*, No. 55 (Spring 1979): 3–14.

13. Francis FitzGerald, *America Revised: History Schoolbooks in the Twentieth Century* (Boston: Little, Brown, 1979).

14. Ibid.

15. Again, it is close to impossible to estimate how many schools employed this kind of curriculum. There is no question, however, that many articles appeared in professional journals of English during the 1970s that discussed problems of teaching these authors. See the issues of *English Journal* and *Media and Methods* during this period. For an example of the teaching of Simon and Garfunkle, see Frederick Wiseman's classic film, *High School* (1968).

16. Randall Collins, *The Credential Society* (New York: Academic Press, 1979); and David Tyack and Elisabeth Hansot, *Managers of Virtue: Public School Leadership in America, 1820–1980* (New York: Basic Books, 1982).

17. Contemporary conservatives, for example, are probably overly impressed with the degree to which courses in values clarification and moral development have become widespread, William J. Bennett and Edwin J. Delattre, "Moral Education in the Schools," *The Public Interest*, No. 50 (Winter 1978): 81–98.

18. Neil Postman and Charles Weingartner, *Teaching as a Subversive Activity* (New York: Dell, 1969).

19. J. Charles Park, "Preachers, Politics and Public Education: A Review of Right Wing Pressures against Public Schooling in America," *Phi Delta Kappan*, Vol. 62 (May 1980): 608; and George Hillcocks, Jr., "Books and Bombs: Ideological Conflict and the Schools—A Case Study of the Kanawha County Book Protest," *School Review*, Vol. 86 (August 1978): 632–654.

20. Burton Clark, *Educating the Expert Society* (San Francisco: Chandler, 1961); and Clark Kerr, et al., *Industrialism and Industrial Man* (New York: Oxford, 1974).

21. For an extreme example of this view, see Alvin Toffler, *Future Shock* (New York: Random House, 1970).

22. Sarane S. Boocock, *An Introduction to the Sociology of Learning* (New York: Houghton Mifflin, 1972) p. 151; and James S. Coleman, *The Adolescent Society* (New York: Free Press, 1961).

23. Talcott Parsons, "The School Class as a Social System," *Harvard Educational Review* 29 (1959): 297–308; and Robert Dreeben, *On What Is Learned in School* (Reading, Mass.: Addison-Wesley, 1968).

24. Dreeben, *On What Is Learned*.

25. Alex Inkeles and David Smith, *Becoming Modern* (Cambridge: Harvard University Press, 1974).

26. Nevitt Sanford (ed.), *The American College* (New York: Wiley, 1962).

27. Samuel Bowles and Herbert Gintis, *Schooling in Capitalist America* (New York: Basic Books, 1976).

28. Ivan Illich, *Deschooling Society* (New York: Harper and Row, 1970); Pierre Bourdieu and J. C. Passerow, *Reproduction* (Beverley Hills, Calif.: Sage Publications, 1977); and Michael W. Apple, *Education and Power* (Boston: Routledge and Kegan Paul, 1982).

29. For a partial empirical test, see Frank M. Howell and Lynn W. McBroom, "Social Relations at Home and at School: An Analysis of the Correspondence Principle," *Sociology of Education*, Vol. 55 (January 1982): 40–52; and Jeannie Oakes, "Classroom Role Relationships: Exploring the Bowles and Gintis Hypothesis," *Sociology of Education*, Vol. 55, No. 4 (October 1982): 197–212.

30. Bowles and Gintis, Schooling in Capitalist America, p. 137.

31. Ibid., p. 134.

32. Ivan Illich, "Vernacular Values and Education," *Teachers College Record*, Vol. 81 (Fall 1979): 31–75.

33. Illich, "Deschooling."

34. Ibid.; and Apple, *Education and Power*.

35. Bourdieu and Passerow, *Reproduction*.

36. Ibid.

37. Collins, *The Credential Society*.

38. John W. Meyer, "The Effects of Education as an Institution," *American Journal of Sociology*, Vol. 83 (July 1977): 55–77.

39. Ibid., p. 60.

40. Ibid., p. 65.

41. Ibid., pp. 69–70.

42. Ibid., p. 74 (emphasis added).

43. Alex Inkeles, "National Differences in Scholastic Performance," *Comparative Education Review*, Vol. 23 (October 1979): 386–407.

44. This problem has bedeviled much research in the field. See James W. Trent and Leland L. Medsker, *Beyond High School* (San Francisco: Jossey-Bass, 1968).

45. Research showing that school effects are more powerful in science and mathematics achievement than in reading or language achievement supports this view. In subjects that are taught more or less exclusively in schools school effects are relatively large; in subjects where much is also learned in the home these effects are smaller. See Inkeles, "National Differences."

46. Harvey Averch, et al., *How Effective Is Schooling? A Critical Review and Synthesis of Research Findings* (Santa Monica, Calif.: The Rand Corporation, 1972).

47. Christopher Jencks, et al., *Inequality* (New York: Basic Books, 1972), p. 87.

48. Ibid., p. 87.

49. Ibid., p. 87.

50. Barbara Heyns, *Summer Learning and the Effects of Schooling* (New York: Academic Press, 1978).

51. Patricia Greenfield and Jerome Bruner, "Culture and Cognitive Growth," *International Journal of Psychology*, Vol. 1 (1966): 89–107.

52. Michael Cole and Barbara Means, *Comparative Studies of How People Think* (Cambridge: Harvard University Press, 1981).

53. Ibid.

54. Ibid. It should be noted, however, that Cole and his associates are skeptical about whether such styles of thinking should be regarded as more developed or more advanced in an absolute sense.

55. Herbert H. Hyman, Charles R. Wright, and John Shelton Reed, *The Enduring Effects of Education* (Chicago: University of Chicago Press, 1975).

56. Ibid., pp. 67–74. See also S. B. Withey, *A Degree and What Else?* (New York: McGraw-Hill, 1972).

57. Trent and Medsker, *Beyond High School*.

58. Ibid.

59. Herbert McClosky and Alida Brill, *What Americans Believe about Civil Liberties* (New York: Basic Books, 1983).

60. Inkeles, "National Differences."

61. For the Nazi case, see Richard Grunberger, *The 12 Year Reich: A Social History of Nazi Germany 1933–1945* (New York: Holt, Rinehart & Winston, 1971).

62. V. S. Naipaul, *Among the Believers: An Islamic Journey* (New York: Knopf, 1981).

63. Joseph I. Zajda, *Education in the U.S.S.R.* (New York: Pergamon Press, 1980).

64. James Coleman, Thomas Hoffer, and Sally Kilgore, *High School Achievement* (New York: Basic Books, 1982).

65. Glen G. Cain and Arthur S. Goldberger, "Public and Private Schools Revisited," *Sociology of Education*, Vol. 56 (October 1983): 208–219; Karl Alexander and A. M. Pallas, "Private Schools and Public Policy: New Evidence on Cognitive Achievement in Public Schools," *Sociology of Education*, Vol. 53 (October 1983): 170–182; William R. Morgan, "Learning and Student Life Quality of Public and Private School Youth," *Sociology of Education*, Vol. 56 (October 1983): 187–202; Jay Noell, "Public and Catholic Schools: A Reanalysis of 'Public and Private Schools,'" *Sociology of Education*, Vol. 55 (1982): 123–132; and Peter H. Rossi and James D. Wright, "Best Schools—Better Discipline or Better Students? A Review of *High School Achievement*," *American Journal of Education* (November 1982): 79–89.

66. Alexander and Pallas, "Private Schools and Public Policy."

67. David A. Squires, William G. Huitt, and John K. Segars, *Effective Schools and Classrooms: A Research-Based Perspective* (Washington, D.C.: A.S.C.D., 1983).

68. Sarah Lawrence Lightfoot, *The Good High School* (New York: Basic Books, 1983).

69. Ibid.

70. For a relatively recent example, see the evidence assembled for the success of open classrooms in Charles Silberman, *Crisis in the Classroom* (New York: Random House, 1969).

71. Torsten Husén, *The School in Question* (Oxford: Oxford University Press, 1979), Chapter 6.

72. Joseph I. Zajda, *Education in the U.S.S.R.* (New York: Pergamon, 1980).

73. Inkeles, "National Differences."

74. Ibid., p. 406.

75. Ibid., p. 405.

76. National Commission on Excellence in Education, *A Nation at Risk: The Imperative for Educational Reform* (Washington, D.C.: U.S. Government, 1983).

77. Report of the Advisory Panel on the S.A.T. Score Decline, *On Further Examination* (New York: College Entrance Examination Board, 1977); and Brian K. Waters, *The Test Score Decline: A Review and Annotated Bibliography*, Technical Memorandum 81-2 (Washington, D.C.: Department of Defense, 1981).

78. Frank Armbuster, *Our Children's Crippled Future* (New York: Quadrangle Books, 1977); and Gilbert R. Austin (ed.), *The Rise and Fall of National Test Scores* (New York: Academic Press, 1982).

79. Patricia A. Graham, "Literacy: A Goal for Secondary Schools," *Daedalus* (Summer 1981): 119–134. Graham cites evidence that standards for what constitutes literacy have steadily risen in recent decades.

80. Jencks, "Inequality," p. 63.

81. *On Further Examination.*

82. Ibid.

83. Ibid., Appendix B.

84. Ibid., Appendix D.

85. National Assessment of Educational Progress, *Writing Achievement: 1969–1979* (Denver: Educational Commission of the States, 1980).

86. Armbruster, *Our Children's Crippled Future;* and Austin, *The Rise and Fall.*

87. Ibid.

88. Ibid.

89. National Assessment of Educational Progress, *Writing Achievement.*

90. U.S. Department of Health, Education and Welfare, *Toward a Social Report* (Washington, D.C.: U.S. Government, 1969), pp. 66–70.

91. Jencks, op. cit., p. 63.

92. Ibid.

93. Thus even if schools do effectively teach the traits that the neo-Marxists argue (and I am skeptical), there is no evidence that such traits are specific to schooling in capitalist societies as opposed to socialist societies.

94. Thus there seems little doubt that such institutions as the famous English public schools and the Julliard School of Music have powerful effects on student attitudes and values. These institutions have long and proud traditions, a relatively homogeneous study body and faculty, and confer very powerful identities on their students. Precisely because most schools are not at all like this, however, we would not expect such effects for most schools. See also Meyer's discussion of chartering effects versus socialization effects in Meyer, "The Effects of Education."

chapter 8

Schools
as Organizations:
Problems of Order,
Control, and Motivation

So far in this book we have treated the institutions we call
schools as a "black box" that somehow produces, or fails to produce,
particular valued educational outcomes. In the course of that discussion
much has been said about the effects of schooling and the discrepancy
between these effects and widely held ideas about what schools should
do. But little has been said about how schools in fact produce these
outcomes and why, in particular, there appears to be such a large
gap between stated goals for schooling and the often rather meager
effects we can observe. Perhaps, as I implied in the last chapter, our
disappointments with schools are partly a result of our perceptions
about what schools do rather than objective failings of schools themselves—the sheer difficulty of measuring the effects of schooling makes
the temptation to attribute outcomes to schools that fit our particular
prejudices and preconceptions almost irresistible. And almost certainly,
as a host of observers point out, many of our recent objectives for
education are so grandiose that it seems unlikely that any institution
staffed by mere mortals could satisfy them.[1] One might question, for
example, whether any conceivable institution could achieve, in a literal
sense, the objective of maximizing emotional or moral development
or teaching all students the ability to learn how to learn. But if dissatisfaction with schooling almost inevitably flows from our contemporary

views of what education should achieve, it may also have another rather different explanation. If schools fail to teach the values, skills, and ideas we expect them to teach, the reasons may lie in the special character of schools as organizations and in the constraints they face in motivating, controlling, and coordinating the activities of large numbers of people who are there not entirely of their own free will.

This chapter is not intended as a comprehensive review of the literature on the sociology of the school as a complex organization.[2] Rather, our interest here is to show how a sociological perspective on the school as an organization both contrasts with most current educational thought and illuminates the problem of why the effects of schooling seem so often disappointing. As my chief illustration of this analysis, I shall examine the comparative failure of the alternative school movement of the late 1960s and early 1970s. In the second part of the chapter I will develop a theory of why school achievement has generally declined in the last twenty years and then connect that decline with changes in schools over that period, focusing particularly on how schools have lost a considerable part of their previous authority to motivate and control the activities of young people.

As formal organizations, schools defy simple classification. Like all complex organizations, schools can be seen as more or less rational instruments for organizing people to accomplish particular goals. Like business corporations, hospitals, or government departments, schools are *bureaucratic* organizations with a hierarchy of command, where clearly defined responsibilities are defined for all employees, and where explicit rules rather than personal relationships shape behavior.[3] Thus there are analogies between school boards and boards of directors of corporations, between school administrators and managers, and between teachers and foremen in business corporations or nurses in hospitals. In each case, the top of the hierarchy is occupied by individuals whose job it is to represent the organization to the outside world and to justify its activities. Because of these responsibilities, these individuals are thought entitled to give orders to other people in the organization.

In large school systems, in particular, this bureaucratic analogy is quite apt. In many large city school systems the goal of educating the young, like the goal of producing particular products at a profit or healing the sick, leads to an elaborate bureaucratic structure where administrators and clerical personnel often outnumber teachers and where teachers in turn are often subject to quite detailed controls.

But if there are useful analogies between administrators and managers, teachers and production-line or office workers, and even between students and raw material that must be processed or transformed, there is one crucial respect in which this bureaucratic model of a hierarchy of command does not apply. The basic work of schools is performed in a setting that is considerably insulated from the kind of detailed supervision and control that characterizes work in almost all other bureaucratic organizations.[4] Work in factories and offices is usually monitored and observed by supervisors or managers who check constantly that it is being performed efficiently and satisfactorily. But the work that takes place in classrooms is, by these criteria, extraordinarily free of direct supervision. Teachers are often required to submit lesson plans and expected to follow a particular curriculum, but they would regard it as a violation of their professional autonomy if principals routinely entered the classroom to check their performance. Teachers may call on principals to help them deal with troublesome students, they may be held accountable if their classrooms are excessively noisy, but they regularly enjoy a great deal of discretionary authority once the classroom door is closed.[5]

This freedom is greatest in college and universities (where visits to the classroom by other professors or administrators are almost unknown), and least in some modern elementary classrooms (where there are several teachers and many different "activity areas"). These variations are of differences of degree rather than differences of kind. In the overwhelming majority of cases teachers are alone with their students, charged only with such general responsibility as covering the syllabus by the end of the school year, handing in grade reports, and maintaining minimum standards of order. In these respects the basic work of schools is organized in a highly decentralized manner in comparison with the work of most other organizations.

The Professional-Client Metaphor

The decentralization of authority in schools has led some sociologists and many educators to characterize these institutions as places where *professionals* and their *clients* come together. Like lawyers, doctors, and architects, teachers have clients for whom they are performing a service that is clearly in their clients' interests. Like these other professionals, teachers have a body of knowledge and professional expertise that makes them uniquely qualified to serve their clients. Just as these other professionals require considerable autonomy from direct supervision to serve their clients' best interests, so the authority teachers enjoy in the classroom can be seen in this light. Although lawyers and doctors, unlike teachers, traditionally earn their living from client fees rather than in the form of fixed salaries, this departure from the classical professional-client model of fees for service seems relatively minor. Large numbers of physicians and attorneys are employed, like teachers, by large organizations, paid a fixed salary, and regularly evaluated by superiors. Nevertheless, they continue to enjoy considerable autonomy in how they conduct their day-to-day work with clients.

The professional-client metaphor of schools is very popular with most contemporary educators. Educators speak a great deal about the "profession" of teaching and the importance of public understanding that teachers have a body of expertise and professional competence that entitles them to equivalent status with lawyers, architects, and engineers. They complain, understandably, that a professional who performs such a vital service is rewarded with salaries that are often below those obtained by manual workers who perform the most menial tasks. Professional educators also refer regularly to students as "clients" and stress how their work involves individualized instruction tailored to the needs of particular students. Thus contemporary educators often write as though the work of teachers in diagnosing particular learning problems, recommending particular courses of study, and evaluating and monitoring progress toward particular goals is directly analogous to the work of doctors with their patients or lawyers with their clients.[6]

Although the professional-client metaphor is a fairly accurate description of what professional educators *believe* schools are doing, at least in their public pronouncements, it is misleading in two crucial respects from a sociological point of view. First, because teaching remains an art rather than a science, with no set of agreed upon or objectively valid principles, the claim of elementary and secondary school teachers to fully professional status is dubious.[7] Physicians can and do misdiagnose the nature of their patients' illnesses, just as engineers or architects sometimes build structures that collapse, but these failures are usually the result of individual incompetence or carelessness rather than the collective ignorance of the profession to which they belong. Despite the existence of literally hundreds of books on the subject, however, the principles of teaching remain in dispute.[8] There are good and bad teachers who would be recognized as such by the great majority of observers, and there are undoubtedly ideas or tips that experienced teachers and professors of education can pass on to beginning practitioners. But there is neither universal agreement nor a body of research evidence showing that one particular set of techniques and practices is always more efficacious than another.[9]

Part of the problem, of course, is our sheer ignorance of the basic character of the educational process: the transfer of ideas, information, and concepts from one mind to another and, in general terms, the nature of human learning. Compared with our understanding of the body and the causes of its sickness and health, our knowledge of the vastly more complex world of the brain is in its infancy. Psychologists remain divided as to precisely how and in what circumstances human beings learn, and the nature and varieties of human intelligence.[10] The neurological and chemical changes in the brain corresponding to this learning are only beginning to be studied. But even if we knew far more about learning than we know now, a formidable barrier to the development of a science of teaching would remain. Disputes about the effectiveness of different teaching methods are disagreements about the worth of different educational goals as well as about the best way to achieve particular ends. Those who advocate traditional highly structured pedagogical techniques, for example, are likely to value similarly traditional learning outcomes: mastery of a particular subject matter and quite specific useful skills. Those who disagree frequently have rather different objectives in mind as the primary goal of their favored pedagogical techniques: understanding rather than specific factual material and general cognitive and emotional development rather than simple literacy or numeracy. It is only a slight exaggeration, therefore, to describe teaching as an activity that employs techniques of unknown and uncertain efficacy to achieve goals that are frequently vague and almost always controversial.

Students as Clients

The professional-client metaphor of schooling is also misleading in its description of the role of students. There is little question that students benefit a great deal from education and, most research indicates, generally enjoy being in school.[11] Quite obviously, however, students are not clients in the sense that the term applies to such groups as patients seeking medical attention or those who need legal counsel. First, elementary and secondary school children are required, usually until age sixteen, to be in school whether they might choose to go or not. Once on school grounds, furthermore, they are required to attend particular classes and to be instructed by teachers regardless of their personal inclinations. Adolescent students do not, for the most part, seek out teachers, as adult patients routinely try and then reject particular physicians; they are *assigned* to particular classes and threatened with negative sanctions if they are inclined to resist. Thus if the heart of the professional-client relationship is a voluntary contract between individuals, the teacher-student and school-student relationship is compulsory.

The sheer number of students and their relative immaturity also shape the character of the teacher-student relationship. Like the ideal relationship between professionals and their clients everywhere, the educational ideal is an individual relationship between the teacher and his or her student. But despite much recent rhetoric about individualization of instruction and meeting the needs of individual students, teaching and learning take place in a crowd of others.[12] Teachers who spend time with individual students in the classroom risk alienating the majority; those who address the class as a whole almost exclusively cannot in any meaningful sense attend to individual learning problems, or the large differences in knowledge and ability that exist in every classroom.

Furthermore, to teach large numbers of students inevitably requires considerable controls over behavior in the classroom. Even with adult students in colleges without mandatory class attendance, teachers cannot do their work without some rules, implicit or explicit, restricting student talk and physical movement. In elementary and secondary schools these rules are typically far more elaborate and detailed. Students are forbidden to talk to their neighbors even in whispers, reprimanded for gazing out of the window, and prohibited from walking around the room.[13] Whereas teachers may dislike these injunctions as much as their students, it is difficult to see how they could be avoided. Given the crowded character of classrooms, the immaturity of students, and the nonvoluntary character of schooling, order in the classroom tends to be problematic and often precarious. Teachers must maintain order, partly because teaching is almost impossible without it and partly because disorderly or noisy classrooms are viewed by principals and other teachers as an indication of incompetence. But the efforts to maintain control over the behavior or deportment of two dozen students often interferes with the educational work of the classroom. Classroom management and disciplinary activities frequently take a great deal of time; they also can poison the atmosphere of mutual confidence and trust that, almost all of us believe, is necessary for effective learning.[14]

All of this suggests, therefore, that the metaphor of the professional-client relationship has only limited use in describing the distinctive character of the relationship between schools and students. Compared with social workers in a welfare agency, nurses in hospitals, or clerical workers in a business corporation, teachers are remarkably free from detailed controls over their work routines. In this sense schools may be viewed more as a collection of semi-autonomous professionals practicing their craft rather than as strictly bureaucratic organizations in which work is always monitored by superiors. But although teachers are relatively free of detailed supervision in the classroom, their autonomy is restricted by other kinds of constraints. The necessity of managing and controlling the activities of large numbers of individuals means that teachers must devote a fair proportion of their time and energy to noneducational tasks. Teachers must act as police officers and disciplinarians as well as educators, and in some schools at least, these roles become dominant. At the same time, the goals of education and the methods for achieving these goals are, by contrast with most other service professions, highly uncertain and characterized by considerable disagreement. There is no equivalent in education to the overriding goal of health or freedom from disease; nor does the teaching profession possess a body of knowledge which, once mastered, gives relatively predictable results with virtually all individuals and in most situations. Some teachers are clearly more effective than others, but it is not obvious that this effectiveness is the result of particular techniques or knowledge that can be readily conveyed to others rather than personal qualities like enthusiasm or commitment, which cannot readily be taught.

Although the professional-client model is misleading in its account of what schools actually do, it is, paradoxically enough, a relatively accurate metaphor for what educators and teachers, and perhaps the general public as well, think schools should be doing. Educators refer to students as clients for whom schools are providing a service, and refer to teachers as professionals who devote their full time and attention to meeting the needs of their clients. Teachers and educators frequently complain that the financial resources available to them make it difficult to achieve such lofty educational goals as cognitive or emotional development. But they rarely admit the possibility that other kinds of constraints limit the school's ability to attain these goals. Educators are not inclined to air whatever doubts they have about the efficacy of particular pedagogical techniques in public, nor do teachers stress that management and discipline problems inevitably take a substantial proportion of their time and energy.

An important and paradoxical conclusion follows from these considerations. Schools are organizations that, compared with most other institutions, are characterized by almost uniquely lofty and grandiose aims and that claim to be places where professionals and their clients come together.[15] Yet the constraints schools face in achieving these goals are fully comparable with and may even exceed those of organizations with far less ambitious goals. To develop this paradox, I will now examine some similarities between schools and other (at first sight) entirely different organizations: prisons, mental hospitals, and adult work organizations.

Schools as Custodial Institutions

Elementary and secondary schools face a number of the same basic problems as prisons, mental hospitals, and army training camps. All these organizations are custodial institutions.[16] They must deal with an essentially captive audience who cannot be presumed to be there of their own free will and who may not leave the grounds or building of the organization without permission. Whereas most students would willingly attend schools in a way that virtually no prisoners would voluntarily remain, all these institutions must compel all their inmates to be present whatever their motivations might be. Inevitably, therefore, compulsion and coercion play an important role in all custodial institutions. Most students wish to attend classes, just as most mental patients desire to attend therapy sessions, but there will always be some individuals who will not so choose and must be compelled to attend. Most students, like most prisoners in low-security prisons, will not be particularly disruptive, but because only a few highly troublesome individuals can interfere with the work of the institution, these people must be coerced to do what others do voluntarily. Thus the rules and controls that custodial institutions use to ensure compliance tend to be designed for the worst possible case.[17] Because some students might bang their bags or satchels against lockers in the corridor, all students must be reminded that this is forbidden. Because a few mental patients might use razors, stockings, or matches to attempt suicide, all patients must be prevented from gaining access to these items except under strict supervision.[18] Because some prisoners might use the exercise yard time to plot an escape or an assault on a guard, silence for all must be enforced.

The result in most custodial institutions is the proliferation of extremely detailed rules of behavior that often have the effect of undermining whatever spontaneous cooperation and good will that exists. To minimize the risk of disorder and disruption that is always present where large numbers of individuals must be compelled to perform what are often rather onerous tasks, custodial institutions tend to control their captive populations in ways that would be considered demeaning outside these organizations. The result of these controls over physical movement, talking, dress, and demeanor is that individuals comply sullenly and resentfully. In small elementary schools, perhaps, this vicious circle of detailed controls leading to resentment and alienation and in turn to further controls does not fully apply. Young children are more malleable and more in awe of adult authority than teenagers. They are perhaps less likely to resent being told to sit up straight and to pay attention and more likely to obey these instructions. Because elementary schools are small and because students tend to remain in one classroom for much of the day, furthermore, organization and management problems outside the classroom tend to be less severe. But in large comprehensive high schools, particularly those serving students from diverse backgrounds, control problems are often acute. Many fifteen- or sixteen-year-old adolescents are, in contemporary society at least, not at all in awe of the school's authority. They are also likely to resent what they regard as demeaning controls over their behavior that characterize virtually all schools and that contrast sharply with the relative freedom they enjoy outside. This is particularly the case for those students who believe, perhaps correctly, they are learning little which is of benefit to them. Thus even if the majority of the student body does not share these views, schools are highly vulnerable to disruption by a relatively small number of individuals who have little to gain by conformity and for whom the standard penalties of suspension or expulsion hold few terrors.

Like prisons and mental hospitals, therefore, schools are places where order and authority are problematic.[19] If most students have more positive incentives to conform to school rules than prisoners in a typical penal institution, only a few determined individuals can make life miserable for the majority. To control these individuals, schools have rather fewer resources at their disposal than prisons and mental hospitals. Disruptive students cannot, like mental patients, be sedated by drugs and physically restrained in a strait jacket. Nor can schools sentence students to long periods of solitary confinement or an additional term in the institution. The sanctions that schools do possess, moreover, are not always effective with the most troublesome students. The threat of suspension or expulsion ceases to deter disruptive behavior if the student positively welcomes removal from the classroom.

Schools as Work Organizations

If schools share common problems of authority and order with other custodial institutions, they also share with such organizations as factories and offices the problem of motivating individuals to engage in what are often rather onerous and demanding tasks. Regardless of which educational goals schools attempt to realize, students are expected to engage in relatively sustained activities that both they and the school define as work.[20] Whereas some of these activities may be intrinsically pleasurable or self-motivated activities for some students, there is abundant evidence that many students find that the tasks they are assigned are difficult and often tedious. In this respect school work is similar to adult work, but schools lack the crucial incentives that adult work organizations possess to motivate this activity. Adults are not only praised for good work, they are also *paid* for it. Although most adults would perhaps continue to do some kind of work if they possessed independent means, it seems unlikely that most routine tasks in factories and offices would be adequately performed without this powerful incentive.

Thus schools must rely on other, and one suspects, rather less universally effective incentives to persuade students to work conscientiously at assigned tasks. Teachers publically praise students who do good work, and schools have honor rolls and award ceremonies where the whole community can celebrate the value placed on academic prowess. At the same time, appeals are made to idle students that their futures are in jeopardy and their parents would be shocked by their indolence. Teachers may ridicule and attempt to humiliate recalcitrant students by enlisting peer pressure, and they even plead with students to "not let me down." Most important of all, schools motivate students by giving them grades that serve both as rewards and punishments.

Grades are the closest equivalent to a currency that academic life possesses.[21] Students, we hope, do not work only for the sake of grades any more than adults work solely for money. But if other motivators fail, grades constitute a reward that is more tangible and enduring than often fleeting expressions of praise. Grades can be exchanged for parental and adult approval; they can also be exchanged, in the long run, for other even more tangible and concrete rewards: admission to the college preparatory curriculum, to college itself, or ultimately to a better job.

There is little question that for most students in most schools, grades (or the marks or examination results in other countries) are, in combination with more informal expressions of teacher approval, effective motivators of student work.[22] Unless they have little or no aptitude for school work, students who work hard know they will receive concrete signs of approval that are not only rewarding in themselves, but have important consequences for how others think of them and for their future careers. At the same time, however, grades suffer from several disadvantages when compared with money, particularly as motivators of students who tend to perform poorly in schools. First, the effectiveness of grades depends on the degree to which students value their consequences. If students do not value college attendance highly, or if they have given up on the possibility of attending college, if they do not care about the approval of their teachers, then grades will be much less effective. And, of course, this is frequently the case. There are many high schools where a significant proportion of the student body is disaffected with the "straight" norms of academic achievement and where students gain prestige from each other by flaunting the norm of hard work and academic success. From these students' point of view, the currency in which they are "paid" for their efforts is close to worthless.

Second, grades are used in schools as motivators and as ways of evaluating students in relationship to each other. A single grade in a particular class serves as a reward for effort and accomplishment (or in the case of a D or F, a punishment for lack of accomplishment) *and* an evaluation of where that student stands in relation to other students. It can readily be seen, however, that such a system gives little incentives to low-achieving students. Because such students rank at or close to the bottom of the class they inevitably will receive low grades which they will perceive as negative sanctions. Even if the shock of this low grade spurs them to further effort, it is unlikely they will be able to achieve a grade of A or B in the near future. To obtain a grade of A, these students would have to do work that surpasses the work of most other students in the class. Thus most low-achieving students must resign themselves to the prospect of receiving evaluations that are consistently negative.

In both these respects, therefore, grades are probably less effective as motivators of student effort than is the payment of wages or salaries in adult work organizations. Adults who are disaffected with their jobs and who care little for the opinion of their supervisors are still paid with a currency that is rewarding because it can be exchanged for a great number of things they may desire. And if all else fails the negative sanction of losing this income is probably a spur to a modicum of effort. Although grades and teacher approval are perhaps as highly rewarding as money for high-achieving students, their limited flexibility makes them less effective for the minority who find themselves at or near the bottom of the class. Schools cannot threaten students with the loss of their livelihood, nor, given the present system of education, can they hold out the prospect of grades of A or B for students whose abilities are such that only with the greatest effort can they achieve minimal levels of accomplishment.

This relative lack of resources for motivating student effort takes on particular importance when we compare the character of student work in schools with the work of most adults. For some students, of course, almost all school work is relatively easy and undemanding and perhaps inherently pleasurable as well. But many students probably find at least part of their school work to be as hard, arduous, and monotonous as adults find work in most offices and factories. School work, moreover, unlike most adult work, tends to become more difficult and demanding over time. If students have mastered the skill of reading two-syllable words or simultaneous equations, they will soon be assigned the task of mastering four- or five-syllable words and quadratic equations. Although these latter tasks are not necessarily more difficult if the previous tasks have indeed been mastered, school work is a process of continued acquisition of new skills rather than the constant repetition of skills that have been learned thoroughly and completely. Adult work, although with obvious exceptions, tends to be less demanding in this respect. Secretaries, salespeople, and physicians may learn new skills on the job, but most of their work consists of applying knowledge and techniques that were acquired years ago to predominantly routine situations.

Finally, school work tends to be monitored and controlled by others at least as much as the work of most adults. Teachers assign students tasks that must be completed in a specified period of time. Rarely do students choose their own assignments and/or enjoy the kind of discretion and control over the pace of their work that is routine in such varied occupations as janitors, salespeople, physicians, or even teachers.[23] In few other occupations, furthermore, are workers as closely monitored as students in the classroom. More than most adult workers, students are expected to be "on task" virtually all the time. They may not talk to their neighbors, gaze out of the window, or walk around the room without permission. Their behavior is regularly scrutinized for signs of inattention and potential violations of rules of deportment and demeanor.[24] Thus if we constructed a hypothetical index of the frequency with which workers can receive commands, school work would rank at or close to the top, followed at a considerable distance by such low-status occupations as household servants and secretaries, with jobs like physicians, professors, architects, or lawyers at the other end of the scale. In some schools, of course, many students work at tasks without such close supervision: at computer consoles, in individual study carrels, or in resource rooms during free periods. And it may be that the rapid development of computer software and the falling price of these machines will make these kinds of individualized learning experiences far more common in the future. But for the present at least, close supervision is the rule. Student work in schools bears many resemblances to those kinds of adult work that have been consistently found to be most associated with low morale and resentment in studies of work satisfaction: little choice and control over tasks and their pacing, and highly detailed monitoring of the work by superiors.

Implications

This discussion suggests that there is a wide gulf between our goals and objectives for schools and the heavy constraints under which these institutions operate. Our objectives for schools are frequently stated in quite grandiose terms, and we often talk of schools as though they were simply places where teachers, who know how to achieve their objectives, and students, who wish only to learn, come together. In this model, educational discussion often focuses on the individual relationship between a particular student and the teacher, with only passing reference to the fact that teaching and learning take place in a crowd of others. Given these assumptions, it is not surprising that educators are continually and chronically dissatisfied with schools. If teachers had a body of knowledge about how to produce particular outcomes fully equivalent to that possessed by physicians, if there was agreement about which outcomes are most desirable, if teachers taught students individually, if all students attended school of their own volition, if schools could effectively motivate these students to give their best effort, if schools did not have to sort and select people as well as educate, then, almost certainly, learning outcomes would be very different and public satisfaction with schools would be much greater. But, of course, none of these conditions exists in virtually any school. All educational institutions must struggle under the first three of these constraints; elementary and high schools must contend with all of them. Even in the close to ideal conditions of exclusive liberal arts colleges, educational outcomes are uncertain and unpredictable.

In many high schools the combination of compulsory attendance, large heterogeneous classes, and students who find academic work unappealing leads to a preoccupation with problems of authority, order, and control that makes close to a mockery of our noble educational ideals. In their hostile, anti-academic student culture, their absence of trust that students will voluntarily do anything that they should do, and in their minutely detailed controls over behavior, some schools do indeed resemble prisons or army training camps more than voluntary associations of professionals and their clients. Although these are extreme cases, most schools in contemporary society, no less than in the past, face control, motivation, and authority problems that undermine or sabotage their educational efforts. In almost all schools, therefore, there is a large discrepancy between what teachers and principals say that teachers and students do together, and what actually takes place in the classroom on a day-to-day basis.[25]

SCHOOL REFORM: THE EXPERIMENTS OF THE 1960S AND 1970S

The school reform movement of the latter part of the 1960s and first half of the 1970s attempted, in quite explicit terms, to reduce or abolish many of the constraints and dilemmas I have described.[26] Its relative success or failure, therefore, can suggest some tentative answers to questions about whether these difficulties arise from the nature of schooling in general or are specific to a particular form of schooling: the traditional school of the past.

During the second half of the 1960s, a radical critique of U.S. schools became popular among many professional educators and, judging by the sales figures of such books as John Holt's *Why Children Fail* and A. S. Neill's *Summerhill,* among the general public as well.[27] The critics drew a sharp contrast between what they saw as the natural intelligence and curiosity of young children, the importance of active involvement on the part of the learner, and the regimentation and control they believed characterized most schools. What schools should and could be, these critics argued, were places where students could be active, self-directed, and self-motivated in their learning; existing schools, by contrast, were seen as authoritarian institutions that required passive roles rather than active engagement and that drilled students in a climate of fear and intimidation.[28] This romantic critique was too overstated for most educators, but a large number accepted the basic thrust of the argument phrased in less polemical terms: Traditional teaching methods and the traditional curriculum took little or no account of the needs of individual students, and many of the problems of motivation and discipline that characterized the schools of the past would disappear if instruction were individualized, the curriculum made more relevant and interesting to students, and the detailed controls of the traditional school over student behavior relaxed.[29]

There is a great deal of controversy about how much the school reform movement succeeded in changing schools during the late 1960s and early 1970s. One view, popular among conservative educators, is that these changes were both widespread and close to disastrous for the learning of fundamental skills. The declining achievement of U.S. students during the past twenty years is, in other words, a direct consequence of the all too successful effort by educational reformers to abolish traditional teaching methods and the traditional curriculum. The cult of relevance, the abandonment of the authority of the teacher, and the pursuit of such chimerical objectives as individualized instruction and intrinsic motivation led directly, in the conservative view, to the degradation of standards and falling achievement.[30] Other observers, by contrast, have stressed the contrast between the widespread acceptance of the rhetoric of school reform in the early 1970s and the paucity of evidence that the character of day-to-day interaction in the classroom changed even moderately in most schools. In the overwhelming majority of schools, even at the height of the reform movement, they argued, teachers still relied on lecture and recitation methods of instruction, still addressed the class as a whole virtually all the time, and continued to enforce the traditional close controls over student behavior.[31]

What is clear, however, is that *some* alternative schools, employing nontraditional teaching methods and attempting to resolve some of the problems of order, authority, and motivation that plague many conventional schools, did arise during the late 1960s and early 1970s. Most students in most schools were not perhaps directly touched by these innovations, but an examination of the small number of schools that were deliberate efforts to break away from the dilemmas and difficulties we have described can throw light on what is possible for most schools.

Do Alternative Schools Work?

Alternative schools are hardly new in our country's educational history. As early as 1902, for example, John Dewey and his colleagues established a laboratory school at the University of Chicago that differed profoundly in curriculum, methods of student assessment, and teaching styles, not only from most schools of the period but from most schools today.[32] A. S. Neill's Summerhill in England anticipated by a couple of decades most of the innovations of the free school movement of the late 1960s. And it should not be forgotten that many quite conventional kindergartens or nursery schools have for many years been doing much of what recent educational radicals have said all schools should be doing. Nonetheless, there are good grounds for considering the free school movement of the late 1960s a watershed in educational innovation.[33] Despite disagreements among its members in aims and objectives, this movement represented a conscious attempt to solve all the dilemmas I have described: to rid schools of bureaucratic constraints, to free teachers from traditional authoritarian roles, and to free students to participate in and choose their own education. It was and is, to the extent that the movement still exists, a movement to create schools without coercion where the "natural intelligence" and creativity of students will flourish.

Free Schools

The free school movement merits attention because it represents what we might call a theoretically extreme case: an attempt to create altogether different kinds of schools rather than to introduce piecemeal changes into existing institutions. First, the movement attempted to free schools from bureaucratic constraints by establishing a network of schools outside the public school system. If such schools were not free in a financial sense, they could at least be free from the tyranny of state-imposed regulations. They were free not only from rules about the appropriate credentials for teachers, about lesson plans, and about rules that required particular subjects to be studied, but also free of the kind of detailed behavioral controls over student conduct that characterized most publicly supported schools. Instead of a bureaucratic model of a hierarchy of authority and a series of impersonal rules applying equally to all, most free schools substituted a democratic model. In this model, decisions about such matters as curriculum, class attendance, and even grading practices were made by students as well as by teachers, and by parents as well as by administrators. The implication of such a model was that no rules were legitimate unless those who are affected by the rules participate in making them.

Second, such a democratic model of schooling implied a profound shift in the role of the teacher. In most free schools the teacher was not seen as a professional with a particular body of expertise to be transmitted to the student. Instead, the teacher was asked, as Herbert Kohl suggested, to become a "human being": teachers must show their emotions, they must reveal something of their personal lives, and they must not cut themselves off from students by the use of titles or by hiding behind a mask of professional anonymity.[34] In many free schools teachers were called by their first names, they formed personal relationships with students outside school, and there was a quest for a genuine relationship based on the "natural authority of adults over children," rather than a relationship based on the arbitrary authority of professional teachers over their students.

Free schools could not, of course, change state laws requiring that children attend school. But they attempted significantly to attenuate the impact of such coercive legislation. Compulsory attendance, I think it is fair to say, was not vigilantly enforced. In many schools children were free to choose whether or not to attend class, and they were permitted substantial freedom within the classroom (to move around, to leave the room). Few schools were characterized by a complete absence of any explicit rules governing student behavior in the classroom, but the fact that such rules were potentially subject to democratic discussion significantly reduced the custodial character of classroom life. There was a world of difference, free school advocates believed, between self-imposed rules regulating one's freedom of action and the "arbitrary" authority of the traditional school to coerce students for what was thought to be for their own good.

Third, free schools attempted to redefine the nature of school work and its evaluation by teachers. The conventional distinction between classroom work and play was rejected. The job of children was not to work at tasks prescribed by teachers, but to choose activities that would enable them to understand, to question, and to grow emotionally as well as intellectually. And if such "work" was to be evaluated, it was for the purpose of providing the child with "feedback" on his or her progress, rather than for the purpose of comparing the child's progress with other children. Children must not be motivated to work for the sake of good grades or by the fear of failure; motivation, it was believed, must come from the desire of the child to master his or her environment.

I have described free schools in the past tense as though they no longer exist. Literally, of course, this is not true. A number of the schools started in the late 1960s remain as flourishing enterprises, particularly in California and New England. Nonetheless, the peak of the free school movement is now past, and the existence of the majority of these schools was short-lived. The free school movement may yet be considered a success (many of its innovations were later adopted by public schools), but in its own terms, as a movement to found an enduring network of schools outside the public school system, it must be considered a failure. Let me suggest some of the reasons for this failure.

The Failure of Free Schools

First, it rapidly became apparent that the emancipation of free schools from the bureaucratic constraints of public schools meant a corresponding dependence on the consensus of many parents, staff, and students. Such schools were financially dependent on parents who were far from united on the particular educational experience that was best for their child, while perhaps united in their opposition to the public schools. But free schools were also committed to the principle that any prescriptive rule must be legitimated by the consensus of those who were affected by that rule. In effect, this implied that parents, teachers, and students either had to agree unanimously on a particular procedure (on rules of punctuality, sanctions for disruptive behavior) or face the charge of the arbitrary exercise of personal power on the part of the teacher. As Firestone points out, an extraordinary amount of time was often taken up by debates about basic rules of procedure, with attempts to evolve a formula that was not arbitrary, yet provided for some degree of predictability and regularity in student behavior.[35]

Second, the ambiguity in many free schools on what constituted appropriate behavior for both teachers and students led to a great deal of dissatisfaction and conflict. A tenet of radical educational ideology, as Dennison puts it, is that "most learning is not the result of teaching." It was also believed to be appropriate for the teacher to relate to students as a human being rather than as an authority figure.[36] But for all but the most gifted teachers such a conception of the role of the teacher led to considerable strains. On the one hand, the teacher could attempt to be a "facilitator" of learning, to provide learning opportunities for the child, and to be a resource person rather than an instructor. However, to the extent that students did not take advantage of such learning opportunities or engaged in disruptive behavior and interrupted the activities of other students, difficult problems arose. These problems were compounded further when many lower-class children were confronted with an upper middle-class white and antiauthoritarian teacher. The norms of teacher conduct in most free schools provided little clear-cut guidance in this situation. If the teacher instructed the students in the conventional sense, or if the teacher punished disruptive behavior, he or she could be accused (or accuse himself or herself) of exercising arbitrary and coercive authority. On the other hand, if the teacher attempted to encourage the child to engage in a different kind of activity corresponding more closely to his or her "true needs," the teacher could be accused of manipulation—one of the primary objections of radical critics to progressive public school education. Nor was it clear that the admonitions to be open, honest, and spontaneous were adequate guides to teacher behavior. What, for example, if teachers formed an intense dislike of some students or an intense affection for others? To act on such preferences would likely lead to resentment among students that the teacher was playing favorites, but not to act on them would mean that the teacher was hiding behind his or her official role.

None of this suggests that some teachers could not succeed in resolving these dilemmas in free schools, nor that they could not motivate students to give of their best, to work hard and creatively without the promise of grades or formal evaluations. There is, in fact, some evidence that initially many free schools produced a veritable outpouring of creative effort and enthusiasm on the part of students and teachers.[37] But there is also reason to believe that after an initial burst of enthusiasm, many schools found it very difficult to institutionalize *routine patterns of behavior* satisfactory to parents, teachers, and students alike. Problems of authority, discipline, and motivation, largely quiescent in the initial stages of some free schools, became increasingly difficult to resolve to everyone's satisfaction. Out of profound ideological conviction, free schools could not use conventional methods of resolving these problems. They could not motivate students by grades; they could not discipline students by making them "an example" in front of the class; they could not rely on the taken-for-granted character of the teacher's authority in the traditional school to prescribe work for students. Lacking these orthodox solutions, many free schools became dependent on the personal charisma of unusually talented teachers to inspire effort and loyalty in their students. To the extent that free schools were able to recruit and hold such rare individuals, these problems could be held at bay. Clearly, however, no system can endure as an effective organization if it makes extraordinary demands on its participants: Demands can be met by most people for only a short period of time, or by very few talented individuals over the long haul. The problem of school reform, as we shall see, consists in devising a set of roles and relationships in which ordinarily talented individuals can do a better job than they do in traditional schools. We cannot solve the problem by devising a school that requires extraordinary commitments or extraordinary talents for its effective operation.

Open Schools
If free schools represented an attempt to create wholly different kinds of schools freed from all the constraints of traditional

schools, open schools are a little more modest and perhaps more realistic in their objectives. Most schools that call themselves "open," in the United States and in Great Britain, are publicly supported institutions subject to the same state laws and regulations as other state-supported schools. Whereas most free schools were opposed to any form of competitive evaluation of students (and indeed many regarded grades as something close to moral horror), many open schools grade students in traditional ways and most provide systematic evaluation of all students at regular intervals. Nor are open schools necessarily innovative in matters of curriculum. Like traditional schools, many open schools teach punctuation, spelling, English grammar, and multiplication tables.[38]

What is most distinctive about open schools is their classroom organization and the pattern of student-teacher interaction within the classroom. Open schools decisively reject the model of simultaneous instruction of the traditional classroom and the kinds of strict behavioral controls over student behavior implied by that model. Instead of teaching all students at the same time, the teacher moves around the classroom from one small group of students, or from one individual student to another. Students have a great deal more freedom than in the traditional classroom to talk to their neighbors (cooperative work is often encouraged) and to move around or even leave the classroom without the teacher's express permission. Although there are important differences among open classrooms in this regard, students have, by contrast with traditional schools, considerable discretion in how they pace and schedule their work and even in what kind of work they do at a particular time.

There are two rationales underlying this model of classroom organization: a theory of social order in the classroom and a theory of student learning. The theory of social order argues that if the nature of the classroom organization is fundamentally changed, there will be less necessity for the detailed behavior controls over student behavior that characterize the traditional school. In traditional classrooms students must remain silent and they are not allowed to walk around the classroom. These rules are necessary for students to be able to concentrate their individual attention on what the teacher is teaching them. If such rules are relaxed in the traditional classroom, students will engage in disruptive behavior that makes it difficult for other students to learn. In the traditional classroom, as Willard Waller suggested long ago, order is a precarious achievement made possible only by a high degree of control over the natural inclinations of students to talk to each other and to move around the classroom.[39]

Open classroom advocates argue, then, that if teachers abandon the effort to teach all students simultaneously many of these rules will no longer be necessary. The vicious circle of the traditional class-room—detailed control of student behavior that leads to resentment and then in turn to more controls leading to even greater resentment—can be broken by redefining the nature of the classroom. If a variety of learning activities are available to students, if students can work together on different projects, and if the teacher then circulates among these groups rather than instructing the whole class at one time, it is no longer necessary that the students simultaneously pay attention to the teacher and ignore their neighbors. In such classrooms a constant, steady, but subdued noise of productive work replaces the silence of the traditional classroom. Minor deviance or disruptive activity by individual students are not necessarily a threat to the work of the class as a whole, as they tend to be in the traditional classroom. Indeed, such deviant behavior should be less common because the amount of coercion required by open classrooms is much reduced. Hence this theory suggests that a redefinition of roles of both teachers and students will largely solve the problem of order in the traditional classroom.

Open classroom advocates also argue that the abolition of the behavioral controls of the traditional school should lead to improved learning in open schools. In traditional schools the student has little choice and discretion in what he or she learns and in when he or she learns it. Students listen to teachers, they follow instructions, they "parrot" back answers in response to questions or instructions. In open classrooms the student role is much more active: Students work with other students on cooperative tasks whose pacing and scheduling is not determined in detail by the teacher. Students are not likely to have to listen to extended lectures from teachers; they can explore and discover solutions to problems that they have had some part in devising. The relaxation of controls over student behavior should lead to greater motivation and greater interest on the part of the student, the emphasis on an active rather than a passive student role should lead to a greater understanding and to a greater degree of mastery over what is learned. In open classrooms students should learn not only more information, not merely memorize and repeat what they have learned—they should learn to understand what they have learned.[40]

In some educational circles these arguments are self-evident. Many progressive educators have considered it obvious for some time that the traditional classroom is very badly adapted to furthering cognitive growth and intellectual understanding among students. They have also believed that many of the restrictive behavioral controls over students in those classrooms are not only morally repugnant, but in fact counter-productive: The traditional classroom is simply an inefficient way of teaching students. What sense does it make, they ask, to force students to sit silently, passively, and relatively motionless, and to ask them to absorb a mass of information, later to regurgitate that information in examinations? What sense does it make to tell students that we want them to gain an intellectual autonomy and an ability to take responsibility for their actions, when the institutions designed to produce these outcomes are organized in ways that carry precisely the opposite message? Let me now examine what we know about the effects of open classrooms, and the validity of the arguments I have described.

The Effects of Open Schools: The Problem of Order

By the simplest possible criterion of success, survival, open schools have been more successful than most free schools. We know, for example, schools that conform closely to the model I have described have existed for several decades in Great Britain, and many U.S. schools strongly influenced by this model in the late 1960s continue to exist. In this very limited sense, then, we can say that the theory that social order in the classroom is possible without the detailed behavioral rules of traditional classrooms is correct. Hundreds of schools presently exist that permit much greater freedom of action on the part of their students than the traditional schools. It thus seems plausible to assume that ordinarily talented individuals working with an unselected student body can dispense with a great deal of the detailed behavioral control over student behavior that characterizes the classic model of the traditional school.

However, there is also evidence that social order in open classrooms is rather more problematic than open classroom advocates assumed. Joyce Epstein and James McPartland, for example, in a large-scale study of open and traditional schools in Maryland, reported that students in open classrooms were *more* likely to report being reprimanded in class for disciplinary reasons than students in traditional schools.[41] The relative absence of universally understood rules for behavior in open schools, they argued, leads to the problem of teachers having to spend more time establishing specific limits for behavior in the open than in the traditional classroom. Although we do not know how serious such incidents were, nor how much of the teacher's time was taken up with discipline problems in these classrooms, the greater frequency of reprimands in open classrooms cannot be lightly dismissed: Open classrooms do not necessarily solve the problem of order better than traditional classrooms.

Observational studies of open classrooms also suggest that order may not be entirely unproblematic in open classrooms. The work of Roland Barth and Leila Sussman suggests that open classrooms may require a certain minimal commitment to norms of good manners and goal-oriented work among their students that cannot always be taken for granted.[42] It perhaps sounds patronizing to say that many lower-class students lack such commitments and they disrupt the activity of other students and do not work effectively without direct teacher supervision. Whatever the reasons for this behavior, there is evidence that open classrooms do not work effectively in the presence of highly disruptive behavior and that such behavior among lower-class youth does not simply disappear when the constraints of the traditional classroom are relaxed. Open classrooms serving predominantly lower-class populations have run into serious difficulties both for this reason and because the parents of many students disapprove of innovative teaching methods and prefer techniques that provide more formal instruction and less student discretion and choice. Unusually talented teachers backed up by an administration committed to open education can perhaps work effectively under such circumstances, but it seems clear that many ordinarily gifted teachers find it difficult to institutionalize open classroom methods with lower-class populations in the United States.

The Effects of Open Schools on Student Learning

Clearly the most crucial issue is the effect of open classrooms on what students learn. Is it true that students in such classrooms are more highly motivated, that they work more creatively, that they understand what they are doing better than in traditional classrooms? It is important to understand that it is very difficult to test such arguments. We do not have very satisfactory measures of creativity or intellectual understanding, and the tests that we do use to measure student learning may discriminate against the kind of learning that open classrooms encourage in favor of the skills that traditional classrooms teach. The distinctive things that open classrooms teach may be precisely what is most difficult to measure.

There are difficulties in measuring the degree of "openness" or "closedness" in the classroom. Most of us probably have a relatively clear idea of what we mean when we talk about an open classroom; it is quite different, however, to spell out precisely these distinguishing features and then to measure them in a real classroom. Different investigators use different measuring techniques, and these differences in measurement may explain differences in findings.

Finally, the apparent effects of open classrooms on student learning may in fact turn out to be artifacts of quite different variables that we have failed to measure. How do we know, for example, that if students in an open classroom score higher on a particular test, this is not because (1) these students were more able to begin with; (2)

their teachers were unusually motivated or gifted; or (3) such class-rooms differed in other respects besides openness or closedness—grading practices, curricula, etc.? No definitive answers are possible to any of these problems with our present knowledge. All we can do is examine research that at least attempts to deal with each of these difficulties and to indicate what seems to be the most plausible but tentative conclusions that can be drawn from this research.

The largest and most methodologically sophisticated U.S. study of open classrooms is the work of Joyce Epstein and James McPartland on over 14,000 students in Howard County, Maryland.[43] In this study school openness is assessed by a student questionnaire that asks students to report how often they must or can do the following things: (1) sit next to the same students; (2) talk to other students while they work; (3) move about the room without asking the teacher's permission; (4) choose their own work assignments; (5) fall behind in their work without the teacher's knowledge; (6) work on different tasks from other students in the class; (7) listen to the teacher talking to the class as a whole. They then combine the responses to this questionnaire to form a scale of openness-closedness, and assign each classroom in all the schools studied a rank according to this scale. This permits an investigation of the impact of classroom openness on a series of measures of cognitive skills for both elementary and high school students, and a comparison of these effects with the effects of student family background, family authority patterns and decision-making style, and the past achievement of students.

The results of Epstein and McPartland's research indicate that school openness is much less powerful a predictor of student achievement than any of these other variables. They conclude, "School openness accounts for a very small proportion of the variance in achievement: less than 1% in 15 of the 16 cases, and always less than 2%."[44] There is no consistent relationship between school openness and test scores across all grades in language skills, reading comprehension, or mathematics. Students in fifth grade gained somewhat in more open classrooms, but students in seventh grade seemed to lose. In no case are these positive or negative effects very powerful.

The openness or closedness of classroom social organization has, in this study, no consistent effects on measured student learning. The investigators do report, however, that open classrooms seem to increase the self-reliance of students. In open classrooms children are less likely to report being uncomfortable in disagreeing with their friends, in putting forward new controversial ideas, and in thinking about the possibility of leaving their home and their families. These effects persist when past student achievements and family background are controlled. They write, "Because the openness of schools has the effect of increasing the level of self-reliance at each grade, it could be interpreted that exposure to open schools has a maturing effect on the average student."[45] Although the results of this U.S. research are not altogether discouraging to open school advocates (who can claim that the specific kinds of learning that open schools most encourage are not being adequately assessed by general measures of basic skills), a recent British study suggests more pessimistic conclusions. It is worth describing this research by Neville Bennett in some detail.[46]

Bennett's conceptualization of openness-closedness is similar to that of Epstein and McPartland, but his measurement of this variable relies on teacher reports of their behavior rather than on student reports. In a long questionnaire teachers are asked to report on the seating arrangements of their classrooms, the degree of freedom they allow students to move around, the extent to which students are permitted to talk to each other, and the percentage of time they spend addressing the class as a whole and working with students individually or in groups. A factor analysis of answers to these questions yields twelve different teaching styles, which were then validated by visits to the classrooms of some teachers to discover where the reports of teaching styles did indeed correspond with actual teacher behavior. Bennett then selected only those teachers for the study whose teaching styles fall into one of three relatively pure types—informal or open, mixed, and formal—and excluded those teachers whose teaching styles could not be so simply classified. This procedure results in thirteen teachers representing the informal or open style and twelve teachers for each of the mixed and formal styles. All the students in the study are from ten to twelve years of age.

Bennett uses a variety of measures to assess student learning: measures of specific skills in a variety of subject areas, measures of general comprehension, and even assessments of creative writing. He does not possess the kinds of data that McPartland and Epstein have on the social background of their students; he does, however, have the records of the prior achievement of each student on virtually all the tests administered. Essentially, therefore, his study is concerned with relative gains or losses over the period of a school year for students in informal, mixed, and formal classrooms. His procedure is to examine whether students in each of these types of classrooms made relatively greater or lesser gains during the course of the year than would have been predicted on the basis of their prior achievement scores.

The results of Bennett's study are almost uniformly disappointing for the proponents of open classrooms. Tests of several different kinds of reading ability—comprehension of sequences, retention of main ideas, vocabulary—show that pupils in informal or open classrooms did significantly worse than would be predicted by their prior scores on these tests the previous school year. The difference between formal and mixed pupils on the one hand and informal pupils on the other, is, Bennett reports, equivalent to some three to five months' difference in reading age. Two tests of mathematical progress, a test of mathematical understanding and a test of computational skills, provided no support for the argument that open classrooms are more effective than traditional classrooms in fostering understanding. Gains in mathematical comprehension over the year were significantly greater among students in the most formal classrooms, and the difference between these and less formal classrooms was equivalent to four to five months' progress in mathematical understanding. The three types of classrooms showed similar relationships in student progress in computational skills. Significantly, perhaps, the gap between the informal and formal learning styles were greatest in this area in the case of students of *highest ability*.

Tests of progress in English comprehension, punctuation, and sentence completion showed the same trend toward the inferiority of informal teaching styles. The relationship was close to linear for the three learning styles, and the effects were consistent for all but the lowest ability groups. English achievement was significantly lower in informal classrooms than in mixed classrooms, and mixed classrooms were significantly inferior to formal classrooms. In an effort to provide a test of the argument that open classrooms teach different kinds of learning than formal classrooms, which might not be measured by objective tests, Bennett provides data on ratings of student stories by teachers. Students were asked to write an imaginative story entitled "Being Invisible for a Day," and they were also asked to write a descriptive essay entitled "What I Did At School Yesterday." Each essay was then evaluated by three different teachers who differed in their teaching styles and an average score was computed for each essay or story. In both tests girls scored significantly higher than boys, but differences between classrooms were very small, with only a slight tendency toward the superiority of both formal and informal teaching styles, and of the inferiority of mixed teaching styles. By this criterion, therefore, open or informal classrooms do not seem to foster the development of creative abilities any more than formal, more traditional classrooms.

Bennett provides two kinds of data that help us make some sense of these findings. First, he observed in some detail one informal classroom whose pupils performed consistently better than would be predicted on the basis of their past achievement. What Bennett calls the "high gain, informal classroom" differed from other informal classrooms in several respects. It was characterized by a high degree of work orientation, a clearly organized and well-structured curriculum, and an orientation toward the cognitive rather than the affective and emotional growth of the students.[47]

Second, Bennett gathered detailed observations of pupil behavior in a sample of all the classrooms studied: observations of patterns of interaction between students and teachers and data on the frequency of work-related activity. The major findings of this observational research indicated that work-related activities (primarily the amount of time spent on reading, writing, computing, or preparing to do these things) were sharply lower in informal classrooms than in formal classrooms. High-achieving students in informal classrooms, Bennett reports, engaged in work-related activity far less than high-achieving students in formal classrooms. His data show that in all classrooms, students who did well spent more time in "on-task" activity than students who did less well, but that virtually all students spent less of their time working in informal classrooms. Bennett provides some fascinating data on the relationship between personality types of students and their work activity in informal and formal classrooms. Highly anxious students, he reports, spent much less time in work activity in informal classrooms than less anxious students, but work activity did not vary by anxiety level in the more formal classrooms. In the more traditional settings, Bennett reports, anxious pupils fidgeted more, but they did not work less. In informal classrooms, by contrast, anxious students spent a great deal more time chatting and gazing into space than less anxious students. For these students, at least, it does not appear that informal classrooms are effective in motivating consistent work.

Finally, Bennett examined a number of measures of attitude change over the course of the school year in the different classrooms. He found that changes in self-esteem or self-conception over the course of the year did not have any consistent relationships with type of classroom.[48] Attitudes toward school and student anxiety, however, were related to classroom organization. In informal classrooms, he reports, students gained in favorable attitudes toward school, but paradoxically their anxiety levels increased during the course of the year. In formal classrooms no change occurred over the year in these attitudes. In mixed classrooms the pattern reversed: Students developed less favorable attitudes toward school, but experienced less anxiety at the end of the year than at the beginning of the year.

Implications of Research on Alternative Schools

None of this research allows us to reach an entirely satisfactory answer to the question, Do alternative schools work? There were, and still are, many different kinds of alternative schools about whose effects we know little or nothing. Some of these, like the Black Muslim schools, used highly authoritarian teaching techniques of drill and unison chanting by the whole class to teach young children how to read. Other schools employed methods derived from behavioral psychology.

Instead of rewarding students by grades, they were given tokens, candy, or money for good work.[49] Whereas open classrooms and free schools were perhaps the common varieties of alternative education in the early 1970s, these rather global terms also conceal a host of variations in curricula, teaching methods, and ways of motivating students.

What does seem clear, however, is that most of the schools that have been studied do not appear to have been able to make a decisive break with those problems described as typical of traditional schools. Once the initial burst of creativity and enthusiasm diminished, almost all of these schools appear to have experienced, perhaps in even more acute form, the problems of authority and motivation that characterize conventional schools. Most free schools, for example, collapsed after a relatively short existence because the abandonment of teacher authority and traditional methods of motivating student work placed quite extraordinary demands on all participants—demands that could be met by only unusually talented and charismatic individuals over the long haul.[50] Although the evidence from open classrooms is more encouraging, it is suggestive that students in these schools may spend rather less time "on task" and more time talking to their neighbors and in getting organized than in formal classrooms. The relaxation of traditional controls over student behavior may be (and probably is) experienced by students as a blessing, but it does not seem, by itself, to result in an outpouring of intrinsic motivation to learn, either by the criteria of time spent on educational tasks or the criteria of measured learning outcomes. The relative decline of open classrooms in recent years, furthermore, also suggests that the majority of such classrooms made demands of time and energy which, though perhaps more tolerable than in free schools, were not matched by correspondingly clear gains in student enthusiasm and learning.

Without question, unusual teachers can make open classrooms more productive and more pleasant places than most traditional classrooms. It remains unclear, however, whether ordinarily talented individuals without special training can do so.

THE DECLINE IN ACHIEVEMENT IN U.S. SCHOOLS: AN ORGANIZATIONAL PERSPECTIVE

So far in this chapter I have suggested that schools face serious problems of authority, control, and motivation, which interfere with and undermine their specifically educational objectives and which were not resolved by the best-known experiments of the 1960s and 1970s. In now turning to the problem of declining achievement in

U.S. schools, I want to consider the possibility that changes in schools during the period from 1965 to 1980 made these problems even more severe and in this way contributed to the test score decline. More specifically, I will suggest that the ability of schools and teachers to motivate and control student behavior significantly diminished during this period. In part this was because of changes in schools themselves, and in part because in the society as a whole more emphasis was placed on the rights of individuals and less emphasis on the rights of consti- tuted authority. Between 1965 and 1980, I will argue, high schools in particular became less solidary institutions, characterized by declin- ing trust and falling morale, increasingly less able to inspire young people to give their best efforts and to control disruptive, rebellious students.

In beginning to make sense of the test score decline, the first step is to describe what we know about its extent and character in some detail. First, there appears to be almost no evidence of a test score decline among younger elementary school students over the last fifteen or twenty years, but as we saw in Chapter 7, a great deal of evidence showed a clear decline among secondary school students.[51] Since reports of test score declines appear to increase as we progress through the elementary grades to junior high school, it seems that the decline is concentrated among adolescent students rather than among young children. Second, the decline in test scores appear to apply quite generally to almost all tests of academic achievement: sci- ence and mathematic achievement, reading comprehension, general verbal skills, and knowledge of current affairs.[52] Most tests show sharper declines in verbal achievement than on tests of numerical skills, but it is notable that there is virtually no over-time comparison in any area of achievement that showed an increase in skills between 1965 and 1980. Third, the decline in achievement in secondary schools seems to be quite general in different regions of the country, in public and private schools, and among high- and low-achieving students. Data collected by the National Longitudinal Survey of high school students, for example, shows only small variations between regions and between private and public schools in the extent of the decline in mathematics and reading achievement between 1972 and 1978.[53] At both periods of time scores of private school students and students living in the Northeast are higher than public school students and Southern stu- dents, with no clear differences between type of school and region in the extent of the change over time.[54] Only in the case of black students, whose scores remain stable from 1972 to 1978, does the evi- dence suggest that different groups of students experienced signifi- cantly different rates of change.[55] Test scores of valedictorians and salutatorians, for example, show equally marked or even sharper de- clines during the 1970s as the majority of high school students.[56]

No simple explanation can do justice to these puzzling and disturbing trends. To blame the decline on the educational innovations of the 1960s and 1970s, for example, as some conservative critics allege, ignores the obvious fact that while elementary schools experienced the largest share of such experiments as open classrooms and individualized instruction, there is almost no evidence of decline in the early grades during this period. Recent observational studies of schools, moreover, indicate that teachers continue to teach in relatively traditional ways in the great majority of classrooms, addressing the class as a whole rather than moving from one group to another, and relying on lecture and recitation methods rather than trying to maximize student participation. Although our knowledge of trends in classroom interaction over time is very limited, there are no data that the reforms of the last twenty years have led to a revolution in teaching methods in more than a tiny minority of schools.

There is, however, considerable evidence that teachers and schools found the task of controlling and motivating student activity more difficult toward the end of this period than in the early 1960s. Studies of student violence and vandalism, for example, show sharp increases in the number of schools affected and the severity of the incidents during the first half of the 1970s.[57] Most schools remained relatively nonviolent, but assaults on teachers and fighting between students involving deadly weapons became common in the urban schools during the last decade.[58] Scattered evidence on rates of absenteeism indicates a similar trend.[59] In the mid–1970s, many urban high schools reported absenteeism rates in excess of 25 percent, a figure that does not take into account the substantial number of students who attended school but skipped some of the classes to which they were assigned during the day. There is also evidence that homework assignments were reduced during this period in many high schools.[60] In the mid–1960s, homework assignments were routinely made for most classes every day. By the mid–1970s, although most teachers continued to require some homework, its average frequency and duration decreased. Finally in this regard, the period of the test score decline was characterized by rising grade point averages in most high schools.[61] If most students worked less hard and achieved less in the late 1970s than ten years before, therefore, this lower productivity was not reflected in increasingly negative evaluations on the part of teachers but in less rigorous evaluations and less demanding standards.

None of this evidence demonstrates that such trends as increasing violence or vandalism, increasing absenteeism, or declining homework assignments *caused* the decline in achievement. Even under ideal research conditions, such a conclusion would be very difficult to substantiate. I believe it is at least plausible to argue, however, that if students are more likely to be absent from school or from individual classes, if they do less homework, and if schools are more unpleasant and occasionally dangerous environments in which to work, then students will learn less.

Changing Conceptions of Authority

Why did schools apparently become less able to motivate and control student behavior over this period? I suggest that these trends were part of a process of change in the scope and character of the school's authority, resulting in part from changes in schools themselves and in part from changing conceptions in the wider society of the appropriate kind of relationship that ought to exist between schools and their students. Beginning in the mid–1960s the traditional broad view of the school's authority over student's behavior was challenged by a much narrower conception that stressed the *rights* of students as well as their duties and responsibilities, and in which many of the traditional controls that schools exercised came to be seen as arbitrary and unjustified power rather than as legitimate authority.[62]

Evidence that the scope of the school's authority has become narrower and more limited is abundant. In 1960, for example, virtually all high schools controlled student deportment and conduct outside the classroom in ways that would be considered quite demeaning two decades later. Dress codes, for instance, regulated the length of the skirts worn by female students, prohibited the wearing of sneakers, and regulated the hair length of male students. High school students were uniformly prohibited from smoking anywhere on school grounds and from chewing gum in school buildings.[63] Male and female students were forbidden to hold hands in school, and a strict system of chaperones prevailed at school dances. Students who broke these rules were subject to, by contemporary standards, a clearly understood series of punishments with no rights of appeal: detention, followed by progressively longer periods of suspension, and ultimately expulsion. Students might and probably did dislike these rules and associated punishments; faced with the virtually unanimous weight of adult authority, however, they had little choice but to obey.

By the mid–1970s a large number and perhaps the majority of schools had relaxed these detailed controls. In part, these changes occurred because the courts began to restrict the scope of the school's authority. In *Tinker* v. *DesMoines* (1969), for example, the Supreme Court ruled that schools could not control student dress unless they could show that such regulations were necessary for some clear educational purpose.[64] The school, the Court found, did not have the same general rights to control student behavior that parents possessed. It did not stand *in loco parentis;* and it was no longer sufficient for the school to argue that rules controlling student dress and deportment were needed for good discipline. Instead, the Court placed the burden of proof on the schools to demonstrate that specifically educational goals would be jeopardized if the rules did not exist. Even more far reaching in its implications for the traditional authority of the school was the *Goss* v. *Lopez* decision (1975).[65] The Court ruled that students facing disciplinary proceedings could not be simply told that they were suspended but must be given notice of the charges against them, and that students had the right to state their side of the case in a hearing before the school authorities. In the same decision, the Court implied that in cases of suspension for more than a few days, more elaborate due process proceedings would be necessary, involving the right to a formal hearing and the right to call witnesses who would testify on the student's behalf.[66]

These court decisions made it more difficult to discipline students, yet these changes were only a part of a much more general change in public attitudes toward the rights of individuals and the responsibilities of institutions and organizations to protect those rights. During the 1970s almost all organizations, from government agencies and business corporations to prisons, mental hospitals, and welfare agencies, came under increasing scrutiny by a public that suspected the rights of the individual were frequently abridged in the name of organizational or bureaucratic convenience.[67] In almost all government organizations and most large corporations, for example, employees began to insist on personnel procedures that offered protection against arbitrary or summary dismissal, and formal grievance procedures in the case of firings or demotions became increasingly common. Consumers began to organize to protect what were increasingly recognized as their rights to seek damages for unsafe products and to obtain replacements for shoddy merchandise. Prisoners, mental patients, and the mentally retarded were all partially successful in obtaining recognition that their rights, while more limited than those of other adults, were not entirely surrendered at the door of these institutions.[68]

A full discussion of these broader changes is beyond the scope of this book, but it is worth noting that the increasing limits placed on the school's authority during the late 1960s and 1970s was paralleled by similar trends in relationships between individuals and a great variety of institutions. In the relationship between welfare clients and welfare agencies, prisoners and prisons, citizens and government agencies, patients and doctors, consumers and business corporations, as well as students and schools, there was a shift toward more emphasis on the rights of the individuals vis-à-vis the institution, and corresponding limitations on the power and privileges of established authorities.

These changes were far more than an administrative inconvenience: an extra burden of paperwork because of new procedures that must be followed if the institution was not to be sued for negligence or discrimination. This new emphasis on individual rights and the rising suspicion of arbitrary authority during the 1960s and 1970s posed a challenge to the traditional relationship between schools and students. If students were increasingly regarded as adults with rights rather than as immature children, then much of the broad discretionary authority schools had traditionally enjoyed came to be seen arbitrary and even capricious. To the extent that the school stood in the same relationship to its students as did parents to their children, such punishments as raking leaves on school grounds for insolent behavior might seem entirely legitimate. But to the degree that adolescents (with considerable adult support) came to define themselves less as children with privileges than as adults with rights, such broad discretionary activity was regarded as increasingly arbitrary.

During the 1970s, therefore, many if not most schools faced increasing challenges to their traditional authority. On the one hand, court decisions, new state regulations, and pressure from liberal opinion had reduced their previously great discretion to punish and discipline students as they saw fit. Students could still be expelled or suspended, of course, but unless relatively strict guidelines and procedures were followed, schools ran the risk that their decisions would be overturned by the courts. As their power to punish students became more circumscribed, schools became increasingly dependent on their students' goodwill and cooperation: on acceptance of the principle that schools had the right to enforce, and students the duty to obey, the multitude of controls and commands that continued to characterize life in classrooms. Most students no doubt continued to believe that schools had the right to insist that they remain silent unless called upon during classroom lessons, that homework assignments be completed on time, and that permission be required to visit bathrooms during classtime. Nonetheless, it also seems clear that an increasing minority of students began to raise questions about these long taken-for-granted rules, to see them as both demeaning and unnecessary, and to demand that they participate in or at least be committed about decisions that had traditionally been made in unilateral fashion by school authorities.[69] The result, by the mid–1970s, if hardly a revolutionary situation of near universal rebellion, was a reduction of the schools' moral authority to inspire and motivate students to give of their best, and a weakening of the mutual trust and good will upon which that moral authority ultimately depended.

The Weakening of the School Community

Between the mid–1960s and the end of the 1970s high schools became less solidary institutions capable of inspiring loyalty and commitment. At the beginning of this period most high schools held weekly assemblies at which all students were expected to be present, maintained large numbers of clubs and voluntary societies that met after school, and celebrated and feted exceptional achievement in award and prize ceremonies.[70] All these activities helped create a sense that the school was a community to which one owed allegience rather than simply a place where students came to work. Solidarity was expressed by singing the school song on ceremonial occasions, by rooting for the school team, and by wearing school letter sweaters or class rings. In clubs and societies like the Future Homemakers of America, the Key Club, and the Senior Pride Committee, the school presented a more benign face than in the day-to-day routines of classroom work. Such organizations helped harness adolescent energies to approved and socially controlled purposes; they also provided ways in which students who were neither athletic stars nor academically outstanding could have their place in the sun.

My own research on high schools in New England suggests that many of these symbols of school solidarity were greatly weakened by the end of the 1970s. An examination of high school yearbooks, for example, shows that far fewer students belonged to school clubs and societies in the late 1970s than in the mid–1960s.[71] A number of activities that used to be held after school hours (glee club, for example) began to be offered for credit during classroom time. None of the schools I studied held the weekly or even monthly assemblies that seem to have been regular features of school life twenty years before. Other symbols of solidarity and community also declined during this period. The younger teachers to whom I spoke in one school, for example, were not aware of the existence of a school song, although it had been sung regularly on ceremonial occasions in the late 1960s. Nor was there any evidence that more than a few students wore sweaters, rings, or carried purses that displayed the school or class insignia. Shortly after the class day ended, all the schools I observed were virtually deserted with virtually no evidence of the after-hours activity that reportedly characterized most high schools in the past.

If these observations are representative, and it must be emphasized that there is virtually no research on these trends against which they might be compared, they suggest high schools lost a significant part of their previous ability to sustain a sense of community and shared purpose among their students during the period of declining test scores. Perhaps because these institutions were typically larger and more bureaucratic at the end of this period than at the beginning,[72] and perhaps because the culture of young people became increasingly separate from and even hostile to the culture of the adult world,[73] schools found it increasingly difficult to engage the loyalties of their students and to harness their energies for socially approved goals. As solidarity declined, many schools seemed to have become simply places where teachers and students came to work, largely irrelevant to students' deepest concerns and sympathies, which increasingly lay elsewhere.

CONCLUSION

Schools are organizations characterized by a large discrepancy between the loftiness of their objectives and the limited resources available to them for achieving these goals. And while this is true of the schools of the past and schools in other societies as well as schools in contemporary United States, there are reasons to believe that the gap between ideals and goals and available resources has substantially increased in recent decades. Contemporary lists of school objectives tend to be phrased in quite grandiose terms: cognitive development rather than the modest goal of acquiring specific skills, learning how to learn rather than the acquisition of any particular body of knowledge, and moral or emotional development rather than the learning of specific moral precepts. But if our expectations for schooling have risen in the last two or three decades, there has been no proportionate increase in the ability of these rather refractory institutions to meet these new ambitious objectives. Indeed, I have argued in this chapter, contemporary schools probably find it harder to motivate student effort, to gain student loyalty and good will, and to control disruptive behavior than the schools of twenty or thirty years ago.

Compared with most adult work organizations, in a number of respects schools are resource-poor institutions. First, schools lack a highly developed technology or body of knowledge that can be relied on to produce successful outcomes in all but a few cases. Factories may turn out shoddy goods that break down, engineers may build bridges that collapse, and hospitals may occasionally kill patients who could have been made healthy. But these are exceptions to what is, in general, a successful process of applying a technology or body of knowledge to produce predictable results. Students learn in schools, of course, but we know surprisingly little about how and why they learn. Although professional educators are often convinced that one particular teaching technique is far superior to another, there is precious little evidence to support these claims. At best, therefore, schools possess a highly uncertain technology for producing the outcomes that are the official purpose of these institutions.

Second, compared with most adult work organizations, schools have fewer and less effective resources for motivating individuals to work steadily and diligently at assigned tasks. If every teacher had one or two students and could therefore ignore the problems of coordinating and controlling the activities of twenty or more young people in a confined space, the nature of school work might be very different. Under these circumstances, teachers would not have to assign the same tasks to most students regardless of their personal inclinations or interests, nor would teachers have to insist on relative silence and lack of movement during classroom lessons. Since teaching takes place in a crowd of others, however, school work is often no less tedious or onerous than much low-status adult work. Indeed, students have little discretion and control over the pacing of their work and little choice over the nature of their assignments. To motivate this work schools must rely on sanctions that are probably less universally effective than the payment of money or the threat of termination of employment. Such sanctions as grades, teacher or parental approval, and threats of suspension or public ridicule have the crucial weakness that their effectiveness depends on the degree to which students *believe* that success in school is important to them and value the approval of school authorities. Since grades are used to evaluate students in relation to each other, as well as indicators of relative progress, it is inevitable that a substantial minority of students will obtain consistently low grades and find it very difficult to obtain positive evaluations of their efforts. For low-achieving students, in particular, therefore, grades are of questionable effectiveness in motivating diligent and sustained effort.

All these difficulties are compounded when we consider that schools, like prisons and mental hospitals, must compel individuals to be present no matter what their personal inclinations might be. Unlike colleges and universities, public and private schools are custodial institutions—a fact that helps explain the greater role of coercion and control over student behavior in these latter organizations. Because students must attend class no matter what their personal inclinations might be, some of them will almost inevitably be disruptive and recalcitrant. Because only one or two students can make teaching and learning impossible for the whole class, schools must control and, if necessary, coerce their behavior. But classroom order is often purchased at the heavy price of undermining the good will and cooperation upon which effective learning depends. To ensure good order, schools often resort to close and detailed supervision of minute aspects of students' demeanor and deportment. Yet these controls, which in effect say to students "We do not trust you to act responsibly," probably have the effect of increasing student resentment and undermining good will.

To what extent can schools resolve these dilemmas and difficulties? In the optimistic climate of the late 1960s and early 1970s it was widely believed that problems of student motivation, order, and control, while characteristic of the traditional schools of the past, could be resolved or greatly alleviated by changing the character of the authority relationship between teachers and students and changes in the social organization of classroom instruction. If traditional controls were relaxed, and teachers were no longer required to act as police officers, if students were no longer forced to attend class, and if conventional grades were abolished, the results would be a more humane and propitious environment for learning, especially for the kind of learning the critics of the day most favored: cognitive and emotional development rather than the inculcation of facts and moral precepts.

Although the evidence is scattered and somewhat inconclusive, it does appear that this optimism was partly unfounded. Problems of order and control did not disappear in free schools; indeed, the routine management of classroom activities seems to have occupied a large share of time and energy in those schools that abolished most traditional controls over student behavior. Whereas unusually talented individuals seem to have produced exceptional levels of student energy and creativity in such settings, free schools often floundered when these individuals departed. The evidence for the success of open classrooms is more mixed, but it too suggests that learning outcomes in alternative schools were not significantly different than in conventional schools. Students do not appear to learn less in open classrooms, but there is no evidence that the new more individualized teaching methods were associated with higher levels of student effort or motivation. Bennett's research suggests that most teachers in informal classrooms found it more difficult to motivate students to work steadily and consistently at assigned tasks than teachers in conventional classrooms. Like free schools, open classrooms often produced exceptional bursts of enthusiasm and energy, but the problems of sustaining that motivation and of managing the activities of twenty or more students appear to have placed unusual demands on most conventionally trained teachers.

Changes in schools in the last two decades provide another opportunity of testing the usefulness of the model of schooling developed in this chapter. During the late 1960s and throughout most of the 1970s, schools were faced with increasing demands to abandon some of their traditional controls over student behavior and to move closer to the professional-client model of the teacher-student relationship. These changes were not, as conservative critics often claim, merely the result of a "take over" of public education by professional educators hostile to traditional schools. Nor is there much evidence that alternative or innovative teaching methods made great inroads in most schools. It is more accurate, I believe, to see the challenges to the traditional authority of the school that were characteristic of this period as an outcome of a broader shift toward more emphasis on rights of individuals (and of course proportionately less emphasis on duties) and greater suspicion of the traditional prerogatives of virtually all authorities: changes that effected prisoners, welfare clients, army recruits, and consumers as well as students in schools.

This attack on traditional authority had its origins outside the field of education, but its effects on schools were probably more important than on organizations with relatively greater resources. As the courts and liberal opinion came to define students as clients with rights rather than as children who possessed merely privileges, so much of the discretionary authority that schools had traditionally exercised began to seem arbitrary and illegitimate. Schools lost part of their previously very broad authority to discipline and punish students as they saw fit and thus became more dependent on moral authority and their students' good will—qualities that appear to have been in increasingly short supply in the skeptical and suspicious mood of the late 1960s and 1970s.

At the same time, and partly for the same reasons, high schools appear to have lost part of their ability to command the loyalty and affection of young people during this period. Schools became larger and more bureaucratic, and many of the rituals and ceremonies that affirmed the presence of a common community of purpose seem to have fallen into abeyance. School songs were no longer sung, weekly assemblies disappeared. Schools ceased to be the central focus of the huge varieties of adolescent activities that characterized high schools in the 1950s and early 1960s.

In view of these developments it is not surprising that absenteeism rates and violence and vandalism increased during this period. Nor is it remarkable that, faced with increasing numbers of unmotivated and recalcitrant students, many teachers generally assigned less homework and gave slightly higher grades for the same quality of work than was the case twenty years before. None of these changes were as dramatic as some critics allege—most schools after all were not characterized by violence or assaults on teachers or by precipitous declines in academic standards. Nonetheless, it seems evident that large numbers of schools experienced a decline in their resources to control disruptive behavior and to motivate student effort during this period. This decline, I have argued, contributed to the trend in falling academic achievement from the mid–1960s to 1980.

Difficult questions about the meaning and implications of these trends are raised by this analysis. One set of questions concerns the permanence of the changes I have described: Should we see the trends in the authority of the school over the past twenty years as a temporary oscillation in the swing of the educational pendulum, or as part of a long-term shift toward more emphasis on the rights of students and increased suspicion of arbitrary authority? Will schools in the future regain both the coercive and moral authority they possessed in the past, or must schools adjust to a more or less permanently changed definition of the appropriate rights and responsibilities of students? Equally difficult to answer is the problem of the effects of changes in the traditional relationship between schools and students on a variety of learning outcomes. Is it the case, as some conservative critics argue, that *any* reduction in the traditional authority of the school necessarily results in a reduction in student effort and motivation? Or is it possible to institutionalize new and more humane relationships between schools and students that both minimize control and coercion and that can motivate students to give their best efforts? Are the dilemmas of schooling that I have described in this chapter only solvable within the framework of primarily traditional schools—with all their attendant disadvantages—or can we devise alternative organizational arrangements that combine respect for students' rights, ways of containing disruptive activity, and effective means of obtaining more simply passive compliance from students?

In the next chapter I will give some tentative answers to these questions—answers that are, in their implications, perhaps more sanguine than the analysis this chapter has suggested. It is important to note, however, that this analysis has strongly argued against the easy optimism of most professional educators in this regard. Schools cannot readily abandon their authoritarian heritage without jeopardizing their control over what is necessarily still a captive audience. Nor is it obvious that, while grades have many disadvantages from the point of view of ideal educational practice, any effective substitutes can be found. New formal rules and elaborate lists of student rights and responsibilities, precisely because they are less personal and more bureaucratic in character, may weaken the school as a solidary and cohesive community. In all these respects, I regret to say, educational reformers have greatly underestimated the difficulty of their task, resting their case for reform, in many instances, on the presumption that once traditional controls over student behavior are removed, problems of order and problems of student motivation will be substantially resolved.

Endnotes

1. Diane Ravitch, *The Troubled Crusade: American Education, 1945–1980* (New York: Basic Books, 1983), p. vii.

2. The most comprehensive discussion of schools as social organizations is Charles Bidwell, "The School as a Social Organization," in J. G. March (ed.), *Handbook of Organizations* (Chicago: Rand McNally, 1965).

3. See Ronald G. Corwin, "Education and the Sociology of Complex Organizations," in Donald A. Hansen and Joel E. Gerstl (eds.), *On Education: Sociological Perspectives* (New York: Wiley, 1977), pp. 156–223; and Roland J. Pellegrin, "Schools as Work Settings," in Robert Dubin (ed.), *Handbook of Work, Organization and Society* (Chicago: Rand McNally, 1976).

4. Bidwell, "The School as a Social Organization."

5. Ibid.

6. John I. Goodland, *A Place Called School* (New York: McGraw-Hill, 1983).

7. Dan Lortie, *School Teacher: A Sociological Study* (Chicago: University of Chicago Press, 1975).

8. Ibid.

9. N. L. Gage, *The Scientific Basis of the Art of Teaching* (New York. Teachers College Press, 1978); and Robert Dreeben, *The Nature of Teaching* (Glenview, Ill.: Scott Foresman, 1971).

10. Howard Gardner, *Frames of Mind: The Theory of Multiple Intelligences* (New York: Basic Books, 1983).

11. Goodland, *A Place Called School,* pp. 116–117.

12. Philip W. Jackson, *Life in Classrooms* (New York: Holt, Rinehart and Winston, 1968).

13. Ibid.; and Willard Waller, *The Sociology of Teaching* (New York: Wiley, 1961).

14. For a discussion of trust, see R. P. McDermott, "Social Relations as Context for Learning," *Harvard Educational Review,* Vol. 47 (1977): 198–213.

15. For a current example of grandiose objectives, see Ernest L. Boyer *High School* (New York: Harper, 1983).

16. See Erving Goffman, *Asylums* (New York: Doubleday, 1961) for what remains the most illuminating discussion of the common features of many custodial institutions.

17. Ibid.; c.f. Waller, *The Sociology of Teaching.*

18. Goffman, *Asylums.*

19. Ibid.; c.f. Waller, *The Sociology of Teaching.*

20. Howard S. Becker, Blanche Geer, and Everett C. Hughes, *Making the Grade* (New York: Wiley, 1969).

21. Ibid.

22. Robert Dreeben, *On What Is Learned in School* (Reading, Mass.: Addison-Wesley, 1968); and Mary Haywood Metz, *Classrooms and Corridors* (Berkeley: University of California Press, 1978). Metz notes that for students who perform poorly grades "have little value as an incentive" (p. 98).

23. Jackson, *Life in Classrooms.*

24. Waller, *The Sociology of Teaching.*

25. Ibid.; and Goodlad, *A Place Called School.*

26. For an enthusiastic account of the reform movement, see Allen Graubard, *Free the Children* (New York: Pantheon, 1972).

27. John Holt, *Why Children Fail* (New York: Delta, 1964); and A. S. Neill *Summerhill* (New York: Hart, 1960).

28. In addition to Holt, Neill, and Graubard, see George Dennison, *The Lives of Our Children* (New York: Random House, 1969).

29. The classic "moderate" statement is Charles E. Silberman, *Crisis in the Classroom* (New York: Random House, 1969). For a skeptical account, see Ravitch, *The Troubled Crusade,* Chapter 7.

30. Frank Armbruster, *Our Children's Crippled Future* (New York: Quadrangle Books, 1977).

31. Goodlad, *A Place Called School,* provides evidence of the persistence of traditional teaching techniques.

32. John Dewey, *Schools of Tomorrow* (New York: Dutton, 1962).

33. Graubard, *Free the Children.*

34. Herbert Kohl, *The Open Classroom* (New York: New York Review Books, 1969).

35. William Firestone, "Ideology and Conflict in Parent Run Free Schools," *Sociology of Education,* Vol. 49 (1976): 241–252.

36. Dennison, *The Lives of Our Children.* For a discussion of authority problems in free schools, see Ann Swidler, *Organizations without Authority: Dilemmas of Social Control in Free Schools* (Cambridge: Harvard University Press, 1979).

37. See Swidler, *Organizations without Authority.*

38. Joseph Featherstone, *Schools Where Children Learn* (New York: Liveright Publishing, 1971); Roland Barth, *Open Education and the American School* (New York: Schoeben, 1972); and Silberman, *Crisis in the Classroom.*

39. Waller, *The Sociology of Teaching.*

40. For a full discussion of these assumptions and the psychological theories that underlie them, see Roland Barth, *Open Education.* See also the discussion of Piaget in Silberman, *Crisis in the Classroom,* pp. 215–219. What strikes the sociologist in this respect is how the collective character of school learning is ignored in all this work: The implicit model throughout is that of the individual student learning from one individual teacher.

41. James McPartland and Joyce Epstein, "The Effects of Open School Organization on Student Outcomes," *The Center for Social Organization of Schools,* Report No. 195, The Johns Hopkins University, 1975, p. 70.

42. Barth, *Open Education,* Chapter 3; and Leila Sussman, *Tales Out of School: Implementing Organizational Change in Elementary Schools* (Philadelphia: Temple University Press, 1978).

43. McPartland and Epstein, "The Effects of Open School."

44. Ibid., p. 15.

45. Ibid., p. 42.

46. Neville Bennett, *Teaching Styles and Pupil Progress* (London: Open Books Publishing, 1976).

47. Ibid.

48. See the findings of W. D. Ward and P. R. Barcher, "Reading Achievement and Creativity as Related to Open Classroom Experience," *Journal of Educational Psychology* 67 (1975): 683–691.

49. Robert Hamblin, *The Humanization Process* (New York: Wiley, 1971).

50. Swidler, *Organizations without Authority.*

51. See endnote 77, Chapter 7.

52. Report of the Advisory Panel on the S.A.T. Score Decline, *On Further Examination* (New York: College Entrance Examination Board, 1977); Ira Mullis, "Citizenship and Social Achievement Trends over Time," paper presented to the American Educational Research Association Meetings, April, 1978; and National Council for the Social Studies, *National Assessment and Social Studies Education* (Washington, D.C.: U.S. Government, 1975), p. 111.

53. Calculations by the author and his associates. The National Longitudinal Survey sampled high school students in 1972 and then, using almost identical

tests, again in 1978. Since these tests were given to all students, in contrast to the S.A.T., trends in these data are probably more accurate a guide to the test score decline than trends in S.A.T. scores.

54. There are, of course, clear regional differences at both points in time, with the highest scores in the Northeast and the lowest scores in the South.

55. Calculations by the author from the N.L.S.

56. Thomas Donton and Gary Echternacht, "A Feasibility Study of the S.A.T. Performance of High Ability Seniors from 1960 to 1974 (Valedictorian Study)," in *On Further Examination,* Appendix C.

57. National Institute of Education, *Violent Schools—Safe Schools* (Washington, D.C.: U.S. Government, 1978). See also Jackson Toby, "Crime in American Public Schools," *The Public Interest,* No. 58 (Winter 1980): 18–42.

58. Ibid.

59. National Association of Secondary School Principals, "Student Attendance and Absenteeism," *The Practitioner* (March 1975); and *On Further Examination,* p. 29.

60. *On Further Examination.*

61. Ibid., p. 29.

62. Metz, *Classrooms and Corridors,* though not explicitly concerned with changes over time, gives excellent examples. See also her "Clashes in the Classroom," *Education and Urban Society,* Vol. 11 (November 1978): 12–35. For a polemical but useful discussion of student rights, see Edward A. Wynne, "What Are the Courts Doing to Our Children?" *The Public Interest* (Summer 1981): 3–18; and Gerald Grant, "Children's Rights and Adult Confusions," *The Public Interest* (Fall 1982): 83–99. The legal changes during the 1970s are described in David L. Kirp, "Proceduralism and Bureaucracy: Due Process in the School Setting," *Stanford Law Review,* Vol. 28 (1975): 841–876. See also David Schimmel and Louis Fischer *The Civil Rights of Students* (New York: Harper, 1975).

63. My unpublished research on high school handbooks or rule books suggests this conclusion, as do my interviews with older teachers in high schools.

64. See Kirp, "Proceduralism and Bureaucracy"; and Wynne, "What Are the Courts Doing?"

65. Kirp, "Proceduralism and Bureaucracy."

66. Ibid.

67. Martin Schapiro, "Judicial Activism," in Seymour Martin Lipset (ed.), *The Third Century* (Chicago: University of Chicago Press, 1979); and Carl F. Kaestle and Marshall S. Smith, "The Federal Role in Elementary and Secondary Education, 1940–1980," *Harvard Educational Review,* Vol. 52 (1982): 384–408.

68. James Q. Wilson, "Response to Kaestle and Smith," *Harvard Education Review,* Vol. 52 (1982): 415–418.

69. Grant, "Children's Rights"; and Metz, *Classrooms and Corridors.*

70. Unfortunately these matters have been thought to be relatively trivial and as a result I know of no research on trends in such ceremonies.

71. My calculations from data in two series of high school yearbooks suggest that about two-thirds of the student body belonged to one or more such organizations in 1968, and about one-third in 1980.

72. Gerald Grant, "The Character of Education and the Education of Character," in "America's Schools: Public and Private," *Daedalus* (Summer 1981): 135–150.

73. James S. Coleman, et al., *Youth: Transition to Adulthood* (Chicago: University of Chicago Press, 1974).

chapter 9

Conclusion:
The Limits
and Possibilities
of Schooling

When I began work on the original version of this book in the early 1970s, optimism about the efficacy of schooling was at its height. Few educators or sociologists at that time challenged the consensus that education was the key to solving problems of equality of opportunity, that the expansion of schooling would enable the children of disadvantaged groups to claim their just place in society, or that more education would help reduce prejudice and discrimination. There was similar agreement that educational expenditures were one of the best investments a society could make to ensure its own future: Only more schooling, it was commonly believed, could provide the increasing levels of cognitive competence that the future economy would require; more and better education would also lead to a more humane, tolerant, and democratic social order, a society where reason and knowledge rather than tradition and prejudice played the dominant role.[1] This faith in education was combined with considerable criticism of existing schools. Many schools, it was widely believed, employed curricula and teaching methods that were now anachronistic and out of step with the needs of the time. But there was much faith that school reform could greatly reduce the gap between educational ideals and the sometimes meager results of educational practice.[2] Existing schools, perhaps, might be less than perfect instruments for reducing inequality of opportunity or for promoting cognitive or emotional development. New schools, however, with better teaching methods and modern relevant curricula, could do far better.

In the last ten or fifteen years, most of this optimism that more and better schooling could transform our quality of life has disappeared among people who think and write about education. None of these ideas has escaped serious challenge; many of them, in the mid–1980s, seem positively naive to many contemporary observers. Few now believe that the school reform movements of the early 1970s were successful in achieving their objectives; indeed, some would claim that these reforms were directly responsible for many of our present discontents. Many sociologists, I suspect, would now regard the impact of schooling on equality of opportunity over the past half century as almost negligible.[3] Integrated schools, we now know, do not dramatically close the gap between black and white children's achievements, nor do policies of expanding educational opportunities necessarily result in proportionately large gains for disadvantaged students. Equally important in puncturing the liberal optimism of the early 1970s was mounting evidence that school expenditures and school resources bear little relationship to any measurable student outcomes. Although this did not imply that no conceivable strategy of school improvement would be effective, it did suggest a pessimistic view of the likely outcome of most politically feasible reforms.[4]

Finally, questions began to be raised about the most fundamental tenets of the liberal faith in education—that modern societies did indeed require even higher levels of cognitive competence, and that more schooling actually produced rising levels of such competence. Against the background of large numbers of underemployed or unemployed college graduates competing for scarce professional and technical positions, and during a period of declining rates of economic growth, new skeptical theories of the relationship between education and society began to arise. The main effect of schooling, these theories argued, was to categorize and label people rather than to change them. Schools provided credentials that would impress future employers instead of developing sophisticated cognitive skills. What is important about schooling, from this point of view, is not that it produces skills or attitudes that are indispensable to modern society, but that educational credentials have, in the modern era, become almost the sole legitimate basis for rationing access to scarce and desirable positions.[5]

How much of this new skepticism and pessimism is justified by the evidence we have reviewed? Does that evidence suggest that schools cannot realistically achieve most of the objectives with which they have been charged? Or is it rather the case that much of the current pessimism among social scientists, if not among the general public, is no more justified by the evidence than was the exaggerated optimism of fifteen or twenty years ago? These are the questions I will address in this concluding chapter.

THE NEW SKEPTICISM ABOUT THE BENEFITS OF SCHOOLING

The relationship between schooling and equality of opportunity has been the single most important issue in the sociology of education in the last twenty years. Opinions about what schools can and cannot do have shifted dramatically over that period. Several kinds of evidence undermined the optimism that characterized most investigators in the mid–1960s. First, the research of Coleman and Jencks showed convincingly, if not perhaps conclusively, that class and race differentials in student achievement were remarkably insensitive to variations in school characteristics.[6] There were small and often inconsistent differences between the performance of black and white students in integrated schools compared with segregated schools; there were also very weak relationships between school expenditures or measures of teacher quality and student performance, suggesting that differences between students attributable to different backgrounds were resistant to almost any politically feasible program of school reform. Research on preschool intervention programs, while somewhat more optimistic in its implications, nowhere suggested that such programs could close more than a small part of the gap between the performances of young children from different social origins.[7] In all these respects, the research seemed to say, schools could do little to reduce inequalities resulting from differences in home environments.

Research on trends in school achievement in the United States and in many other countries attacked the optimism of the functional paradigm in a different way. Judged by the single criterion of years of school completed, U.S. schooling in the last fifty years has become somewhat more equally distributed among rich and poor and black and white. But in access to credentials that are most significant for future status, the picture is less encouraging. Low-status students have closed much of the gap between themselves and other students in high school graduation rates, but large and perhaps even increasing differences persist in rates of college graduation and entry to graduate school.[8] The expansion of education has increased everyone's educational opportunities but, because high-status groups have been better positioned to take advantage of those opportunities, it has done little to close the relative gap between individuals from different social origins. Much the same trends are apparent in a number of European countries. In each case, many of the large increases in the number of university students in recent decades has taken the form of more enrollments by middle-class students rather than working-class students.[9] In no country, furthermore, is there clear evidence that the expansion of schooling has substantially reduced the dependence of adult status on social origins over time.[10]

Many sociologists and most radical critics have seen these findings as evidence not for the limitations of education to solve problems of inequality, but as evidence for class bias or racism in schools. Much has been written that purports to show that if schools used different testing techniques or evaluation procedures, if tracks were abolished, if the curriculum were different, or if teachers did not expect lower-class students to fail, then inequality of educational outcomes would be much reduced. But the evidence for this conscious or implicit bias has not always been convincing; indeed, the proponents of such a view have often weakened their case by claiming that since schools are obviously class biased or racist institutions, no detailed empirical comparisons are necessary. Studies of secondary school tracking, for example, suggest that track assignments are by no means perfectly meritocratic, but the greater part of the differences between high- and low-track students are attributable to differences *prior* to track assignments rather than to the consequences of those assignments.[11]

Nor does the evidence from studies of IQ tests clearly support the radical position. Critics maintain that such tests do not measure intelligence in some pure sense, and that the tests have long been misunderstood as providing evidence that disadvantaged students are less intelligent than other students. But it is also likely that the major reason why disadvantaged students score lower on these tests is because they possess fewer of the skills needed for success in school. To abolish the use of these tests, therefore, while perhaps desirable on other grounds, may divert attention from these important and enduring differences between students of which the results of testing are a symptom rather than a cause.

Research on teacher expectations is also inconclusive in its support for the argument that schools themselves cause much of the inequality between students. There is some evidence that teacher expectations can become self-fulfilling prophecies, helping the achievement of favored students and hindering the achievement of unfavored students.[12] And there are some data suggesting that teachers base their expectations of future performance on class and race-linked stereotyped characteristics of students as well as on their actual present or past performance.[13] However, this hardly amounts to a strong case that most schools (or most teachers) produce inequalities *because* they are prejudiced against students from disadvantaged origins. Expectation effects, in all but a few studies, are relatively small. After a decade of research, there is little evidence for the kind of systematic prejudice against, or differential treatment of, low-status students by most schools.

If there is a key to the puzzle of unequal achievement of students from different social origins, therefore, it does not lie in attacking schools as class-biased or racist institutions nor in rejecting the strong evidence that much of this difference lies outside the school's control. More promising, I believe, is research that focuses on grouping and organizational practices in the early years of school which, while accepting that students from different origins come to school with different aptitudes and skills, examines how these differences are often magnified by assignment to different groups. Thus research by a number of different investigators working in different conditions seems to agree that students assigned to low-ability groups in the first years of school have fewer opportunities to practice and demonstrate their reading skills.[14] The sheer organizational problems of managing the activities of children who find the student role unfamiliar or difficult to play, may have the unintended consequence that these children fall further behind. This research also suggests there would appear to be no easy solutions to this problem. Teachers face real difficulties in managing the activities of a heterogeneous group of students—difficulties that cannot be resolved simply by admonitions that they should become more sensitive to the special needs of disadvantaged children. Abolishing or modifying grouping practices may reduce some of the differences between the achievement of students from different social origins, but it might also create more management and control problems and hurt the achievement of the more advantaged students. Here, as elsewhere, the research suggests that there are dilemmas and choices that schools face but no cost-free solutions where all goals are simultaneously maximized.

Must we then conclude that schools can do little or nothing to reduce the disadvantages of students from low-status origins and to help create a society of greater opportunities for all? I do not think the research warrants such a pessimistic conclusion. First, the evidence clearly shows that some groups have greatly benefited from the expansion of educational opportunities in the past three decades. Black students, for example, have closed a considerable part of the gap between themselves and white students in rates of college attendance and high school graduation. The same is true for Japanese-Americans and Chinese-Americans. For each of these groups there are good grounds for believing that, had the educational expansion of the past twenty or thirty years not occurred, their relative position, in terms of access to scarce and desirable occupations, would have been worse than it is today. In addition, much of the evidence upon which we have relied refers to the effects of changes that took place some considerable time ago. As rates of college attendance ceased to expand significantly in the mid and late 1970s, it may be that low-status students in general, as well as black students, began to catch up with other students in college and in high school graduation. We simply do not yet know.

What is clear, however, is that the expansion of schooling has not been a panacea for creating equality of opportunity in the wider society. In the long run, perhaps, greater educational opportunities may reduce some of the handicaps under which children of poor and disadvantaged groups suffer. But schools cannot compensate, in more than a very limited way, for inequalities in the wider society. If one wishes to reduce such inequalities, the research implies, the best way to do so is to attack them directly: transferring resources from privileged to less privileged people rather than simply providing formally equal educational opportunities for all. Creating equal educational opportunities has appealed to many people as a relatively cheap and painless solution to the problem of gross inequalities between groups in access to desirable jobs and other scarce resources. But schools cannot create more jobs, more income, and more status. If everyone has more schooling that does not mean that everyone has greater access to desirable high-status positions. And it is, in retrospect, rather extraordinary that many people have acted as though they believed this: that the expansion of educational opportunities alone would enable the poor and disadvantaged to claim their just place in society.

Although the naivete of this view is now widely recognized, it is important to stress that the expansion of schooling need not be justified solely in terms of its purported effects on equality of opportunity in the wider society. Most of us would agree, I suspect, that it is good that low-status students today have double or triple the chances of attending college that their parents enjoyed, even if it is not true that they have experienced similar gains in chances for high-status jobs. Higher levels of formal education have been valued only partly because they are thought to lead to higher-status jobs or more equality of opportunity. They have also been justified for quite different reasons: because knowledge is good and ignorance is bad, and because education allows people to participate in a wider, richer, more tolerant, and less parochial culture. I now turn to an examination of these broader effects of formal education.

The Debate about What Schools Teach

Until the late 1960s, the benefits of schooling were thought to be sufficiently obvious to be in little need of empirical demonstration. It was almost universally believed that schools taught fundamental skills and basic knowledge of the society's culture and institutions, promoted cognitive development, and fostered such essentially modern attitudes and values as tolerance, respect for rationality, and openness to new ideas. This consensus was challenged by essentially three different critiques. First, beginning at the end of the 1960s, radical theorists argued that schooling fostered passive conformity rather than active engagement, and unthinking obedience to the status quo rather than independent and critical thought. The expansion of schooling, these critics argued, was not a process of intellectual emancipation, but produced docile and compliant consumers of the official mythology of our society. Beneath the official rhetoric of grandiose goals and objectives, neo-Marxist critics argued, lay the real function of schooling: to produce employees who would submit to the repressive demands of work in a hierarchical, capitalist society, and to conceal the dominance of inherited power and privilege by persuading people that intelligence and effort were the sole determinants of success.

The conservative critique, of course, contains assertions that contradict this analysis at almost every point. Radical theorists claim schools are major props of the established social order; conservatives claim schools promote cultural and moral relativism. New curricula and progressive teaching methods, conservatives believe, have not only under mined the mastery of the basic skills that used to be taken for granted, they have also fostered the view that one person's opinion is as good as another, that there are no general moral principles that can be applied to almost any situation, and that our own society is undeserving of our respect, loyalty, or affection.[15] Whereas radical critics picture schools as still essentially controlled by capitalist elites, conservatives believe that schools have been captured in the last twenty years by liberal and progressive educators who have abandoned the traditional educational mission in favor of such essentially chimerical objectives as moral and emotional development and learning how to learn.

Finally, in this regard, the liberal optimism of the functional paradigm has been challenged by theories that stress the credentialling function of schooling rather than the effects that schools have on skills, attitudes, or values. Collins and Jencks, for example, are skeptical that schools have the substantial enduring effects on attitudes, values, and even on intellectual development that are claimed for them.[16] Collins argues that much of what is learned in school is rapidly forgotten and makes little contribution to the effectiveness of adult role performance. The importance of schooling, therefore, lies not in its dubious efficacy as an instrument of socialization but in the general acceptance of the principle that educational credentials are a fair and rational way of allocating positions. Modern societies have an image of themselves as knowledge-based and preeminently rational; to ration access

to scarce and desirable positions on the basis of educational qualifications, therefore, confirms that self-image. The fact that employers insist
on college graduation as a condition for employment does not imply
that the job in question requires skills that only such graduates possess.
Nor, as Meyer argues, does evidence that college graduates have different attitudes from nongraduates imply that they learned these attitudes
in college.[17] Because educational credentials in modern society function
as a kind of cultural currency, those who possess them come to think
of themselves differently than those who lack them; because these
qualifications have high prestige, employers who insist on impressive
educational credentials can better sustain claims that their particular
occupations are entitled to high status and commensurate monetary
compensation.

Each of these theories, I believe, offers us important insights about
the process of cultural transmission in modern societies and the role
of the institutions that we charge with that task. But each of them is
also a highly selective account of schooling, shaped as much by the
ideology of the theorist as by any available empirical evidence. Radical
and neo-Marxist theories correctly emphasize that schooling in modern
societies involves conflicts between groups with different values and
different conceptions of what is worth knowing. As Bourdieu and Illich
point out, schools do not simply teach knowledge or culture; they teach
a particular form of knowledge or consciousness and the values and
ideals of one group rather than another. Behind disputes over educational philosophies, therefore, are struggles between *groups* for control
over the hearts and minds of the young, struggles in which those who
have economic and political power have considerable advantages.

But radical theorists, I believe, tend to assume that the results
of this conflict are today, as in the past, entirely predictable. They
overestimate the homogeneity of elite groups and underestimate the
extent to which contemporary schools increasingly mirror the real cultural diversity of the society. No doubt contemporary schools still *attempt* to teach the virtues of the free enterprise system, the traditional
Protestant virtues, patriotism and punctuality, but both the hidden
and the explicit curricula also convey rather different messages as well.
Thus radical theorists tend to miss what is perhaps the most important
difference between the schools of today and the schools of the past:
Students are exposed to multiple and conflicting values and ideals both
in and out of school, to liberal and cosmopolitan attitudes that are
critical of the status quo as well as to the traditional virtues of the
Anglo-Protestant elite, to popular and middle-brow culture as well
as to high culture, to moral relativism as well as to moral absolutism,
and, finally, I also suspect, to the very ideas that the radical theorists
themselves promulgate.

The conservative account is strong precisely where the radical theory is weak. Conservative critics, although they probably overestimate the magnitude of the transformation, are correct in stressing that schools no longer convey a homogeneous set of moral and cultural ideals, and that they have lost a considerable part of their authority to cajole or inspire the young to learn what they have to teach. Most schools, of course, do not have courses in values clarification, feminist history, or popular culture, but there is little question that the explosion in the number of elective courses in the last two decades has meant that the curriculum, perhaps for the first time, has begun to reflect something of the real diversity of U.S. society. Although teaching methods and controls over student behavior that many educators find demeaning and arbitrary have not perhaps been radically transformed, there is good evidence that both the moral and coercive authority of the school has been increasingly limited in recent decades. The schools of the 1970s had more difficulty than the schools of the 1950s and 1960s in controlling disruptive behavior, in motivating most students to give of their best, and in inspiring loyalty and commitment.

The weakness of the conservative critique, however, is in its assumption that such changes necessarily mean decline and decay. Conservatives speak of a decline in the schools' authority as though it were obvious that the kinds of authority that schools enjoyed in the past were appropriate for all time.[18] They also assume that any redefinition of relationship between schools and students away from the *in loco parentis* model inevitably means that students will learn less. What is more plausible, I will suggest at the end of this chapter, is to see many of our current problems as an outcome of the difficulties in moving from a traditional authoritarian model of schooling to schools with new kinds of authority relationships with their students. Conservatives point out that schools in the 1970s were not generally successful in solving the problem of that transition, but I believe that does not imply that, in another less turbulent age, such a transformation could not be achieved without the unfortunate effects of the last ten years.

The third and most fundamental critique of the liberal optimism of the 1960s questions both the efficacy of schooling in fostering significant intellectual or moral development and challenges the functional interpretation of the effects of schooling upon society. I think the evidence on both of these issues is mixed, slightly favoring the functional or conventional view on the effects of schooling on cognitive development and attitudes, but suggesting that the functional interpretation of the link between schooling and societal complexity is seriously misleading.

Assessing the effects of schooling on intellectual development and on such attitudes as toleration and open-mindedness is extraordinarily difficult. No doubt it is true that students learn much in school that they would not have learned had they not attended these institutions: rules of English grammar, names and dates of historical figures, the formulae for solving quadratic equations. But to move from these specific and perhaps temporary kinds of learning to propositions about general intellectual development requires that we separate the effects of schooling from the effects of maturation and the wider environment. Of course this is extremely difficult in a society where virtually all children attend school. The best evidence for the effects of schooling, therefore, comes from studies of societies where only a modest proportion of students attend school and from research in industrialized countries on students who have been the victims of extended school closings. That evidence suggests that, while intellectual development proceeds without benefit of schooling, students who attend schools more rapidly acquire the reasoning and analytical skills that we conventionally call intelligence.[19] In developing countries, attending schools appears to have very important consequences for the development of these general abilities. Although research on school attendance in industrialized societies is not quite so clear cut, there is good evidence that for disadvantaged students in particular, schooling is important for the learning of general intellectual skills as well as the acquisition of specific information.[20]

There is also some evidence that schooling does tend to promote attitudes of toleration of divergent opinions and intellectual open-mindedness. Contrary to the claims of some neo-Marxist critics, students who have attended college score significantly higher on tests of these attitudes than they did four years before, and higher than matched samples of college dropouts.[21] In these respects, we can also say that, at least in Western societies, the optimism of the functional paradigm receives support for empirical research.

These limited findings hardly begin to answer the larger questions raised by the proponents of the benefits of schooling, however. If schools promote the development of general intellectual skills among individuals, has the expansion of schooling increased the intellectual sophistication of the population as a whole? Has increased schooling helped produce a society that tolerates unpopular views and supports civil liberties? Has it stimulated the development of culture and the arts, contributed to a more informed and mature political debate, emancipated people from narrow parochial concerns, and fostered involvement with a wider or more cosmopolitan world? It is, I think, impossible to reach more than the most tentative and subjective conclusions to these questions. Depending on our preconceptions we can pick and choose among the vast array of impressionistic evidence over the past half century. One could stress, for example, that surveys of book readership among the U.S. population have shown a steady rise since World War II,[22] but one might also emphasize that the best-seller lists continue to be dominated by pulp fiction and by self-improvement or home repair books. Those who would argue that expanding education has promoted interest and engagement in cultural activities can point to the explosion in museum going, in music performance and attendance at concerts, and booming interest in the visual arts in the last three decades.[23] But others could emphasize that network television has steadily reduced its serious drama and music programming over the past twenty years and that much commercial popular culture remains mindless and shallow. Defenders of public education, finally, could point to increasing support for civil liberties, greater knowledge of foreign affairs, and increased demands that government be accountable and responsive.[24] But these arguments, in turn, could be countered by evidence that only a minority of the U.S. public supports the particular freedoms envisaged in the Bill of Rights, declining newspaper readership, and substantial reductions in the percentage of people who choose to vote in national or local elections.[25]

On balance, I believe, the evidence favors a generally optimistic interpretation, but both the ambiguous character of many of these trends and the difficulty of attributing any of them to the effects of schooling rather than changes in the wider intellectual and cultural climate suggests considerable caution. Few would claim that the expansion of schooling has been anything other than a very good thing. It is equally clear, however, that many of the dramatic benefits that were foreseen for this process have not so far materialized.

If this evidence only gives modest support to the more optimistic versions of the functional paradigm, much of what we have learned about the relationship between schooling and society in the past ten years suggests that this theory is, at key points, mistaken in its account of this relationship. Modern societies are undoubtedly more complex and more dependent on formal knowledge than their predecessors, and part of the heightened importance of schooling in these societies can be seen as a response to this complexity. An increasing number of professional and technical jobs can be said to require extensive educational preparation. The new knowledge that the great research universities provide is probably more critical than ever before to the society's future economic growth. In all these respects the functional argument is correct. Where that argument is misleading, however, is in its assumption that what is true for some occupations and some limited sectors of the economy is true in general. Projections of the Bureau of Labor Statistics, for example, indicate that the five most rapidly growing occupations in the 1980s will be secretaries, janitors, nurses' aides, truck drivers, and sales clerks.[26] The so-called "high tech" occupations, although expanding rapidly in percentage terms, will provide far fewer new openings. The majority of these jobs are projected to be quite modest in their skill requirements: computer operators rather than programmers, and data processing clerks rather than systems analysts.[27] If these projections are even remotely accurate, therefore, it is implausible to argue that most young people now alive will require vastly more complex skills than their parents. Such skills and the education that provides them can be justified on many grounds, but the changing complexity of work would not appear to be one of these grounds.

Perhaps the most serious error of the functional paradigm is that in its haste to justify the importance of education in modern society, it ignores the ways in which scholarly credentials serve as a highly legitimate way of rationing access to scarce and desirable positions. Excessively credulous of official rhetoric, the theory tends to accept at face value claims that ever increasing levels of educational qualifications are necessary and rational if a particular occupation is to be adequately performed. But as conflict theorists like Collins and Meyer point out, many kinds of individuals have interests in making such claims whether or not they are true. Educational qualifications, like noble birth in many past societies, are almost universally regarded as entitling their possessor to rights and privileges that those who lack them do not possess. Such advantages derive from an official mythology that modern society, in contrast to previous societies, is more rational, more meritocratic, and more dependent on expert knowledge than any previous social order. Whether or not we privately believe that such qualifications are necessary, therefore, there are strong pressures on us to publicly affirm their value.

The irony, of course, is that this official mythology is partly true and partly false. In part, educational qualifications denote real differences in skills and attitudes among individuals, which affects their adult role performance—differences which are attributable, at least in part, to what has been learned in school. It is also the case that the enormous proliferation of experts in new fields—from family counselors to management consultants, or from systems analysts to sex therapists—correspond to real knowledge these individuals possess. But it is also true that formal educational qualifications have consequences for the way those who possess them are treated that are separable from these socialization or learning effects. Thus college graduates and high school dropouts are different from one another in part because these social categories are *thought* to denote real differences in skills and attitudes and have important consequences for future status. People in modern societies seek out the advice of such experts as family counselors or management consultants in part because they *believe* that such categories of expertise and specialized knowledge exist and that particular kinds of educational qualifications are an accurate guide to whether an individual possesses that expertise. On the one hand, therefore, schooling and educational qualifications can be interpreted as a somewhat rational way of producing knowledge and of making distinctions between people who do or do not possess that knowledge. But at the same time, we can also speak without much exaggeration of a "cult" of schooling in modern society: We believe, with less real evidence than we like to admit, that formal educational qualifications denote real differences between people, and we tend to accept, also often with little evidence, claims that using educational qualifications as the chief way to sort and select people is preeminently rational.

The Problem of School Reform

The last article of liberal faith to be challenged by the results of the research of the last twenty years is in some ways the most fundamental of all. I refer to the belief that if existing schools do not have all the beneficial effects that are claimed for them then new, alternative, more effective schools can be devised that will succeed where existing schools have failed. Three rather different kinds of evidence have challenged this belief in recent years: the apparent failure of the alternative school movement to produce demonstrably different results in student learning, the decline of high school achievement in recent decades, and the failure of sociological research to show that virtually any measurable school characteristic bears a consistent relationship to student learning when student characteristics are held constant.

I do not think it is an exaggeration to say that in the late 1960s and early 1970s most educators and sociologists of education believed that a set of reforms, which can be broadly described as progressive, would have substantial impact on the effects of schooling on students. If student roles were less passive and if instruction were more individualized, if some of the more demeaning controls over student conduct were relaxed, if new, more research-based curricula were introduced, and if teachers were trained to teach by these new methods, then, it was believed, quite clear-cut benefits would result. It is also true, I believe, that a large number of educators still maintain that such reforms would be efficacious, believing that the disappointing results of the past do not reflect the failure of these reforms but the limited scale on which they were tried.[28]

Although the research on alternative schools cannot resolve this controversy in any final sense, its results suggest that at least much of the easy optimism of the late 1960s was misplaced. There is virtually no evidence, for example, that students in alternative schools learned more, as measured by standardized tests, than students in conventional schools. It may be true that other skills and other learning not measured by conventional tests were fostered by such schools, but there is as yet no hard evidence, as opposed to impressionistic observations by those in favor of alternative schools, that clearly supports these claims. Contrary to the claims of some proponents of open classrooms and individualized instruction, problems of student motivation, and issues of order and the control of student disruption, loomed as large, and perhaps even larger, in open or informal classrooms as in traditional settings.[29] It seems reasonable to conclude that alternative schools place greater demands on the time and energy of teachers and administrators—demands that, if met, can resolve problems of motivation and order, but which are difficult to sustain over the long haul.

Evidence of declining test scores from the mid–1960s to 1980 also weaken the liberal argument that educational reform along progressive lines would increase the effectiveness of schools. Relatively few schools over this period, of course, profoundly changed their teaching methods or classroom organization. But if most schools remained relatively traditional in these respects, it is hard to deny that the direction of change over this period was in an, albeit modestly, progressive direction: toward innovative, more relevant curricula, more student discretion and choice, and toward less explicitly didactic and authoritarian teaching methods. The declining achievement of U.S. high school students during this period does not imply that these innovations are the cause of such a decline, but it clearly does not support the view that progressive reforms will produce demonstrably superior outcomes. Simply stated, the curricula and teaching methods of most high schools in 1980, although still far removed from the ideal of many liberal educational critics, were closer to that model than in the schools of the 1950s and early 1960s; yet, a great deal of evidence suggests academic achievement in these schools in the early 1980s was lower than twenty years before.[30]

Taken together with the evidence for alternative schools, therefore, these findings pose a serious challenge to the conventional liberal wisdom that has prevailed among most educators and sociologists for much of the last thirty years. That conventional wisdom was exemplified in countless proposals for curriculum reform in fields as various as mathematics and English, and also in characterizations of traditional teaching techniques as authoritarian and geared toward memorization rather than understanding. These characterizations clearly implied that the traditional school was less effective in producing intellectual development and higher-order cognitive skills than contemporary schools employing more up-to-date techniques. Such views are not, of course, conclusively refuted by the evidence we have reviewed. It is possible, for example, that some generally positive effects of the school reforms of this period were entirely dwarfed by changes in the society at large quite beyond the school's control. It is also possible that with the ending of social turmoil of the 1960s and 1970s, school achievement will resume what has been, historically, a generally upward course. But it nonetheless seems likely that the implicit theory that guided the school reform movements of this period is partly or wholly misleading. That theory underestimated the difficulties of motivating an essentially captive audience of students to give of their best, the fragility of order and control in many classrooms, and the very great demands that less authoritarian relationships between schools and students placed on educational institutions.

Finally, sociological and educational research on the effects of different schools suggests, at first sight at least, an even more pessimistic conclusion. Not only is it more difficult to create new, more effective schools than we had previously believed, and not only are the changes we advocate likely to have unforeseen consequences, but it is possible that almost no conceivable school reform program would create dramatically different results from those we observe in existing schools. This is one implication that could be drawn from almost twenty years of research comparing the effects of different schools on student learning—research that conspicuously fails to find any identifiable school characteristics that have consistently powerful and positive effects on student learning. Students learn a considerable amount in school, the research shows, but there is very little evidence that the rate of such learning varies substantially with any identifiable school characteristics.[31] That research, of course, does not deny that unusual schools with unusual effects of both a positive and negative variety exist, and all of us will have our own list of such exceptionally good or exceptionally bad institutions.[32] What it does imply, however, is these schools are exceptions not because they use different teaching methods, curricula, evaluation systems, or different kinds of classroom organization, but because they employ unusual individuals who develop unusual relationships with each other.[33] Almost by definition, therefore, these exceptional circumstances cannot be duplicated on a large scale. We cannot say this practice or that method will work better than any other practice or method. All we can say is that, for largely unpredictable reasons, some individuals or some combination of individuals will produce either very good or very bad results. The implications of this for deliberate strategies of school reform on a national scale are, it is hardly necessary to add, pessimistic.

THE POSSIBILITIES OF SCHOOLING

Much of what we have learned about schooling in the last twenty years suggests that the limits of schooling are greater than we had previously believed. Schools have not proved to be the solvent that dissolves barriers preventing the talented children of the poor from claiming their just place in society. They do not, I believe, reinforce inequalities in society, but neither have they been effective in emancipating people from the limitations of their social origins. Going to school undoubtedly promotes cognitive development and intellectual skills, but it is not so obvious that the expansion and democratization of schooling in the last fifty years has had the dramatic effects on intellectual, political, and cultural life that were envisaged by its most fervent supporters. Rationing access to scarce and desirable occupations by educational qualifications is a fairer and probably more efficient method of social selection than rationing on the basis of ancestry or privilege, but it has also led to a cult of educational credentials in which formal qualifications operate as a kind of cultural currency that often bears little relationship to what has actually been learned. The real enduring aims of education, many social scientists now believe, have been perverted in the name of largely unnecessary vocational training, and the result has been a steady rise in cynicism and disillusionment with the educational process. And finally, of course, we know rather less than we believed twenty years ago about how to create more effective schools. Schools have proved to be almost uniquely refractory institutions, resistant to our efforts to change them. What changes have taken place, furthermore, have had few of the positive effects that their proponents hoped for.

Although all this needs to be emphasized, there are dangers in overstating the case and falling victim to a pessimism which, in future years, may seem no more justified than the excessive optimism of the early 1960s. Schools have not met the high and often contradictory expectations that we have had for them. But that does not mean that no future institutions could satisfy more modest and realistic expectations. The experience of the last two or three decades has been largely disappointing and dispiriting for those who had placed great hopes in formal education. It may also be true, however, that the strains placed on schools by the events of those years were unique and will not reappear in the foreseeable future. The problems of creating more effective schooling are more formidable than we first thought. That hardly implies, however, that no new developments in the technology of teaching and new methods of classroom organization are possible.

The great problem in assessing the possibilities as well as the limits of schooling is in determining which of the findings we have reviewed are generally true for schools at virtually any time and place and which are the product of what may turn out to be a highly unusual period in American history. Given the closeness of these events in time and the gross imperfections of our knowledge, such a task is inevitably speculative and problematic. But intelligent thought about the prospects for formal education requires that we make an attempt, at least, to separate the enduring dilemmas and limitations of schooling from the perhaps unique problems and difficulties that these institutions faced in recent decades.

The Enduring Dilemmas of Schooling

All schools in modern Western societies face a series of dilemmas and constraints that can perhaps never be satisfactorily resolved. Transmitting the cultural heritage to the young involves the problem of selecting some kinds of knowledge and some particular ideals and values rather than others. Because modern societies are so culturally diverse, and because so much knowledge is of recent origin, no one set of educational objectives is likely to gain universal consent. Schools cannot teach everything, nor can all values be simultaneously affirmed. In comparison with most past societies and with contemporary communist or socialist states, therefore, what schools teach inevitably becomes controversial. No matter how excellent these institutions may be in promoting some educational objectives, some groups will be highly critical of schools because they have other aims and goals in mind.[34]

Mass secondary and higher education, of course, compounds this problem. Formal education beyond the three R's and a few rudimentary facts about their societies' history and culture used to be confined to a small elite, which, it could be assumed, shared most of the cultural assumptions and values that lay behind the traditional liberal arts curriculum. Contemporary societies face the problem of adapting and modifying this curriculum to the demands and needs of a much larger and more culturally diverse body of students. And if it is admitted that not everyone needs to know or should study calculus, physics, or the works of Plato and Aristotle,[35] problems of what proportion of students should study these things and on what basis they should be selected remain. European schools and colleges, by and large, have chosen to ration access to this "high-culture" curriculum in order to preserve traditional standards of excellence, believing, rather pessimistically, that only a small minority of the population can benefit by such study. The solution in the United States, on the other hand, has been to democratize access to the traditional arts and science curriculum, believing that the costs of a simplified and watered-down version "science" rather than physics or "great ideas of philosophy" rather than Plato) is worth the benefits of the exposure of the great mass of students to ideas and knowledge that were previously reserved for the elite.

Problems of what should be taught, therefore, are almost inseparable from problems of to whom this should be taught. And while at any one time and in a particular society, workable compromises are devised, it is difficult to imagine any definitive solution. Put starkly but not I think inaccurately, schools have not found a satisfactory resolution to the problem of what to teach to the large numbers of students who lack academic aptitudes and inclinations, who have mastered basic skills of literacy and numeracy some years before, but who are required by law or by social convention to remain in formal education until the age of seventeen or eighteen. In the name of relevance and job training, one can teach these students vocational skills, but evidence suggests that some training is only marginally predictive of occupational success.[36] In the name of opportunity or general education, schools can insist that these students should be exposed to some form of the traditional arts and sciences, with the probable result that large numbers of students are bored and academic standards lowered. Neither solution is satisfactory, but short of abolishing compulsory schooling beyond the age of fourteen or fifteen, it is difficult to conceive of an alternative.

Related to this dilemma are problems of equality and equality of opportunity. Schools have been charged, particularly in the United States, with tasks that are probably entirely unrealistic: creating a more equal society, abolishing poverty, and eradicating hereditary privilege. Even if we scale down such expectations to the more modest goal of providing equality of opportunity and facilitating the mobility of talented low-status individuals, difficulties and dilemmas remain. A student's social origins, partly through their effects on measured ability and partly through effects on a host of other student characteristics, powerfully shapes performance in school. One can, of course, proclaim that since the schools do not cause these differences they have no responsibility for the great variations in educational outcomes between individuals from different backgrounds. But such a position is far too simplistic empirically, and for most people, morally unacceptable. At the very least schools should strive to break the cumulative cycle of disadvantage, failure, and discouragement, characteristic of so many students from low-status backgrounds.

There is little question that schools *could* take steps in this direction, and by deliberate policy, reduce the disadvantages these students suffer. For example, schools could abolish ability grouping in the elementary grades, and colleges and graduate schools could reserve far more places specifically for students from disadvantaged backgrounds. Most dramatically of all, schools *could* concentrate much of their teaching effort on students who have the most difficulty in learning, placing much less emphasis on teaching those students who, in all probability, can learn most of the skills taught in elementary schools without much assistance. Such a strategy would probably substantially improve the performance of students who currently achieve at very low levels. All of these policies, however, to a greater or lesser degree, involve high costs for other students. These costs would take the form of reduced opportunities for learning or reduced access to professional positions as resources and scarce places are shifted around. Costs might also take the form of widespread sentiments that such reallocation of time and resources would be unfair and unjust: that academic merit is no longer rewarded and that schools now discriminate against people from nondisavantaged origins. These are some of the enduring dilemmas of the problems of inequality in school achievement.

Finally, all schools face constraints imposed by the problems of organizing, motivating, and controlling the activities of large numbers of young people who are not present entirely of their own free will. Because schooling is compulsory, and because teaching and learning take place in a crowd of others, order in classrooms tends to be problematic. Order and relative tranquility is usually achieved by most teachers, but only at the price of large numbers of detailed controls over student behavior that are doubtless resented, and with the diversion of a lot of time and attention away from instruction toward management activities.

Furthermore, since schools lack the ability to pay students, and grades are often ineffective motivators of student effort, elementary and secondary schools lack many of the positive and negative sanctions that most adult organizations possess to motivate individuals to give their best effort. Schools make very great demands on their participants, both in terms of the difficulty of the tasks they ask individuals to perform, and in terms of the commitment and good will we believe is indispensable to effective learning, yet they are, in many respects, resource-poor institutions. If students do not learn what they are taught, or if their intellectual curiosity declines rather than increases during their school careers, or if many students are sullen or bored much of the time, this is not only because of the deficiencies or feelings of individual teachers, the curriculum, or particular schools, but because of the organizational constraints under which all schools, to a greater or lesser degree, suffer. Reform proposals that take no account of these constraints (and I regret to say that many proposals of the recent past imply that problems of motivation and problems of authority will largely disappear if only the right curriculum or pedagogical technique is followed) are likely to be ineffective in achieving their objectives.

The Unique Problems of Schooling in the 1960s and 1970s

All these constraints and dilemmas, while hardly timeless, represent enduring problems that place limits on what schools can achieve in the future as well as what they have achieved in the past. But it is also true, I believe, that the experiences of schooling in the last two or three decades are a misleading guide to what is possible in the future. Schools, and of course society in general, went through unprecedented strains during the post-World War II period, some of which are unlikely to be repeated. To assess the possibilities of schooling, therefore, we need to examine in what respects our current pessimism is colored by the events of what may, in retrospect, prove a highly unusual period in the history of formal education.

First and most obviously, these decades were a time of extraordinary growth in the number of students that had to be accommodated by the educational system, a rate of growth that will not be repeated in the next three decades barring completely unforeseen demographic shifts. That growth was the result of a combination of high birth rates from 1945 to the early 1960s and, until the mid–1970s, a steadily increasing percentage of the population who chose to remain in school beyond the age of compulsory education. The sheer press of these consistently increasing enrollments placed strains on schools, and such effects were magnified, in many institutions, by increases in the cultural and social diversity of the student population. Large-scale migration during the 1950s and 1960s of black and Hispanic populations to the large cities of the North and Midwest, the integration of many public schools, and the replacement of small high schools serving one community with large comprehensive institutions, meant that by the early 1970s far fewer schools were as homogeneous, in terms of race, ethnicity, or class, as they had been twenty or thirty years before. Most of the problems and dilemmas I have described were magnified by these developments. As students became more heterogeneous in their academic aptitudes and styles of demeanor and deportment, schools faced even more acutely the problems of prescribing an appropriate curriculum, the problem of sorting and selecting students into different tracks, and the problems of authority and motivation. Many schools, particularly in large cities, were overwhelmed by these problems.[37]

The past two decades were also a time of unprecedented criticism of our society and its institutions, of which schools were a principal target. Schools were expected to contribute to the creation of a less unequal, less authoritarian, less racist, and more democratic society. To do this, however, they were expected by many critics to set an example by abolishing such traditional procedures as IQ testing, tracking, sexist or racist curricula, and reducing much of their discretionary authority to punish or discipline students as they saw fit. Faced with such criticism, even though it remained a distinctly minority view, it is understandable that many teachers and school officials became confused and uncertain about their mission, and that students, confronted with this reduction in the moral authority of the school, became less convinced that the educational enterprise was worthwhile.[38]

All these difficulties were compounded by changes in the role and self-conceptions of young people during the 1960s and 1970s. These changes made the controls and constraints to which students were subjected in schools seem considerably more onerous and unjustified than they had seemed in the past. Starting around 1960, a youth culture, with distinctive tastes in music and clothes, and with cultural attitudes often antagonistic to those of the adult world, began to emerge.[39] Individuals of thirteen to fourteen years of age, considered in the 1940s and 1950s as unambiguously childlike, began to be defined and to define themselves as a group no longer under the exclusive control of their parents or teachers. They came to share values and interests that were separate if not always hostile to those of the adult world.[40] These young people claimed, and to a substantial degree were granted by the courts and by adults in general, rights that had not been recognized in previous decades. The traditional *in loco parentis* relationship between schools and students, in which students had duties, responsibilities, and privileges, was challenged by a new conception of student rights. Such rights included the right of students to dress as they saw fit and to know the reasons for any disciplinary action. They might also include the right to question or to have a role in deciding the myriad rules that regulated school life, or even the right to know the reasons for a particular educational assignment.

In the broadest terms, therefore, the new youth culture of the 1960s and 1970s represented a challenge to traditional adult authority. That authority, even at the height of the counter-culture movement, was never entirely rejected by any but a tiny minority, but it became less taken for granted and more skeptically viewed by most young people than in the past. Parents found it more difficult to control and restrict the activities of their teenage children, organizations like the Boy Scouts and Girl Guides found it harder to recruit members to their traditionally adult-approved organizations, and, of course, schools faced increasing difficulties both in inspiring the young to give of their best and in disciplining and punishing recalcitrant students who were no longer intimidated by threats of suspension or expulsion. During the 1960s and 1970s, schools were increasingly faced with students who were less in awe of adult authority than they had been in the past, more inclined to be critical of the rules and controls over their daily life, and, one suspects, rather less involved or engaged with the traditional ceremonies and rituals of school life. The result was that, with the possible exception of school sports, much of the affect and emotional energy of young students moved away from the school during this period. Increasingly schools became simply places to which one went, more or less willingly, to work, rather than communities for which they felt loyalty and affection.[41]

We are still too close in time to the many changes in U.S. society that took place in the 1960s and 1970s to fully understand their impact upon schooling. Many other trends, changes in family life, national self-confidence, or even the impact of increased television watching, could also plausibly be connected to the difficulties schools faced during those decades.[42] Nor, apart from the evidence of declining birth rates in the 1970s, can we make any but the most speculative projections about the likely persistence or reversal of such trends in future decades. Predictions about future changes in the educational system have been almost spectacularly wrong in the past, and there is no *a priori* reason why our foresight today should be any keener than that of our predecessors.

Nevertheless, it is probable that some if not all of these difficulties will not soon recur. It seems likely, for example, that the period of very rapid expansion of higher education came to an end in the mid–1970s and will not resume in the foreseeable future. Even if the birth rate begins to rise again in the 1980s, it will be some considerable time before high schools again experience the acute pressure of steadily increasing numbers of the 1960s. A return to the more culturally and socially homogeneous schools of the past is unlikely, although increasing enrollment in private schools represents a disturbing change in that direction.[43] But schools in the next few decades will not have to face the problems of socializing a steadily more heterogeneous student body that many of the schools in the last two decades confronted.

Judging by the first half of the decade, it is also plausible to argue that the 1980s will prove to be a time of reaffirmation of more traditional American values of hard work, self-denial, achievement, and patriotism, with proportionately less emphasis on self-expression and the questioning of authority. Certainly there is more concern today, both among the general public and in the schools, with the importance of excellence and high academic achievement. There is also increasing criticism of what are now widely seen as misguided attempts to sacrifice those standards in the name of greater equality.[44] Whether these trends are to be applauded or condemned, I leave it to readers to decide; it seems likely, however, that this change of emphasis will make the traditional tasks of schooling rather easier to achieve.

What is much less clear is the future of recent changes in the relationship between students and schools. On the one hand, it could be argued that the widespread questioning of adult authority that took place throughout the 1970s was a temporary aberration that is already being replaced by less rebellious and more conforming styles of youthful behavior. Some polls of the attitudes of young people, for example, show a distinct trend toward more conventional attitudes during the

1980s.[45] At the same time, it is possible that the shift toward a greater emphasis on student rights and the attack on the *in loco parentis* conception of the school may constitute a long-term shift in the way in which contemporary societies view the responsibilities, rights, and duties of young people and in how these individuals view themselves. There is as yet little indication that colleges and universities, for example, are moving in the direction of regulating the extra-classroom activities of their students by reimposing controls over life in dormitories. Nor are there signs that the courts are reconsidering rulings that limited the discretionary authority of high schools to punish and discipline students or to control student dress. If young people are perhaps more respectful of adult authority than was the case fifteen years ago, it is by no means clear that they are willing to exchange the rights they won in the 1970s for the privileges and duties that characterized their status in earlier decades. In other words, adolescents show little inclination to meekly allow themselves to be regarded as children in need of extensive guidance and direction. They continue to claim, with substantial support from their elders, that although they do not have the responsibilities of adults they are nonetheless entitled to many of the rights that adults enjoy.

To the extent that this remains the case, it would seem that schools cannot easily return to the time when teenagers would accept their myriad rules and controls as part of the natural order of things. Many students are less intimidated by threats of such punishment as suspension and expulsion than they were in the past. Unless this changes, and unless schools regain the wide and, by contemporary standards, arbitrary power they once enjoyed, they will experience continuing difficulty in dealing with older students who would much prefer to be elsewhere. Sanctions that affect the majority of students are also problematic. If teenage students continue to regard the ceremonials and rituals of school life as childish things, inappropriate for individuals whose self-conceptions are closer to those of adults than children, then schools will have lost one important means of obtaining loyalty and commitment. If large numbers of students are no longer willing to accept the premise that the requirements and tasks imposed on them are made in good faith and in their own interests, then schools will continue to experience severe difficulties in stimulating young people to give their best efforts. In these respects, therefore, the legacy of the 1960s and 1970s may be a source of enduring problems for the schools.

The Future of Schooling

Although schools are quite ancient institutions, the great transformation in the experience of young people's lives that we have described as the schooling revolution is very recent in origin. One implication of this fact, I believe, is that whatever our current disappointments with schooling, it is far too soon to regard this revolution as a failure. Universal secondary education and mass higher education are now a permanent feature of modern Western societies, yet the most recent and dramatic phase of this revolution has taken place within the life time of most people who are now alive. Is it then not arrogant or presumptuous to conclude that the limits of schooling are already known and that its possibilities are restricted to what has been discovered in a few decades of experimentation?

There is much to be said for this view. The present limitations of schooling derive in part from our sheer ignorance of the nature of human intelligence, the nature of learning, and the best ways of promoting the development of higher order cognitive skills. Educators have long believed that they knew far more about these matters than they really knew, not because of any special arrogance on their part, but because they live in a society that believes there are expert solutions to *all* problems, and in a society that demands that professionals, to ensure their legitimacy, make claims of knowledge and expertise they often do not possess. Sometime in the future, though probably not in the next decade, this situation should change. Recent, though no longer fashionable, arguments for the individualization of instruction, for example, rest on the premise that different children learn in different ways and that teaching methods appropriate to one child are not necessarily appropriate for another. That premise, I believe, will probably prove to be correct *in the long run*. But we do not yet know nearly enough about different learning styles, and the fit between those styles and teaching techniques, to make such individualization dramatically more effective than the more common methods of instruction. We have made progress in the last ten years in understanding some of the blocks and difficulties that prevent some children from learning to read with facility, but we know very little about how to promote higher order thinking processes in individuals. At present, only a minority of students learn such higher order skills, and many of us privately believe, whatever our public declarations to the contrary, that the limits of their intelligence rather than the limits of our ability to teach are responsible. When we learn far more than we know now about the precise character of these skills and the character of the mistakes that most children commonly make in attempting to acquire them, then, I suspect, much of this private pessimism about the limitations of the average intelligence will disappear.

In addition, the help we now give to disadvantaged children consists of little more than additional instruction of a conventional kind before they attend school or, if they are fortunate, remedial teaching in the first or second grade. If we knew more about the thinking styles of children from different social origins, however, we could prescribe more effective learning procedures and probably narrow the gap between their achievement and that of more advantaged students. If schools were truly places where children daily acquired more intellectual mastery, furthermore, some of the present problems of motivation and widespread boredom would disappear. Such a happy condition will not arise soon, I believe, and probably not in our life times, but in the long run, at least, research into human intelligence and the nature of learning will probably revolutionize schooling.

But what of the shorter-term prospects? Here too it is possible that developments in scientific research and technology could make a considerable impact. Anyone over the age of forty might shudder at the suggestion that new technology can transform the classroom, remembering the failures of such innovations as teaching machines, programmed instruction, and instructional television.[46] But it seems conceivable, if not probable, that rapid development of instructional software and very cheap computer consoles could provide a way of eliminating the present dominance of simultaneous instruction of the whole class and the many problems of order and control that this entails. Even if effective learning programs were confined to instruction in mathematics and science, their employment would free many teachers and students from the tyranny of daily battles over attention and involvement, and the problems of pitching instruction to the average student at the expense of the top and bottom thirds of the class.

Barring such a transformation, however, it is difficult to see how schools in the near future are likely to have dramatically different effects than contemporary schools. In the next decade, schools will probably not have to face some of the acute problems that were experienced during the late 1960s and 1970s. A stable or declining student body, a societal reaffirmation of the importance of some of the more traditional academic goals, a reduction in hostility between the generations—all these, I suspect, will help produce a modest increase in academic effort and reverse a trend of declining test scores almost regardless of whether such current proposals as merit pay for teachers or increasing graduation requirements are adopted. If the percentage of students attending college remains stable, moreover, it is conceivable that students from disadvantaged origins will begin to catch up in access to college degrees as they have closed the gap between themselves and other students in high school graduation. In this respect, schooling may make a modest contribution toward equality of opportunity in a period of stable or declining enrollments, despite the fact that societal preoccupations with such an objective is currently at a low ebb.

At the same time, however, both the character of the aims we have for schooling and the dilemmas and problems I have described would seem to make future disappointments inevitable. Contemporary public discussion of schooling, for example, is now divided between what seems a majority view that scientific and technological change will soon require far more complex skills among the population and a more traditional emphasis on the restoration of the central role of the liberal arts and science curriculum. In the extravagance of its rhetoric—school reform is seen as necessary for national survival and for the restoration of the United States' competitive position in the world—the first view is reminiscent of the arguments of the late 1960s. Schools are again asked to transform our society, but to do so by producing dramatically higher levels of cognitive, mathematical, and scientific competence rather than producing economic or social equality. Such assertions obviously raise questions about to what extent schools can produce such dramatically different outcomes. But they also gloss over the fact that there is very little data linking educational excellence to economic growth, and even more important, the great probability that *most* jobs in the near future will not require highly sophisticated cognitive skills.[47] And while we may expect temporary shortages during the next decade of skilled workers in some highly specialized fields, this hardly amounts to a general shortage of skilled labor.[48]

Taken literally, therefore, the rhetoric of this argument is close to nonsense. Indeed, a stronger case could be made for almost the opposite claim: Modern societies have failed to provide skilled or challenging work for all but a minority of the population, and for very large numbers of individuals the training they receive in schools is largely unnecessary or irrelevant.[49] For perhaps 15 or 20 percent of the population elaborate and extensive education is probably necessary for effective performance of their occupational roles, and the quality of this education, particularly its deficiencies in developing mathematical and scientific competence, may adversely affect job performance and societal economic growth. Effective mathematical and scientific education for the rest of the population can be justified on many grounds, but economic growth or societal survival would not appear to be one of them.

The argument that we should return to traditional aims—education rather than job training, and the liberal arts and sciences rather than the pursuit of relevance—is neither nonsensical nor foolish. This is, after all, what schools best know how to do. But if this is interpreted as an injunction to return to tne craditional school of the past, it is likely that here, too, disappointment is in store. The revolution in human knowledge in our time, and the sheer diversity of most modern societies has eroded agreement on what an ideal core curriculum should be. Many university faculty, for example, believe that the time has come to put an end to the smorgasboard of elective courses that now constitute the curriculum and to replace this with a core of broad courses essential to every educated person. Although agreement that there *should be* such a core is common, consensus about which kinds of knowledge and ideas it should include is rare. This is not only because of interdisciplinary rivalries and desires to protect one's own turf, it is also because reasonable and thoughtful people no longer *agree* on what knowledge is of most worth. The traditional subjects of the past have been challenged by claims of new disciplines; all subjects, furthermore, are far more fragmented and specialized than they were in the past. We can and do conceal our disagreement by phrasing our educational objectives in such global terms that consensus is virtually guaranteed. The fact remains, however, that people in contemporary societies are deeply divided on what specifically students should learn and there is little prospect of a return to the consensus of the past.

A second obstacle to the revitalization of more traditional forms of schooling lies in the changing character of these organizations. Schools probably can, and to some extent have already, found ways to adapt to the problems of diminished authority to punish and discipline recalcitrant students. Schools can relax some of their previously tight controls over student behavior and deportment, they can provide resource rooms and free periods for students to break the monotony of the school day, they can cease to require that all students be present for weekly or monthly assemblies, they can publish handbooks stating explicit rules governing school life and formal procedures for resolving disputes, and they can, of course, provide more choice and direction in the courses that students take. And many schools, of course, have done all of these things, partly from a conviction that these changes represent good modern educational practice and partly because more traditional controls proved unworkable with contemporary students.

The result of these changes, however, may be that schools of the future may be less able to inspire loyalty and affection and may be less solidary institutions than the schools of the past. If students share fewer experiences in common, in the form of the same classes or weekly assemblies, they may be less likely to identify with the school. If informal disciplinary proceedings are replaced with the impersonal application of rules and formal grievance procedures, this may undermine the personal relationships between teachers and principals and students in favor of a more bureaucratic conception of a system that, although less arbitrary and unfair, has no human face. The price of these changes, in other words, may be that the high school may become increasingly like a commuter junior college, offering choice and diversity and exercising fewer controls over student behavior, but unable to stimulate any but the most modest sentiments of commitment, community, and shared purposes.[50]

CONCLUSION

The traditional school, born at a time when education was seen as the inculcation of a body of enduring truths, and confined to a privileged few, no longer commands the allegiance of educators or students, its rationale undermined by the destruction of an authoritative cultural heritage, by the transformation in the character of its student body, and by changing conceptions of the rights and responsibilities of young people. Ever since Dewey this school has been attacked as largely irrelevant to the lives of many students, as unnecessarily coercive, and as inimical to the development of those qualities which a modern education requires: the ability to think critically and independently, the promotion of moral judgment, and learning how to learn.

I believe these critics, though they probably overstate the case against the traditional school, are basically correct. If these are the qualities one wishes formal education to develop, then traditional schools, or even schools as they are presently organized, are not well adapted to those purposes. If we are after understanding rather than learning formulae and facts, lecturing twenty-five or thirty students who are forced to be present is probably not the ideal way to proceed. The traditional school interferes with learning by the need for extensive controls over student behavior; it also makes the task of tailoring instruction to the needs of particular students close to impossible.

If the traditional school is, in this sense, anachronistic and obsolete, the irony is that it is very difficult, in the near future at least, to change it in any fundamental way. The compulsory character of schooling, the fact that learning takes place in a crowd of others in a confined place, and the paucity of positive incentives that schools have to offer as rewards for good work are all constraints that are not easily removed. And they are more important than the constraints that can more readily be changed: higher paid or more qualified teachers, improved curricula, changed requirements for graduation. In the long run, we will probably know dramatically more than we know now about how students learn and about how to foster intellectual growth, enough perhaps to make some of these constraints largely irrelevant. Although that day is still far off, we have for some decades now held expectations that are more appropriate for these *hypothetical schools of the future* than the schools that we *actually possess.* Many educators have convinced themselves, if not always the general public, that these expectations could be realized if only whatever educational reforms are currently fashionable are instituted. Almost inevitably, such unrealistic expectations have led to disappointment and disillusionment. Schooling, it is now often said, is a failure. Because schools can do less than we hoped, we are inclined to ignore the real evidence that its benefits have been very considerable. Because our faith in schooling as a panacea for our social ills has been disappointed, many of us, including some of my fellow sociologists, have reacted with a cynical vision that sees formal education as nothing more than a rationing or credentialing device.

The truth, I have argued in this book, is much more complex. We know surprisingly little about schools, much less than most of our educational and sociological theories suggest, in part because we thought we knew or already had most of the answers. What we have learned suggests that the limits of schooling are narrower than we previously believed, and that reforms that fail to take account of the constraints under which schools labor are likely to fail. If this implication seems pessimistic, it is only so for those who confuse action today or next week with effective reform strategies based on real knowledge. Schools remain among our most unstudied institutions. If we wish to make them work better we must first learn more about them.

Endnotes

1. Burton Clark, *Educating the Expert Society* (San Francisco: Chandler, 1961).

2. Charles Silberman, *Crisis in the Classroom* (New York: Random House, 1969). Silberman explicitly connects his proposals for school reform with the need for more cognitive competence in a more complex society and the promotion of a more just and tolerant society.

3. Though not, I suspect, most educators.

4. Thus Jencks argues that we should reform schools to make them more pleasant places to be and shed the illusion that such changes will have wider demonstrable effects upon learning or inequality. Christopher Jencks, et al., *Inequality* (New York: Harper and Row, 1973).

5. Randell Collins, *The Credential Society* (New York: Academic Press, 1979).

6. Jencks, *Inequality.*

7. Milbrey W. McLaughlin, *Evaluation and Reform* (Cambridge: Ballinger, 1975). See also the comprehensive review and references in Carl F. Kaestle and Marshall S. Smith, "The Federal Role in Elementary and Secondary Education, 1940–1980," *Harvard Educational Review*, Vol. 52 (November 1982): 384–408.

8. But it should be noted the most recent data do not yet take account of trends during the late 1970s and early 1980s when higher education enrollments were quite stable.

9. Raymond Boudon, *Education, Opportunity and Social Inequality* (New York: Wiley, 1974).

10. Ibid.; and Maurice Garnier and Lawrence Raffalovich, "The Evolution of Equality of Educational Opportunities in France," *Sociology of Education,* Vol. 57 (January 1984): 1–10.

11. See the discussion in Chapter 6.

12. Ray Rist, "Social Class and Teacher Expectations: The Self-Fulfilling Prophecy in Ghetto Education," *Harvard Education Review* 40 (1970): 411–451.

13. Ibid.

14. Donna Eder, "Ability Grouping as a Self-Fulfilling Prophecy: A Micro-Analysis of Teacher-Student Interaction," *Sociology of Education,* Vol. 54 (July 1981): 151–162.

15. Conservatives, of course, said this of previous as well as contemporary schools.

16. Collins, *The Credential Society,* Chapter I; and Jencks, et al., *Inequality,* p. 135.

17. John W. Meyer, "The Effects of Education as an Institution," *American Journal of Sociology,* Vol. 83 (July 1977): 55–77.

18. Edward A. Wynne, "What Are the Courts Doing to Our Children?" *The Public Interest* (Summer 1981): 83–99.

19. Michael Cole and Barbara Means, *Comparative Studies of How People Think* (Cambridge: Harvard University Press, 1981).

20. Jencks, et al., *Inequality.*

21. James W. Trent and Leland L. Medsker, *Beyond High School* (San Francisco: Jossey-Bass, 1968).

22. U.S. Department of Commerce, Bureau of the Census, *Statistical Abstract of the United States, 1981* (Washington, D.C., 1982), pp. 369–371. The number of books published more than doubled between 1960 and 1981, with big increases in poetry, literature, and drama. The sharpest increase, however, was in books about medicine—primarily self-help and diet books.

23. Thus the number of copyright registrations of works of art, musical compositions, and plays more than doubled between 1960 and 1975. Ibid., p. 569.

24. For civil liberties, see Herbert McCloskey and Alida Brill, *What Americans Believe about Civil Liberties* (New York: Basic Books, 1973).

25. For newspaper circulation, see U.S. Department of Commerce, Bureau of the Census, *Statistical Abstract of the United States, 1983,* p. 565. For voting, see Ibid., p. 262. See also McCloskey and Brill, *What Americans Believe.*

26. " 'High Tech' No Curative for Job Ills, Experts Say," *New York Times,* September 18, 1983, p. 1.

27. "High-Tech Openings Limited," *New York Times,* April 4, 1984, p. 27.

28. Thus the reforms called for in John Goodlad, *A Place Called School* (New York: McGraw-Hill, 1984) are not essentially different from those proposed in 1969 by Silberman, *Crisis in the Classroom.*

29. Ann Swidler, *Organizations without Authority: Dilemmas of Social Control in Free Schools* (Cambridge, Mass.: Harvard University Press, 1979); and Mary Haywood Metz, "Clashes in the Classroom," *Education and Urban Society,* Vol. 11 (November 1978): 12–35.

30. It is noteworthy, however, that while by common consent changes along progressive lines were greater in elementary than in secondary schools, test scores fell more among the older students.

31. For a minority view, see the review in Rebecca Barr and Robert Dreeben, *How Schools Work* (Chicago: University of Chicago Press, 1983), Chapter 2.

32. Sarah Lawrence Lightfoot, *The Good High School* (New York: Basic Books, 1983).

33. Ibid.

34. We can also say that professional educators in their public pronouncements will minimize the extent of these conflicts.

35. For a contrary view, see Mortimer Adler, et al., *The Paideia Proposal: An Educational Manifesto* (New York: MacMillan, 1982).

36. Bruce Fuller, "Educational Evaluation and Shifting Youth Policy," *Evaluation Review,* Vol. 5 (April 1981): 167–188.

37. See, for example, the description of "Hamilton" school in Mary Haywood Metz, *Classrooms and Corridors* (Berkeley: University of California Press, 1978).

38. Metz, "Clashes in the Classroom."

39. James S. Coleman, et al., *Youth: Transition to Adulthood* (Chicago: University of Chicago Press, 1974), Chapter 7.

40. Neil Postman, *The Disappearance of Childhood* (New York: Delacorte Press, 1982).

41. For a similar analysis, see Joseph Adelson, "What Happened to the Schools," *Commentary* (March 1981): 12–17.

42. See the analysis in Report of the Advisory Panel on the S.A.T. Score Decline, *On Further Examination* (New York: College Entrance Examination Board, 1977).

43. Disturbing, that is, to those who support public education.

44. Though recent reports on the crisis in education pay lip service to equality, and talk about "excellence for all," there is no question that priorities have shifted in this regard.

45. Dean R. Hoge, "Changes in College Students' Value Patterns in the 1950's, 1960's and 1970's," *Sociology of Education,* Vol. 49 (April 1976): 155–163.

46. For an account of this earlier movement, see Silberman, *Crisis in the Classroom,* Chapter 5, "The Failures of Educational Reform."

47. See endnote 27.

48. See endnote 28.

49. James O'Toole, *Work, Learning and the American Future* (San Francisco: Jossey Bass, 1976).

50. It is noteworthy that these ideals are missing from most contemporary tests of school objectives. See, for example, Ernest L. Boyer, *High School* (New York: Harper, 1983).

bibliography

References marked with an asterisk (*) are particularly recommended for further reading.

* Adelson, Joseph. "What Happened to the Schools," *Commentary* (March 1981): 12–17.

Adler, Mortimer et al. *The Paideia Proposal: An Educational Manifesto* (New York: MacMillan, 1982).

The Advisory Panel on the S.A.T. Score Decline. *On Further Examination* (New York: College Entrance Examination Board, 1977).

Alba, Richard D., and Lavin, David E. "Community Colleges and Tracking in Higher Education," *Sociology of Education*, Vol. 54 (October 1981): 223–227.

* Alexander, Karl L., and Cook, Martha A. "Curricula and Coursework: A Surprise Ending to a Familiar Story," *American Sociological Review* 47, No. 5 (October 1982): 636.

Alexander, Karl L.; Eckland, Bruce K.; and Griffin, Larry J. "The Wisconsin Model of Socio-Economic Achievement: A Replication," *American Journal of Sociology*, Vol. 81 (1975): 324–342.

Alexander, Karl, and McDill, Edward. "Selection and Allocation within Schools," *American Sociological Review*, Vol. 41 (December 1976): 963–980.

Alexander, Karl, and Pallas, A. M. "Private Schools and Public Policy: New Evidence on Cognitive Achievement in Public Schools," *Sociology of Education*, Vol. 53 (1983): 170–182.

Anderson, Ronald S. *Education in Japan* (Washington, D.C.: U.S. Government, 1975).

Apple, Michael W. *Education and Power* (Boston: Routledge and Kegan Paul, 1982).

Armbuster, Frank. *Our Children's Crippled Future* (New York: Quadrangle Books, 1977).

Austin, Gilbert R. (ed.). *The Rise and Fall of National Test Scores* (New York: Academic Press, 1982).

Averch, Harvey et al. *How Effective Is Schooling? A Critical Review and Synthesis of Research Findings* (Santa Monica, Calif.: The Rand Corporation, 1972).

Baratz, Stephen S., and Baratz, Joan C. "Early Childhood Intervention: The Social Science Basis of Institutional Racism," *Harvard Educational Review*, Vol. 40 (Winter 1970): 29–50.

* Barr, Rebecca, and Dreeben, Robert. *How Schools Work* (Chicago: University of Chicago Press, 1983).

Barth, Roland. *Open Education and the American School* (New York: Schoecken, 1972).

Becker, Gary. *Human Capital* (New York: National Bureau of Economic Research, 1964).

Becker, Howard S.; Geer, Blanche; and Hughes, Everett C. *Making the Grade* (New York: Wiley, 1969).

Bell, Daniel. *The Coming of Post-Industrial Society* (New York: Basic Books, 1973).

Bennett, Neville. *Teaching Styles and Pupil Progress* (London: Open Books Publishing, 1976).

Bennett, William J., and Delattre, Edwin J. "Moral Education in the Schools," *The Public Interest,* No. 50 (Winter 1978): 81–98.

* Berg, Ivar. *Education and Jobs: The Great Training Robbery* (New York: Praeger, 1970).

Berman, Paul, and McLaughlin, Milbrey W. *Federal Programs Supporting Educational Change, Vol. VIII: Implementing and Sustaining Innovations* (Santa Monica, Calif.: Rand Corporation, 1978).

Bernstein, Basil (ed.). *Class, Codes and Control,* three volumes (London: Routledge and Kegan Paul, 1973, 1974, 1976).

Bernstein, Basil. "Education Cannot Compensate for Society," *New Society,* Vol. 26 (February 1970): 345.

Bestor, Arthur. *Educational Wastelands* (Urbana, Ill.: University of Illinois Press, 1953).

Bidwell, Charles. "The School as a Social Organization," in J. G. March (ed.), *Handbook of Organizations* (Chicago: Rand McNally, 1965).

Bird, Caroline. *The Case against College* (New York: McKay, 1975).

Blau, Peter, and Duncan, Otis Dudley. *The American Occupational Structure* (New York: Wiley, 1967).

Blaug, Mark. "The Empirical Status of Human Capital Theory: A Slightly Jaundiced Survey," *Journal of Economic Literature,* Vol. 14, No. 3 (September 1976): 827–855.

Block, N. J., and Dworkin, Gerald (eds.). *The I.Q. Controversy* (New York: Random House, 1976).

Bock, Philip K. *Modern Cultural Anthropology* (New York: Knopf, 1969).

Body, Bertha. *A Psychological Study of Immigrant Children at Ellis Island* (Baltimore: Williams and Wilkins, 1926).

Bonner, Stanley F. *Education in Ancient Rome* (London: Methuen, 1977).

Boocock, Sarane S. *An Introduction to the Sociology of Learning* (New York: Houghton Mifflin, 1972).

Boudon, Raymond. *Education, Opportunity and Social Inequality* (New York: Wiley, 1974).

Bourdieu, Pierre, and Passerow, J. C. *Reproduction* (Beverly Hills, Calif.: Sage Publications, 1977).

* Bowles, Samuel, and Gintis, Herbert. *Schooling in Capitalist America* (New York: Basic Books, 1976).

Boyer, Ernest L. *High School* (New York: Harper, 1983).

Bronfennbrenner, Urie. *Two Worlds of Childhood: U.S. ana U.S.S.R.* (New York: Russell Sage, 1970).

Brooks, Charlotte. "Some Approaches to Teaching English as a Second Language," in S. W. Webster (ed.), *The Disadvantaged Learner* (San Francisco: Chandler, 1966), pp. 516–517.

Brophy, Jere, and Good, Thomas. *Teacher-Student Relationships* (New York: Holt, Rinehart and Winston, 1974).

Burn, Barbara B. *Higher Education in Nine Countries* (New York: McGraw-Hill, 1971).

Cain, Glen G., and Goldberger, Arthur S. "Public and Private Schools Revisited," *Sociology of Education*, Vol. 56 (October 1983): 208–219.

Carlson, Gosta. *Social Mobility and Class Structure* (Lund, Sweden: Almquist, 1958).

Carnoy, Martin (ed.). *Schooling in a Corporate Society* (New York: McKay, 1975).

Cicourel, Aaron V., and Kitsuse, John I. *The Educational Decision-Makers* (New York: Bobbs-Merrill, 1963).

* Clark, Burton. *Educating the Expert Society* (San Francisco: Chandler, 1961).

Clark, Burton. *The Open-Door College* (New York: McGraw Hill, 1960).

Clignet, Remi. *Liberty and Equality in the Educational Process* (New York: Wiley, 1974).

Cole, Michael, and Means, Barbara. *Comparative Studies of How People Think* (Cambridge, Mass.: Harvard University Press, 1981).

Coleman, James S. *The Adolescent Society* (New York: Free Press, 1961).

Coleman, James. "The Concept of Equality of Opportunity," *Harvard Educational Review* 38 (1968): 7–32.

* Coleman, James; Hoffer, Thomas; and Kilgore, Sally. *High School Achievement* (New York: Basic Books, 1982).

Coleman, James et al. *Equality of Educational Opportunity* (Washington, D.C.: U.S. Government, 1966).

* Coleman, James S. et al. *Youth: Transition to Adulthood* (Chicago: University of Chicago Press, 1974).

* Collins, Randall. *The Credential Society* (New York: Academic Press, 1979).

Comber, L. C., and Keeves, John P. *Science Education in Nineteen Countries* (New York: Wiley, 1973).

Corwin, Ronald G. "Education and the Sociology of Complex Organizations," in Donald A. Hansen and Joel E. Gerstl (eds.), *On Education: Sociological Perspectives* (New York: Wiley, 1977), pp. 156–223.

Coser, Lewis. "Presidential Address: Two Methods in Search of Substance," *American Sociological Review*, Vol. 40 (1978): 691–700.

Crandall, Virginia. "Achievement Behavior in Young Children," *Young Children* 20 (1964): 77–90.

de Francesco, Corrado. "Myths and Realities of Mass Secondary Schooling in Italy," *European Journal of Education*, Vol. 15, No. 2 (1980): 135–152.

Dennison, George. *The Lives of Our Children* (New York: Random House, 1969).

Dewey, John. *Schools of Tomorrow* (New York: Dutton, 1962).

* Di Maggio, Paul. "Cultural Capital and School Success: The Impact of Status Culture Participation on the Grades of U.S. High School Students," *American Sociological Review*, Vol. 47 (April 1982): 189–201.

Dore, Ronald. *The Diploma Disease* (Berkeley: University of California Press, 1976).

Douglas, J. *The Home and the School* (London: McGibbon and Kee, 1964).

Dreeben, Robert. "American Schooling: Patterns and Processes of Stability and Change" in Bernard Barber and Alex Inkeles (eds.), *Stability and Social Change* (Boston: Little, Brown, 1971).

Dreeben, Robert. *The Nature of Teaching* (Glenview, Ill.: Scott Foresman, 1971).

Dreeben, Robert. *On What Is Learned in School* (Reading, Mass.: Addison-Wesley, 1968).

Durkheim, E. *Moral Education* (Glencoe, Ill.: Free Press, 1961).

Durkheim, Emile. *The Evolution of Educational Thought* (London: Routledge and Kegan Paul, 1977).

Eckland, Bruce K. "Genetics and Sociology: A Reconsideration," *American Sociological Review*, Vol. 32 (1967): 173–194.

* Eder, Donna. "Ability Grouping as a Self-Fulfilling Prophecy: A Micro-Analysis of Teacher-Student Interaction," *Sociology of Education*, Vol. 54 (July 1981): 151–162.

Eger, Martin. "The Conflict in Moral Education: An Informal Case Study," *The Public Interest* 63 (Spring 1981): 62–80.

Entwisle, Dorris, and Hayduk, Leslie. "Academic Expectations and the School Attainment of Young Children," *Sociology of Education*, Vol. 54 (January 1981): 34–50.

Featherman, David, and Hauser, Robert M. *Opportunity and Change* (New York: Academic Press, 1978).

Featherstone, Joseph. *Schools Where Children Learn* (New York: Liveright Publishing, 1971).

Felmlee, Diane, and Eder, Donna. "Contextual Effects in the Classroom: The Impact of Ability Groups on Student Attention," *Sociology of Education*, Vol. 56 (April 1983): 77–78.

Firestone, William. "Ideology and Conflict in Parent Run Free Schools," *Sociology of Education*, Vol. 49 (1976): 241–252.

Firth, Raymond. *We, The Tikopia* (Boston: Beacon Press, 1957).

* FitzGerald, Francis. *America Revised: History Schoolbooks in the Twentieth Century* (Boston: Little, Brown, 1979).

Ford, Juliette. *Social Class and the Comprehensive School* (London: Routledge and Kegan Paul, 1973).

Freeman, Richard. "Black Economic Progress Since 1964," *The Public Interest*, No. 52 (Summer 1978): 52–68.

Freeman, Richard. *The Overeducated American* (New York: Academic Press, 1977).

Fuller, Bruce. "Educational Evaluation and Shifting Youth Policy," *Evaluation Review*, Vol. 5 (April 1981): 167–188.

Gage, N. L. *The Scientific Basis of the Art of Teaching* (New York: Teachers College Press, 1978).

Gardner, Howard. *Frames of Mind: The Theory of Multiple Intelligences* (New York: Basic Books, 1983).

Gardner, John W. *Excellence* (New York: Harper, 1961).

* Garnier, Maurice, and Raffalovich, Lawrence. "The Evolution of Equality of Educational Opportunities in France," *Sociology of Education*, Vol. 57 (January 1984): 1–10.

Gerth, Hans, and Mills, C. Wright (eds.). *From Max Weber: Essays in Sociology* (London: Routledge and Kegan Paul, 1948).

Goffman, Erving. *Asylums* (New York: Doubleday, 1961).

Goldthorpe, John H. *Social Mobility and Class Structure in Modern Britain* (Oxford: Clarendon Press, 1980).

Goodlad, John. *A Place Called School* (New York: McGraw-Hill, 1984).

Goodman, Paul. "The Present Moment in Education," *New York Review of Books*, April 10, 1969.

Gottfredson, Denise C. "Black-White Differences in the Educational Attainment Process: What Have We Learned?" *American Sociological Review*, Vol. 46 (October 1981): 542–557.

Graham, Patricia A. "Literacy: A Goal for Secondary Schools," *Daedalus* (Summer 1981): 119–134.

* Grant, Gerald. "The Character of Education and the Education of Character," in "America's Schools: Public and Private," *Daedalus* (Summer 1981): 135–150.

* Grant, Gerald. "Children's Rights and Adult Confusions," *The Public Interest* (Fall 1982): 83–99.

Graubard, Allen. *Free the Children* (New York: Pantheon, 1972).

Green, Philip. "Race and I.Q.: Fallacy of Heritability," *Dissent* (Spring 1976): 181–196.

Greenfield, Patricia, and Bruner, Jerome. "Culture and Cognitive Growth," *International Journal of Psychology*, Vol. 1 (1966): 89–107.

Greer, Colin. *The Great School Legend* (New York: Viking Press, 1973).

Grunberger, Richard. *The 12 Year Reich: A Social History of Nazi Germany 1933–1945* (New York: Holt, Rinehart and Winston, 1971).

Grusky, David B., and Hauser, Robert M. "Comparative Social Mobility Revisited: Models of Convergence and Divergence in 16 Countries," *American Sociological Review*, Vol. 49 (February 1984): 19–38.

Guthrie, James et al. *Schools and Inequality* (Cambridge: M.I.T. Press, 1971).

Haller, Emil J., and Davis, Sharon A. "Teacher Perceptions, Parental Social Status and Grouping for Reading Instruction," *Sociology of Education,* Vol. 54 (July 1981): 162–173.

Halsey, A. H. "Equality and Education," *Oxford Review of Education,* Vol. 1, No. 1 (1975): 1–28.

* Halsey, A. H.; Heath, A. F.; and Ridge, J. M. *Origins and Destinations* (Oxford: Clarendon Press, 1980).

Hamblin, Robert. *The Humanization Process* (New York: Wiley, 1971).

Hanushek, Eric. *Education and Race* (Lexington, Mass.: D. C. Heath, 1972).

Harbison, Fred, and Myers, Charles. *Education, Manpower and Economic Growth: Strategies in Human Resource Development* (New York: McGraw Hill, 1964).

Hauser, Robert M. "Contextual Analysis Revisited," *Sociological Methods and Research,* Vol. 2 (February 1974): 365–375.

Hauser, Robert. "Temporal Change in Occupational Mobility: Evidence for Men in the U.S.," *American Sociological Review* (October 1976): 585–589.

* Hauser, Robert, and Featherman, David. "Equality of Schooling: Trends and Prospects," *Sociology of Education,* Vol. 49 (April 1976): 99–119.

Herrnstein, Richard. "I.Q.," *Atlantic Monthly* (September 1971): 43–64.

Herrnstein, Richard J. *I.Q. in the Meritocracy* (Boston: Little, Brown, 1973).

Hess, R.; Shipman, V.; and Jackson, D. "Some New Dimensions in Providing Equal Educational Opportunity," *Journal of Negro Education,* Vol. 34 (1965): 220–231.

Heyneman, Stephen P., and Loxley, William A. "Influences on Academic Achievement across High and Low Income Countries: A Reanalysis of IEA Data," *Sociology of Education,* Vol. 55 (January 1982): 13–21.

Heyns, Barbara. *Summer Learning and the Effects of Schooling* (New York: Academic Press, 1978).

Hillcocks, George, Jr. "Books and Bombs: Ideological Conflict and the Schools— A Case Study of the Kanawha County Book Protest," *School Review,* Vol. 86 (August 1978): 632–654.

Hodgson, Geoffrey. "Do Schools Make a Difference," *Atlantic* (March 1973): 35–46.

Hoge, Dean R. "Changes in College Students' Value Patterns in the 1950's, 1960's and 1970's," *Sociology of Education,* Vol. 49 (April 1976): 155–163.

Howell, Frank M., and McBroom, Lynn W. "Social Relations at Home and at School: An Analysis of the Correspondence Principle," *Sociology of Education,* Vol. 55 (January 1982): 40–52.

Hunt, John. "The Psychological Basis for Using Pre-School Environment as an
Antidote for Cultural Deprivation," *Merrill-Palmer Quarterly* 10 (1964).

Hurn, Christopher. "The Vocationalization of American Education," *European Journal of Education,* Vol. 18 (1983): 45–64.

Husén, Torsten. *The School in Question* (Oxford: Oxford University Press, 1979).

Hyman, Herbert H.; Wright, Charles R.; and Reed, John Shelton. *The Enduring Effects of Education* (Chicago: University of Chicago Press, 1975).

Illich, Ivan. *Deschooling Society* (New York: Harper and Row, 1970).

Illich, Ivan. "Vernacular Values and Education," *Teachers College Record*, Vol. 81 (Fall 1979): 31–75.

* Inkeles, Alex. "National Differences in Scholastic Performance," *Comparative Education Review*, Vol. 23 (October 1979): 386–407.

Inkeles, Alex, and Smith, David. *Becoming Modern* (Cambridge: Harvard University Press, 1974).

* Jackson, Philip W. *Life in Classrooms* (New York: Holt, Rinehart and Winston, 1968).

Jencks, Christopher. *Who Gets Ahead?* (New York: Basic Books, 1979).

* Jencks, Christopher et al. *Inequality* (New York: Basic Books, 1972).

Jencks, Christopher, and Brown, Marsha. "The Effects of High Schools on their Students," *Harvard Educational Review*, Vol. 45 (1975): 273–324.

Jensen, Arthur. "Arthur Jensen Defends His Heresy," *Psychology Today* (October 1969): 24.

* Jensen, Arthur. "How Much Can We Boost I.Q. and Scholastic Achievement?" *Harvard Educational Review* 39 (1969): 1–123.

Juster, Thomas (ed.). *Education, Income and Human Behavior* (New York: McGraw-Hill, 1975).

Kaestle, Carl F., and Smith, Marshall S. "The Federal Role in Elementary and Secondary Education, 1940–1980," *Harvard Educational Review*, Vol. 52 (November 1982): 384–408.

Kamin, Leon. *The Science and Politics of I.Q.* (Potomac, Maryland: Erlbaum Associates, 1974).

Karabel, Jerome. "Community Colleges and Social Stratification," *Harvard Educational Review*, Vol. 42 (1972): 521–562.

Karier, Clarence (ed.). *Shaping the American Educational State* (New York: Free Press, 1976).

* Kasun, Jacqueline. "Turning Children into Sex Experts," *The Public Interest*, No. 55 (Spring 1979): 3–14.

Katz, Michael. *Class, Bureaucracy and Schools* (New York: Praeger, 1975).

* Katz, Michael (ed.). *School Reform, Past and Present* (Boston: Little, Brown, 1971).

Keddie, Nell. "Classroom Knowledge," in M. F. D. Young (ed.), *Knowledge and Control* (London: Collier, 1971).

Kerr, Clark. *Priorities for Action: Carnegie Commission on Higher Education, Final Report* (New York: McGraw-Hill, 1973).

Kerr, Clark (ed.). *A Digest of Reports of the Carnegie Commission on Higher Education* (New York: McGraw-Hill, 1974).

Kerr, Clark et al. *Industrialism and Industrial Man* (Cambridge: Harvard University Press, 1960).

Kilson, Martin. "Black Social Classes and Intergenerational Poverty," *The Public Interest*, No. 64 (Summer 1981): 58–78.

* Kirp, David L. "Proceduralism and Bureaucracy: Due Process in the School Setting," *Stanford Law Review*, Vol. 28 (1975): 841–876.

Kohl, Herbert. *The Open Classroom* (New York: New York Review Books, 1969).

Kohlberg, Lawrence, and Mayer, Rochelle. "Development as the Aim of Education," *Harvard Educational Review*, Vol. 42 (1972): 449–496.

Kohn, Melvin. "Social Class and Parent-Child Relationships: An Interpretation," *American Journal of Sociology* 68 (1968): 471–480.

Krug, Edward A. *The Secondary School Curriculum* (New York: Harper, 1960).

Krug, Charles. *The Shaping of the American High School, 1880–1920* (Madison: University of Wisconsin Press, 1969).

Labov, William. "The Logic of Non-Standard English," in F. Williams (ed.), *Language and Poverty* (Chicago: Markham, 1970).

Lavin, David E.; Alba, Richard D.; and Silberstein, Richard A. *Right versus Privilege: The Open Admissions Experiment at the City University of New York* (New York: Free Press, 1981).

Leacock, Eleanor. *Teaching and Learning in City Schools* (New York: Basic Books, 1969).

Levin, Henry M. "Assessing the Equalization Potential of Education," *Comparative Education*, Vol. 28 (February 1984): 11–27.

Levine, Donald M., and Bane, Mary Jo (eds.). *The Inequality Controversy: Schooling and Distributive Justice* (New York: Basic Books, 1975).

Levitas, Maurice. *Marxist Perspectives in the Sociology of Education* (London: Routledge and Kegan Paul, 1974).

Lewis, Oscar. "The Culture of Poverty," *Scientific American*, Vol. 215 (October 1966): 19–25.

* Lightfoot, Sarah Lawrence. *The Good High School* (New York: Basic Books, 1983).

Lipset, Seymour Martin. *The First New Nation* (New York: Basic Books, 1963).

Lortie, Dan. *School Teacher: A Sociological Study* (Chicago: University of Chicago Press, 1975).

Mackler, B. "Grouping in the Ghetto," *Education and Urban Society*, Vol. 2 (1969): 80–96.

McDermott, R. P. "Social Relations as Context for Learning," *Harvard Educational Review*, Vol. 47 (1977): 198–213.

McClosky, Herbert, and Brill, Alida. *What Americans Believe about Civil Liberties* (New York: Basic Books, 1983).

McDill, Edward L.; Rigsby, Leo C.; and Meyers, Jr., Edmund D. "Educational Climates of High Schools: Their Effects and Sources," *American Journal of Sociology*, Vol. 74 (1969): 567–568.

McLaughlin, Milbrey W. *Evaluation and Reform: The Elementary and Secondary Education Act of 1965* (Cambridge: Ballinger, 1975).

McPartland, James, and Epstein, Joyce. "The Effects of Open School Organization on Student Outcomes," *The Center for Social Organization of Schools*, Report No. 195, The Johns Hopkins University, 1975.

* Metz, Mary Haywood. *Classrooms and Corridors* (Berkeley: University of California Press, 1978).

Metz, Mary Haywood. "Clashes in the Classroom," *Education and Urban Society*, Vol. 11 (November 1978): 12–35.

* Meyer, John W. "The Effects of Education as an Institution," *American Journal of Sociology*, Vol. 83 (July 1977): 55–77.

Meyer, John W. "High School Effects on College Intentions," *American Journal of Sociology*, Vol. 76 (July 1970): 59–70.

Meyer, John W. et al. "Public Education as Nation Building in America: Enrollments and Bureaucratization in the American States, 1870–1930," *American Journal of Sociology*, Vol. 85 (November 1979): 591–613.

Miller, Harry. *Education for the Disadvantaged* (New York: Free Press, 1967).

Moynihan, Daniel P. *The Negro Family* (Washington, D.C.: U.S. Department of Labor, 1965), pp. 31–34.

Mullis, Ira. "Citizenship and Social Achievement Trends over Time," paper presented to the American Educational Research Association Meetings, April, 1978.

Naipaul, V. S. *Among the Believers: An Islamic Journey* (New York: Knopf, 1981).

National Assessment of Educational Progress. *Writing Achievement: 1969–1979* (Denver: Educational Commission of the States, 1980).

National Association of Secondary School Principals. "Student Attendance and Absenteeism," *The Practitioner* (March 1975).

* National Commission on Excellence in Education. *A Nation at Risk: The Imperative for Educational Reform* (Washington, D.C.: U.S. Government, 1983).

National Council for the Social Studies. *National Assessment and Social Studies Education* (Washington, D.C.: U.S. Government, 1975).

National Institute of Education. *Violent Schools—Safe Schools* (Washington, D.C.: U.S. Government, 1978).

National Science Board Commission on Precollege Education in Mathematics, Science and Technology. *Educating Americans for the 21st Century* (Washington, D.C.: National Science Foundation, 1983).

Oakes, Jeannie. "Classroom Role Relationships: Exploring the Bowles and Gintis Hypothesis," *Sociology of Education*, Vol. 55, No. 4 (October 1982): 197–212.

* O'Toole, James. *Work, Learning and the American Future* (San Francisco: Jossey Bass, 1977).

Park, J. Charles. "Preachers, Politics and Public Education: A Review of Right Wing Pressures against Public Schooling in America," *Phi Delta Kappan*, Vol. 62 (May 1980): 608.

* Parsons, Talcott. "The School Class as a Social System," *Harvard Educational Review* 29 (1959): 297–308.

Parsons, Talcott. *Structure and Process in Modern Societies* (New York: Free Press, 1960).

Parsons, Talcott, and Platt, Gerald M. *The American University* (Cambridge, Mass.: Harvard University Press, 1973).

Passow, A. Harry et al. *The National Case Study: An Empirical Comparative Study of Education in Twenty-One Countries* (New York: Wiley, 1976).

Pellegrin, Roland J. "Schools as Work Settings," in Robert Dubin (ed.), *Handbook of Work, Organization and Society* (Chicago: Rand McNally, 1976).

Pincus, Fred L. "The False Promise of Community Colleges," *Harvard Educational Review,* Vol. 50 (1980): 332–360.

Pintner, Rudof. *Intelligence Testing: Methods and Results* (New York: Henry Holt, 1923).

* Postman, Neil. *The Disappearance of Childhood* (New York: Delacorte Press, 1982).

Postman, Neil, and Weingartner, Charles. *Teaching as a Subversive Activity* (New York: Dell, 1969).

Purves, Alan. *Literature Education in Ten Countries* (New York: Wiley, 1973).

Ralph, John H., and Rubison, Richard. "Immigration and the Expansion of Schooling in the U.S., 1890–1970," *American Sociological Review,* Vol. 45 (1980): 943–954.

Rehberg, Richard A., and Rosenthal, Evelyn R. *Class and Merit in the American High School* (New York: Longman, 1978).

Richardson, John G. "Variations in Date of Enactment of Compulsory School Attendance Laws: An Empirical Inquiry," *Sociology of Education,* Vol. 53 (1980): 153–163.

Rickover, Hyman. *Education and Freedom* (New York: Dutton, 1959).

* Rist, Ray. "Social Class and Teacher Expectations: The Self-Fulfilling Prophecy in Ghetto Education," *Harvard Educational Review,* Vol. 40 (1970): 411–451.

Rosenbaum, James E. "Track Misperceptions and Frustrated College Plans: An Analysis of the Effects of Tracks and Track Perceptions in the National Longitudinal Survey," *Sociology of Education,* Vol. 53, No. 2 (April 1980): 74–88.

Rosenbaum, James E. *Making Inequality* (New York: Wiley, 1976).

Rosenthal, Robert, and Jacobson, Lenore. *Pygmalion in the Classroom* (New York: Holt, Rinehart and Winston, 1968).

Rowan, Brian, and Miracle, Jr., Andrew W. "Systems of Ability Grouping and the Stratification of Achievement in Elementary Schools," *Sociology of Education,* Vol. 56 (July 1983): 133–144.

Rutter, Michael et al. *Fifteen Thousand Hours* (London: Open Books, 1979).

Ryan, William. *Blaming the Victim* (New York: Pantheon, 1971).

St. John, Nancy. *School Desegregation: Outcomes for Children* (New York: Wiley, 1975).

Sanford, Nevitt (ed.). *The American College* (New York: Wiley, 1962).

* Scarr, Sandra, and Weinberg, Richard A. "The Influence of 'Family Background' on Intellectual Attainment," *American Sociological Review*, Vol. 43 (October 1978): 674–692.

Schafer, Walter E., and Blexa, Carol. *Tracking and Opportunity: The Locking-out Process and Beyond* (Scranton, Penn.: Chandler, 1971).

Schapiro, Martin. "Judicial Activism," in Seymour Martin Lipset (ed.), *The Third Century* (Chicago: University of Chicago Press, 1979).

Schimmel, David, and Fischer, Louis. *The Civil Rights of Students* (New York: Harper, 1975).

Schultz, Theodore. "Investment in Human Capital," *American Economic Review* 51 (March 1961): 1–17.

* Sewell, William H., and Hauser, Robert M. "Causes and Consequences of Higher Education: Modes of the Status Attainment Process," in William H. Sewell, Robert M. Hauser, and David L. Featherman (eds.), *Schooling and Achievement in American Society* (New York: Academic Press, 1976), pp. 9–28.

Sexton, Patricia. *Education and Income* (New York: Viking, 1961).

Sherman, Mandel, and Key, Cora B. "The Intelligence of Isolated Mountain Children," *Child Development*, Vol. 3, No. 4 (1932): 284.

* Silberman, Charles. *Crisis in the Classroom* (New York: Random House, 1969).

* Sowell, Thomas. "New Light on the Black I.Q. Controversy," *New York Times Magazine* (March 27, 1977): 56–63.

Spring, Joel. *Education and the Rise of the Corporate State* (Boston: Beacon Press, 1972).

Squires, David A.; Huitt, William G.; and Segars, John K. *Effective Schools and Classrooms: A Research-Based Perspective* (Washington, D.C.: A.S.C.D., 1983).

Stinchcombe, Arthur. *Rebellion in a High School* (New York: Quadrangle Books, 1964).

Stodolsky, Susan, and Lesser, Gerald. "Learning Patterns in the Disadvantaged," *Harvard Educational Review*, Vol. 37 (1967): 546–593.

Sussman, Leila. *Tales out of School: Implementing Organizational Change in Elementary Schools* (Philadelphia: Temple University Press, 1978).

* Swidler, Ann. *Organizations without Authority: Dilemmas of Social Control in Free Schools* (Cambridge, Mass.: Harvard University Press, 1979).

Terman, Lewis. *Intelligence Tests and School Reorganization* (New York: World Books, 1923).

Thernstrom, Stephan. *The Other Bostonians* (Cambridge: Harvard University Press, 1973).

Thomas, W. I. *The Child in America* (New York: Knopf, 1928).

Thorndike, Robert L. *Reading Comprehension in Fifteen Countries* (New York: Wiley, 1973).

Thornton, Clarence, and Eckland, Bruce K. "High School Contextual Effects for Black and White Students: A Research Note," *Sociology of Education*, Vol. 53 (October 1980): 247–252.

* Toby, Jackson. "Crime in American Public Schools," *The Public Interest*, No. 58 (Winter 1980): 18–42.

Toffler, Alvin. *Future Shock* (New York: Random House, 1970).

Treiman, Donald. "Industrialization and Social Stratification," in Edward Laumann (ed.), *Social Stratification: Research and Theory for the 1970s* (New York: Bobbs-Merrill, 1970), pp. 207–234.

Trent, James W., and Medsker, Leland L. *Beyond High School* (San Francisco: Jossey-Bass, 1968).

* Trow, Martin. "The Second Transformation of American Secondary Education," *International Journal of Comparative Sociology*, Vol. 2 (1961): 144–166.

* Tyack, David. *The One Best System* (Cambridge, Mass.: Harvard University Press, 1974).

Tyack, David, and Hansot, Elisabeth. *Managers of Virtue: Public School Leadership in America, 1820–1980* (New York: Basic Books, 1982).

U.S. Department of Health, Education and Welfare. *Toward a Social Report* (Washington, D.C.: U.S. Government, 1969).

Valentine, Charles. "Deficit, Difference and Bicultural Models of Afro-American Behavior," in "Challenging the Myths: The Schools, the Blacks and the Poor," *Harvard Educational Review* (Reprint Series No. 5, 1975), pp. 1–21.

Vernon, Philip. *Intelligence and Cultural Environment* (London: Methuen, 1970).

Vogel, Ezra P. *Japan as Number One.* (New York: Harper, 1980).

* Waller, Willard. *The Sociology of Teaching* (New York: Wiley, 1961).

Ward, Martha C. " 'Teaching' Them Children to Talk," in Joan I. Roberts and Sherrie K. Akinsanya (eds.), *Schooling in Cultural Context* (New York: McKay, 1976), pp. 386–400.

Ward, W. D., and Barcher, P. R. "Reading Achievement and Creativity as Related to Open Classroom Experience," *Journal of Educational Psychology* 67 (1975): 683–691.

Waters, Brian K. *The Test Score Decline: A Review and Annotated Bibliography*, Technical Memorandum 81-2 (Washington, D.C.: Department of Defense, 1981).

Williams, Raymond. *The Long Revolution* (New York: Columbia University Press, 1960).

Williams, Robin. *American Society* (New York: Knopf, 1970).

* Willis, Paul. *Learning to Labor* (New York: Columbia University Press, 1981).

Wilson, James Q. "Response to Kaestle and Smith," *Harvard Education Review*, Vol. 52 (1982): 415–418.

Wilson, William J. *The Declining Significance of Race* (Chicago: University of Chicago Press, 1979).

Withey, S. B. *A Degree and What Else?* (New York: McGraw-Hill, 1972).

Wynne, Edward A. "What Are the Courts Doing to Our Children?" *The Public Interest* (Summer 1981): 83–99.

Zajda, Joseph I. *Education in the U.S.S.R.* (New York: Pergamon, 1980).